CAMBRIDGE STUDIES IN AMERICAN LITERATURE AND CULTURE

Robert Lowell

Cambridge Studies in American Literature and Culture

Editor: Albert Gelpi, Stanford University

Advisory Board

Nina Baym, *University of Illinois, Champaign-Urbana*
Sacvan Bercovich, *Harvard University*
Richard Bridgman, *University of California, Berkeley*
David Levin, *University of Virginia*
Joel Porte, *Harvard University*
Mike Weaver, *Oxford University*

Other Books in the Series

Robert Zaller, *The Cliffs of Solitude*
Peter Conn, *The Divided Mind*
Patricia Caldwell, *The Puritan Conversion Narrative*
Stephen Fredman, *Poet's Prose*
Charles Altieri, *Self and Sensibility in Contemporary American Poetry*
John McWilliams, *Hawthorne, Melville, and the National Character*
Barton St. Armand, *Emily Dickinson and Her Culture*
Elizabeth McKinsey, *Niagara Falls*
Albert J. Von Frank, *The Sacred Game*
Marjorie Perloff, *The Dance of the Intellect*
Albert Gelpi, *Wallace Stevens*
Ann Kibbey, *The Interpretation of Material Shapes in Puritanism*
Sacvan Bercovich and Myra Jehlen, *Ideology and Classic American Literature*
Karen Rowe, *Saint and Singer*
Lawrence Buell, *New England Literary Culture*
David Wyatt, *The Fall into Eden*
Brenda Murphy, *American Realism and American Drama, 1880–1940*
Jerome Loving, *Emily Dickinson*
Paul Giles, *Hart Crane*
Richard Grey, *Writing the South*

Robert Lowell

Essays on the Poetry

Edited by
STEVEN GOULD AXELROD
University of California, Riverside
AND
HELEN DEESE
Mount St. Mary's College, Los Angeles

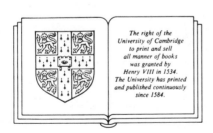

The right of the
University of Cambridge
to print and sell
all manner of books
was granted by
Henry VIII in 1534.
The University has printed
and published continuously
since 1584.

CAMBRIDGE UNIVERSITY PRESS
Cambridge
London   New York   New Rochelle
Melbourne   Sydney

Published by the Press Syndicate of the University of Cambridge
The Pitt Building, Trumpington Street, Cambridge CB2 1RP
32 East 57th Street, New York, NY 10022, USA
10 Stamford Road, Oakleigh, Melbourne 3166, Australia

First published 1986

Printed in the United States of America

Library of Congress Cataloging in Publication Data
Robert Lowell : essays on the poetry.
(Cambridge studies in American literature and
culture)
Includes index.
1. Lowell, Robert, 1917–1977 – Criticism and
interpretation.   I. Axelrod, Steven Gould, 1944–
II. Deese, Helen.   III. Series.
PS3523.O89Z855   1986   811'.52   86–12916

British Library Cataloguing in Publication Data
Robert Lowell: essays on the poetry –
(Cambridge studies in American literature
and culture)
1. Lowell, Robert – Criticism and
interpretation.
I. Axelrod, Steven Gould   II. Deese, Helen
811'.52   PS3523.O89Z/

ISBN 0 521 30872 0

Contents

     HELEN DEESE   180

11   *Day by Day:* His End Game
     A. KINGSLEY WEATHERHEAD   217

12   "Prose or This": What Lowell Made of a Diminished Thing
     GEORGE MCFADDEN   231

     Works Cited   256

     Index   263

Illustrations

Preface

 This collection of essays attempts to reassess Robert Lowell's poetry and to restimulate critical thinking about it. In recent years, readers interested in Lowell have paid an increasing amount of attention to his private life – to what he termed his difficulty with ordinary living. Without wishing to repress that concern, the authors of these essays seek to refocus attention on his texts, to raise new sorts of questions about them.

 The introductory essay by Steven Gould Axelrod locates criticism in the present "era of biography" and attempts to clarify interpretative issues by analyzing one of Lowell's late poems, "George III." Jay Martin studies the interior drama of Lowell's oeuvre from a psychoanalytic perspective. He describes the poet's painful but successful artistic efforts to deal with his sense of loss and his need to mourn.

 The succeeding essays progress through Lowell's canon in a roughly chronological fashion. Albert Gelpi reevaluates *Lord Weary's Castle,* finding that in its prophetic witness to the world and its suggestions of a spiritual realm of being, it is indeed the masterwork Randall Jarrell initially proclaimed it to be. Sandra M. Gilbert and Lawrence Kramer both uncover new literary meanings in *Life Studies.* Gilbert perceives mythic and revisionist elements in "Skunk Hour," and Kramer redefines the relationship between language and psychological content in a major rereading of the "Life Studies" sequence. Marjorie Perloff, after taking the disturbing revelations of recent biography into account, suggests that Lowell both uses and transcends his experiential materials in the stronger poems of *Life Studies* and *For the Union Dead.* Alex Calder analyzes Lowell's sonnet sequences of 1969–73 as process poems, whereas Calvin Bedient studies them as dialogic compendia of metaphors and metonyms. Although the former critic focuses on form and the latter emphasizes style, both redefine the terms by which Lowell's sonnets may be understood.

 The final four essays consider Lowell's last book of poetry, *Day by Day.* Taking an intertextual approach, Alan Holder connects the poems to each other and to poems from the entire Lowell canon. He discerns underlying patterns of returning, descending, and disintegration in Lowell's last major text. Helen Deese explores the importance of painting and photography to "Epilogue," to "Marriage," to *Day by Day* as a whole, and to Lowell's final thinking about the art of poetry. A. Kingsley Weatherhead finds *Day by Day* wanting in Coleridgean imagination and judges it a despairing coda to Lowell's career. George McFadden, however, eloquently defends the book. Like Bedient, he notes that Lowell infused his poetry with the style and matter of prose fiction, thereby renewing his gift.

The divergent and frequently controversial voices in this book testify to radical disparities among Lowell's "endless experiments" – to borrow a phrase from Ralph Waldo Emerson – and to the complexity, perplexity, and endurance of his poetic utterance.

Nine of these essays are entirely new. Three others contain material previously printed, though all have been extensively revised. The authors and editors thank the following: the editors of *Psychoanalytic Inquiry* for permission to reprint material in Jay Martin's "Grief and Nothingness" (3, no. 3 [1983]: 451–84); Greg Kuzma and Best Cellar Press for permission to reprint material in Sandra M. Gilbert's "Mephistophilis in Maine" (*Book of Rereadings* [Crete, Nebr., 1979], pp. 254–64); and the editors of *American Poetry Review* for permission to reprint material in Marjorie Perloff's "*Poètes Maudits* of the Genteel Tradition" (12, no. 3 [1983]: 32–38).

Frank Bidart, Literary Editor for the Estate of Robert Lowell, has granted Steven Axelrod permission to quote from the manuscript draft of Lowell's unpublished essay "New England and Further," and has granted Alex Calder permission to quote from drafts of *Notebook 1967–68* and *Notebook*. The authors and editors are grateful to him and to the Houghton Library of Harvard University.

Thanks are due to Mount St. Mary's College for a generous Faculty Research Grant that greatly assisted Helen Deese in the completion of her essay and of this book; and to the Research Committee of the University of California, Riverside, for financial assistance with the typing of the manuscript.

We dedicate our portions of this book to Rummy and Rise, and to Tom and Martha, Mary Ann and Dave, Frank, Sam, and Jem.

STEVEN GOULD AXELROD
HELEN DEESE

Contributors

STEVEN GOULD AXELROD is Professor of English at the University of California, Riverside. He has written *Robert Lowell: Life and Art* and has coauthored, with Helen Deese, *Robert Lowell: A Reference Guide*. The author of numerous articles on American literature, he is presently completing a book-length study of Sylvia Plath.

CALVIN BEDIENT is Professor of English at UCLA. His publications include *Architects of Self: George Eliot, D. H. Lawrence, and E. M. Forster; Eight Contemporary Poets;* and *In the Heart's Last Kingdom: Robert Penn Warren's Major Poetry.*

ALEX CALDER tutors at the University of Auckland, New Zealand. He is completing a doctoral thesis on Lowell and the long poem.

HELEN DEESE is Assistant Professor of English at Mount St. Mary's College in Los Angeles. A specialist in the English Renaissance as well as in modern literature, she is coauthor, with Steven Gould Axelrod, of *Robert Lowell: A Reference Guide*. She is presently studying the relations between poetry and the other arts.

ALBERT GELPI is William Robertson Coe Professor of American Literature at Stanford University and editor of Cambridge Studies in American Literature and Culture. He has written *Emily Dickinson: The Mind of the Poet; The Tenth Muse: The Psyche of the American Poet;* and (forthcoming) *A Coherent Splendor: The American Poetic Renaissance, 1910–1950*. In addition, he has edited *The Poet in America* and *Wallace Stevens: The Poetics of Modernism* and has coedited, with Barbara Charlesworth Gelpi, *Adrienne Rich's Poetry*.

SANDRA M. GILBERT is Professor of English at Princeton University. A poet as well as a critic, she has written *Acts of Attention: The Poems of D. H. Lawrence* and several books of poetry, including *In the Fourth World* and *Emily's Bread*. With Susan Gubar she has coauthored *The Madwoman in the Attic* and coedited *Shakespeare's Sisters: Feminist Essays on Women Poets* and *The Norton Anthology of Women's Literature*.

ALAN HOLDER is Professor of English at Hunter College of the City University of New York. He has written *Three Voyagers in Search of Europe: A Study of Henry James, Ezra Pound and T. S. Eliot; A. R. Ammons;* and *The Imagined Past: Portrayals of Our History in Modern American Literature.* His essays and reviews have appeared in a number of periodicals.

LAWRENCE KRAMER teaches English and comparative literature at Fordham University, Lincoln Center, and works as both a critic and a composer. Widely published on literary and musical subjects, he is the author of *Music and Poetry: The Nineteenth Century and After.*

GEORGE MCFADDEN lives and writes in Southold, New York, and is currently working on Henry James. His most recent publication is *Discovering the Comic.*

JAY MARTIN is Leo S. Bing Professor of Literature at the University of Southern California and also teaches in the Southern California Psychoanalytic Institute and in the California College of Medicine at the University of California, Irvine. In addition, he has a private practice in psychoanalysis at Irvine, California, where he lives. Among other books, he has written *Harvests of Change: American Literature, 1865–1914; Robert Lowell;* and biographies of Conrad Aiken, Nathanael West, and Henry Miller. Two new books will appear next year: *Psychoanalysis and the Life of Literature* and *The Fictive Personality.*

MARJORIE PERLOFF is Professor of English and Comparative Literature at Stanford University. Her books include *The Poetic Art of Robert Lowell; Frank O'Hara: Poet among Painters; The Poetics of Indeterminacy: Rimbaud to Cage;* and *The Dance of the Intellect: Studies in the Poetry of the Pound Tradition.* Her most recent book, *The Futurist Moment: Avant-Garde, Avant-Guerre, and the Language of Rupture,* has just been published.

A. KINGSLEY WEATHERHEAD is Professor of English at the University of Oregon. His books on modern American and English poetry include *The Edge of the Image: Marianne Moore, William Carlos Williams, and Some Other Poets; Stephen Spender and the Thirties;* and *The British Dissonance: Essays on Ten Contemporary Poets.*

1

Lowell's Living Name:
An Introduction

STEVEN GOULD AXELROD

I

"Biography first convinces us of the fleeing of the Biographied," Emily Dickinson once wrote (318). Since Robert Lowell's death in 1977, a good deal of biographical writing has appeared and more is on the way. Lowell's readers must now try to read his work in the shadow of these biographies. But how do we avoid reading the life that biography has invented in place of the poems we have been given? Why are we tempted to let these readerly fictions of a life master and enslave the writerly poems that justify them? The fascination with biography may simply be a way to domesticate Lowell's wild words, a way to control the anarchic energy of texts that perversely attract and evade us, threaten us and give us pleasure. Surely the desire to tame, to define as an object, is evident in all the major works of Lowell criticism. Perhaps that effort has now been joined by a more disingenuous attempt to define the poems by placing the poet. And perhaps, as writers and readers of biography, we have been tempted to go further still, to dispose of the troublesome poems entirely by writing the poet off. If that is indeed our unconscious goal, is it any wonder that Lowell has fled?

Powerful works of art provoke powerful hostilities: Strong texts generally go through a prolonged period of challenge after making their initial impact, and the challenge they face often reflects their own character. It is not surprising, therefore, that a writer best known for his autobiographical poetry should be tested on the ground of his life. The general biographical strategy thus far has been to reveal Lowell as an empty and trying individual. The poems are viewed as anything but central to his being since his being has no center. He is conceived as existing primarily to make others miserable – wives, children, friends, strangers, biographers. According to this biographical fiction, the texts simply underwrote a life that had no other means of support.

1

Despite these Herculean efforts at denial – these efforts to diminish the man in order to liberate ourselves from the incomprehensible and demanding words that he wrote – Lowell's words will not leave us alone, though we do not know what to make of them. We now encounter the difficulty of initiating a new stage of appropriation, one beyond the initial (largely appreciative) interpretive stage and the present (largely deprecatory) biographical stage. The contributors to *Robert Lowell: Essays on the Poetry* have attempted to foster this new stage by rigorously reconsidering the poetry. They hope to revitalize the inherited critical tradition, in part through controversy. But before we consider either their contribution to the ongoing dialogue or the nature of the texts that generate such dialogue, let us examine more closely the biographies that have appeared and the problems they raise for criticism.

II

Soon after Lowell's death in 1977, although harsher representations still awaited their hour, a host of benign memoirs by Lowell's friends ushered in the era of biography. Many of these were collected in Rolando Anzilotti's *Robert Lowell: A Tribute* (1979) and a special Lowell issue of the *Harvard Advocate* (November 1979). In addition, Lowell's former wives, Jean Stafford and Elizabeth Hardwick, both published fictionalized memoirs. Often amusing, revealing, and moving, these various reminiscences provide insight into Lowell's character and a rich sense of the man, though their implication for the reading of Lowell's texts remains unclear.

Perhaps the most evocative of these works is Hardwick's *Sleepless Nights* (1979). Lowell does not make an appearance until the final third of this book, though he is prefigured obsessively in such locutions as a "*perfido*" (19), "treachery" (21), "alone here in New York, no longer a *we*" (61), and "the distresses of New Yorkers, . . . divorce, abandonment, the unacceptable and the unattainable, ennui filled with action, sad, tumultuous middle-age years shaken by crashings, uprootings, coups, desperate renewals" (49–50). Finally, Hardwick introduces Lowell into the narrative, though not by name. He appears initially as an italicized "*he*" (98), the narrator's cohabitor during a stay in the Netherlands in the early 1950s. He reenters occasionally as a lover, a teller of anecdotes about himself, a man who reads and writes all day and does not seem to belong anywhere or to anyone. Finally the narrator remembers Lowell simply as "him who has left" (148). Lowell is a barely mentioned ghost, a deliberately evoked mystery, a foil to the "Lowell" of the official biographies who is mentioned constantly yet bears no profound relation to a living human being.

Although Lowell hardly appears in Hardwick's memoir, he makes his presence known in her voice – her pained, hopeless, hopeful eloquence. "To live a life is not to cross a field," she quotes Pasternak at the beginning of her narrative (11), not acknowledging that she is in fact quoting Lowell's translation of Pasternak. At the end of his own poetic memoir, *Notebook 1967–68,* Lowell wrote:

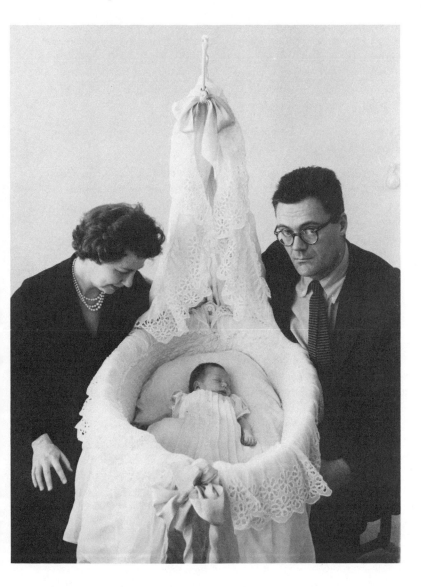

Lowell and his wife, Elizabeth Hardwick, with their baby, Harriet, 1957. Photograph by Alfred Eisenstaedt, *LIFE* Magazine, © 1957 Time Inc.

I have flashbacks to what I remember, and notes on old history. My plot rolls with the seasons. The separate poems and sections are opportunist and inspired by impulse. Accident threw up subjects, and the plot swallowed them – famished for human chances. . . . In truth I seem to have felt mostly the joys of living; in remembering, in recording, thanks to the gift of the Muse, it is the pain. (159–60)

Hardwick's similarly intended work concludes in the very same tones, balancing a similar weight of joy and pain:

On the battered calendar of the past, the back-glancing flow of numbers, I had imagined there would be felicitous notations of entrapments and escapes, days in the South with the insinuating feline accent, and nights in the East, showing a restlessness as beguiling as the winds of Aeolus. And myself there, marking the day with an I.

In truth, moments, months, even years were magical. Pages turned, answering prayers, and persons called out, Are you there?

And yet the old pages of the days and weeks are splattered with the dark-brown rings of coffee cups and I find myself gratefully dissolved in the grounds as the water drips downward. (150)

One could plausibly argue that *Sleepless Nights* is the best biography yet written of Lowell because it acknowledges his elusiveness, it highlights the limits of its own perspective, and it demonstrates the way Lowell's unique voice enters into those who are his survivors, the way he lives on not only in his own texts but in the discourse of those who have closely attended him.

The first full-scale biographical work was C. David Heymann's *American Aristocracy: The Lives and Times of James Russell, Amy, and Robert Lowell* (1980). Despite the exhaustive effort that went into it, and despite its seemingly mainstream attempt to explain the poetry by explaining the poet, this book has curiously become the great repressed text in Lowell studies, read by few, praised by none, footnoted nowhere. To all outward appearance, the book simply does not exist. Clearly Heymann in some way did not supply the myth that was wanted. Lowell himself seems to have given Heymann permission to see his papers at Harvard, though even that, like so much else in Heymann's career, is a matter of dispute. Lowell's executors, however, inaugurated the general disapproval of Heymann's work by refusing him permission to quote the materials he had researched. Upon publication, most reviewers regarded *American Aristocracy* as *outré*, perhaps because Heymann was so plainly identified as an outsider and arriviste by Lowell's executors, or perhaps because his popularistic prose did not tell scholars what they wished to hear about themselves, while the narrative itself failed to provide enough scandalous specifics to justify a temporary descent into the gutter.

Heymann's study does contain some worthwhile material. For example, its discussion of Lowell's imprisonment in 1943 (324–39) provides information and commentary not available elsewhere. Heymann analyzes the political attitudes that impelled Lowell to refuse the draft and speculates that "the enforced conditions and prolonged artificial lighting" of prison "might have played a catalytic role in helping set off his manic-depressive condition" (339). In contrast, Ian Hamilton's later, rival biography merely quotes documents (86–91) while remaining relatively silent about the poet's beliefs, the political and military situation in 1943, and the possible effect of Lowell's incarceration on his subsequent life.

Nevertheless, one must admit that the scholarly neglect of *American Aristocracy*, though exaggerated and somewhat disturbing in its social implications, has fundamental merit. Even the strong passages are marred by factual and interpretive gaffes. Heymann often paraphrases secondary sources as if he had invented the language himself. And his comments on intellectual and artistic matters tend toward the bizarre. For example, he writes that Lowell's "conversion to Roman Catholicism was . . . inspired in part by his college readings: Hawthorne, Melville, English seventeenth-century preachers, Calvin himself, Gilson and others, some of them Catholics" (320). Later he adds Jonathan Edwards to this list (321). He never explains why reading Hawthorne, Melville, seventheenth-century Protestant preachers, Calvin, and Edwards should have pushed Lowell toward, rather than away from, Roman Catholicism. He calls Eliot's *The Waste Land* a "blank-verse sequence" (353), dismisses "Waking in the Blue" and "Home After Three Months Away" as mere "syntactic jottings" (341), claims that Lowell's translations of Baudelaire surpass the original, and so on. Lowell's final volumes are "slack and confused, their language flaccid, their tone self-serving" (513). In sum, Heymann provides a biography that is occasionally shrewd but generally superficial, frequently in error, and overtly hostile at its close. It portrays a man whose life was a senseless sequence of events but whose art, at least in its early phases, surmounted its origins.

When Ian Hamilton's *Robert Lowell: A Biography* appeared in 1982, it elicited a reception dramatically different from the one accorded *American Aristocracy*. It was widely reviewed, widely praised, and widely read. One major critic typically termed it "an absorbing and sympathetic account" (Procopiow, *Robert Lowell* 33). Since its publication, almost every article and monograph on Lowell has referred to it, and many have reflected its viewpoint. It has become the most influential book yet written about the poet.

One initially wonders at its success since in many respects Hamilton's biography seems little different from Heymann's. It too dwells on surface details. Indeed, because Hamilton received the access and permissions that Heymann lacked, his book provides many more facts than Heymann's. Like Heymann, Hamilton writes as a literary journalist rather than a scholar. He regularly quotes reviews of Lowell's books but almost never extended analyses; his intellectual center is the daily press, not the library. And also like his predecessor, but to an even greater degree, Hamilton appears to be antagonistic to his subject, though he masks his bias in a style of seeming objectivity. How then to account for Hamilton's triumph in the light of Heymann's failure? First, of course, Hamilton's ability to persuade Lowell's intimates and executors to help him has seemed to give his book an official imprimatur. Second, Hamilton does indeed reveal more information about Lowell's private life, especially its scandalous side: drunken brawls; extramarital affairs; recurrent episodes of madness and institutionalization; abuse and betrayal of friends, wives, lovers, acquaintances; red-baiting of the director of Yaddo writer's colony; troublemaking south of the border and across the Atlantic; hiding *Mein Kampf* in the dust jacket of *Les Fleurs du mal;* and so on. But I believe that another factor has played a crucial role in the book's success. Hamilton's genius is in relating the most sordid personal details in a tone of effortless, agreeable superiority. Reading *Robert Lowell: A Biography* is like reading the *National Enquirer* firm in the conviction that one is actually perusing the *Times Literary Supplement.*

Those who work their way through Hamilton's biography may think they are learning about the "real" Robert Lowell, but they are not. As in the Heymann biography, they are reading about an outline of a man, whose intellect and life-shaping character are missing. This depicted individual, with his mindless caroming from one activity to another, from one disaster to another, more closely resembles a literary embodiment of modern nihilism – Faulkner's Popeye perhaps, or O'Connor's Misfit – than he does a living human being, not to mention a human being with a remarkably developed consciousness. The figure created by Hamilton produces poetry at frequent intervals, but he does not live very deeply in his imagination. Yet one knows from every word that Lowell ever wrote that poetry was central to his existence: "Nothing is real until set down in words" (*N* 246). Because Hamilton generally devalues the imagination, and particularly discredits *Lowell's* sort of creativity, the essential Lowell never appears in this biography.

Hamilton's "Lowell" is a continual source of annoyance and concern, a half-educated, half-civilized problem child who never grows up, never can keep himself out of scrapes, never accomplishes anything of lasting value. One wonders why Hamilton bothered to write about such a lamentable individual. His book reads less like a literary biography than a probation report. At an early point in the narrative, for example, Hamilton observes that Lowell "elected to sulk his way through the first stages of his education" (14). Yet perhaps it is unfair to suggest that a six-year-old boy "elected" his behavior. Possibly that behavior might be interpreted as an unwilled consequence of pathologies in the family life. Possibly Lowell's childhood withdrawal and aggression might be sympathetically examined in psychological or other terms rather than simply condemned. The narrative pattern thus appears at the outset: irony directed at Lowell's conduct and an almost complete lack of interest in what was going on in his mind.

When Lowell marries Jean Stafford, Hamilton blames their conflicts on him. Until Stafford collapses into mental illness, a condition certain to lose Hamilton's sympathy, he treats her as a heroine. Yet anyone who has read Stafford's papers dating from this period (Hamilton apparently did not) soon senses that blame in this marriage must be shared, and indeed Lowell and Stafford did eventually agree to share it. Stafford's later comments, quoted by Hamilton, starkly contrast to his own assessment. "My dear," she wrote to Lowell, "please never castigate yourself for what you call blindness – how blind we both were, how green we were, how countless were our individual torments we didn't know the names of" (307). Hamilton nearly always sides against Lowell when domestic disputes arise. What if Lowell's third wife, Caroline Blackwood, did leave the ailing poet locked and abandoned in her house in Ireland while she disappeared to London? In this narrative, the wives can do almost nothing wrong and Lowell nothing right. On the basis of this biography, even so canny a reader as Marjorie Perloff can wonder (ch. 6, this volume) why Lowell's wives and friends put up with him. The answer, surely, is that Hamilton tells only one side of the story.

Hamilton similarly criticizes Lowell's treatment of his parents. He calls Lowell's reaction to his mother's death "callously brisk" (205), yet almost immediately after this event Lowell was hospitalized in the most extended psychotic episode of his life. Perhaps a more sensitive biographer might have connected that apparent "callousness" to other feelings, hardly callous, that he was also harboring. Hamilton also insists that Lowell was "hard" on his father in "91 Revere Street" (227), though family friends have asserted just the reverse. Indeed, on the evidence Hamilton himself provides, one might as easily accuse Lowell of covering up for his father, not only in the prose memoir but in the many poems about his father as well, almost all of which are suffused with affection, remorse, and a devastating sense of loss. The poems about his mother are sometimes sharper in tone, but they too express affection and grief: "tears ran down my cheeks" (*LS* 77), "I almost lifted the telephone to dial you, / forgetting you have no dial" (*DBD* 78). Yet Hamilton will have Lowell guilty of filial impiety, and no amount of evidence that the case is much more complex than that can sway him.

Hamilton regards Lowell's behavior in mania as similar to that of a "naughty boy" (218), similar indeed to the behavior of the naughty boy Lowell himself once was. For example, he finds something "boyish" about this letter:

> I've been out of my *excitement* for over a month, I think, now, and am in good spirits, though I don't feel any rush of eloquence to talk about the past. It's like recovering from some physical injury, such as a broken leg or jaundice, yet there's no disclaiming these outbursts – they are part of my character – me at moments. (218)

What I would see as Lowell's honest attempt to avoid "disclaiming" his actions, Hamilton regards as "boyish." Perhaps he wishes for a sort of public self-humiliation.

Yet Lowell's letter goes on to do almost precisely that: "The whole business was sincere enough, but a stupid pathological mirage, a magical orange grove in a nightmare. I feel like a son of a bitch." Perhaps, simply, no amount of contrition would suffice for Hamilton. He seems to regard mental illness as consciously willed and morally culpable behavior. There is no forgiveness possible – only, in lieu of outright condemnation, irony.

Hamilton terms Lowell's hopes that nuclear war might be avoided "optimistic musings" (361), while labeling his involvement in anti-Vietnam War protests a "political adventure" (383). He even satirizes Lowell's comments about writing a new play following "Benito Cereno," reporting that "perhaps to enliven" his brief trip to London for the opening of his play, Lowell "announced" to the press that "he might now write plays about either Trotsky or the recently killed Malcolm X: 'I could probably get him talking. But all the Negroes around him, – I don't know how they'd talk.' His worries on this score were respectfully reported in the quality London papers" (359). It is not quite clear why Lowell's personal relations, politics, and comments about his work should be treated with this consistent tone of contempt. Why is it absurd that Lowell should worry about the accuracy of his dialogue in a contemplated play about American blacks, and that the London press should "respectfully" report his comments? Why is political involvement reduced to the status of a boyish "adventure," and why are his politics so often scorned as "radical"-in-quotation-marks?

By the end of Lowell's life, Hamilton's bias becomes quite explicit. A more objective observer might discern a degree of pathos, even tragedy, in the situation of a great poet, prematurely dying, without a home, menaced by mental illness and by the unpredictable temperament of his wife, and still, despite everything, possessed by the rage to write, and writing what are arguably among the most moving of his lyrics. Yet Hamilton notes only Lowell's "exhilaration at reappearing at the scene of his most recent crime," as if he were a delinquent (435); his "winter antics," as if he were a clown (454); his "Easter dramas," as if he were an actor and his sufferings unreal (462).

These interpretations contradict the facts, which make Lowell seem wiser and saner than many of those around him, and they contrast with Lowell's eloquent letters. In the quoted comments of Lowell's friends one also catches glimpses of the sides of Lowell that Hamilton cannot show: "He was, as always, working hard" (Frank Bidart) (467); "I'll never forget how touched I was at the boring writers' sessions when I would glance over and let my eyes rest on the brooding, sorrowing Beethovenesque head. I don't know why that head and face so often touched me through sheer presence – so much suffering contained there, I suppose" (William Styron) (466–67). It is a virtue of this biography that it gives us the tools with which to begin to construct an alternate version of Lowell's life. The narrative is not skillful enough to produce a coherent myth; the quotations stand out from the surrounding materials and subvert them.

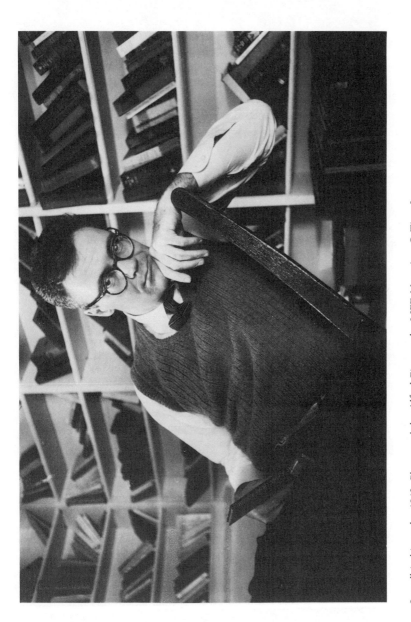

Lowell in his study, 1962. Photograph by Alfred Eisenstaedt, *LIFE* Magazine, © Time Inc.

The biographer clearly came to dislike his subject – not an unprecedented phenomenon. But what does he make of Lowell's art? The first thing to note is that Lowell's poetry plays a relatively minor role in Hamilton's narrative. Hamilton's *modus operandi* is to wait until each volume is published and then to quote selectively from reviews, appending his own evaluation. Because these passages are brief and occur at widely spaced intervals, we may easily overlook them, as virtually all reviewers of the book have in fact done. Let us now examine them rather closely to discern the pattern that emerges.

Hamilton gives short shrift to Lowell's first book, *Land of Unlikeness* (1944), focusing on negative aspects of two "key reviews" (99), those by Randall Jarrell and R. P. Blackmur. After disputing elements of praise in Jarrell's review, Hamilton vigorously endorses Jarrell's criticisms:

> Jarrell, though, is too good a critic not to see that Lowell's political satires have "a severe crudity," that his literary punning, his ubiquitous allusiveness, is often no more than "a senseless habit," that there is something "Bismarkian" in his surveillance of the moral world, and a tendency throughout to slip into an "Onward Christian Soldiers" style of battle rhetoric. (99)

Whereas Hamilton faults Jarrell for keeping such censure "well hidden," he praises Blackmur for meeting "the book's essential character head on," quoting the passage in which Blackmur called Lowell "distraught about religion," "fractiously vindictive" in dealing with human beings, and "nearly blasphemous" in dealing with faith (99).

Lord Weary's Castle (1946), usually thought of as Lowell's first major work, fares little better in Hamilton's analysis. He perceives "excessive strain" in Jarrell's famous laudatory review. After praising "perhaps thirty" lines in the book as "haunting" (specifying only the final verse of "Quaker Graveyard in Nantucket"), Hamilton proceeds to make sport of the book:

> Although Lowell had certainly become craftier and more resonant since writing *Land of Unlikeness,* in most of the new poems his posture – and, intermittently, his posturing – remained essentially the same: the hectic, crunchingly enjambed iambic line, the welter of grabbed myths and pseudosymbols, the impudent and hortatory prayers, the barely controlled retributive gusto and the linguistic flagellation – both of self (so that the poet's noble rage will not lazily abate) and of the fallen world (which, if it will not be redeemed, surely deserves further punishment). (105)

Although in *Lord Weary's Castle* Lowell eliminated the "sillier" puns as well as "the more hysterical 'political' gesturing," his tone remains "manic," his structures still deteriorate into "myth and melodrama," and his texture remains an "elemental moonscape" (105–7).

Nor does *The Mills of the Kavanaughs* (1951) find favor. After claiming that Jarrell was right in his review to "single out 'Falling Asleep Over the Aeneid' as the most effective poem" in the volume (actually Jarrell called "Mother Marie Therese" the best poem, revising his judgment only some years later), Hamilton goes on to lambaste "the cardboard characters, the dramatic monologues that all sound the same, the classical myths that don't quite fit, the narratives that weave in and out of dreamed and 'real' experience, past and present actions, without ever yielding enough clues for us to sort out which is which" (182). In the light of such analysis, one begins to suspect that it does not really matter very much which poem wins the contest to be called "best." "Altogether," Hamilton concludes, "*The Mills of the Kavanaughs* is a confused, self-punishing, bleakly secular performance – and a crucial one in Lowell's development" (186).

That last clause prepares us to expect a version of the most popular current paradigm for understanding Lowell's career, the paradigm that Albert Gelpi and A. Kingsley Weatherhead challenge in their essays in this volume and that the other contributors (myself included) assume. According to this model, Lowell discovered his authentic, strong voice in *Life Studies* (1959). But we are in for a surprise. Hamilton does not much like *Life Studies* either. He judges Richard Eberhart's positive review to have gone "overboard" (270), and his own commentary is markedly restrained. Of Lowell's stylistic breakthrough in Part I, he judiciously asserts: "The only 'task' of Lowell's new style will be to prove its own disconsolate and modest propositions; his one remaining faith, if one can call it that, is in the imaginable moral power of perfect speech. At worst, no one could say of *this* new book: 'But who believed this? Who could understand?'" (260). At worst, then, one is forced to admit that the book makes easy reading. But what can one say at best? Hamilton judges Part II, Lowell's prose memoir, to be "highly polished" and "sorrowing" but also a "merciless exercise" in "ridicule," resentful and malicious (260). He dismisses the poems of Part III as "minor" (261).

That leaves Part IV, the "Life Studies" sequence proper, in which Lowell's "'new style' is unequivocally on display" (261). "There are times," Hamilton begins, "when the 'poetry' adds nothing to the prose [of the memoir]" – and we note the quotation marks around the word "poetry" (261). The early poems in the sequence are "pedestrian" and "one would be hard pressed to insist that they *need* to be set out as verse" (263). The line breaks "seem random, and there is none of the rhythmic or imagistic subtlety that marks the later . . . poems" (261). In the later poems, however, "there is a noticeable tightening: alliterations and assonances seem more deliberate, more shrewd and menacing; the dramatic shifts more calculated, brutal" (263). Hamilton explains this improvement by suggesting that "by this stage Lowell was more sure – technically – of what he was about" (263). We should note that Hamilton here confuses order in the sequence with order of composition. Actually the last poem in the sequence, "Skunk Hour," was composed first, and all the poems were revised more or less simultaneously. We should also note how ambiguous Hamilton's praise is. "Menacing" and "brutal," "shrewd" and "calculated," these seem to be Mafia bosses, not poems. Perhaps the truth is that Hamilton simply feels more comfortable with Lowell's subject matter when he moves away from his parents and toward his adult self, though he never feels truly at ease when reading Lowell's poetry. Hamilton enthusiastically praises only one poem in the volume, "Waking in the Blue," which he describes as a "supreme example of Lowell's new 'informality,' an informality seamed with high instinctive artifice (if such were possible!)" (246). The grounds that permit this poem to be praised above the others remain obscure.

So it goes. *Imitations* (1961) is pockmarked with "limp translatorese," "stale archaisms," and "mechanical poeticizing" of the sort produced by "an amateur poet or an overworked professor" (292). *For the Union Dead* (1964), despite the "fullsome" praise it received (308), contains "exercise poems" (304). Even its celebrated title poem is in truth "overdeliberate and without . . . energy and grace," though it does make a positive step "towards extending the possibilities of [Lowell's] self-centeredness" (279). *The Old Glory* (1964) seems "threadbare," its political concerns "crudely underscored" (311). With the possible exception of "Waking Early Sunday Morning," *Near the Ocean* (1967) lacks "great assurance, or even clarity" (330). Lowell's decision to publish the volume in such a state revealed "a strain of vulgarity" (348). *Notebook* (1969, 1970), a sprawling, uneven epic written in "slack fourteen-liners" (368), is frequently impenetrable without a biographical key (387). A "weird, unshapely monument" to Lowell's belief that he must transmute his experience into literature, it is only "near-literature" (388). Hamilton curiously does not evaluate *The Dolphin* (1973), but spends three pages quoting from negative reviews. Finally, he calls *Day by Day* (1977) "almost meandering" (436), a terminus and a sort of confession of life-long failure:

> Many of these poems are loose, chatty, confidentially *verbatim,* and there are moments throughout the book when Lowell calls into question his whole "way of writing"; he envies the imaginers, the mythmakers, the fabulists. . . . "Alas, I can only tell my own story," he writes in "Unwanted," and the suggestion throughout *Day by Day* is that perhaps the last chapter of the story has been told. (470–71)

Looking through Hamilton's entire biography, we find less than a handful of poems he feels he can honestly endorse: "Waking in the Blue," one stanza of "Night Sweat," the "charming" "Soft Wood." A few others he refrains from explicitly condemning. Those meager poems apart, it is all a poetic acid pit, requiring not exegesis but detoxification.

With such a view of Lowell the man and the poet, Hamilton certainly seems an odd choice for a biographer. But the most important limitation of his biography lies elsewhere: in his failure to take account of Lowell's intellectual and creative life. This is the biography of an outward shell, who eats and drinks, has sexual intercourse, makes and breaks friendships, works at universities, takes trips, sees doctors, publishes books. The being within the shell – the Lowell of ideas, the Lowell who had creative impulses that he alternatively fought to express and fought *against,* the Lowell who achieved greatness despite the sins and follies committed by that shell who shared his existence – *that* Lowell is almost totally absent. That Lowell, of course, is the only one that matters to us, and the only one that mattered to Lowell himself, who wrote of his "life spent in life work" (*N* 143). Harold Bloom has distinguished between the "poet-in-the-poet" and the "person-in-the-poet" (*Map* 19). That distinction helps us see what goes so terribly wrong in this unremittingly factual, subtly malicious narrative: Hamilton tells the story of the "person-in-the-poet." Lowell's struggles to be an artist and to be one again and again at every stage of his life, and his concomitant struggle against art, against the overweening claims of the imagination – these are all left out. The paradox is that if Lowell *had* been only the person Hamilton describes, this biography would have had no reason to exist.

Perhaps the problem is ultimately an aesthetic one. Hamilton's notion of the poetic vocation and Lowell's embodiment of it come to two quite different things. Hamilton allies poetry with "rhetoric . . . argument pursued for the sake of wit and wordplay rather than for any just or true solution" (18). No wonder that he should feel consistently uncomfortable in the presence of an imagination conceived so differently. For Lowell, poetry was not just "wit and wordplay" but an all-consuming passion: "If I stop writing I stop breathing" (*H* 169). He insisted that "poetry isn't a craft that you can just turn on and off. It has to strike fire somewhere, and truth, maybe unpleasant truth about yourself, may be just the thing that does that" (Alvarez, "Robert Lowell" 19). We can trace his conception of the poetic act to the intense examples set by his mentors Allen Tate and William Carlos Williams, and ultimately to the writing of Ralph Waldo Emerson, whom Lowell called the "master" of American literature (ms. at Harvard). As uncomprehending as Hamilton is in Lowell's presence, we can imagine him all the more so in Emerson's. Hamilton lacks sympathy with the main tradition of American poetry.

W. H. Auden, in a remarkable essay on modern American verse, supplies the terms that allow us to see Hamilton's problem most clearly. Connecting a nation's literature to its history and landscape, Auden describes American poetry as individualistic, democratic, and Puritan, whereas British poetry remains more traditional, inhabiting a universe with a familiar face: "The only Americans I can possibly imagine as British are minor poets with a turn for light verse like [James Russell] Lowell and Holmes; and the only British poets who could conceivably have been American are eccentrics like Blake and Hopkins" (10). Auden analyzes the difference in this way:

> Every European poet, I believe, still instinctively thinks of himself as a "clerk," a member of a professional brotherhood, with a certain social status irrespective of the number of his readers (in his heart of hearts the audience he desires and expects are those who govern the country), and taking his place in an unbroken historical succession. In the States poets have never had or imagined they had such status, and it is up to each individual poet to justify his existence by offering a unique product. . . . To some degree every American poet feels that the whole responsibility for contemporary

> poetry has fallen upon his shoulders, that he is a literary aristocracy of
> one. . . . There are advantages and disadvantages in both attitudes. A Brit-
> ish poet can take writing more for granted and so write with a lack of
> strain and over-earnestness. American poetry has many tones, a man talk-
> ing to himself or one intimate friend, a prophet crying in the wilderness,
> but the easy-going tone of a man talking to a group of his peers is rare; for
> a "serious" poet to write light verse is frowned on in America and if, when
> he is asked why he writes poetry, he replies, as any European poet would,
> "For fun," his audience will be shocked. (18)

As early as his school days at St. Mark's, Lowell was speaking of "literature's urgency" (Hamilton, *Robert Lowell* 22). This conviction never left him. In 1965 he
commented to A. Alvarez that whereas the English seem to regard poetry as something "done with your left hand," in America "it's always done with both your
hands":

> I've never lived anywhere else, but I feel it is extreme (and perhaps unique,
> even) about America, that the artist's existence becomes his art. He is re-
> born in it, and he hardly exists without it. . . . I don't know enough about
> Englishmen or any other country to make a comparison. But I feel this
> in meeting people, that we have a feeling the arts should be "all out" –
> you're in it, you're all out in it, and you're not ashamed to talk about it
> endlessly, sheerly. That would seem embarrassing to an Englishman, and
> inhuman, probably, to be that "all out" about it. (Alvarez, "Talk" 43)

On another occasion, he wrote that Whitman was "our best and the wind of the
great dream let loose" – the archetype of the American poet ("Digressions" 66). "To
a sour foreign eye," he went on, "most American literature is a sequence of demoli-
tions, the bravado of perpetual revolution, breakthrough as the stereotype with nothing preserved." Yet Lowell defended against such a charge, quoting Henry Adams:
"The American mind exasperates them as a buzz-saw might exasperate a pine forest"
(67). Lowell declared himself ambivalent about the figure that emerges from American history and literature – "this angel, devil, firebringer, Milton's rebel, the first
American." Yet since "national characteristics outlast the national fortunes" ("Digressions" 67), he himself resembled this prophet-rebel-hero, self-liberated from
"cautions and nots" (Alvarez, "Talk" 43). He believed that in America "the artist
finds new life in his art and almost sheds his other life" (Alvarez, 43).

In the last essay published in his lifetime, Lowell summed up the reciprocal relations between his poetry and his life. Significantly, the mood of "urgency" links this
summation with his schoolboy comments of forty years before:

> I am not an authoritative critic of my own poems, except in the most press-
> ing and urgent way. I have spent hundreds and hundreds of hours shaping,
> extending and changing hopeless or defective work. I lie on a bed staring,

crossing out, writing in, crossing out what was written in, again and again, through days and weeks. Heavenly hours of absorption and idleness . . . intuition, intelligence, pursuing my ear that knows not what it says. In time, the fragmentary and scattered limbs become by a wild extended figure of speech, something living . . . a person. . . . Looking over my *Selected Poems,* about thirty years of writing, my impression is that the thread that strings it together is my autobiography, it is a small-scale *Prelude,* written in many different styles and with digressions, yet a continuing story – still wayfaring. . . . I pray that my progress has been more than recoiling with satiation and disgust from one style to another, a series of rebuffs. I hope there has been increase of beauty, wisdom, tragedy, and all the blessings of this consuming chance. ("After Enjoying" 112–15)

One recalls Albert Gelpi's argument in *The Tenth Muse: The Psyche of the American Poet* that American poetry *is* the poet's psyche (x), that the American artist is "thrown back on himself more than his counterpart in England or on the continent" (10), that the "insistent and subsuming theme" of American poets is the "enigma of their identity" (11). Observers ranging from Tocqueville to Phillip Rahv, R. W. B. Lewis, Roy Harvey Pearce, and Harold Bloom (*Agon*) have made similar points. The problematic of American poetry involves the twin tropes of self and newness. It is a problematic in which Hamilton simply has no interest. Unfortunately his critical blindness occurs precisely at a crucial point in the American poetic character and, more specifically, in Lowell's. Hamilton cannot fathom Lowell's impulse to revise his sonnet to John Berryman so that it reads not "these are words" (*N 1967–68* 151) but "we are words" (*H* 203).

It is this Lowell, the poet who could so completely identify himself with his words, who is absent from Hamilton's telling of the life. Hamilton observes that *The Mills of the Kavanaughs* was "crucial" in the development of Lowell's "voice" (186) without ever showing Lowell struggling for his voice. He occasionally alludes to Lowell's "ambitions as a poet" (42), but such references are almost lost in the narrative and in any case Hamilton seems to understand poetic ambition merely as a synonym for careerism (see 334). Lowell himself understood his poetic ambition in quite different terms. For example, Hamilton quotes Lowell commenting that "a man's struggle with the text" may consume him (350), that he spends his days "writing and rewriting" (353–54), that "to write we seem to have to go at it with such single-minded intensity that we are always on the point of drowning" (337). Hamilton even quotes Elizabeth Hardwick commenting about Lowell that "texts had been his life" (468). Yet except in such quoted phrases, this theme evaporates in Hamilton's account. Thus Hamilton has missed his essential story: the place the imagination has made for itself in our age and in America.

Perhaps the true story involves Lowell's perpetual quest to decenter his work, which Joseph Riddel and others have identified as a central feature of American poetics. As early as 1944, when Lowell had not yet published his first book and was in fact without any established style at all, he wrote of his desire to discover a "new style" (Hamilton, *Robert Lowell* 98). This desire recurs like a leitmotif in Lowell's self-references, including, as we have just seen, the last essay he published in his lifetime. This obsessive, self-propelled drive was motivated less by objective facts than by inner need and was thus insatiable. It contributed to Lowell's poetic achievement but perhaps limited it also, producing a poetry of constant change and inconclusiveness. Like Melville's Ishmael (ch. 32), Lowell prayed never to complete anything; like the speaker of Baudelaire's "Le Voyage," he engaged in a lifelong search for *le nouveau*, for perfect freedom. Without that unquenchable thirst, his poetry itself might have dried up.

Lowell felt so personally contingent that he dedicated himself to a task of self-creation in an unfinishable discourse, spent his life pushing beyond the borders of his previous texts, lived only in the ever-shifting frontier of an immanence he variously termed his "style," his "voice," his "texts," his "poems," his "living name." Part Sisyphus, part Prometheus, part democratic American, and part shadow haunted by his own passing and the fear of having never existed, Lowell lived a life of almost unimaginable inner drama. Out of his self-doubt and his faith in himself, out of his daily life and his immersion in the world of words, he created texts that have become crucial to our time.

III

How then do we think, speak, and write about Lowell's poetry, a decade after his death and in the aftermath of a highly influential, narratively forceful, but intellectually deficient biography? We may seek to derive an alternate, profounder image of the poet from his own words and from the information Hamilton has collected. Jay Martin accomplishes just that in his essay in this volume, a brilliant reading of Lowell's texts as a prolonged encounter with grief. Or we may acknowledge Hamilton's portrait of the artist as a sot, while returning nevertheless to the poetry as if to a separate reality, as Marjorie Perloff does in her essay. Finally, we may simply study the poetry freshly, eager to extend the critical tradition that has grown up around it. That is essentially the method of the rest of the essays in this volume.

Following Martin's analysis of the psychological patterns of Lowell's life and work, Albert Gelpi commences the critical debate by attempting to revise the Lowell canon. Radically departing from orthodoxy, he argues for the supremacy of *Lord Weary's Castle* over the later works on the ground that it represents the poet's most sustained and powerful engagement with the world. Sandra M. Gilbert and Lawrence Kramer elaborate on *Life Studies,* the volume in which Lowell broke through to a more personal-seeming voice. Gilbert interprets "Skunk Hour" as an evocation of a magical world in which the poet must face, among other things, the anxiety that his strong male and female precursors provoke in him. Kramer treats the entire "Life Studies" sequence as an address to a "silent, anonymous Other" who supersedes the speaker's Oedipal object-choice, and as a discourse in which rhetoric and experience reciprocally implicate each other. Kramer's psychoanalytic method parallels Martin's, though his major finding differs significantly: He concludes that *Life Studies* is predominantly the instrument of Lowell's "resistance to cure," a creative evasion, though a potent one. Marjorie Perloff, discussing Lowell and Berryman together, focuses on the poems of *Life Studies* and *For the Union Dead*. Although, like Gilbert and Kramer, she regards this middle phase as the nub of Lowell's achievement, she views that achievement more skeptically than they, arguing finally that "the 'Age of Lowell' can now be understood as marking the end of an era rather than ushering in a new one."

Alex Calder and Calvin Bedient take divergent but complementary approaches to Lowell's next distinct grouping, the sonnets of 1969–73. Calder discusses *Notebook* in its various versions as a "process poem." He finds Lowell's poem more adaptable to Derridean and Foucaultian systems of reference than similar poems by Olson, Ginsberg, and Berryman since it reveals "a process of constant revision rather than a process more committed to speech as a model." Bedient also studies the language of the sonnet sequences, emphasizing not Lowell's revisions but his "opening of the poetic gates" to "heteroglossia," to multiple quotation and the competition of discourses. Finally, Alan Holder, Helen Deese, A. Kingsley Weatherhead, and George McFadden debate the merits of Lowell's last phase, the darkened yet transparent eloquence of *Day by Day*. Holder and especially Weatherhead argue that these poems represent a falling away from Lowell's earlier achievement, a poetic curtailment, a manifestation of loss. Deese and McFadden, however, defend them as a fitting conclusion to Lowell's career-long search for new ways of writing poetry. Deese finds Lowell perfecting and defining his "art of the eye" through an intertextual encounter with Vermeer, Rembrandt, Van Eyck, and photography, and through his reshaping of pastoral elegy. McFadden suggests that although Lowell suffered from a narcissistic fixation that produced mania and depression, he turned this "reduction of his powers" into an asset by struggling "to snatch one last word from the claws of his personal devil."

As I have suggested and as the dialogue among our contributors attests, Lowell's career exhibited the same profile he mockingly attributed to American literature in general: "the bravado of perpetual revolution, breakthrough as the stereotype with nothing preserved" ("Digressions" 66). But just as that is only a part of the truth about American literature, so it is only part of the truth about Lowell. Although I think it accurate to call "breakthrough" Lowell's personal stereotype when he contemplated his career, I doubt that his different phases left "nothing preserved" from the earlier ones. Rather, I suspect that his desire for breakthrough was a defense against a strong need to stabilize, repeat, and even at worst to regress. As he once confessed in a different context, "I wish to turn the clock back with every breath I take" ("Liberalism" 19); it was this wish, or something allied to it, that he continually fought to break through. Therefore, critics like Bernard Duffey (290–94) and Marjorie Perloff (*Poetic Art* x, 1–54) who emphasize elements of consistency in

Lowell's work make a valid point. The dynamics of Lowell's poetry attest to a tension between his desire to change and his equally strong need to preserve.

Beneath the perpetual revolutions, I can identify three constants in Lowell's poetry. One is his language, which strains against the limits of the "poetic" so brilliantly and unremittingly that the effort unites his various new styles, despite their surface differences. The second is psychological insight, peripherally present in the earliest poems and centrally present from *The Mills of the Kavanaughs* on. The third is social and historical awareness, a quality that seems to come to the fore in his most ambitious work but that is implicit throughout his oeuvre. Lowell recognizes the inherent rhetoricity of poetry, its condition of being bound in and as opaque language, and at the same time seeks to retain poetry's ancient gift of illuminating the world outside itself.

Criticism of the 1980s has tended to emphasize the linguistic and psychological aspects of Lowell's poetry over its social-historical aspect, perhaps because of an antihistorical temper to the times, perhaps because Lowell's sense of history involves ambiguity rather than clarity. Nevertheless, I would like to conclude this essay by examining a late poem in which social-historical awareness is paramount: "George III." I have chosen this particular poem because it has thus far received no critical commentary and because it seems to me to epitomize Lowell's art. We see in it Lowell's last complex and moving attempt to voice an utterance both connected to and independent of the world.

From the beginning of his career, Lowell sought to create his poetic identity out of an involvement with history. His development as an artist in the shadow of the Modernist giants only confirmed his historicism, his sense that, as T. S. Eliot put it, in penetrating the life of another age "one is penetrating the life of one's own" (xii). In his first books, *Land of Unlikeness* (1944) and *Lord Weary's Castle* (1946), Lowell allied himself with the Christian poetics of Eliot as well as the Christian historiography of Christopher Dawson, Arnold Toynbee, Etienne Gilson, and E. I. Watkin. The basic concept goes back to Saint Augustine: Secular history is but an aspect of God's design and has a preordained, redemptive end. Responding to the cataclysmic violence of World War II, Lowell wrote as if that end were now at hand: "The Lord survives the rainbow of his will" (*LWC* 14). Eliot, himself ambivalent toward time, had come to the position in *Four Quartets* that "only through time time is conquered," but Lowell, who called himself "a red arrow on this graph / of Revelations" (*LWC* 69), implied that only the end of time could conquer time. Although many of the Modernists subordinated historical data to an overriding myth, Lowell went furthest in prophesying an imminent apocalypse. When history refused to die – when, as he later put it, instead of civilization breaking down, *he* did (Alvarez, "Robert Lowell" 19) – he felt compelled to reconceive the problem.

By 1953, Lowell was asserting that "the greatest historians were those who recreated people, not simply those who gave an accurate or even an interesting account of events. . . . History is an art, not a science" (McCormick 269). Influenced by nineteenth-century historians like Macaulay who believed that history is a province of literature – and perhaps also by mid-twentieth-century historians who had begun to emphasize the "historical imagination" (Collingwood 231–48), the "poetry of history" (Neff 4), and the idea that "no historian can be 'great' if he is not also a great artist" (Toynbee 44) – Lowell came to regard historiography as a creative act analogous to that of poetry. Although by calling history an art he meant to refute the objectivism of scientific historiography, he equally opposed himself to all systems that claim to stand outside history in order to define it as an object. Lowell had moved from a preoccupation with general laws to an immersion in particulars. He still wished to bear witness to the world but no longer from a superior vantage point, no longer supposing, as Michel Foucault was later to put it, that his own analysis could "remain stable in itself or escape the movement of History" (*Order* 370). Foucault, in fact, provides an illuminating context for understanding Lowell's shift when he observes that in the modern era, "Behind the history of positivities, there appears another, more radical, history, that of man himself – a history that now concerns man's very being, since he now realizes that he not only 'has history' all around him, but is himself, in his own historicity, that by means of which a history of human life, a history of economics, and a history of languages are given their form" (*Order* 370). Although Foucault goes on to prophesy the demise of such humanistically oriented historicism, Lowell remained allied to it throughout the rest of his life.

In such volumes as *Life Studies* (1959), *For the Union Dead* (1964), and *Near the Ocean* (1967), Lowell acknowledged that his grasp on the historical world could at best be only fragmentary. As the philosopher Maurice Natanson has written, the reality of history is "the reality of the subjectivity that creates and defines it, that bears its meaning, and that is witness to its truth" (177). Therefore, the historian must face "the radical status of his own existence, his own being in the historical world" (183). Lowell now placed himself and his language at the center of his historical imagination. He said that he mingled personal memories with cultural memories in "For the Union Dead," for example, in order to avoid a "fixed, brazen tone" (ms. at Harvard) – "brazen" implying both arrogance and claims to permanence. Through what I have called its art of analogy (*Robert Lowell* 173), the poem sets in dynamic interaction childhood memories and the movements of history; the Civil War and the modern world; Colonel Shaw and the eloquent speaker of the poem. Lowell became "our truest historian," as Richard Poirier has called him (1), not by discovering the objective truth about the past but by making a truth that takes into account the radical role of his own discourse in formulating it.

In the sonnet sequences of *Notebook* (1970) and *History* (1973), Lowell carried his notion of history as art as far as he could, seeming to use historical people and events merely as raw materials for his machine of signifiers. But in "George III," published in his last collection, *Day by Day* (1977), he regained the balance of *For the Union Dead*. The poem portrays King George in a deliberately ambiguous manner. One might argue from a Marxist perspective that Lowell's ambiguities simply expose the contradiction in his ideology: The conflict between his progressive impulses and his unacknowledged allegiance to a hierarchical, imperialist capitalist system results in guilt feelings and a need to obfuscate by discovering ambiguities and ironies. Although there may be justice in such a charge, we do well to recall Lowell's own position on such matters. He was fully aware of his divided loyalties: "A poem needs to include a man's contradictions. One side of me, for example, is a conventional liberal. . . . My other side is deeply conservative, wanting to get at the roots of things. . . . In the writing of a poem all our compulsions and biases should get in, so that finally we don't know what we mean" (Kunitz 36). Moreover, he rejected the authority of any totalizing world view. He thought history *inherently* a repository of ironies and ambiguities. No system or ideology could answer all its questions or solve all its riddles.

Lowell's method as a poet of social and historical awareness probably owes most to Yeats. Yeats observed that "we make out of the quarrel with others, rhetoric, but of the quarrel with ourselves, poetry" (331). Lowell intentionally turned his social-historical poems of the 1950s, 1960s, and 1970s into quarrels with himself, often by identifying himself with his subject. His adherence to the Yeatsian formula is clear in his remark about including personal elements in "For the Union Dead" to avoid a "brazen" tone. The poems may lose prophetic power, as Albert Gelpi suggests in this volume, but they gain authenticity. Through turning on themselves, they avoid the dangers of bombast or oversimplification. And whatever their limits, they have found a language that makes a political poetry possible in our time.

Along with "For the Union Dead," "George III" (*DBD* 133–35) is one of only two poems Lowell composed for a specific public occasion. Commissioned by *Newsweek* for its July 4, 1976, issue, it commemorates two hundred years of American independence. Lowell being Lowell, he chose to write his bicentennial poem about the wrong George, not Washington but George III, whom he describes as lying "relegated to the ash-heap, / unvisited in this Bicentennial year – / not a lost cause, but no cause." Unlike Pound in the "Adams Cantos," Lowell does not reproduce historical documents verbatim in the belief that documents equal objective truth, nor does he even reproduce them as Williams does in *Paterson,* to create a collagelike interchange between poetry and prose. Instead he assimilates his sources into his own poetic language, altering, rearranging, and in a sense reimagining the material. Borrowing incidents from Oscar Sherwin's *Uncorking Old Sherry,*[1] Lowell describes King George dancing with his appalled apothecary, reviewing imaginary troops, and bowing to an elm as if it were a Chinese emissary. In relating these anecdotes, the poet aims for something beyond analysis: He seeks to vitalize and epitomize the historical character he has recreated. Like a Herder or a Collingwood, he empathizes with his subject. Indeed, Lowell's own experiences when sick must have informed his understanding of George's delusive behavior. For example, the time that George talked "for thirty-two hours / on everything, everybody" parallels Lowell's own "nonstop talk" in mania (Hamilton, *Robert Lowell* 341). Thus Lowell's quarrel with the "mad" king becomes also a quarrel with himself.

In addition to portraying George III, the poem portrays another historical personage closer to home. It concludes in this way:

> George –
>
> once a reigning monarch like Nixon,
> and more exhausting to dethrone . . .
>
> Could Nixon's court,
> could Haldeman, Ehrlichman, or Kissinger
>
> blame their king's behavior
> on an insane wet nurse?
>
> Tragic buffoonery
> was more colorful once;
>
> yet how modern George is,
> wandering vacated chambers of his White House,
> . . . .
> in his last lucid moment,
> singing a hymn to his harpsichord,
>
> praying God for resignation
> in his calamity he could not avert . . .
>
> mercifully unable to hear
> his drab tapes play back his own voice to him,
>
> morning, noon, and night.

Lowell superimposes his present historical moment on the past, modern breakdowns on more ancient ones, *The Final Days* on the life of George III. The poet seeks to "re-create people," as the great historians do, penetrating the past and the present at the same time. Aware of historical difference, he also senses the threads that tie human being to human being. "George III" does not pretend to give us the absolute truth about history, but in juxtaposing two widely separated historical characters, it creates its own order of truth.

"George III" puts into play four contrasting and complementary elements – five if we count the reader. The four are the "young George" of 1776, a figure of some nobility though tyrannical; George grown "old" and mentally ill; Richard Nixon in his Watergate disgrace; and the poem's voice or language-generator or "author-function" (to adopt Foucault's phrase [*Language* 124–31]), which puts these forces into action, juxtaposes these historical images, and creates ironies through its comparisons and contrasts. The poem implicitly moves from a historicist retrieval of particulars to a poetic sense of something more universal than historical data: the tragicomedy of human existence.

The generator of the text begins by rather sympathetically evoking the youthful George who is paradoxically both victim and tyrant (lines 1–13). He then contrasts this figure with the image of the aged George, who is also paradoxical: "mad, bad" in theory but largely whimsical and sweet-tempered in the specific anecdotes told about him (lines 14–54). Indeed, as the stories accumulate, the elderly George becomes increasingly attractive. Even the generalization "mad, bad, old" gives way to the less judgmental "old, mad, deaf, half-blind." Whereas the initial anecdotes include some damaging material – he picks a page's pocket, he holds a candle threateningly close to his wife's face, and so on – the later ones emphasize only his pathos and humor. He writes his own epitaph in order to proclaim himself "a good man"; he monologues for hours, seemingly in a desperate effort to communicate *something* to *somebody*; he reads *Don Quixote* and the Bible aloud, simultaneously; he sings a hymn not on but *to* his harpsichord; he prays for resignation. Like the mother skunk in "Skunk Hour" and the title character of "Jonathan Edwards in Western Massachusetts," this George is diminished, absurd, and yet somehow heroic.

Writing, reciting, and singing, he is perhaps a figure of the poet. On this level of interpretation, we may construe the poem as an allegory of the voice that utters it, an ironically deflationary vision of the poet-prophet reduced to an apparently absurd status. What is introduced as George's fall from sanity and rectitude ("not yet the mad, bad, old king") transforms itself, as it is elaborated, into a spiritual rise. George progresses from the "lust for dominion" to a Bible-reading, hymn-singing, "tragic buffoonery" – a buffoonery that injures no one, oppresses no one, and results in no casualties of war. Although mad, he speaks, through the poetry of his actions, a kind of truth to power. Perhaps he is God's fool.

The last half of the poem contrasts George III to President Nixon. The narrator conflates the two: Nixon is a "monarch" with a "court" whereas George resides in a "White House." Although Nixon is mentioned in only a few lines, this conflation keeps him continually in mind. When the narrator depicts George III "praying God for resignation," for example, we think of Nixon insisting to Henry Kissinger that they kneel down and pray together "for help, rest, peace and love" during the darkest days of Watergate, and Kissinger's fear that the president had lost his mind (Woodward and Bernstein 423–24). When George addresses imaginary congresses, we think of Nixon "talking to the pictures on the wall" (Woodward and Bernstein 395); when George wanders vacated chambers, we recall Nixon doing likewise. The juxtaposition of George and Nixon exposes a host of similarities between them: delusions of grandeur, erratic behavior, loss of lucidity, and a compulsion to talk alternating with morose introspection and a haunted isolation. But it also brings out differences, which redound in George's favor: He is "colorful" whereas Nixon is "drab"; he has the capacity to amuse himself and others whereas Nixon is solemn and self-absorbed; he is physiologically diseased whereas Nixon is morally responsible for his acts.

Nevertheless, despite Lowell's continuing motive of "telling off the . . . president" (*LS* 85), he ultimately makes Nixon something of a sympathetic character too. The text introduces Nixon as one who was less "exhausting to dethrone" than George, a reminder that he has indeed been forced to resign. The poem then provides more illustrations of George's "colorful" buffoonery, implying by its lack of corresponding anecdotes about the American president the appalling poverty of Nixon's personal life. George ends by praying for resignation (unlike Nixon who prayed only to *avoid* resignation); he is "mercifully unable to hear / his drab tapes play back his own voice to him." Certainly the poem ironically suggests that in electing Nixon, America chose a leader as autocratic as the one it rebelled against two hundred years before, but it also captures the man's pathos: the crazed seclusion of his last days in office, his Dantesque punishment of having to endure a world inhabited only by the sound of his own voice playing back to himself time without end. Like Faulkner's Quentin Compson, Nixon remains trapped in his own story, which he hears everywhere. He is, in a sense, Lowell's dreaded anti-self, powerless to "break through" to the future, powerless to discover a new style that would allow him to reengage the world. For him, "nobody's here" (*LS* 90), not even skunks – just the redundant language of the past that the obsessed, solipsistic, and atrophied listener cannot bear to switch off.

Ultimately, all three of these figures – Nixon and the young and old George – are juxtaposed with the "image or lie of voice" that utters them (Bloom, *Breaking* 4). This voice artfully arranges the figures to create a moral landscape in which violence – whether in the form of an individual flogging or a ruler's lust for dominion that results in mass death – contrasts to affliction. Significantly, the poem does not simplistically divide violence and affliction but locates them together in the same individuals. The poem exposes moral complexity so that the reader, the fifth character in the poem, recognizes it in himself, undoing his repression. Furthermore, the poem's landscape is informed by the narrator's eye for absurd humor, a quality that allies the poem with "Skunk Hour" and empties it of its latent desire for sweeping statement. And the landscape is informed by forgiveness as well, indicated at the outset by the modification of "poor George" and at the conclusion by the wish for mercy for the poem's subjects. As I have suggested, the narrator implies through his act of empathic identification with George and Nixon a relation between them and himself. They function as his doubles who, by reflecting back his poetic self to him, create a self-reflexive space in the poem. Yet he is greater than they. The speaking voice or language-generator is the most complex and capable character in the poem: able to witness, order, and create; to provide a moral frame of reference by means of irony and pity; and to set into motion interacting sets of words, images, and themes that dynamically charge each other with significance.

Although "George III" is an act of keen historical insight, its use of reflexive characters and ironic structures of juxtaposition discloses an awareness that poetry cannot capture history as an object. At about the same time as Lowell wrote this poem, he attempted to encapsulate his poetics in "Epilogue," much as Yeats did in "Under Ben Bulban." After expressing a wish to "say what happened," in the manner of classical empirical historicism, "Epilogue" concludes with a more delimited commitment:

> We are poor passing facts,
> warned by that to give
> each figure in the photograph
> his living name.   (*DBD* 127)

Although Lowell's poems may nostalgically yearn for the authority to name reality directly, they settle for naming figures, for representing what is already laden with representation. In that spirit, Lowell humbled "George III," his poem about history, by terming it a "translation" (*DBD* 133). Lowell's poems prize their link to the world; they also acknowledge their separation from it, their inability to free themselves from the history and structure of their own discourse. "George III" is Lowell's last demonstration of the way art can illuminate history and psychology while remaining cognizant of itself as necessarily other.

At his strongest, Lowell created an art unlike anyone else's – sophisticated, brilliant, insightful, humane. This art, and not his difficulty with ordinary living, is the central meaning of his existence. He has bequeathed us not merely the "poor passing facts" of his experience on earth but a "living name."[2]

NOTES

1   Lines 15–22, 25–26, 32–33, 37–42, and 44–52 of "George III" are based on two separate sections of Sherwin's biography of Richard Sheridan (228–31, "The King's Madness"; 322–23, "Plots of the Regency"). Throughout his career, Lowell selectively integrated other writers' words and other artists' representations into his own texts, creating, as Donald Carne-Ross has said of *Imitations,* a "probing encounter between two linguistic and cultural mediums" that gives us "the uniquely liberating experience of living within two areas of reality, two systems of reference" (169). I might add that in works like "For the Union Dead," *The Old Glory,* and "George III," Lowell stages an encounter not only between different languages and cultures but between representations of different historical eras and individuals as well.

These are the original sentences in Sherwin along with Lowell's "translation" of them:

"He makes a page go to sleep as an anodyne for his own insomnia and then immediately picks his pockets" (230): ". . . not yet the mad, bad old king, / who whimsically picked the pockets of his page / he'd paid to sleep all day outside his door . . ." (lines 14–16).

"He fancies himself a Quaker and is dressed like one from head to foot" (231): ". . . who dressed like a Quaker . . ." (line 17).

"On November 27, the King is removed to Kew. His antics are sad and ludicrous. He dances a minuet with his apothecary in a new tie wig which he orders for the purpose" (231): ". . . who danced a minuet / with his appalled apothecary in Kew Gardens . . ." (lines 17–18).

"He sits with young Court ladies embroidering and pretends to play the fiddle" (228): ". . . who did embroidery with the young ladies . . ." (line 19).

"His majesty, whose curt answers and suspicious bluntness indicate a phlegmatic temperament, is really the reverse" (228): ". . . and criticized them with suspicious bluntness . . ." (line 20).

"To see his wife he pushes the candle into her face and nearly sets her on fire" (229): ". . . who showed aversion for Queen Charlotte, almost / burned her by holding a candle to her face" (lines 21–22).

"He bows to an oak, seizes one of the lower branches, and shakes it with the most apparent cordiality and regard – just as a man shakes his friend by the hand" (229): ". . . aghast / his retinue by formally bowing to an elm, / as if it were the Chinese emissary" (lines 24–26).

"Some there are who rumor that his wet nurse was a lunatic and that quack medicines unhinged his balance" (228): ". . . could Haldeman, Ehrlichman, or Kissinger / blame their king's behavior / on an insane wet nurse?" (lines 31–33).

"He loves to wander through the corridors, a venerable figure with a long silvery beard, attired in a silk morning gown and ermine night cap, holding imaginary conversations with ministers long since dead" (323): ". . . yet how modern George is, / wandering vacated chambers of his White House, / addressing imaginary congresses, / reviewing imaginary combat troops . . ." (lines 36–39).

"The belief that he is dead is one of his regular delusions. 'I must have a new suit of clothes,' he says one day, 'and I will have them black in memory of George the Third, for he was a good man" (323): ". . . thinking himself dead and ordering black clothes: / *in memory of George, for he was a good man*" (lines 40–41).

"He talks for thirty-two hours on end – of everybody and everything" (229): ". . . he talked for thirty-two hours / on everything, everybody . . ." (lines 43–44).

"At Windsor he sits dictating Cervantes and the Bible – at the same time and with incredible speed – to pages whom he afterwards creates Baronets and Knights of the Holy Roman Empire" (229): ". . . read Cervantes and the Bible aloud / simultaneously with shattering rapidity . . ." (lines 45–46).

"'Can it be so late?' he asks. 'Quand on s'amuse, le temps vole'" (323): *"Quand on s'amuse, que le temps fuit –"* (line 47).

"The Queen enters his apartment during one of his lucid intervals and finds him singing a hymn and accompanying himself on the harpsichord. When he has concluded, he kneels down and prays aloud for his consort, for his family, and for the nation, and lastly for himself, that it might please God to avert his heavy calamity, or if not, give him resignation under it" (322): ". . . in his last lucid moment, / singing a hymn to his harpsichord, / praying God for resignation / in his calamity he could not avert . . ." (lines 48–51).

2 I wish to thank Rise B. Axelrod, John M. Ganim, and David Thomas for their helpful suggestions about this essay.

2

Grief and Nothingness: Loss and Mourning in Lowell's Poetry

JAY MARTIN

Between grief and nothing, I will take grief.
—Faulkner, *The Wild Palms*

Robert Lowell was the most important poet in America during the 1960s and 1970s. Not only was his poetic achievement high, he also, like his ancestors James Russell Lowell and Amy Lowell, occupied a prominent position as a literate spokesman on social and cultural issues. At the same time, more privately, he was preoccupied with death, and he gave the richest expression that twentieth-century poetry has to offer of the varieties of the experience of loss and mourning. He wrote solidly and continuously in the great tradition of the literature of grief.

In retrospect, his whole life seemed to have been lived under the shadow of death. When, late in life, Lowell wrote in the autobiographical poem "Night Sweat," "always inside me is the child who died, / always inside me is his will to die" (*N 1967–68* 103), he seems to be making a point similar to the one Elliott Jacques made: "How each one reacts to the mid-life encounter with the reality of his own eventual death . . . will be markedly influenced by his infantile unconscious relation to death" (507).

In this essay I trace, through Lowell's poems, how his earliest fantasied encounters with "death" in experiences of separation, loss, mourning, and self-fragmentation affected his later efforts to face numerous losses and eventually his own death. Lowell's sense that inside him was a "child who died" had an early origin and remained powerfully at the core of his being throughout his life. But what allied Lowell, as a child, to loss?

Lowell's Childhood

On March 1, 1917, Robert Traill Spence Lowell IV was born, the issue of two of the most prominent families in New England: the Winslows, who traced their ancestry directly to the *Mayflower,* and the Lowells, who arrived in Massachu-

setts Bay in 1639. The "spectacularly correct" match of Lowell's parents was based
more on genealogy than on romance (Hamilton, *Robert Lowell* 4).[1] Arthur Winslow,
Lowell's grandfather, had already rejected several possible suitors for his daughter
Charlotte's hand, due to deficiencies of ancestry. He found R. T. S. Lowell III ac-
ceptable, but unfortunately, apart from his bloodlines, Lowell's father had little to
recommend him. He seems to have been passive, weak-willed, too genteel; as a consequence he was completely dominated by his wife. She disparaged him to one and
all – and to herself. In a notebook that she kept in connection with her psychotherapy
in 1937, Lowell's mother bitterly described her feelings about her marriage. According to Robert Lowell, she married

> because she thought it was time to. She was not at all in love with the
> man, nor did she really admire him. But he seemed the best that was of-
> fered. She rather enjoyed his admiration, and thought she might improve
> him, and would be free herself, and away from the constant family fric-
> tions and quarrels, which she thought degrading.
>
> But she also thought she was doing a very wrong thing in marrying this
> man whom she did not love, and often felt that she would be punished for
> it, as she was always punished for doing what was wrong.
>
> After this marriage . . . having to live in constant companionship with
> this comparative stranger, whom she found neither agreeable, interesting,
> nor admirable, was a terrible nervous strain. She became increasingly crit-
> ical and unappreciative. She wished to do nothing and see no one. She was
> utterly hysterical, and would have liked to die, but the idea of (Playing the
> game) kept her from doing it. So to the world, her family, and her friends
> she appeared happy and serine [sic]. She was determined not to whine and
> be a Coward; but what a lot of care she made for herself.
>
> Her husband "could not understand at all, was always kind, though irre-
> sponsible; and thought her half crazy." [The final words are direct quo-
> tations from her notebook.] (quoted in Hamilton 386)

The effects on the boy of his disappointed and angry mother soon became obvious. He never found a satisfactory way to identify with his mother and was always
troubled in his relations with her. Nor could he get close to his father, who was the
butt of his mother's constant criticism. Lowell told his friend, Allen Tate, that from
a very early time he had come to see his father through his mother's eyes as ineffectual and that, "unseen and all-seeing," he had listened to his parents' nightly quarrels
(Simpson 124). Of course, despite his mother's influence, the boy would not have
entirely taken his mother's point of view. He seems to have partly idealized and
identified with both his parents and therefore been very confused by their enmity.
Then, too, what was the little boy to think about his own sufficiency when Charlotte soon turned him over to a nurse? Did that mean that Mother really had as

little regard for him as she did for Father? The answer seemed all too clearly to be a resounding Yes! Lowell's feeling that by the age of two he understood, "with despair, that I was second fiddle even in my nurse's affection" (Hamilton, *Robert Lowell* 229) – her first fiddle was Jesus – might well be a displacement of his awareness of his early disappointment in his mother; it would have been too difficult for him to confront his fear that he was second fiddle – or, even worse, that she did not care about him at all, but only about herself. That he was disappointed and terrified by his mother there is no doubt. Her "exaggerated humor" hurt him; he felt belittled. She seemed all-powerful. Certainly, the little boy's experience was that women were more powerful than men. He wished he had been born a girl so that he could have been, like his mother, strong; to "be a boy . . . was to be small, denied and weak" (*LS* 27). He saw his mother as full of complaints and disappointments, narcissistically demanding attention and affection and making him feel that *her* needs were primary and his of no account. Even years later, in Mrs. Lowell's old age, Lowell's second wife Elizabeth Hardwick saw Mrs. Lowell as "nervous and insecure and very conventional" (Hardwick, Letter).

Lowell later said that by the age of three, "I could no longer see Mother as that rarely present, transfigured, Sunday-best version of my nurse. I saw her as my mother, as a rod, or a scolding rusty hinge. . . . I tried to remember Mother when she was happier . . ." (Hamilton, *Robert Lowell* 9). But that thought only led to a hallucinatory core of fantasies about annihilation; for Mother would have been happier, the child concluded, only without Father – *and* therefore without the son whom they had produced – Robert Lowell himself.

Lowell received mixed, confusing, double-binding messages from his parents. They exhibited steadfast hostility, rather than affection, toward each other; they did not even spend nights in the same house. Mrs. Lowell was bent on robbing her husband of all dignity: She criticized him openly to her son, who concluded that his father was "spineless." Through his father's example the boy was properly wary of the evident danger of getting too close to his mother. He could not respect his father, and he was afraid to get too close to his mother. When he was eight and his father was called out of the house for the night on naval affairs, his mother burst into the boy's bedroom, hugged him, and said, "Oh, Bobby, it's such a comfort to have a man in the house!" to which her son replied: "I am not a man. I am a boy!" (Hamilton 12). In short, childhood was a set of contradictions: He idealized but feared his mother, while he depreciated but secretly admired his father. He thus developed what Erik Erikson calls a "negative identity": He made the best of a thoroughly bad lot of possible identifications.

The narrow field available to him for active identification with his parents was through aggression: His father was spineless, but Lowell became a battler and bully in school and was infatuated with Napoleon (and later, Hitler) and military uniforms; his mother insisted on order and discipline, but Lowell was notoriously messy in his habits. His parents were orderly, mannerly, and neat; Lowell, as a young man, was "rude and diffident, a kind of Yankee Stephen Daedalus" (Aaron, Letter), and unruly and "lumbering" (Hardwick, Letter). His parents were so mismatched and they so evidently proclaimed their differences that to the child it was clear that to identify with either parent would be to alienate the other, and so he was unable to develop a strong unambivalent attachment to either (cf. Bowlby, "Making" 202, *Attachment* 442). Even as he was deeply anxious and fearful of being rejected, he still yearned for his parents' love and burned with frustration in not being able to give and receive love. Into young manhood Lowell remained on terms of mutual hostility with his father, finally finding an occasion to bully him and knock him down in his own house. His mother was not so easily defeated, but very early Lowell began to antagonize her indirectly by announcing engagements to women of whom she would certainly disapprove.

John Bowlby's approach to early childhood disorder and mourning applies to Lowell in an exemplary fashion: "Once the child has formed a tie to a mother-figure, which has ordinarily occurred by the middle of the first year, its rupture leads to separation anxiety and grief and sets in train processes of mourning" ("Processes" 317). In such an occurrence, Bowlby adds, "these mourning processes not infrequently take a course unfavorable to future personality development and thereby predispose to psychiatric illness" (317). Lowell's continuing ambivalent tie to both his parents – not ceasing with their deaths – gives sound reason to infer that he had formed attachments that were shaken but neither broken nor strengthened.

The clinical picture that begins to emerge can be summarized in this way: Two kinds of experiences worked into two sorts of psychic distortions. The experience of loss associated with his idea that he was "second fiddle" led him down a path of self-doubt and neurotic depression. His deeper and more complex experience of total rejection thrust him toward an inner sense of not holding together, toward struggles with unintegrated and fragmented hostile internalizations. These two experiences, as we shall see, were linked as are two sides of a coin: They showed up separately and alternately. Whenever one side was dealt with, relieved, and made to subside in intensity and urgency, the other would make its appearance. As an adult Lowell attempted to work with and even turn to artistically productive uses his experience of loss by composing poetry, especially poetry about loss, grief, and mourning. He could do little on his own to control the effects of his experience of self-fragmentation, which usually made its first defensive appearances in grandiose identifications and manic flights and often ended in hospitalization.

Exactly when Lowell's psychiatric illness was detected is not certain. By the mid-1930s his mother was seeing Merrill Moore, the poet-psychiatrist, on her own. She brought her son to see Moore in the spring of 1935, while Lowell was still a student at St. Mark's prep school. He evidently continued to see Moore periodically during 1935 and 1936, Lowell's freshman year at Harvard. Later, in 1939, Moore arranged for Mrs. Lowell to see Jung in Zurich. According to Lowell, Jung said to her, "If your son is as you have described him, he is an incurable schizophrenic" (*DBD* 122).

Thenceforth Lowell was never entirely free from attacks, which put him, as psychiatrists at McLean Hospital said, "truly under the complete domination of childhood fantasies" (Hamilton, *Robert Lowell* 243). He described himself as in "a condition of blank drifting broken by manic enthusiasms" (Hamilton 175). Quite early in his career Lowell's mental state became the subject of frequent gossip in literary circles. In 1949, for instance, the poet Weldon Kees wrote to a friend: "I suppose the most hair-raising news is about Robert Lowell. . . . [A]fter years of behavior that charitable people described as somewhat odd, he has gone completely off his rocker and has been put away in a sanitarium in Boston. Paranoia plus a God-complex, it seems; he had been threatening to 'get' Jean Stafford because he felt he had been singled out to 'root out evil'" (Kees, Letter). He was hospitalized more than twenty times, with such varied diagnoses as "psychotic reaction, paranoid type," "hypomanic," "acute schizophrenic," and "manic-depressive"; and treated with hydrotherapy, electric shock, dynamic analysis, and a wide variety of medications, of which chlorpromazine and lithium were the most frequent. Recently surveying the record of Lowell's treatments, the psychoanalyst E. James Anthony has remarked that Lowell "seems to have been diagnosed and treated almost at whim," which leads Anthony to conclude that "the creative mind, when disordered, can quite befuddle the strict diagnostician" (Anthony, Letter).

Lowell wove the anguish and grief connected with his early traumas of loss and fragmentation into his literary work. Defeated in personal life by illness, he could defend against grief and, moment by moment, day by day, tenuously triumph in literature. By bringing something new and valuable into existence – a poem, an autobiographical sketch, a drama, even a translation – he could counterbalance and compensate for what had gone out of existence. Poetry and autobiography temporarily substituted for the lost mother, the loss of hope, and the shaken self. What could be held together, poetry held. Poetic grief was really his only defense against psychic nothingness. Scarcely another poet in the history of literature has been so preoccupied with loss, death, and mourning; few have been so sensitive to the vicissitudes of grief; seldom has a poet taken up elegiac themes so continuously; no other poet, perhaps, has given such anguished expression to his personal encounter with sorrow and mourning. He was so keenly sensitive to loss from an early time that he continued to be aware of the varieties of the small losses that we all experience continually throughout life: He *noticed* loss wherever he looked and thereby helped his audience to see how fundamental in life loss is (see Peretz 9). What he lost in life he partly recovered through literature; as Bowlby puts it, "loss of [an] object almost always results in an effort to recover it" ("Pathological Mourning" 509). At the least he momentarily staved off fragmentation by recovering the illusion of capacity, unity, and approval through artistic form and achievement in art. The richly accomplished though often tormented body of work that was made possible by Lowell's struggles with loss remains a permanent testimony to the capacity of the artist to turn parts of his suffering into creative accomplishments. If he had no other stable identity, he could count on an identity as a writer. Poetry gave lost things a way of continuing; it gave to Lowell a way of surviving.

Unlike many other poets, Lowell's theme is not how to achieve love but how to endure grief. In his review of Lowell's first book, *Land of Unlikeness* (1944), R. P. Blackmur wrote: "Dante loved his living Florence and the Florence to come and loved much that he was compelled to envisage in hell, and he wrote throughout in loving meters. In Lowell's *Land of Unlikeness* there is nothing loved unless it be its repellence; and there is not a loving meter in the book" ("Review" 38). Certainly he wrote poems in which the effort to secure love was primary – "Night Sweat" (*FUD* 68–69), *The Dolphin*, and "We Took Our Paradise" (*DBD* 57), for instance, come quickly to mind; but loss and grief and one's own capacity to survive them form the iron thread that runs through his work from beginning to end. Like Faulkner, Lowell seemed to have had no choices between nothingness and grief: He chose both, facing blank nothingness in a succession of breakdowns while making grief blossom into art.

Lowell's work is a virtual museum of the varieties of object loss and mourning. In this essay I can discuss or even refer to only a few poems representative of his preoccupation with loss and grieving. I have chosen to discuss Lowell's work according to the increasingly personal focus of his experience of loss, beginning with his poems on the deaths of his ancestors; continuing on to poems responding to the deaths of his contemporaries; to poems memorializing his parents; to those that described his own personal losses through his sickness, divorce, and the aging process; and finally I look at poems in which he directly confronted his own expected death. These are his "subjects" on the level of manifest content. Lowell wrote of death most of his life because he spent his life mourning his early abandonment, a trauma so painful that until just before his death he could deal with it only through mirrors, by writing about the deaths of others.

Lowell's Ancestral Elegies

As Marjorie Perloff has observed, Lowell's most celebrated work has been his elegies, especially for relatives on his mother's side (*Poetic Art* 131–63). It is worthy of note, indeed, that Lowell's early elegies for members of the maternal side of his family exhibit his changing relation to his mother, from a wish to vent his rage and spite on her to an acceptance of her frailty and insufficiency as a mother.

Lowell's first major book of poetry, *Lord Weary's Castle* (1946), contains three elegies for his Winslow ancestors. "The Quaker Graveyard in Nantucket" (8–14), the first poem by Lowell to attract widespread critical praise, was written for a cousin who was drowned at sea during the Second World War. Despite its personal subject, however, this is in every sense a highly formal poem. The cousin is referred to impersonally as "the drowned sailor" or "you, my cousin." His personality is less important than his symbolism as a victim of modern warfare, and secondarily as a symbol of the redemptive possibilities still existing in the traditions of the Catholic faith. The poem begins with an image of Winslow's dead body caught in a dragnet and ends with his and (more generally) modern man's hope for salvation through penance, grace, and finally through world apocalypse. The poem is full of condensed, brilliant images:

> Gobbets of blubber spill to wind and weather,
> Sailor, and gulls go round the stoven timbers
> Where the morning stars sing out together
> And thunder shakes the white surf and dismembers
> The red flag hammered in the mast-head. Hide,
> Our steel, Jonas Messias, in Thy side.   (12)

Although this elegy appears to be classical in its formal approach to emotion, in retrospect it is possible to see that Lowell was drawing on his personal grief from a safe impersonal distance, and the passionate intensity of the work derives as much from unconscious repression and defensive condensation as from deliberate poetic technique.

The subject of "In Memory of Arthur Winslow" (19–22) is his maternal grandfather. Far from being a lamentation, the poem castigates and condemns his grandfather, whom Lowell's mother idolized. Mrs. Lowell had insisted on living in close proximity to her father throughout Lowell's youth, even when this required living separately from her husband. She actually referred to her father as "Napoleon," while ridiculing her husband's mild personality. Lowell's condemnation of Arthur Winslow, then, could scarcely be read within the family as other than an oblique, but fully explicit, attack on Winslow's daughter – Lowell's mother.

Indeed, aggression against Arthur Winslow is full-blown, almost outrageously excessive. In the first section, subtitled "Death from Cancer," the old man is pictured in the most vivid terms as struggling against cancer in the hospital. The astrological sign for Cancer, the crab, picks at his flesh:

> Your people set you up in Phillips' House,
> To settle off your wrestling with the crab –
> The claws drop flesh upon your yachting blouse . . .

He foresees Winslow being carried into the land of the dead. Likewise, he says in the second section ("Dunbarton"), the old energy of the Pilgrim and Puritan fathers has been dissipated in modern times: Only tottering members of the Winslow and Stark genealogy attend the burial, supported by crutches and speaking through ear trumpets. No powerful sermon is given – only "preacher's mouthings," hollow echoes of past times.

In the third section, "Five Years Later," Lowell castigates his mother's father for his capitalist enterprise, the craft

> That netted you a million dollars, late
> Hosing out gold in Colorado's waste,
> Then lost it all in Boston real estate.

He was led on, Lowell plainly says, by "devil's notions." Lowell concludes the poem ambiguously, implying that his grandfather will "Sink like Atlantis in the Devil's jaw" unless, like Lazarus, he is raised up by a special intercession of the Virgin Mary.

Though it is a short poem, "Mary Winslow" (25) is equally harsh. Lowell portrays his mother's aged relative at the moment following her death, just as "the body cools." A demanding, narcissistic patient, she had claimed constant attention, had to be fed mush and orange juice, and was loud with complaints. Now death "stops her hideous baby-squawks and yells." The entire description is mocking and satiric; she who was so pretentious and "grandiloquent" in life appears ridiculous in death.

These three poems were published when Lowell was twenty-nine. His mother died eight years later, and his writing about the Winslows showed a new and different orientation toward his mother's family. In *Life Studies* (1959), Lowell broke with the characteristic approach and methods of his previous poems to write in a more personal, confessional style. As if to exhibit the change clearly, the first three poems in *Life Studies* are Winslow elegies, paralleling the three in the earlier collection. In a psychologically clear gesture, the 1959 sequence "undid" the anger in the 1946 series, replacing defensive anger with the beginnings of acceptance and sorrow and the acknowledgment of loss on the level of the ego.

To make the parallel unmistakable he even wrote "My Last Afternoon with Uncle Devereux Winslow" (59–64) in four parts, like the earlier elegy on Arthur Winslow; but between the two lies a world of difference. The poem describes Lowell's first encounter with death, in 1922, when he saw his mother's brother Devereux dying of Hodgkin's disease. Mixed with confusion over the approaching death is the little boy's love for his grandfather – the same Arthur Winslow he had formerly censured: "Nowhere was anywhere after a summer / at my Grandfather's farm" (59). He lovingly recalls all the particulars of his grandfather's presence on the farm. He tells his parents that he wants to stay with his grandfather, he does not want to return to Boston with them. But the summer is over, the farm has to be closed down. Uncle Devereux, who "was closing camp for the winter," was dying: "Come winter / Uncle Devereux would blend to . . . one color" (64). This elegy is a poem of great beauty, in which the small boy's confusion over death is mingled with the adult poet's grief, not only for his uncle, but even more for his grandfather.

In "Dunbarton," the next poem in *Life Studies* (65–67), the intensely intimate feelings he had for his grandfather are treated directly. Lowell's father was away on sea duty in the Pacific, and everyone referred to Arthur Winslow as "your father." "He was my Father. I was his son," the poet flatly says. On "yearly Autumn getaways from Boston / to the family graveyard in Dunbarton," he helped his grandfather rake the leaves "from our dead forebears" (65–66). The boy felt numbed by death, but relished the living love he shared with the old man. He presents the two sides of this love in the first three lines of the poem, which exhibit his loving projection of his grandfather's love:

> My Grandfather found
> his grandchild's fogbound solitudes
> sweeter than human society.

Love is the subject, again, in the last three lines, which convey his own, nearly sexual, pleasure in "being close" to grandfather:

> In the mornings I cuddled like a paramour
> in my Grandfather's bed,
> while he scouted about the chattering greenwood stove.

In the third Winslow poem in *Life Studies,* "Grandparents" (68–69), Lowell explicitly acknowledges his relation to his grandparents: He is their inheritor. He has literally inherited the summer farm where once he had been a visitor. Then, for the first time in his Winslow elegies, the adult poet fuses with the little boy and, reexperiencing now the love that the boy felt then, he cries in grief and mourning and regret for his loss. Is he also perhaps expressing his longing for the idealized, loving parent he had never had except in his grandfather?

> Never again
> to walk there, chalk our cues,
> insist on shooting for us both,
> Grandpa! Have me, hold me, cherish me!
> Tears smut my fingers. . . .

In these poems, we see Lowell beginning to replace the anger that characterized his first response to death with grief and mourning. His earlier anger had clearly been tied up with the continuing difficulties of his relation to his mother. Each of Lowell's succeeding books contains at least one poem dealing with the death of a Winslow. In these, he continues to work out his own primary depression through mourning for his ancestors.

Two poems in *Notebook 1967–68* (1969) concern Winslows. The first is a recollection of his mother's sister, Aunt Sarah ("For Aunt Sarah"), in which he can lightly and humorously treat their lifelong differences (34). And the second is another poem concerning Arthur Winslow ("My Grandfather"), in which Lowell meditates on his grandfather's probity and dedication to simple virtues:

> I begin to know why he stood the frost
> so many weekends with his little grandson
> sawing up his trees for a penny a log –
> Old Cato. . . .   (40)

Lowell has moved far from his first volumes, where rage against his mother and her family predominated.

Lowell's cousin Harriet Winslow, the poet once told his mother, was "really a lot like you – tells the same kind of story. But I doubt if either of you would see the likeness" (Hamilton 129). In his imagination she symbolized the good mother he had wanted. Of all his relatives he felt closest to her, and she returned the feeling, eventually willing her summer residence in Castine, Maine, to him. He called her "a true lady," and she in turn valued his talents: "There have been too many afternoon naps in the Winslow line," she said wittily. Perhaps because she was like his mother but was not his mother, Lowell could express toward her some of the love, and do the work of mourning, that was much more difficult for him to do directly, without displacement. In any event, in three of his later volumes of poetry he wrote commemorative poems for his cousin Harriet. Not unimportantly, too, he named his daughter after this cousin.

The first of these poems appeared in *For the Union Dead* (1964) and is entitled "Soft Wood" (64). This is a work of memory and a meditation on the theme of change and permanence.

> Yet the seal pack will bark past my window
> summer after summer.
> This is the season
> when our friends may and will die daily.

This, Lowell says, is because the life of nature is duplicable – one animal or one flower is like another of the same kind – whereas humans are unique. What does remain, what he inherits, is remembrance and the acceptance that he can still possess not only the house she willed to him, but also his memory of her and his continuing love for her:

> Harriet Winslow, who owned this house,
> was more to me than my mother.
> I think of you far off in Washington,
> breathing in the heat wave,
> and air-conditioning, knowing each
> drug that numbs alerts another nerve to pain.

With every loss comes a benefit, with every benefit a loss, Lowell says in the final line. The penalty of being human is to be irreplaceable; the benefit is that human uniqueness allows for memory.

Lowell wrote of his cousin Harriet on two other occasions. In "Fourth of July in Maine" (*NO* 27–34), he writes of watching the patriotic celebrations in Castine; the white colonial frame house itself seems a symbol of the American Revolution, isolated and displaced in the present. He recalls how Harriet would telephone from her hospital bed in Washington, D.C.:

> How often when the telephone
> brought you to us from Washington,
> we had to look around the room to find
> the objects you would name – lying there,
> ten years paralyzed . . .   (31)

Perhaps, he thinks, what is lost does live on to the extent that it can be lovingly remembered. In his very last book, *Day by Day* (1977), published the month before his death, Lowell returned to his meditations about Harriet ("Endings" 49–50). Three memories arose: of his first visit to her as a child; of a later visit, twenty-four years later, when their affection had reached a more intimate level; and of her death, when "the immortal / [was] scraped unconsenting from the mortal" (50). After death, Harriet lived entirely in his memory, and though this loss was painful, Lowell writes, he was able to accept it because nothing, after all, was lost to the reconciling memory.

Elegies on Other Poets

Writing about the deaths of his Winslow relatives allowed Lowell to establish an internally supportive network of relations with his ancestry and family and also to reflect on or examine, at different stages, his relation to his real mother and fantasied mother, living and dead. Through reflections on others, that is to say, he could incorporate them and also, obliquely, conduct a search for a lost mother along with a self-investigation at a safe, aesthetic remove from the powerful emotions that were associated with loss.

Precisely the same may be said about his elegies for other poets who were either slightly older or his contemporaries. Poems on the Winslows expressed his private, and poems on "ancestors" and "cousins" among poets his public, associations. Both kinds of poems supported his double sense of his own value – as inheritor of an ongoing family and as heir of a continuing literary tradition.

Lowell's concern for what he inherited from literary tradition was so exclusively masculine in its concept, it seems clear that especially in his elegies for older writers, his literary "fathers," he was working out his grief over the loss of his father, much as he did in the Winslow poems with regard to his mother. The very organization of the volume *Life Studies* suggests this: It includes a long prose autobiography focusing on Lowell's childhood memories of his father. Immediately following are four poems on writers, three of which are elegies – on Ford Madox Ford, George Santayana, and Hart Crane.

It is surely no accident, too, that Lowell placed the poem on Ford just after his memoir of his father. For in 1937 just after Robert struck Commander Lowell and knocked him down, breaking decisively with his father, Merrill Moore suggested that to get him away from his family in some productive way Lowell should be put in touch with Ford Madox Ford, who, Hamilton writes, "was at Harvard on his way to visit Moore's friend Allen Tate in Tennessee. The idea was that Lowell should meet a 'real writer' and if Ford agreed to help, perhaps some arrangement could be arrived at by which Lowell could be separated from his parents without abandoning either his academic prospects or his ambitions as a poet" (42). Ford accepted Lowell as a kind of apprentice in writing, and through this fortunate arrangement the elaborate network of the international literary scene opened up to Lowell: Ford brought the young Lowell to Tate; Tate sent him to John Crowe Ransom, whom Lowell followed to Kenyon College; at Kenyon, in turn, he roomed with the young fiction writer Peter Taylor in the same building with the poet and critic Randall Jarrell; later he took a fellowship at Louisiana State University to work with Tate's former roommate Robert Penn Warren – and so on. That this literary world took in and embraced Lowell gave him a second container to replace his lost family. His elegies for poets allowed him to imagine new ancestors and fathers, new figures to identify with, signifying new, artistic modes of being and becoming. Lowell's summarizing comment in the last line of "Ford Madox Ford: 1873–1939" applies exactly to Lowell's father: "You were a kind man and you died in want" (*LS* 50).

Later works by Lowell, such as *History* (1973), are filled with his tributes to his deceased artistic predecessors. And such a volume as *Imitations* (1961) in which he rewrites (rather than merely translates) the great European poets, from Homer to the present, may be seen as an attempt to fuse with and join the great tradition of his poetic ancestors. If his mother could trace *her* family tree back to the *Mayflower,* he could trace *his* to Homer!

This was all gain, the acquisition of a tradition. In a very clear and direct way Lowell wrote in the tradition of what Daniel Aaron has called "the etiquette of grief," a style "of grief and mourning discernible in a particular group: a generation of American intellectuals and writers who flourished shortly before and during the last half of the 19th century." These included James Russell Lowell, Henry Adams, William Dean Howells, Henry James, Emily Dickinson – all, like Lowell, born in New England or associated with that region. Robert Lowell, who was keenly sensitive to American literary traditions, wrote poems and letters that consciously practiced the "ritual of grief" (Samuels 286) in the tradition of his New England forebears.

Lowell's poetry of loss and mourning was especially reserved for poets he considered to belong to his own generation. He felt very strongly that his generation was cursed and blighted. This was no doubt a projection of his own sense of doom, but it also had some solid evidence behind it. In 1959 he wrote to John Berryman: "It seems there's been something curious, twisted and against the grain about the world poets of our generation have had to live in. What troubles you and I, Ted Roethke, Elizabeth Bishop, Delmore [Schwartz], Randall [Jarrell] – even Karl Shapiro – have had" (Hamilton 275). Certainly, he had good reason to write as he did, and the troubles mounted. In 1963, Sylvia Plath, who had attended Lowell's poetry seminar at Boston University, committed suicide. Before doing so, she had told a

British Council interviewer that in her intensely emotional poetry she had been guided by the example of Lowell's *Life Studies* (Holbrook 289). Lowell wrote a foreword for her posthumously published *Ariel* (1966), containing her anguished work. "These poems are playing Russian roulette with six cartridges in the cylinder," he wrote (x). The same year Robert Frost, Roethke, and Louis MacNeice also died. The first two were, in a sense, rivals for Lowell in poetic preeminence, one older and the other from Lowell's own generation; Lowell genuinely liked MacNeice. But it was a deep, lasting shock when he received news in 1965 that Randall Jarrell had killed himself. Lowell had always thought of Jarrell as rational, sound, and stable; and his suicide, occurring during a period of depression, profoundly shook Lowell's belief in his own capacity to endure. He wrote the obituary for Jarrell in the *New York Times,* but he spoke of Jarrell as if he were still alive. Within weeks of Jarrell's death Lowell was hospitalized for a manic outbreak.

Fearful of his own suicidal impulses and therefore reluctant to admit that Jarrell had killed himself, Lowell projected his present fears and his earliest sense of loss outward in his own full-blown version of what A. H. Chapman has called "the concept of Nemesis." George H. Pollock's description of this belief surely applies to Lowell in the mid-1960s.

> The patient believes he is destined to repeat in his life the pattern of a significant other person's life which ended in tragedy and catastrophe. The conviction that there is an extensive life-pattern mirroring, even in the correlation of events and ages when they occur, may persist over many years or even an entire lifetime and may form the basis of a "personal myth." The person whose pattern is being followed is usually dead or was hospitalized, almost always is the father or mother, and the loss occurred during the childhood of the patient. The "nemesis" feeling is partly conscious and is rooted in the patient's feeling of responsibility for the death or illness of the person whose life he is doomed to imitate. Guilt over hostile or competitive feelings results in symptoms that follow the path of talion principle retribution. ("Anniversary" 352)

Lowell, of course, would have been internally encouraged to believe the catastrophe was cyclical and repetitive because his own mental breakdowns had often followed a cyclical pattern frequently occurring with the first signs of spring. Intimations of hope came on the wings of despair for Lowell. Deeper and more primitive was the belief that he had been cursed at birth and thus that the disasters of his generation were hardly more than confirmations of his own now approaching doom. For Lowell, the Nemesis continued to consume his friends and alter egos. Increasingly his chief interest in the news was in the obituaries. One after another, his earliest ideals, the poets of the previous generation, died. He could scarcely face their deaths with equanimity, for he had founded a large part of his identity on their activities, and his correspondence was full of comment on their passing. But it was at least "natural" that the older generation should die off. However, when, in the mid-1960s his own contemporaries started to go, often by committing suicide, Lowell felt that something of himself died with them: The whole generation seemed cursed. "I think I never met anyone who has somehow as much seeped into me," Lowell wrote of Delmore Schwartz. Schwartz had once seemed the most promising poet of his time; in 1966 he died, half forgotten. Of all the male poets contemporary with Lowell who had been his close friends, that left only John Berryman alive. And then, in 1972, Berryman jumped off a bridge. Lowell wrote his obituary for the *New York Review of Books.* More and more his work was thanatography, his life like the final act of a Shakespearean tragedy – strewn with corpses.

Beginning with *Near the Ocean* (1967), he followed up on the prose obituaries he wrote for some of these writers and composed poetic elegies for all. To Jarrell he gives the fundamental question: "But tell me, / Cal [Lowell's nickname], why did we live? why do we die?" (*H* 135). With reference to each of the dead poets, Lowell himself offers a different answer (*H* 135–42, 203): to give expression to horror (Plath); to honor nature (Roethke); to capture the essence of the dream world (Schwartz); to save "humor and honor from the everlasting dross" of quotidian life (T. S. Eliot); to survive madness or blindness (Ezra Pound, Wyndham Lewis); to take pleasure in fear (Louis MacNeice); to remain sensual (William Carlos Williams); to mourn, especially in the midst of success (Robert Frost); or even to express ultimate freedom by "suicide, the inalienable right of man" (Berryman).

Having written his elegies for his contemporaries seems to have given Lowell some relief from the blighted sense of Nemesis that had gripped him so harshly in the mid-sixties. In his poems he had said, over and over, that his mentors and contemporaries had lived and died with some meaningfulness. He was edging cautiously toward accepting that his own life might have had accomplishment and purpose. "For John Berryman," a poem that appeared in Lowell's last volume, summarizes the hasty, hard life of their generation. "Really we had the same life," Lowell writes, "the generic one / our generation offered" (*DBD* 27). He concludes calmly:

> To my surprise, John,
> I pray *to* not for you,
> think of you not myself,
> smile and fall asleep.   (*DBD* 28)

Father and Mother

The alterations that took place over the years in the way Lowell wrote about his Winslow relatives and his increasing acceptance that his forebears and fellow poets had lived meaningfully reflected Lowell's changing perspective on his relation to his mother and father. In several poems he left a record of these developments.

In the *Introductory Lectures on Psycho-Analysis,* Sigmund Freud wrote: "From [the] time [of puberty] onwards, the human individual has to devote himself to the great task of detaching himself from his parents. . . . For the son, this task consists in . . . reconciling himself with his father if he has remained in opposition to him. . . . These tasks are set to everyone; and it is remarkable how seldom they are dealt with in an ideal manner" (337). Lowell's youth was, as I have said, noisy with rebellion against his father, whom, in identification with his mother, Lowell viewed as a total failure. When Lowell saw an engraving of Alexander the Great in a book, he compared the hero's appearance to his mother's, not his father's. Self-effacing, quiet, unselfish, Father never emerged victorious from domestic battles. His wife steadily opposed him and invariably bested him; their son was determined to do the same – to triumph over him or to rebel against him. His father had gone to St. Mark's: Lowell was enrolled there and forced to go, but he performed badly. His father was an engineer: Lowell would be a poet. His father had attended Harvard: Robert rejected Harvard and followed the poet Ransom to Kenyon. His father was a career naval officer: Robert became a conscientious objector. His father was mild-mannered: Robert was bumptious, demanding, unruly. Eventually he chose a new name for himself: not Robert Traill Spence Lowell IV but Cal – Caligula, after the cruel Roman emperor. His father opposed his choice of a fiancée: Cal knocked his father to the floor. To be sure, there was a good deal of secret, deferred obedience behind all of this rebellious behavior. After he knocked his father to the floor, he almost immediately dropped the girl his father had criticized. And later in life, Lowell was nostalgic for St. Mark's and taught at Harvard. But Lowell's father saw the opposition, not the obedience, and he became increasingly exasperated with, and alienated from, his son. Commander Lowell found his son, Elizabeth Hardwick says, "a stranger. He used to say . . ., 'Well, his friends like him'" (Hardwick, Letter). Lowell, meanwhile, was finding in other men, usually teachers and older poets, substitute fathers to obey and idealize.

Then, in 1950, his father wrote him a note, signing it "affectionately yours." Four days later Commander Lowell said to his wife, "I feel awful," and suddenly died. Robert rushed to Boston and helped to organize the funeral. Later, when he asked his mother about the will, she said that he was not mentioned at all. Crushed, Lowell asked, "Didn't he even leave me his watch, or something?" (Hamilton 169). His mother thought he wanted an inheritance, but what he wanted most was some acknowledgment of a tie to his father.

If reconciliation with his father was no longer possible in life for Lowell, it remained a possibility through his writing: Through literature he could bring his father back to life, see him from a new point of view, and treat his own creation with the affection he could never give his father. This is precisely what he did in a prose piece that he started to write six years after his father's death, "91 Revere Street," the address of the house where he had grown up. On the surface, this was an autobiographical reminiscence, but it gave the adult Lowell a chance to see himself through new eyes, and thus to see his father afresh. Not surprisingly, the hero (even if largely a mock-hero) of Lowell's autobiography was Commander Lowell. In one of his early drafts Lowell reflected on his changed mind: "My own father was a gentle, faithful and dim man. I don't know why I was so agin him. I hope there will be peace" (Hamilton 228).

Written with great joy but also bitterness, and full of the pleasures of remembrance mixed with painful irony, "91 Revere Street" was published in 1959 (*LS* 11–46). Members of the Lowell family, he writes early in the sketch, were worldly, they "seemed to have given my father his character," for they "lacked that granite *back-countriness* which grandfather Arthur Winslow attributed to his own ancestors, the iconoclastic, mulish Dunbarton New Hampshire Starks" (12). Clearly he was stressing the romance of his father's family, and in "91 Revere Street" Father is always at center stage. A varied cast of characters and incidents flows through the narrative – relatives and friends and associates of Father's, trips with Father to look at preparatory schools, and Father's decision to leave the navy – all circling back eventually to Father.

In the midst of the writing, Lowell learned that he was to become a father himself and this fact doubtless kept the question of the relations between fathers and children prominently on his mind. In any event, thoughts about his father spilled into two poems also included in *Life Studies*. "Terminal Days at Beverly Farms" is a meditation – really, an imaginative creation – concerning his father's last days at the Lowell residence in Beverly, Massachusetts:

> Father and Mother moved to Beverly Farms
> to be a two minute walk from the station,
> half an hour by train from the Boston doctors.
>
> . . . .
>
> Father's death was abrupt and unprotesting
> His vision was still twenty-twenty.   (73–74)

What Lowell is trying to accomplish, clearly, is to share in the daily life of Father's last days, to get close in death to the father he had not really been able to approach in life. This motive is even more evident in the other poem, "Father's Bedroom" (75). Here he inspects the bedroom after Father's death, even opening his books to read the inscriptions, as if by handling the things Father had used he could save Father from being lost to him. He keeps Father alive by dwelling on the things he had used when alive.

Once started, Lowell continued to reflect on his father to the end of his own life, eventually feeling an identity with him where once there had been only opposition. At the age of forty-five, he wrote:

> At forty-five,
> What next, what next?
> At every corner,
> I meet my Father,
> my age, still alive.

Father, forgive me
my injuries,
as I forgive those I
have injured!   (*FUD* 7)

His father, he says, left "dinosaur / death-steps on the crust / where I must walk."
More and more he saw himself as walking in his father's footsteps. In the 1960s when
he began to think of his own approaching death, he imagined talking to father, saying to him, as if in death or a dream:

"I have never loved you so much in all my life."
You answered, "Doesn't love begin at the beginning?"   (*H* 116)

In 1976, as Lowell was about to become sixty, the feeling of identification was extremely powerful. For the first time he felt almost fused with his father. He composed
a final epitaph for his father – and for himself, since they shared the name – titled
simply, like a gravestone, "Robert T. S. Lowell" (*DBD* 80–81), consisting of a dialogue between father and son who at last are seen talking together calmly. The son
begins by expressing regret he was not present when the father died and by wishing
that his father were still alive now that Lowell had reached the age at which his father
died. And the father, in response, tells the story of his life, stressing how lonely he had
always been and reminding the son that he now has two children of his own to love.

Lowell remained fundamentally more ambivalent about his mother; his relation
with her went deeper and was more crisis-crossed with tension, ambiguity, and
paradox. He never rebelled against her wishes and values so directly as he did against
his father's; but Lowell's biography is littered with transitory love relations and intense but brief liaisons with many women. These affairs had a compulsive quality
and might have had two determinants: first, his childhood fear that he would lose
his mother's love and need to win it over and over; and second, the wish that he
could indicate to his mother – and then to his wives, substitutes for his mother – that
he did not, after all, need her love, that he could easily replace her with another
woman. He would force Mother – and then other women who loved him subse-
quently – to experience the pain of loss of love that had once so tortured him. Twice
he became engaged to and married women of whom his mother plainly disapproved,
and similarly, during his marriages he formed connections with other women, relations about which his wives could be, at best, tolerant. In many ways, his life was
ruled by a continuing, silent, acted-out argument with his mother, seeking to win
her love and then dismissing its importance. He remained desperate for her love, but
his anger made him rage against her. The two sides of his feeling are everywhere
apparent in his behavior: He fell in love time after time, instantly, as if he could not
get enough love from women; yet beneath the romantic yearnings, most of the
women he loved soon saw, with fright, the emergence of a tremendous hostility
toward women, on an emotional and even a physical level, causing his friend Allen
Tate to say flatly that "there are definite homicidal implications in his [internal]

world, particularly toward women . . ." (Hamilton 156). His second wife, Elizabeth Hardwick, found "why one tortures the person he most loves a 'baffling question.'"

But Lowell's paradoxical relation to his mother never emerged so clearly as in the winter of 1954, when he received a cable from Italy that she had suffered a stroke and was dying in the hospital at Rapallo. He delayed, taking a roundabout route, staying with a friend overnight near Paris, even though the original cable had arrived four days late and he was urged to hurry on. Worse still, he began to show signs of a manic attack; he was unable to sleep, but talked and drank all night. An hour before he arrived in Rapallo, his mother had a second stroke and died.

That day and in those immediately following he mixed appropriate mourning, such as weeping for long periods, with grandiose and perhaps guilty behavior, such as buying his mother a black-and-gold baroque casket that resembled the coffin of "her hero," Napoleon. His thinking was bizarre; he claimed, for instance, to have discovered an identification between himself and Hitler. Shortly after the funeral, he suddenly announced that during the week he had spent in Italy making funeral arrangements he had fallen in love with a young Italian woman, and that he intended to divorce his wife immediately in order to marry her. Elizabeth Hardwick suspected that he was "in an elation which is brought about by guilt feelings over his relief, quite unexpected, at his mother's death, guilt feelings complicated by his profiting from her death [through inheriting her estate]" (Hamilton 207–8). And she was not far wrong. But he was also trying to keep Mother alive through marrying a woman from the place where she had died. What George Pollock calls the "separation reaction" was very strong in Lowell; like one of the patients Pollock mentions, Lowell found it really impossible to acknowledge his mother's death. Perhaps, like that patient, "to mourn [would be] to acknowledge the nothingness of [his] mother, and this meant emptiness" inside him ("Mourning" 349). He certainly was very close to facing his own emptiness, and whenever this occurred, a psychotic break was likely to follow. He used religion, grandiose identifications, and the replacement of one woman with another as aids in warding off his guilt, emptiness, and fragmentation. But these (chiefly manic) defenses made everything speed up for him, so that he soon felt "tireless, madly sanguine, menaced, and menacing" (Hamilton 215). Less than two months after his mother's death, he was hospitalized as completely delusional.

Immediately following the poems in *Life Studies* in which Lowell memorialized his father, he placed his poem on the voyage home from Rapallo in the ship carrying his mother's corpse. The poem circles all around the actual death, referring to the nurse, the Italian landscape, the coffin, the passengers, but it never focuses on the fact of the death itself. Indeed, the poem ends in a way that suggests that it was not really Charlotte Lowell who was in the casket:

> . . . on Mother's coffin,
> *Lowell* had been misspelled *LOVEL.*
> The corpse
> was wrapped like *panetone* in Italian tinfoil.   (78)

Lowell's biographer helps to put an interesting perspective on these lines when he quotes Lowell's comments that his mother had always been punctilious in having her name spelled correctly. Hamilton adds that Lowell himself referred to his mother as "Charlotte Winslon" in a letter written at this time and says her name was misspelled as Lowel on the coffin. Denial reached into Lowell's spelling, as it did into his consciousness and memory.

Lowell never was able to make an internal reconciliation to the loss of his mother, probably because his own primary sense of loss involved, at a very early age and primitive level, loss of her love. Evidence I have already given suggests that his rage was too strong for him to focus it on her directly. He could not face her death any more than he could his earliest loss of her. Just before his death, however, he wrote two poems that offer additional clues concerning his grief in relating to her. In "To Mother" (*DBD* 78–79), he speaks of how he has grown old, as old as his mother was when she died, and he remembers, with fresh pain, how hurtful her humor was to him as a child; he concludes, at once malicious and forgiving and self-doubting,

> I enjoyed hearing scandal on you. Much came
> from others, your high-school friends, themselves now dust.
> It has taken me the time since you died
> to discover you are as human as I am . . .
> if I am.

Manifestly, thoughts of his mother always enmeshed him in doubts of his own value, ending in doubts of his existence and an uncovering of the dead child at the core of his identity.

The reasons for his tremendous sense of rejection and the rage it generated are made clear in the final poem Lowell wrote about his mother. One of the last poems that he finished before his death, "Unwanted" (*DBD* 121–24) is one of the saddest poems in the language concerning mother–son relations. A sense of death, of finality, hovers over the poem: "Too late, all shops closed –," it begins. Then he remembers a comment about John Berryman, with whom Lowell closely identified:

> I read an article on a friend,
> as if recognizing my obituary:
> "Though his mother loved her son consumingly,
> she lacked a really affectionate nature;
> so he always loved what he missed."
> This was John Berryman's mother, not mine.   (121)

"Alas," he continues, "I can only tell you my own story" – but Berryman's obituary is perilously close to his own, except that his own is worse: Lowell's mother did *not* love her son consumingly, and therefore Lowell loved even more desperately the love he had missed. He explains how he knows this. First, he recalls being told by his and Mother's psychiatrist, Merrill Moore:

> When I was in college, he said, "You know
> you were an unwanted child?"   (122)

Lowell wonders if perhaps Moore was criticizing his parents "to help me." He off-handedly replied to Moore that he did not care; "in a medical sense," he quipped, all children are unwanted. Yet even then he realized that his casual answer did not ring true in his own head. His next thought was that in that world an only child "was a scandal." Following this passage in the poem Lowell reaches back to an older memory, which he has kept secret all these years, of his mother telling him that when she was carrying him in her womb she had taken long walks saying bitterly to herself, "I wish I were dead, I wish I were dead" (123). "Unforgivable for a mother to tell a child," Lowell blankly comments. His rage is still so great he wonders if for her bitter rejection of him she will be condemned – with him – to hell:

> Is the one unpardonable sin
> our fear of not being wanted?
> For this, will mother go on cleaning house
> for eternity, and making it unlivable?   (124)

As clear as it is tragic, Lowell here gets as close as he could to his earliest belief that in losing his mother's love he was doomed forever. All through his life he raged against this loss. For other losses he mourned and to them he became reconciled, but not to this, his deepest, sharpest grief.

Personal Losses and Anticipations of Death

About a month after the publication of *Day by Day* (1977), the volume in which "Unwanted" appeared, Lowell died. His third wife, Caroline Blackwood, called his death a "suicide of wish" (Hamilton 473); she felt he wanted to die, that he had given up. Jacques writes of the internal clock that ticks out the parents' lives inside the child's: "The sense of the agedness of parents, coupled with the maturing of [one's] children into adults, contributes strongly to the sense of ageing – the sense that it is one's own turn next to grow old and die" (510). (Lowell's daughter Harriet was twenty in 1977.) Lowell had frequently told people that both his parents had died at sixty, and though this was not strictly true, he felt as if his Nemesis would really appear when he reached that age. He insisted that he did not expect to live past sixty. He could not imagine outliving his parents. Lowell's friends could see – at least in retrospect – that he was preparing for an expected death. "A few months before [Lowell] died," Harvard professor Daniel Aaron writes, "he came to my house for supper. He seemed positively benign, almost saintly, as if he'd already been translated. . . . [I] think now that he was on the point of taking off. He kissed my wife (whom he had met for the first time) and said goodbye the way people do who are planning a permanent escape" (Aaron, Letter).

For years Lowell had written about many of his personal losses – those that all persons experience: the loss of vitality through aging (e.g., "Middle Age," *FUD* 7); the loss of health through illness (e.g., "For Anne Adden 4," *H* 139); the loss of memory (e.g., "Jean Stafford, a Letter," *DBD* 29); and the loss of his family and possible alienation from his daughter through divorce (e.g., *The Dolphin*). Rather than being experienced as the loss of some significant loved one through death, these may be considered "losses of the self" (cf. Peretz 5).

In 1974, writing to Peter Taylor, Lowell summarized very clearly the way that the losses inevitably experienced in aging made him feel that he was living with a defective self, a sense that he had lost part of his true self. Perhaps the self-loss Lowell wrote about most frequently and with the greatest anguish was of his loss of self-regard through the humiliations of which he was conscious following each of his manic attacks. In 1965, when he heard that his friend Randall Jarrell had had a mental breakdown, he wrote to him movingly both of his own despair and of the eventual easing of the feelings of degradation following mental illness:

> I have been through this sort of thing so often myself that I suppose there's little in your experience that I haven't had over and over. What's worst, I think, is the grovelling, low as dirt purgatorial feelings with which one emerges. If you have such feelings, let me promise you that they are temporary, what looks as though it were simply you, and therefore would never pass does turn out to be not you and will pass. (Hamilton 339)

Many of Lowell's poems, beginning with *Life Studies,* exhibit the horror of mania, depression, the side effects of medication, and the consciousness of shame during recovery. In "Home" (*DBD* 113–14), for example,

> "Remarkable breakdown, remarkable recovery" –
> but the breakage can go on repeating
> once too often. . . .
> *I wish I could die.*
> Less than ever I expect to be alive
> six months from now –

This sense of the complete breakup of the self in the final loss of life had, of course, been accumulating for several years. Lowell's childhood experience of the death of the self was now melding into his awareness of aging and his wish for death. Many of Lowell's late poems are examples of what Allan Reed calls "anticipatory grief work" – the preparation for accepting one's own death. In *Notebook 1967–68,* he wrote two poems titled "My Death," and the last poem in the book is called "Obit." In a poem contained in *History,* he became reconciled to the status in literary history that he had earned through his accomplishment. He believed he would have a place "on the minor slopes of Parnassus" and that, therefore, he would live, preserved in his poetic creations like a bee who "lives embalmed in honey" (194). His books, he says, will be like coffins that will hold his mummy.

His final poem on the subject of his approaching death is in *Day by Day*. Lowell's last volume is truly a "book of the dead." In it he consolidated many of his themes, ideas, and feelings concerning loss and mourning. After John Berryman's death, his oldest and closest male literary friend remaining alive was his roommate at college, the fiction writer Peter Taylor. One of Lowell's most beautiful poems, "Our Afterlife I" (*DBD* 21–22), is addressed to him. In this poem Lowell clearly and simply gives a final accounting of his own accomplishments, culminating in the greatest loss of all – his own death. This is a daring poem and worth pausing over. He begins with a memory dating from the time he first met Taylor in Tennessee:

> Southbound –
> a couple in passage,
> two Tennessee cardinals
> in green December outside the window
> dart and tag and mate –
> young as they want to be.

Then, abruptly shifting to the present, he says simply: "We're not." In fact, Lowell adds, he had recently had a second child, and curiously this had made him feel "a generation older." Other writers have recently died: "This year killed / Pound, Wilson, Auden . . . / promise has lost its bloom." By implication, the year is coming when he and Taylor will also die. In "our boyish years . . . time stood on its hands," he says; time seemed to stand still then. But now he sees that this impression was an illusion, a "Sleight of hand." Now,

> After fifty
> the clock can't stop,
> each saving breath
> takes something.

The paradox is stunning in its conveyance of doom. The energy consumed by breathing wears down the body that breathing keeps alive. Is all, then, death and loss? At this point – in his poem and in his life – Lowell says his final, confirming words toward existence. He accepts his accomplishments as sufficient. He asserts that ripening – even if ripening also means decay – is the goal of life. Life, he beautifully says, is an ascent. Above all, he accepts change – especially the change from life to afterlife. What seems "rust" – decay, death – is after all but a change of forms. The poem brilliantly concludes:

> . . . This is riches:
> the eminence not to be envied,
> the account
> accumulating layer and angle,
> face and profile,
> 50 years of snapshots,
> the ladder of ripening likeness.

> We are things thrown in the air
> alive in flight . . .
> our rust the color of the chameleon.

By the time he wrote this, Lowell had arranged to be buried among his ancestors and parents in the private cemetery at Dunbarton, a place about which he had written several times. He had returned to the Episcopal church into which he was born, and he left instructions for his funeral to be celebrated with a solemn High Mass at the Church of the Advent. "That's how we're buried" (Hamilton 468), he said to a young friend, meaning he had accepted his family and their ways; for all his differences, he joined them in the end.

Conclusion

Melanie Klein's statement that when early childhood loss releases internal anxieties, the child needs to develop "methods of defense which are essentially directed against the 'pining' for the lost object" (316) is helpful in conceptualizing Lowell's lifelong preoccupation with loss and his capacity to use literature to create a viable identity. What might simply have remained "pining," Lowell turned into elegies and verse memorials; what might have served only as defense, Lowell transformed into artistic works of great beauty and insight concerning the vicissitudes of loss and mourning. On the occasion of his mother's death, he clearly exhibited enormous grief, rage, and an exhilarating sense of freedom, followed by guilt. These were held in check by their variety and also by a wide array of familiar defenses. For a while he kept his more radically disoriented thoughts under control through work and denial, but finally his defenses, including his poetry, were not adequate to sustain him.

But it is just as clear that Lowell also turned the child's early need to pine for the lost object and lost love into the ability to grieve for his losses in forms of poetry that he inherited from his literary forebears. In many ways he was a very traditional poet. Certainly, too, he wrote for the appreciation of an audience. It was by no means possible that the approval and praise he received from readers could compensate him for the affection he failed to get from his parents. But his very considerable audience did help to make other losses tolerable.

Lowell's style and the poetic forms he chose were important features of his mourning. Hamilton quotes enough of Lowell's manic or schizophrenic speech during hospitalizations to allow us to see that just beneath his ordinary, conventional discourse bubbled a cauldron of idiosyncratic verbal craziness – grandiose, rageful, demanding. Lowell used the more formal language of poetry as a counterbalance to this fragmentation of language. His early poems were highly artificial, elevated in diction, mannered, and rhetorically dense; they were clearly the agonized product of an exalted consciousness straining to communicate perfectly. In short, they moved as far as possible toward expressing the powers of poetic intelligence, whereas his psychotic speech expressed the power of his impulses. Although Lowell's later poems appear more conversational and are certainly more confessional, they are the products of extremely careful poetic contrivance. His manuscripts exhibit a complex, careful process of revision, sometimes indicating several years spent on a single poem. In the late 1960s and early 1970s Lowell used poetic form as a further means of control; he wrote almost exclusively in one of the most traditional of poetic forms, the sonnet, even as he bent the form to his own individual expressive powers. The effort of intelligence required for poetry helped to keep back the crazy talk that always murmured and mumbled inside him.

Lowell's last attempts to work through his anger and anxiety and frustration over his early feelings of abandonment by his mother are in the poem "Unwanted." It ends with the questions:

> Is getting well ever an art
> or art a way to get well?   (*DBD* 124)

These are strategic questions. Lowell must have asked them of himself many times. For Lowell, the answer is both yes and no. Art was undoubtedly his main counterbalance to the feelings of being "unwanted," and thus in the most general terms a substitute for Mother. Writing poetry and living the literary life gave him a great deal: a productive, creative work, a series of inherited forms and traditions, a group of artistic colleagues and friends, teaching jobs, students, an activity that was personally meaningful and also valued by others, and an audience. Perhaps most important, it gave him a vehicle by which he could deal with and to a large degree work through his own early feelings of grief through writing about the losses of his ancestors, parents, and friends, as well as the losses in self, through sickness, despair, and old age.

In retrospect, for all its frailties, Lowell's life seems one of enormous courage; despite considerable psychic disorder, he drove himself again and again back in the direction of health through literature, for the sake of continuing creation, when many of his contemporaries despaired or killed themselves. Despite the always fragile state of his mental health, through his creativity he maintained a powerful, healthy core. He had, Elizabeth Hardwick has noted, a "really startling vitality, humor, learning, and energy, [a] . . . zest for life and, of course, for writing" (Hardwick, Letter). Along with his sense of loss he preserved a tremendous capacity for enduring friendships – mostly with men, but also with women, such as Elizabeth Bishop. Repeatedly, Lowell crawled out of the groveling humiliations of his breakdowns and surmounted the grinding pain of early and late loss. He learned to wager that his illness created a false self, but that his true self was allied with art. Art gave Lowell the will to continue. It did not cure him: It could not ultimately be a way to stay well. But his art was in getting well and in building a monument of poetry over the ruins of his losses.

NOTE

1 All references to Lowell's life are to Ian Hamilton's recent biography. Hamilton (475) says that "some of Lowell's 'memories' should be treated with caution; it is likely that he added colorful details here and there . . . and from time to time simply invented episodes from childhood." I treat the literal truth of Lowell's "memories" with the caution that Hamilton recommends, but I believe that in Lowell's inventions or "fictions," we can detect important aspects of his psychic reality, and this tells us something about how he experienced his childhood.

3

The Reign of the Kingfisher: Robert Lowell's Prophetic Poetry

ALBERT GELPI

There has been something fabulous about Robert Lowell's career from the outset – in part because it was deeply expressive and symptomatic of its period. Allen Tate introduced *Land of Unlikeness* (1944) with magisterial flourishes at the height of the New Critical hegemony as a proud exhibit of its hegemony. Influential friends like R. P. Blackmur and Randall Jarrell hailed this first book in its limited press edition, and *Lord Weary's Castle* (1946) brought Lowell the Pulitzer Prize before the age of thirty for his first commercially published volume of verse. Two decades later Irvin Ehrenpreis was able to speak plausibly of "The Age of Lowell." The fact that his poetry underwent dramatic changes in style and form and meaning during those intervening decades – in fact between *Lord Weary's Castle* and the books beginning with *Life Studies* (1959) – is an aspect of the fabulous and symptomatic character of his career. However, against the current critical consensus that favors the later work, I want to argue emphatically for the centrality of Lowell's early work in measuring his lasting achievement, indeed to argue that the early work of his "Catholic" period constitutes his principal claim to a lasting poetic achievement.

In the twists and turns of Lowell's career the volatile and agonized tension between belief and disbelief is reflected in the oscillation between more closed and more open forms and between more symbolic and more direct statement. I am not suggesting a consistent or irrevocable correlation between disbelief, open form, and colloquial diction; other poets' work would belie such a correlation, and there were self-conscious changes in manner from book to book throughout Lowell's canon. At the same time, the early poems did pack densely symbolic language into intricately worked meters and stanzas, and the collapse of Lowell's Christian prophetic vision was accompanied by an overall shift to more flexible versification and more direct and overtly autobiographical statement.

With uncanny foresight Jarrell fixed attention as early as *Land of Unlikeness* on the contrary drives toward inwardness, necessity, closure on the one hand and freedom, openness, change on the other. Reviewing *Lord Weary's Castle,* he commented again that the poems "have two possible movements or organizations: they can move from what is closed to what is open, or from what is open to what is closed" (20). Critics are correct in seeing the major change in Lowell's manner as roughly coinciding with his loss of faith, and in seeing *Lord Weary's Castle* as the principal volume of the early period and *Life Studies* as the unmistakable transition to the later, agnostic phase. But in retrospect *Lord Weary's Castle* can also be seen as an anticipation of what was to come. That is to say, the fact that the poetic modes and genres pursued in *Lord Weary's Castle* persist into the later volumes foreshadows the shifts in thematic development and technique. Thus dramatic monologues like "Between the Porch and Altar," "Mr. Edwards and the Spider," and "After the Surprising Conversions" lead directly into the dramatic and narrative poems in the next book, *The Mills of the Kavanaughs* (1951). Autobiographical poems like "Rebellion" and "In the Cage" and family elegies like "In Memory of Arthur Winslow" and "Mary Winslow" presage *Life Studies*. Verse renderings of a range of poets – Propertius, Villon, Rimbaud, Valéry, Rilke – into what the prefatory "Note" called imitations rather than translations anticipate the 1961 volume of *Imitations*. The sonnets on historical subjects, both those about New England ("Salem," "Concord") and those on European themes ("Napoleon Crosses the Berezina," "Charles the Fifth and the Peasant") look down the line to the various *Notebook* versions of the late sixties and early seventies.

Nevertheless, it is the explicitly religious and prophetic cast of *Lord Weary's Castle* that gives the book its distinctive voice and character and that raises the issues central to my argument. For despite the enthusiastic, almost astonished acclaim those poems received on their publication, later reviewers and critics have tended to follow Lowell himself in deprecating and dismissing them as overwrought and overwritten. Without question the language is pitched at the breakpoint of form and metaphor, and the violence marks these as war poems in more ways than the obvious one. The poet is at war with self, family, region, country, as well as with the war the country is waging. But my point will be that Lowell's poetry never reached such heights and depths again.

His sense of serious poetic vocation dates from the late thirties, when he defied his family by abandoning Harvard to study with John Crowe Ransom and Tate. Lowell not only absorbed into his writing the dense verbal and metaphorical formalism espoused by the New Criticism, but also found in Tate and Ransom a kindred disgust with secular materialism, which warred against Christian humanism. Just as his mentors held their Southern agrarianism up as a counterideal to industrial capitalism, Lowell focused his outrage on the history of New England, epitomized in his family, which he read as confounding Puritan piety with mercantile greed. By the early forties he had found in the Roman Catholicism that was anathema to his forebears the religious vision he needed to prophesy against his people and his society. Not surprisingly, Tate found these poems remarkable and connected the highly energized and concentrated formalism to their religious perspective:

There is no other poetry today quite like this. T. S. Eliot's recent predic-
tion that we should soon see a return to formal and even intricate metres
and stanzas was coming true, before he made it, in the verse of Robert
Lowell. Every poem in this book has a formal pattern, either the poet's
own or one borrowed. . . . But this is not, I think, a mere love of external
form. Lowell is consciously a Catholic poet, and it is possible to see a close
connection between his style and the formal pattern. The style is bold and
powerful, and the symbolic language often has the effect of being *willed*;
for it is an intellectual style compounded of brilliant puns and shifts of
tone; and the willed effect is strengthened by the formal stanzas, to which
the language is forced to conform. (1)

Tate was speaking of *Land of Unlikeness,* but his remarks remained relevant to *Lord
Weary's Castle,* despite general agreement that the newer poems appeared less willed
in their Catholic symbolism and verbal virtuosity, as satiric denunciation intensified
to apocalyptic prophecy.

However, the waning of the New Critics' influence and of Eliot's example coincided with the waning of Lowell's Catholicism in the late forties, and his Catholic
formalism came to seem clotted and inflated to the disillusioned poet. In fact, disillusionment accorded with the period more than did prophecy, and in the act of pro-
claiming "The Age of Lowell," Ehrenpreis was able to agree with the poet in in-
veighing against the early work:

The defect of *Lord Weary's Castle* is the same as that of *Land of Unlikeness.*
In Whitman, Tate and Hart Crane, one cannot help noticing a habit of
substituting rhetoric, in the form of self-conscious sublimity, for poetry. If
Lowell, their heir, yields to this habit, it is because, like them, he has
the highest conception of the poet's task. But the mere posturing, the air
of prophecy, does not make speech either noble or prophetic. In Lowell's
most commonly over-praised work, "The Quaker Graveyard," the use of
rhetoric joins with a denseness of symbolism to make a poem that seems
more impressive for aspiration than for accomplishment. (165)

The best commentary after Ehrenpreis – including the two most useful overviews,
Steven Gould Axelrod's *Robert Lowell: Life and Art* (1978) and Vereen Bell's *Robert
Lowell: Nihilist as Hero* (1983) – has many illuminating observations to make about
the early poems, but continues to assume *au fond* that they are interesting principally
as precursors to the later poems. Ehrenpreis only voiced the growing consensus when
he dismissed the early work as mere rhetoric and so as questionable or false prophecy.

Without question Lowell's early poems are unashamedly, unabashedly, unreserv-
edly prophetic and apocalyptic as nothing else in contemporary highbrow literature
was, including Eliot's and Tate's compressed, muted meditations. But the first point
to be made is that it is the critical and academic preference for "opaque ambiguities"

(Axelrod, *Robert Lowell* 67) and muted ironies that creates suspicion of, resistance to, embarrassment about the violent emphases and apocalyptic chiaroscuro of Lowell's prophetic manner. And the second point is that prophecy perforce relies on rhetoric as its necessary mode of expression. As Whitman and Hart Crane, Blake and Shelley, Yeats and Pound, Hopkins and Dylan Thomas demonstrate, rhetoric need not be hollow, manipulative, or posturing, though all of these poets have faced that charge from time to time. What disturbs positivist critics is that rhetoric consists in a heightened use of the sensuous and oral, nondiscursive resources of language – heavy stresses, insistent and sustained rhythms, compounded alliteration and assonance and onomatopoeia – to extend language into a dimension beyond denotation and even connotation, to push communication to its limits and (if possible) beyond, toward intimations of the incommunicable. The prophet speaks as voice and vessel for God or the gods or the transpersonal force, and must therefore propel language above or below – in any case, outside – the range of customary human speech. The words must break through the categories of rational proposition and demonstration, and the energy, even violence, of the language is the record of that breakthrough.

In other words, the prophet must transcend his medium, or at least must use the medium as if it can transcend itself. Rhetoric operates by gestalt rather than argument, through resonance rather than statement. Listeners or readers are meant to be overwhelmed and carried along the rhythmic and sonar propulsion toward an area of perception otherwise beyond comprehension. The Lowell of *Land of Unlikeness* and *Lord Weary's Castle* did indeed take the prophetic as "the highest conception of the poet's task," as Ehrenpreis conceded, and dismissed any distrust of rhetorical utterance as evidence of the violent "unlikeness" between the secular view and the religious. He would have echoed Flannery O'Connor's blunt retort to objections about the violent grotesquerie of her stories: "To the hard of hearing you shout, and for the almost blind you draw large and startling figures" (*Mystery* 33–34).

O'Connor and Lowell were not close friends; but her correspondence with him is included in her collected letters, *The Habit of Being,* and their connection is as Catholic prophetic writers. Her stories, like Lowell's poems, fixed on the moment of violence as the moment of grace. The scriptural epigraph to one of her novels supplied its title: "From the days of John the Baptist until now, the Kingdom of Heaven suffereth violence, and the violent bear it away" (Matthew 11.12). The contradictions inherent in temporal existence inevitably move to conflict, and those ruptures and collisions reveal grace kindled at the cross-point of the contradictions, transfiguring the violence in which it is embroiled and made manifest. The rhetoric employed by Lowell and O'Connor (by her, admittedly, with a lacing of humor) registers that kinetic and explosive moment. Listen to "Death from Cancer," the first section of the elegy "In Memory of Arthur Winslow," reprinted in *Lord Weary's Castle* from *Land of Unlikeness.* The rumbling verses rattle like a roller coaster through the stanzas, driving the powerful images headlong to the glimpse of inexplicable mystery at the end-stop climaxing each stanza:

This Easter, Arthur Winslow, less than dead,
Your people set you up in Phillips' House
To settle off your wrestling with the crab –
The claws drop flesh upon your yachting blouse
Until longshoreman Charon come and stab
Through your adjusted bed
And crush the crab. On Boston Basin, shells
Hit the water by the Union Boat Club wharf:
You wonder why the coxes' squeakings dwarf
The *resurrexit dominus* of all the bells.

Grandfather Winslow, look, the swanboats coast
That island in the Public Gardens, where
The bread-stuffed ducks are brooding, where with tub
And strainer the mid-Sunday Irish scare
The sun-struck shallows for the dusky chub
This Easter, and the ghost
Of risen Jesus walks the waves to run
Arthur upon a trumpeting black swan
Beyond Charles River to the Acheron
Where the wide waters and their voyager are one.   (*LWC* 19)

Vereen Bell took syntax as Lowell's device for submitting the verbal dynamics to the rule of reason:

> Syntax in *Lord Weary's Castle* is the order-making force, the instrument of will and reason, the organizing system that constrains and creates the pressure. When the syntax breaks, the rational will has yielded, the union with God has failed, and the poet has entered time to contend with chaos – if such is possible – on its own terms. (11)

But here it is less that syntax exerts restraining pressure on the verbal ferment than that the verbal ferment exerts expansive and distorting pressure on the syntax. What we experience in the poem is not so much rational containment as the irrepressible volatility of the materials. Sentences stretch themselves, sometimes excruciatingly, into modifying phrases and clauses, as if the poet were trying to sweep his whole world into a single synthesizing statement, and the breaking point is not simply a breakdown, as Bell suggests, but a breakthrough – not just a failure of rational will but an incipient dissolution of rational will in wordless and terrified wonder.

Writing before Bell, Tate had taken Lowell's prosody rather than syntax as the ordering device and spoke of the heavily symbolic language being "forced to conform" to the restraints of the stanzaic conventions of meter and rhyme. But again the effect of the verses is less of restraint than of expansiveness; instead, the sense of the language as cramped and explosive in the crucible of form comes from its resistance to the rational control of prosody and syntax. In "Death from Cancer," the sentences unreel in the tight stanzaic structure with its varying line lengths and its pattern of meter and rhyme, but the grid cannot encompass, or can barely encompass, the verbal propulsion. The rhymes serve not to separate verses from each other but to emphasize their almost complete enjambment; far from slowing the sentence down or dividing it into discrete units of sense, they add to the rising clamor, as the local details (Phillips' House, Union Boat Club, Public Gardens) pile up, only suddenly to yawn on illimitable vistas: the Charles now the Acheron, the children's swanboat now Charon's ferry, the dying and bedridden patient now the farthest voyager. The verbal pressure against syntactic and prosodic delimitation parallels the transformation of the limited perception of the sense phenomena into awed apprehension of the absolute.

"To Peter Taylor on the Feast of the Epiphany" works in much the same way:

> Peter, the war has taught me to revere
> The rulers of this darkness, for I fear
> That only Armageddon will suffice
> To turn the hero skating on thin ice
> When Whore and Beast and Dragon rise for air
> From allegoric waters. Fear is where
> We hunger: where the Irishmen recall
> How wisdom trailed a star into a stall
> And knelt in sacred terror to confer
> Its fabulous gold and frankincense and myrrh:
> And where the lantern-noses scrimmage down
> The highway to the sea below this town
> And the sharp barker rigs his pre-war planes
> To lift old Adam's dollars for his pains;
> There on the thawing ice, in red and white
> And blue, the bugs are buzzing for the flight.
> December's daylight hours have gone their round
> Of sorrows with the sun into the sound,
> And still the grandsires battle through the slush
> To storm the landing biplanes with a rush –
> Until their cash and somersaulting snare
> Fear with its fingered stop-watch in mid-air.   (*LWC* 46)

Written for the holy day that annually celebrates the manifestation of the newborn Savior to the Magi, and crackling with puns and symbols, the three long, complex sentences are echo chambers of alliteration and assonance and internal rhyme, as they race through the enjambed couplets. The word "fear" recurs throughout the poem in contrasting permutations – the awe of the Magi, the faith of the Boston Irish Catholics, the materialism of the Puritans' scions – and builds to the dramatic dash and the climactic "until" clause of the final couplet, announcing the dreaded Armageddon no longer to be forestalled by money or worldly distraction.

Not all the poems operate at quite this intensity, but the tone and rhetorical devices for generating pressure within and against formal conventions are characteristic. Here, for example, is the last stanza of "The Drunken Fisherman":

> Is there no way to cast my hook
> Out of this dynamited brook?
> The Fisher's sons must cast about
> When shallow waters peter out.
> I will catch Christ with a greased worm,
> And when the Prince of Darkness stalks
> My bloodstream to its Stygian term . . .
> On water the Man-Fisher walks.   (*LWC* 32)

Or the last stanza of "At the Indian Killer's Grave," in which Lowell prays that he may escape the curse his ancestors sowed:

> I ponder on the railing at this park:
> Who was the man who sowed the dragon's teeth,
> That fabulous or fancied patriarch
> Who sowed so ill for his descent, beneath
> King's Chapel in this underworld and dark?
> John, Matthew, Luke and Mark,
> Gospel me to the Garden, let me come
> Where Mary twists the warlock with her flowers –
> Her soul a bridal chamber fresh with flowers
> And her whole body an ecstatic womb,
> As through the trellis peers the sudden Bridegroom.   (*LWC* 57)

There had been no American writing of such apocalyptic and religious ferocity since the Puritans, and among them none, not Edward Taylor any more than Eliot, charged their religious expression with such baroque energy and "Catholic" sensuality. *Lord Weary's Castle* coincided with a resurgence of interest in Catholicism in postwar America. Thomas Merton's account of his conversion to Catholicism, *The Seven Storey Mountain,* won the serious attention of intellectuals as well as a place on the best-seller lists; Jacques Maritain and Etienne Gilson were quickening interest in Thomist Scholasticism; poets as opposite in temperament as Tate and William Everson became Catholics; the Gothic tales of sin and grace that went into *A Good Man Is Hard To Find* were bringing Flannery O'Connor eager and admiring readers; Bishop Sheen came into living rooms all across the country on prime-time television.

There is no way of telling how Lowell's poetry would have developed had he remained a Catholic, or whether the more direct and colloquial free-verse style of *Life Studies,* which we now associate with his lapse of faith, would have occurred anyway and been accommodated into the expression of a developing religious sensibility. But such was not the case, and we are left with accounting for what did happen. In retrospect we can see with increasing clarity the deepening signs of impending crisis. Tate had a point in feeling that Lowell's expression in the early poems was sometimes too willed, and Ehrenpreis was not entirely wrong in feeling his sublimity too self-conscious. By hindsight we can see that Lowell's prophetic stance was threatened in ways that, even in *Land of Unlikeness* and *Lord Weary's Castle,* foreshadowed its collapse.

It is not just that the critical moments in the poems are sometimes cast into a hortatory imperative: "Gospel me to the Garden, let me come . . ." (*LWC,* 57); or the famous lines from the last section of the elegy for Arthur Winslow:

> O Mother, I implore
> Your scorched, blue thunderbreasts of love to pour
> Buckets of blessings on my burning head
> Until I rise like Lazarus from the dead. . . .   (*LWC* 22)

Religious poetry frequently falls into prayers of petition; think of Donne and Hopkins, Eliot and the Puritan Taylor, who of all the metaphysical poets has a raw verbal energy most akin to Lowell's. And the insecurity that adds to the stress of the petitions is a familiar aspect of the dialectic in much religious verse. The problem lies rather in the force and the focus of Lowell's doubt about the central and essential Christian mystery, the Incarnation itself.

Lowell sought to use his Catholicism to scourge the lapsed Puritanism of his elders, but it was, ironically, the Puritan cast of Lowell's Catholicism that made it difficult for him as prophet to proclaim the Incarnation. That central Christian mystery posits the immanence of God's Spirit in matter, that is, in nature and in human nature. Lowell's ingrained Calvinism gave him so profound a sense of sin – of fallen nature and human fallibility – that he had great difficulty in conceiving of God's presence except as the negation of the natural or the absence of the human. Since matter was corrupt and corrupting of spirit, the Spirit entered matter only to annihilate it. To Lowell's mind, at once fevered and chaste, redemption seemed to ordain destruction of the natural order; grace manifested itself as apocalypse, and salvation required the death of the body.

In Christian belief the Incarnation overcame the schism that Original Sin opened between nature and grace, flesh and spirit, but Calvinists condemned Catholics for accepting that resolution too easily and living in the flesh too comfortably. The formative influence that Saint Augustine exerted on Calvinism stemmed largely from the fact that he infused theology with the Platonist Gnosticism he had imbibed before his conversion. Gnostic Puritans demanded of God and themselves – day by day, again and again – the verifiable demonstration of the divine presence in the material order as a sign of their special election, their personal exemption from accursed nature. Otherwise, lacking such palpable proof, they faced a bitter choice: either to deny God or to accept their personal damnation. A fatal hesitancy or qualification about God's immanent presence is part of the drama – and dramaturgy – of some of the best poems in *Lord Weary's Castle*.

For example, "Colloquy in Black Rock":

> Here the jack-hammer jabs into the ocean;
> My heart, you race and stagger and demand
> More blood-gangs for your nigger-brass percussions,
> Till I, the stunned machine of your devotion,
> Clanging upon this cymbal of a hand,
> Am rattled screw and footloose. All discussions
>
> End in the mud-flat detritus of death.
> My heart, beat faster, faster. In Black Mud
> Hungarian workmen give their blood
> for the martyre Stephen, who was stoned to death.
>
> Black Mud, a name to conjure with: O mud
> For watermelons gutted to the crust,
> Mud for the mole-tide harbor, mud for mouse,
> Mud for the armored Diesel fishing tubs that thud
> A year and a day to wind and tide; the dust
> Is on this skipping heart that shakes my house,
>
> House of the Savior who was hanged till death.
> My heart, beat faster, faster. In Black Mud
> Stephen the martyre was broken down to blood:
> Our ransom is the rubble of his death.
>
> Christ walks on the black water. In Black Mud
> Darts the kingfisher. On Corpus Christi, heart,
> Over the drum-beat of St. Stephen's choir
> I hear him, *Stupor Mundi,* and the mud
> Flies from his hunching wings and beak – my heart,
> The blue kingfisher dives on you in fire. (*LWC* 5)

The reader recognizes the kinesthetic imagery, the enjambed versification, the combustive sound effects, the strongly stressed rhythms and thudding rhymes of the early poetry, but our principal concern now is thematic. In 1944 Lowell lived briefly in Black Rock near the federal penitentiary in Danbury, Connecticut, from which he had been paroled after serving time as a conscientious objector in defiance of the World War II draft law. His neighbors were Hungarian immigrant Catholics who worshipped in the local church of Saint Stephen, protector of Hungary; however, unlike the conscientious objector Lowell, they were contributing to the war in their native Europe by working in the local defense plant. The colloquy is introspective and solipsistic, addressed not to God but to the poet's own heart as its throbbing beats threaten to shake the machine of his body to pieces (the pun in "screw and footloose" links the poet's physical condition with his mental condition). Overlooking the harbor from a spit of land, Lowell's hyperactivated mind seizes on the violent meeting of wave and rock as symbolic of material existence. Things wear each other down, wear each other out, destroy each other. Black Rock worn down to Black Mud: The middle sestet of the poem catalogues the detritus where land confronts sea. But natural deterioration is hastened and debased by human destructiveness. The fishing tubs are armored for war; the Hungarians piously but obliviously contribute their blood to the Red Cross to help save those mangled by the munitions they make for pay. In Lowell's imagination their nationalistic patron Stephen becomes identified (and contrasted) with Stephen the first martyr, who in being "stoned to death" and "broken down to blood" in imitation of "our Saviour who was hanged till death" typifies the Christian as triumphant victim of and victor over the temporal order.

Like many of the early poems, this one is written for a feast day in the Church's calendar. It was called "Pentecost" at one point in its composition (Axelrod, *Robert Lowell* 54). Pentecost recalls annually the institution of the Church, when in fulfillment of Jesus' prophecy the Spirit descended on the Apostles as a symbol of God's continuing incarnational presence in the world even after the resurrection and ascension of Jesus. And in the final sestet Pentecost becomes overlaid with another spring feast, Corpus Christi, which commemorates Christ's informing and unceasing presence in the world's body. Lowell's image of incarnational descent, however, is not a divine indwelling but a divine dive-bombing. Instead of baptismal immersion, the Christ of Black Rock walks *on* the darkened waters, reiterating the image from "Death from Cancer" ("the ghost / Of risen Jesus walks the waves"), "The Drunken Fisherman" ("On water the Man-Fisher walks"), and "The Slough of Despond" ("I walk upon the flood") (*LWC* 19, 31, 62). In this presentation, Jesus' descent is not into flesh but in rejection of flesh ("the mud / Flies from his hunching wings and beak") and in destruction of body ("my heart, / The blue kingfisher dives on you in fire"). In contrast with Flannery O'Connor or with Eliot in "Little Gidding" (Lowell had recently reviewed *Four Quartets*), these lines do not suggest that God works redemptively through and in the violence of nature and of human acts, but rather that Christ must enter the material order in order to obliterate its innate depravity. His descent redeems from body; he is the dive-bomber, and his fire is decreative rather than, as in the Pentecost of "Little Gidding," purifying. The ecstasy of "Colloquy in Black Rock" consists in the anticipation of apocalypse, even the anticipation of the poet's own death, as release from the human condition. Far from dreading his being "rattled screw and footloose," the pacifist exults in the violence of his disintegration. The passive verb "am rattled" becomes, in the refrains of the quatrains between the sestets, an exhortation to his drumming heart to "beat faster,

faster" and pound his body to rubble. Lowell's patron is not the national patron of Hungary but Stephen the protomartyr.

Lowell's anxiety about the Incarnation is the issue in "The Quaker Graveyard in Nantucket" as well (*LWC* 8–14). Far from being "Lowell's most commonly over-praised work," as Ehrenpreis asserts, it is the most ambitious and best poem in the book and indeed in Lowell's oeuvre; and, along with William Everson's poem for Robinson Jeffers, "The Poet is Dead," it is the finest American elegy since "When Lilacs Last in the Dooryard Bloom'd." The poem has been sensitively explicated by Hugh Staples, Axelrod, Bell, and other critics, and there is need here only to relate the long and complex poem to my argument. The mourning for Lowell's cousin Warren Winslow, killed and buried at sea during World War II, comes to be viewed symbolically in the context of salvation history, framed by the epigraph from Genesis and the gnomic last line adumbrating the end of the world: "The Lord survives the rainbow of his will." Lowell's principal literary sources for this feat of sustained rhetorical virtuosity are the Bible, Milton, and the Shakespearean grandiloquence of *Moby-Dick*. Between Genesis and Apocalypse the poem shows all disorder – the amoral violence of nature, the immoral violence of human beings against nature and each other. The overlaying of the "dreadnaughts" of the Atlantic fleet with the Nantucket whalers, particularly the *Pequod*, and with Job's ship fuses biblical history, American history, New England history; the Sailor becomes Everyman, and the hunting of the whale becomes the supreme symbolic enactment, at once grotesque and sublime, of the Incarnation in history.

For Christian theology maintains both the transcendence of God and His immanence in creation. In the epigraph from Genesis the Creator entrusts creation to the dominion and responsibility of His supreme creature, and the theological mystery of history is that in His omniscient and omnipotent providence God has submitted Himself to the uncertain disposition of the human will, a will now weakened by its original fall from grace. Since the responsibility of freedom permits evil as well as good, God's covenant tolerates violation of the covenant. The rainbow that God arched above the receding flood as a sign that He would not again destroy the world by water till the Last Day still arches over the contentions of land and sea, human and beast, human and human: a history of violations in which the violators either claim God's sanction, like the Quakers driven to hunt the whale for profit, or blame God, like Ahab, for whom the whale is the mask of Jehovah: "IS, the whited monster." But so deeply is the Creator implicated in creation that even violation of the covenant brings "fabled news" of His immanence and sovereignty. Prideful human egotism like Ahab's may make the whale seem a monstrous embodiment of the absolute "I Am Who Am," but in the last section of the poem it is the sailors themselves, not the whale, who seem the real "sea-monsters, upward angel, downward fish," human nature a grotesque contradiction between spiritual and animal.

The poem comes to a climax in the fifth of seven sections:

When the whale's viscera go and the roll
Of its corruption overruns this world
Beyond tree-swept Nantucket and Wood's Hole
And Martha's Vineyard, Sailor, will your sword
Whistle and fall and sink into the fat?
In the great ash-pit of Jehoshaphat
The bones cry for the blood of the white whale,
The fat flukes arch and whack about its ears,
The death-lance churns into the sanctuary, tears
The gun-blue swingle, heaving like a flail,
And hacks the coiling life out: it works and drags
And rips the sperm whale's midriff into rags,
Gobbets of blubber spill to wind and weather,
Sailor, and gulls go round the stoven timbers
Where the morning stars sing out together
And thunder shakes the white surf and dismembers
The red flag hammered in the mast-head. Hide,
Our steel, Jonas Messias, in Thy side.

As regularly happens in the prophetic poems, the last line catches up everything that
has gone before and casts it into a different dimension of significance. The first lines
ask the Sailor if he will join in the universal blood-cry for the whale, the symbol of
the creation ravaged and exploited for power and profit by those ordained to be its
caretakers. The massacre of the whale is described in graphic, almost excessive detail,
until ("until" does not occur here, but it marks the breakover point in "To Peter
Taylor" and other poems) the last, brief sentence reveals that the whale contains and
conceals Jonah, the type of Jesus. The dismemberment becomes a crucifixion. If the
graveyard at Nantucket verges on Jehoshaphat, the biblical place of the Last Judgment, the fact that it also verges on Calvary makes a decisive difference in the nature of that Judgment. The phrase "The death-lance churns into the sanctuary" in
the middle of the passage anticipates the final revelation and links the harpooning
Sailor with the centurion at the foot of the cross, and in the last line the poet accepts
"our" universal human identification with the harpooner to beseech Jonas Messias,
as He receives the death-lance, to bless and redeem His desecration. Now "when the
whale's viscera go," "the roll / Of its corruption overruns this world" in a way that
inverts the despairing sense of the first lines of the passage.

However, the poem does not end with this almost unbearably charged moment,
but instead veers away from it in the final two sections. Lowell's Calvinism found
the corruption of the world too radical to sustain the sense of redemptive immanence attained in these lines. Section VI, therefore, presents his Gnostic description of "Our Lady of Walsingham" as the representative and exemplar of the redeemed human:

Our Lady, too small for her canopy,
Sits near the altar. There's no comeliness
At all or charm in that expressionless
Face with its heavy eyelids. As before,
This face, for centuries a memory,
Non est species, neque decor,
Expressionless, expresses God: it goes
Past castled Sion. She knows what God knows,
Not Calvary's Cross nor crib at Bethlehem
Now, and the world shall come to Walsingham.

God here is all inscrutable transcendence and no tormented immanence. Beyond the contradictions of His physical and historical Incarnation ("Calvary's Cross" and "crib at Bethlehem"), Mary's expressionlessness expresses God's inhuman otherness. The way to Walsingham presages not a redemption of the human but a redemption from the human.

Section VII concludes the poem with a reversion to the violence of wind and wave and predatory "sea-monsters," human and inhuman. The last lines seem to call into question the possibility of harmonious order predicated in the epigraph from Genesis:

You could cut the brackish winds with a knife
Here in Nantucket, and cast up the time
When the Lord God formed man from the sea's slime
And breathed into his face and breath of life,
and blue-lung'd combers lumbered to the kill.
The Lord survives the rainbow of His will.

The world is presented here as perverse in and from the Creation; from the very moment "when the Lord God formed man from the sea's slime," the "blue-lung'd combers lumbered to the kill." The phrase "blue-lung'd combers" fuses in the image of violence the waves that wear the land to the detritus of beach, the fish who inhabit the waves, and the scavenging human beachcombers. Earlier in the section Lowell's spare "It's well" pronounced a word of balked resignation, if not benison, on the scene: God transcends His transient and doomed creation, and Apocalypse shall deliver the world even from Walsingham to His inscrutable providence.

In 1974 Lowell drastically shortened "Quaker Graveyard" for the British selected poems, eliminating Sections II and IV, printing "Our Lady of Walsingham" as a separate poem, and reducing VII to only the final lines quoted earlier. Perhaps these last two excisions stemmed from Lowell's realization that the fixation with God's otherness in the last two sections of "Quaker Graveyard" diverged from the incarnational vision attained by the end of Section V; certainly the 1974 version moves more quickly to that climax and then almost immediately (if ambiguously) closes. But

Lowell quickly realized that the revised text diminished the unresolved drama of God's transcendence and immanence (and of his own Gnosticism and incarnationalism), and he restored the full text in the American *Selected Poems* (1976) the year before his death.

In *Lord Weary's Castle,* "As a Plane Tree by the Water" and "Where the Rainbow Ends" actually imagine the Apocalypse descending on Boston. The former concludes exultantly that "vision puts out reason's eyes" and hails the coming resurrection (47). The latter poem concludes *Lord Weary's Castle* with the volume's most unambiguous affirmation, which enfolds the Old and New Testaments, Jahweh and Messiah, from Genesis to Revelation:

> In Boston serpents whistle at the cold.
> The victim climbs the altar steps and sings:
> "Hosannah to the lion, lamb, and beast
> Who fans the furnace-face of IS with wings:
> I breathe the ether of my marriage-feast."
> At the high altar, gold
> And a fair cloth, I kneel and the wings beat
> My cheek. What can the dove of Jesus give
> You now but wisdom, exile? Stand and live,
> The dove has brought an olive branch to eat.   (*LWC* 69)

It is a long way from the volume's opener, "The Exile's Return," to this conclusion. The liturgical decorum of the scene surrounds and tempers and mediates "the furnace-face of IS," and the sequence of shorter sentences, fitted into verses with more end-stops than usual, contributes to the air of serene and ecstatic assurance.

The narrative and dramatic character of the poems in *The Mills of the Kavanaughs* somewhat obscured Lowell's lapse from faith to disbelief, but the first poem in *Life Studies,* "Beyond the Alps" (3–4), traces the inner journey through an allegorical train ride from Rome ("Much against my will / I left the City of God where it belongs") to Paris ("our black classic, breaking up / like killer kings on an Etruscan cup"). The verses resonate with rhetorical and mythological flourishes, but now the vibrations remain teasingly ironic and do not seek a breakthrough into prophetic vision.

Lowell's dating of the poem is not necessarily autobiographically accurate, but it is thematically deliberate. The parenthetical foreword identifies 1950 as "the year Pius XII defined the dogma of Mary's bodily assumption." That dogma extends the Incarnation into an assertion about human destiny: God's descent into flesh is completed in our bodily resurrection and ascension. More explicitly than does previous Christian teaching from which it is an extrapolation, the Assumption says that we are redeemed in fulfillment, not denial, of our humanity, and Lowell pointedly links his ultramontane journey to the doctrinal declaration of the Assumption because his Calvinist Gnosticism can not conceive of salvation in the body:

> The lights of science couldn't hold a candle
> to Mary risen – at one miraculous stroke,

> angel-wing'd, gorgeous as a jungle bird!
> But who believed this? Who could understand?

Mary as gorgeous and angel-winged jungle bird seemed to Lowell more alien and incomprehensible than the expressionless Lady of Walsingham.

"Beyond the Alps" chillingly foreshadowed both the private and political poems of Lowell's later years by making it clear that the inability any longer to believe has left Lowell with a diminished sense of self and circumstance. He is reduced to a "blear-eyed ego kicking in my berth" (the pun connects his cramped train bed with the human condition) in a world where contending powers, whether nominally of church or state, oppress the duped, "monstrous human crush":

> Pilgrims still kissed Saint Peter's brazen sandal.
> The Duce's lynched, bare, booted skull still spoke.
> God herded his people to the *coup de grâce* –
> the costumed Switzers sloped their pikes to push,
> O Pius, through the monstrous human crush. . . .

The rhymes and stresses, the sound and wordplay make for a rhetorical density and energy carried over the prophetic poems but expressive now of the strenuous self-consuming ironies sparked by the recoil from prophecy. This inversion and implosion of linguistic energy animates the colloquial, unmetaphorical, free-verse style of the "Life Studies" sequence that initiates and constitutes the strongest segment of the account of Lowell's "ego kicking in [his] berth," played out in subsequent volumes.

Lowell designated "Skunk Hour" (*LS* 89–90) "the anchor poem" of the sequence. The first four stanzas are written in the wryly humorous and loosely associative descriptive manner that "Life Studies" was substituting for the mythic metaphors of *Lord Weary's Castle*. However, the second half of "Skunk Hour" suddenly moves into a different order of perception and statement: a kind of anti-vision, or black hole of the psyche or spirit. Lowell said that Berryman read it all too accurately as an account of mental breakdown, and he characterized it as a "secular, puritan, and agnostical" dark night of the soul – not a Christian mystical one like Saint John of the Cross's but an "Existential night" ("On 'Skunk Hour'" 107, 108, 99). The fifth and sixth stanzas present a hallucinated sense of physical and psychological existence as an infernal calvary in which mechanical impulses drive dehumanized material objects to a violent end. Then, just as unexpectedly, in the last two stanzas comes an existential deliverance of sorts – not out of but into the squalor and violence of material existence. The poet stands outside his tortured psyche and, contemplating the skunk's world, admires despite himself her brute tenacity and spunk. Here is the metamorphic moment of the sequence:

> I myself am hell;
> nobody's here –

only skunks, that search
in the moonlight for a bite to eat.
They march on their soles up Main Street:
white stripes, moonstruck eyes' red fire
under the chalk-dry and spar spire
of the Trinitarian Church.

I stand on top
of our back steps and breathe the rich air –
a mother skunk with her column of kittens swills the garbage pail.
She jabs her wedge-head in a cup
of sour cream, drops her ostrich tail,
and will not scare.

The metamorphosis is all the more powerful – and symptomatic – for being anti-climactic and ironic. "The skunks are both quixotic and barbarously absurd," said Lowell, "hence the tone of amusement and defiance"; yet their march provides a sort of "affirmation, an ambiguous one" ("On 'Skunk Hour'" 107–108).

In response to a commission from the Boston Arts Festival, Lowell began to write "Colonel Shaw and the Massachusetts 54th" during the early months of 1960 and read it to clamorous applause at the festival on the Common in June of that year. It appeared in the *Atlantic* in November and was tipped into the paperback edition of *Life Studies* after "Skunk Hour." It is one of Lowell's most tightly written and most explicated poems; its ironies rise to prophetic outrage in seeing Boston's decline into barbarous materialism as part of a national and global declension. The doomsday of materialism goes unheeded in the billboard Lowell saw high over Boston Common; the advertisement seeks to demonstrate the security of Mosler Safes for cash profits by displaying an actual photograph of a safe still intact in the rubble of Hiroshima: "the 'Rock of Ages' / that survived the blast" (*FUD* 72). The city that was established on a New England hill to shine as beacon of grace to the Old World has turned out to be the secular city. Its perversion discloses its covert allegiance with "the dark downward and vegetating kingdom / of the fish and reptile." The razing of the old Aquarium to make way for so-called progress merely looses the sleek, finned predators into the streets:

The Aquarium is gone. Everywhere,
giant finned cars nose forward like fish;
a savage servility
slides by on grease.   (*FUD* 72)

In his biography of Lowell, Ian Hamilton claims that "For the Union Dead" provides "a way forward to the next phase of Lowell's work," specifically the political poems, though he notes somewhat bewilderedly that the last lines, just quoted, recall "the poet-prophet of *Lord Weary's Castle*" (*Robert Lowell* 278–79). The poem did of course become the title poem of Lowell's next volume, placed at the end to provide a rousing conclusion. However, without denying Hamilton's point, I would argue that there was a genuine appropriateness about the first appearance of that poem with *Life Studies* in the paperback edition rather than with the poems in the 1964 volume to which it gave the title. For it is the function of poetry as prophecy that gives coherence to *Land of Unlikeness, Lord Weary's Castle,* and (in the vigor of denial and exorcism) *Life Studies* and makes "For the Union Dead" a coda to the poetry before 1960. From this point of view that jeremiad belongs with and brings to a close Lowell's early poetry, and makes a more accurate point of demarcation than *Life Studies* between the early and late phases of his development. The attempt at jeremiad in a later poem like "Waking Early Sunday Morning" (from *Near the Ocean*) merely demonstrates the collapse of inspiration. Rue renders rhetoric hollow; only a prophet can deliver a jeremiad – not an ironist.

William Everson, himself a Catholic prophetic poet, though of a very different sort from Lowell, has made some illuminating remarks on the effect of the loss of faith on Lowell's career. In a 1962 interview, after *Life Studies* but before *For the Union Dead,* he mused about the disruption in Lowell's poetic vocation: "With poetry your initial creative insight carries you on with a great burst of energy and makes a breakthrough. Now to discover how to transfer over into another system, another psychic frame of reference is extremely difficult." Everson explained that he did not mean faith solely in a dogmatic sense but rather, more generally,

> in the sense of an unconscious which affirms the authenticity of reality against its dubious aspects. . . . I think Lowell would have maintained [belief in himself as a poet] if he hadn't gone through the crisis of losing the faith by which he achieved his prime work. When he'd lost that faith, it put a different bend in his career. . . . When you are a Christian poet, or a communist poet, and lose your faith, the loss of commitment reduces you to a different level of activity. (32–33)

I am making much the same point: not that Lowell wrote no good poems after 1960 or ceased to be a serious and significant poet, but rather that because he came to an enabling sense of himself as a prophetic poet, the lapse from that "highest conception of the poet's task" warped his subsequent life and work. The later volumes record, over all, a wavering decline: the narcissistic self-recapitulation of most of *For the Union Dead* ("I am tired. Everyone's tired of my turmoil" [19]); the vacillation in *Near the Ocean,* particularly in the poems that seek political engagement, between moral indignation and self-doubt; the several attempts to sort out into coherent and readable shape the alternations in the running sonnet sequence between private surrealism (or "unrealism" [*N* 262], as Lowell came to prefer to call it) and public commentary; and finally the candid but deflated nostalgia of *Day by Day.* These later volumes contain dazzling lines and passages, and arresting poems, but nothing, in my judgment, to compare with "Colloquy in Black Rock" and "Quaker Graveyard," "Life Studies" and "For the Union Dead." In terms of Everson's typology, Lowell had ceased after 1960 to try to be a poet who "stands witness to a world beyond the world of his making" and had become in his own estimation something lesser: a poet who "creates a world of his own making" (Everson 36) – merely. Lowell's compensatory counterstrategy was to denigrate the prophetic poems while he compulsively wrote and rewrote in his notebook the linguistic microcosms of his own devising. But that "merely" haunted him and, succubus-like, steadily sapped his remaining strength.

Day by Day, published in 1977, the year of Lowell's death, pieces together a self-conscious comment on his life and career. The book is more trenchant and moving than the numbing procession of sonnet volumes; it is in fact his best book since *For the Union Dead* – in good part because of his ability to lift himself above the shambles of his experience, if only to commiserate the prophetic vision he had lost. Again and again these premonitory death-poems crackle and ignite in a final, flaring recognition of his fall from prophecy to irony.

The Gnosticism that all along made him ache for an existence "unembarrassed by the flesh" (34) and free of the "carnivorous harmony of nature" (41) pitched "the unredeemable world" into "the downlook" (125) of a fatal disease:

> Folly comes from something –
> the present, yes,
> we are in it,
> it's the infection
> of things gone . . .   (57)

But true Gnosticism at least looks to an apocalyptic explosion into transcendent otherness, as the blazing poems in *Lord Weary's Castle* did. The phrases in *Day by Day* only light the flickering way to extinction, as in this brilliant conceit of the body as a disposable cigarette lighter glowing with its dying flame:

> Now the lifefluid goes
> from the throwaway lighter,
> its crimson, cylindrical, translucent
> glow grows pale –   (46)

For all the rueful disavowals of his youthful presumptuousness, the combustive energies of poems like "Colloquy in Black Rock" and "Quaker Graveyard" made the later poetry seem anticlimactic even to the poet:

> I cannot read.
> Everything I've written
> is greenish brown,
> as if the words
> refused to sound.   (77)

And from the closing "Epilogue":

> . . . sometimes everything I write
> with the threadbare art of my eye
> seems a snapshot,
> lurid, rapid, garish, grouped,
> heightened from life,
> yet paralyzed by fact.
> All's misalliance. (127)

After inscribing his family's elegies from first book to last, Lowell now pronounces his own: "Under New York's cellular facades / clothed with vitreous indifference, / I dwindle . . . dynamite no more" (48). The same poem, "Death of a Critic," ponders those dynamite days when the kingfisher seemed Christ dive-bombing on a divine mission: "Was my integrity my unique / understanding of everything I damned?" (47). The answer comes a few poems later in "Domesday Book": "The reign of the kingfisher was short" (56).

The past tense of the verb seems definitive. The image concludes "Domesday Book" and emerges from lines in which the intensity of nostalgia concentrates into a sudden rhetorical incandescence:

> The old follies, as usual, never return –
> the houses still burn
> in the golden lowtide steam of Turner.
> Only when we start to go,
> do we notice the outrageous phallic flare
> of the splash flowers that fascinated children.
>
> The reign of the kingfisher was short. (56)

Another of the most moving moments in the book comes near the end in "Home," when, thinking back across his wrecked marriages to the Virgin Mother whom he had left behind in Rome ("much against my will") because he could not accept her incarnational Assumption, Lowell breaks out:

> The Queen of Heaven, I miss her,
> we were divorced. She never doubted
> the divided, stricken soul
> could call her Maria,
> and rob the devil with a word. (115)

What distinguishes these passages and others in *Day by Day* is that the irony is made to press both ways, intensifying the energy it dissipates, elevating the values it deflates. But the verbal energy arises from those foregone values; it flares outrageously and sputters out.

4

Mephistophilis in Maine: Rereading "Skunk Hour"

SANDRA M. GILBERT

"Why, this is hell, nor am I out of it."
—Marlowe, *Dr. Faustus* (I.iii.80)

Some years ago I participated in a weekend symposium in San Francisco titled "Poets on Poetry." At one session, several panelists were discussing "their" contemporaries, and a particularly passionate young man arose, almost trembling with intensity, to declare that "Catullus is my contemporary and Pound is my contemporary, Whitman is my contemporary and Bly is my contemporary, but Robert Lowell is *not* my contemporary." His remarks were greeted with applause, laughter, and some cheers by an audience of fellow poets, all of whom assumed, I imagine, that they too, like Catullus, were this fiery young artist's "contemporaries."

Perhaps this episode still implies, as it surely hinted at the time, that the moment has arrived when poets should *re*read Lowell, though I must confess that it still also causes me to feel some qualms about doing so. Clearly, the sternly negative judgment that emerged from it has been widely shared, especially on the West Coast, where lines are "breath units" and the living is easy. Lowell was "old fashioned," the young poet's speech implied, and yes, his laughing audience agreed, the emperor had been wearing old clothes; he should have given them to the Salvation Army, for as W. B. Yeats put it, "There's more enterprise in walking naked," especially in California.

Lowell's death in 1977 meant, of course, that for a while people were more discreet about the revolutionary impulses they felt toward him, and it meant, as well, that a serious process of rereading his work began, with a biography by Ian Hamilton as well as studies by Steven Gould Axelrod (*Robert Lowell*) and Vereen Bell, among others, supplementing and revising such earlier critical texts as those by Marjorie Perloff, Alan Williamson, and Jerome Mazzaro. But in the long run the problems involved in rereading this poet's writings are not likely to change. For what critics and journalists like to call "the midcentury," Lowell was American poetry's Emperor of Ice Cream. Thus, just as younger Victorian artists could locate themselves only by coming to terms with Tennyson, so most American poets of the sixties and seventies had to define themselves and their art at least partly through some sort of confrontation with Lowell.

For many poets (most famously Sylvia Plath and Anne Sexton, but more recently Alan Williamson and Frank Bidart), such a confrontation involved actually studying with the man himself. For me, however – and my strategy here will be at least partly impressionistic, indeed "confessional" – it meant studying, and being stunned by, his writing, especially by (of course) *Life Studies*. A rereading almost by definition should include and qualify a first reading, but that is no problem for me because I remember so well how, just out of college and with a sensibility formed by studies of Yeats, Pound, Stevens, and Eliot, I was stunned when I first came across *Life Studies* in 1960. Not stunned in the positive sense of gasping admiration, either, but stunned meaning bewildered, dizzied, even curiously sickened.

Obscure and unprepossessing, these poems of the "tranquillized *Fifties*" were not gracefully dramatic (like Yeats), cosmically ambitious (like Pound), sophisticatedly philosophical (like Stevens), or learnedly allusive (like Eliot). On the contrary, they seemed in their earnest privacy both thick-voiced and shrunken, as if they had been written by a forty-year-old Rimbaud who had gotten into manufacturing lawn mowers in Massachusetts instead of gunrunning in Africa. To enter any one of them was like entering a darkened, heavily curtained room where someone has been living a very long time with too many family relics. Dusty, sadly factual, sardonically circumstantial, they were like endless anecdotes told by an Ancient Mariner hooked on "No Doz." Or maybe, better still, they were like the old snapshots he presses on you to lend verisimilitude to his obsessive recitation, smudged and peeling images from an album damp with family shadows.[1]

Yet, despite the aversion I did undeniably feel, I kept on reading these poems. Why were they so charismatic, compelling even in their peculiar shrunkenness, their factual gloom, their ennui? Why did one continue to sit in the darkened parlor of this stammering Mariner as he flung down photo after photo of old friends, teachers, dying uncles, former wives, eccentric parents and grandparents? What was the charm in his verse version of *One Man's Family*?

That I did not understand then quite why I went on reading and rereading *Life Studies* even while I continued to pore (and that seems an appropriate word) over the grimiest details of the poems shows just how valuable an exercise continual *re*reading is. Because I think I know consciously now what I unconsciously intuited then: that Lowell's poems really were the aesthetic paradigms of the "tranquillized *Fifties*," poems of – yes – the midcentury, and this was one source of their almost perverse appeal. To read them was to wiggle the loose tooth of history, to feel the masochistic pleasure/pain of complete immersion in the fatality of one's own "era."

For to be, as I have said Lowell was, the bard of the midcentury is in a way to have been buried in our century (in fact, in what Elizabeth Bishop, eulogizing Lowell, called "our worst century so far")[2] with little or no hope of climbing out of it. Born in 1917, Lowell may not have seriously believed (though according to Ian Hamilton he seriously feared [473]) that he would be dead in 1977; as it happens he was, but he had every reason to suppose that he would not live to see the mystic year 2001. Is it too fanciful to speculate that his inevitable sense of confinement – his sense (shared by poets like Auden and Thomas) of being enclosed by and limited to the twentieth century – had an effect on his work? Surely, after all, some of the openness and exhilaration we feel in Yeats is a function of his delight in having survived and transcended the century in which he was born. Wilde, Johnson, Symonds, Synge and the rest – all were left behind in "the Victorian period" or the "*fin de siècle.*" Yeats, triumphant, lived to tell the tale. So, in a smaller way, did Pound and Eliot, who outlived their nineteenth-century childhoods to "make it new" as twentieth-century men. For Lowell and his contemporaries, however, born not before or after but *with* Modernism, such triumphs were not likely to be achieved. The tranquillized fifties – the dead center of the century – were where, in every sense, Lowell found himself.

No wonder, then, that his *Life Studies* is so helplessly circumstantial. The twentieth century itself was the dreary, family-haunted, photograph-plastered room where Lowell had been living a very long time and where he expected to go on living – with files, photos, and newspaper clippings – quite a while longer. There were no rainbow bridges to be crossed from age to age, no solemn passageways to enter. It would all be the same: the same America, the same auto hulks, the same Miltown, the same damn century. Thus, though history both public and private is naturally the subject of most of these history-imprisoned poems, history here is not a chronicle of grandeur, or even of grandeur diminished, but a compendium of trivial details and tedious repetitions. Where Pound and Eliot weave entrancing webs of quotations, or at least shore fragments of the Western mind against their ruins, Lowell shores his New England up with sandbags full of facts, names, dates. Even his most nobly elegiac poems are cluttered with persons, places, and things, as if snapshots were the promised end of history, and Candid Camera were Clio's other name. This poet's dead mother comes home from Italy "wrapped like *panetone* in Italian tinfoil" (*LS* 78), and he mourns her because, among other things, when he stayed out late as a young man she used to leave "my milk-tooth mug of milk / . . . waiting for me on a plate / of Triskets" (*LS* 79). The night attendant in "the house for the 'mentally ill'" where the poet finds himself is "a B.U. sophomore" who reads Richards's *The Meaning of Meaning* (*LS* 81). The poet himself drives a Tudor Ford, only teaches on Tuesdays, and bookworms "in pajamas fresh from the washer each morning" (*LS* 85). At nineteen, his father was "'the old man' of a gunboat on the Yangtse" (*LS* 72). Now, father dead and dead mother buried in tinfoil, the poet notes that it is 1953, and "the Republic summons Ike, / the mausoleum in her heart" (*LS* 7). But it is a mausoleum where one suffocates not in emptiness, blackness, airlessness – the melodramatic *nil* of the nineteenth century[3] – but in facts and products, Triskets and Tudor Fords, *The Meaning of Meaning,* and "Ike," immortal name.

It is accurate, I think, to say that for a child of the fifties the terrible familiarity of all this was compelling. Yes: Lowell was holding a mirror up to the ill nature of urban–suburban midcentury America, and there I found myself, one of a million blurrily corroborating details. Yet my own inhabitation of a grimy historical background does not seem, even so, quite enough to explain the fascination of *Life Studies.* Sociology is one thing, and poetry, especially this poetry, is something else, no matter how authentically its "reality" is textured. Even a cursory reexamination of, say, "During Fever" (*LS* 79–80), one of the volume's most apparently fact-afflicted poems, suggests this to me now, for while Lowell's evocation of parenthood among three generations – his mother and her Victorian "papá," himself and his mother, his daughter and himself – may *seem* merely random, his verse is really structured by a genealogy of illness that is both purposeful and calamitous.

Creaking in her crib, victim of an obscure guilt inherited from her "dim-bulb father," Lowell's infant daughter – an *un*tranquillized child of the fifties – mutters "sorry" in the first stanza of this poem. Her fever, fostered by the "sick city," recalls the fervor of the speaker's own days as a sardonically "gemlike undergraduate," as well as the prolonged childhood in which, after he had been greeted by the "milk-tooth mug of milk" his mother left for him, he and she "bent by the fire / rehashing Father's character." Compared to the capitalized grandeur of his own parents ("*M*other" and "*F*ather"), this lowercase, modern "*f*ather" is, as Lowell says of "himself" in another poem, "frizzled, stale, and small." Yet such diminishment is clearly his heritage just as guilt is his daughter's: Furtive and curiously culpable, his own paternal parent, despite his capitalized Fatherhood, waited until he thought his gossiping wife and son were asleep to "tiptoe down the stairs / and chain the door."

Inevitably, then, "Mother" – though she possesses the insignia of respectability and wealth ("a silver hot water bottle . . . Italian china . . . [a] nuptial bed . . . as big as a bathroom") – yearns backward into a past dominated by her own "Father," who "groused behind a screen / . . . whenever young men came to court [her], / back in those settled years of World War One." The ferocious irony of that last phrase, however – the "settled years of World War One" – illuminates the ambiguity of this understated but devastating and devastated family history:

> Terrible that old life of decency
> without unseemly intimacy
> or quarrels, when the unemancipated woman
> still had her Freudian papá and maids!

Was it "terrible"? Haunted by a lineage of "Mothers" and "Fathers" whose enigmatic transactions with time have shaped the fevers of their descendants, the "father" and (by implication) the "daughter" of the midcentury must struggle to understand

and resist an "old life" that still encroaches on their sleep, a life whose quotidian facts and maladies – hot water bottles, china, screens, and magazines – begin to resonate like myths.

But if I now sense that "During Fever" at least half transforms a literal genealogy into a monitory and quasi-mythic history, it is in "Skunk Hour" (*LS* 89–90), consistently for me (as for many readers) one of the most fascinating of the *Life Studies* pieces, that I have long felt and continue to feel with particular keenness the resonance of something beyond "mere" factuality. As usual with Lowell's work, my initial response to this text began with bafflement. Who were these people, how did they get into this poem, why did it matter that they were here? Nautilus Island's dotty heiress and her reverent son; that summer millionaire "who seemed to leap from an L. L. Bean / catalogue"; the "fairy / decorator" and his silly orange-brightened shop – I could not help wondering (as I had been trained in college to wonder) what they "represented." And if I thought about the problem this way, it was obviously both possible and safe to conclude, as many critics have and as I guess I too must have at some point, that all these bizarre figures were inhabitants of a sort of updated Waste Land, modernized versions of T. S. Eliot's typist and his young man carbuncular, or of those obnoxious women in "Prufrock" who come and go talking of Michelangelo.[4] Certainly, like the Eliot characters, Lowell's people were isolated and sterile: The heiress was a hermit, the "fairy decorator" would "rather marry," the summer millionaire inexplicably disappeared. More, it seemed significant that in the world of "Skunk Hour" only cars (love cars!) made love, lying sensuously hull to hull "where the graveyard shelves on the town," and only skunks passionately reproduced their own kind.

In fact, many of these points still do seem significant to me, but on the rereading that, as John Berryman proclaimed, "Skunk Hour" requires ("all poems are built of course for rereading, but this more than most" [101]), they do not seem significant enough to account for the poem's continuing charisma. Yes, the human figures in "Skunk Hour" are peculiar, alienated, in some sense sterile or even life-denying: Lowell himself, for instance, explaining the poem as a dramatization of "an Existentialist night," dismissed the characters in the first four stanzas as details intended to sketch "a dawdling more or less amiable picture of a declining Maine sea town" ("On Skunk Hour" 107), emblems of – in Berryman's words – "the past, outworn, gone, or not gone" (101). Yet as Steven Gould Axelrod has shown, the poet's struggle with the first four stanzas of "Skunk Hour" was far more intense than he later admitted (*Robert Lowell* 124–26). Indeed, the weak opening of an early draft of "Inspiration," as the work was originally called, reveals through the complete absence of the monitory figures – heiress and millionaire and decorator – who were eventually to establish the "tone" of the piece, just how important these strange and estranged beings were to become.[5]

In fact, against the readings of Berryman and others, I would argue that, apparently "historical" and socially symbolic as these characters are, they are also, along with the poem's putative speaker, in some sense magical, powerful. Though they are treated ironically, the people in "Skunk Hour," speaker and all, are for the mid-century figures of what Wallace Stevens called "capable imagination," or perhaps, more accurately, figures to be studied by such an imagination. Indeed, when I brood on them as perseveringly as Lowell must have (despite his distracting insistence that he was just thinking of "a blue china doorknob" ["On 'Skunk Hour'" 110]), I begin now to think that they have the mythic strength of hell, the strength of the smoky visions Jonathan Edwards saw in the forests of New England, the strength of a tough underworld that no twentieth-century exorcists – whether Republican, Democrat, or "fire-breathing Catholic C.O." (*LS* 85) – can ever dissipate. But in that case, even strewn with auto corpses or festooned with fake fishnet, our inescapably "modern" world may also be disquietingly (and inescapably) magical. In fact, both auto bodies and fishnet may themselves be part of mysteries we enact in neurasthenic bewilderment, knowing not what we do.

To begin with mysteries: It is fairly clear that if the events of "Skunk Hour," such as they are, do not actually happen on Halloween, they happen somewhere in Halloween's ritually black-and-orange vicinity. The decorator's shop, for instance, is sacramentally orange, and the night on which the speaker strays demonically toward the graveyard on "the hill's skull" is pure black. All souls are abroad, ill spirits sobbing, moon-struck eyes aglow. But a world in which "we've lost our summer millionaire" is, after all, a world of dead and doubtless damned souls; a world no longer inhabited by those archetypal summer millionaires Pan and Christ, Adonis and Attis, Osiris and Orpheus; a world on its gloomy way toward the winter solstice, sun lowering, shadows frowning, "love-cars," like Charon's dread black boats, lying hull to hull on the hill's skull.

It is no wonder, then, that this world is ruled by a "modern" woman who also seems to be very much a witch: "Nautilus Island's hermit heiress." Her "Spartan" cottage links her to the ancient world, as does her abode on Nautilus Island. Moreover, the enduring presences of *her* sheep, *her* son the bishop, and – most inexplicable to twentieth-century minds – *her* farmer, imply her continuing and all-pervasive power. Perhaps "she's in her dotage," and perhaps she secretly wishes not only to be Queen Victoria but to live in "Queen Victoria's century." Yet still, ruling her New England community through sheep and farmer and bishop, manifesting her presence through falling "eyesores," she's Circe, Hecate, Ishtar, Venus, the goddess of love turned goddess of death in an All Soul's Night world where the graveyard shelves on the town.

It is fitting, therefore, that with that vegetation/fertility god, the summer millionaire, mysteriously lost (he who leaped from a marvelously punning "L. L. Bean / catalogue"), the escapades of the "fairy" decorator begin. Weary as Ariel, this enchanted spirit would "rather marry" for – as all enchanted spirits know – "there's no money in his work." Still, if he is "doomed for a certain term to walk the night, / And for the day confined to fast in fires," like Hamlet's father, he will do so, dreary

and dutiful, filling his ineffectual fishnet with orange cork and draping his unfunc-
tional cobbler's bench in orange fiery as the "red fox stain" that "covers Blue Hill."
And after all, though net and bench have no practical roles in the "real" world, they
may well serve some talismanic purpose in the realm of image magic to which it begins to seem clear the "fairy decorator" really belongs.

But if an updated Circe is Queen of this Night, a "fairy decorator" its unwilling
jester/minister, a "summer millionaire" its absent king, then the poem's speaker –
Lowell himself, or the person Lowell has elaborately defined for us as "Lowell himself" – is its crown prince. At first, in fact, as I thought about these strange figures
in "Skunk Hour," this poet-prince seemed to me to be a sort of sad, mad Hamlet,
wandering entranced through the dark in his *Tudor* Ford, and watching pruriently
for love cars hard by the graveyard. All very Hamlet-like activities, of course. Indeed, when the speaker confesses "My mind's not right" and hears a car radio bleat
"Love, O careless Love," I felt certain that, like Eliot's Prufrock, he's primarily a
twentieth-century revision of Hamlet, nerve-worn and impotent, the crown prince
Least Likely to Succeed and thus the very model of a modern minor poet. But when
this speaker confesses "I myself am hell," it becomes clear that he's not *just* Hamlet or
Hamlet's cousin but also, what is more important, the descendant or reincarnation
of a more crucial and burning figure: Mephistophilis, or Lucifer, or Satan, the very
model of a Romantic major poet. As such a poet, however, he is doomed for more
than "a certain term" to walk the night. He is doomed, in fact, to find his ill spirit
everywhere since (like Marlowe's Mephistophilis) he learns wherever he goes that
"this is hell, nor am I out of it," and (with Milton's Satan) he complains that "which
way I fly is hell, myself am hell."[6]

This hell of self, though – what sort of hell is it? Should we identify it with, for
instance, the hell of solipsism into which Byron, like a swashbuckling Satan, continually plunged? Or, more contemporary, is it the hell of psychoanalysis, the dis-
tinctively Freudian inferno that perpetually yawned, as Lowell knew, beneath the
suburbs of the tranquillized fifties? A number of Lowell's other poems suggest that
both these hypotheses are reasonable ones. They suggest, in other words, that this
poet's self-stalking self is both melodramatic and neurotic, both broodingly Byronic
and anxiously psychoanalytic.[7] In "Eye and Tooth," for instance, a piece collected in
For the Union Dead (18–19), the speaker immerses himself in suffering caused by an
infection that turns his "whole eye . . . sunset red." Tormented, like any good analysand, by boyhood memories, he sequesters himself, a petulant modern Childe Harold, in "joyless revery," confessing that

> I lay all day on my bed.
> I chain-smoked through the night,
> learning to flinch
> at the flash of the matchlight.

And despite his demonically energetic chain-smoking in darkness, he concludes, "I
am tired. Everyone's tired of my turmoil."

For such trivial and self-indulgent turmoil, the skunk – as I must have dutifully decided when I first read this poem – is an apt if somewhat mechanical metaphor. After all, small and apparently ineffectual though it is, a single skunk can blanket the world for miles around with the stink of his or her turmoil, a stench of self as exhibitionistic as the Byronic posturings of any neurotic (or indeed, if one wishes to be biographically accurate, the helpless effusions of any manic-depressive). Yet as I reread "Skunk Hour," and as I try to understand the charismatic atmosphere the poem still generates for me, I keep thinking that there is (as we used to say in the fifties) "more to" Lowell's skunks than such a neatly definable, almost allegorical meaning. Similarly, the hellish self this poem constructs and fearsomely displays for us seems far more dreadful than the inner hell of tiresome turmoil we all expect *poètes maudits* to inhabit. Selfish neurotics and symbolically self-seeking skunks are part of this poem, I think, but a comparatively minor part of it. For, inhabited by weird and magical creatures – not only witches and fairies but radios that bleat and cars that make love – the hell Lowell reveals to us here really is Hell, the *ur*-place that burns and freezes at the center of the earth, the kingdom that rules and is ruled by Satan, Prince of Darkness. And Lowell's skunks, therefore, are Hell's totemic animals, fiery familiars who emerge from the shadows of the graveyard to march, as if punning on Milton and Dante, "on their *soles* up Main Street," flaunting their demonic triumph "under the chalk-dry and spar spire / of the Trinitarian Church."

At the same time, it seems to me not insignificant that the first of these fierce familiars is a *female* animal – a *mother* skunk who leads her "column of kittens" to the sour cream, the per-version of maternal milk jammed into the poet's garbage pail. Beginning with a Circean "heiress" and ending with a bestial progenetrix, "Skunk Hour" culminates a volume that also includes such explorations of female potency and male impotence (or distorted potency) as "During Fever," "Sailing Home from Rapallo," "Man and Wife," and "To Speak of Woe That Is in Marriage," among others. That the work may hint, then, at both sub- and pre-texts that explore such matters is perhaps inevitable. To be more specific, is it a coincidence that the literary anxiety articulated in stanza three of "Inspiration" ("Writing verses like a Turk, / I lie in bed from sun to sun – / There is no money in this work. / You have to love it") dissolves into the sexual anxiety felt by the "fairy decorator" ("There is no money in his work, / he'd rather marry")?

More specifically (and perhaps arcanely) still, is it possible that "Nautilus Island's hermit / heiress" (whose "son's a bishop") may subtextually – and no doubt quite unconsciously – allude to Marianne Moore, the "hermit heiress" of American poetry whose "The Paper Nautilus" was an important precursor poem about female power and whose poetic "son" was the very Elizabeth *Bishop* to whom "Skunk Hour" is dedicated?[8] As a, if not *the,* Hamlet of midcentury verse, Lowell clearly felt himself indebted to, and possibly wounded by, a number of Gertrudes, whose dead Modernist husbands, like himself, were "doomed for a certain term to walk the [Existentialist] night," a night whose intertextual echoes evoke not only the magical mysteries of *Faustus* and *Hamlet* but also the male worries of *The Waste Land*, "Prufrock,"

Ulysses, and other Modernist cruxes.[9] In this dark night of the soul from which the triple godhead of patriarchal law, lure, and lore have withdrawn themselves (as the "chalk-dry and spar spire / of the Trinitarian Church" tells us), it is no wonder that the tormentedly hellish presence of a loveless Mephistophilian/Satanic speaker manifests not only the absence of a paternal Father/God but also the frightening encroachment of unruly female figures.

Yet why, despite what I am finally admitting may be a secret, subtextual misogyny, do I find "Skunk Hour" not just fearsome but, to be honest, rather wonderful? Partly, I think, it is because, along with the pain (and possibly the rage) this poem implies, the text suggests something about the power of the artist, the power to see *through,* for instance, what the fifties' media used to call the "wonderful world" of "Ike" to what is on the other side: fierce shadows, myths burning like October leaves in New and old England. For after all, what "Skunk Hour" argues is not primarily that "America is hell" – an old idea and a boring one in its usual (polemical) sense – but rather that the artist-seer can *make* a hell of America, and a magical hell at that, evoking, with his ill spirit, those totemic skunks who incarnate the other, visionary world that abides beneath our dull suburbs. That Lowell managed such prestidigitation without, like Eliot and Joyce, constructing an *overtly* allusive mythical structure – that his "intertextuality" must be speculatively excavated – seems all the more remarkable. But no doubt this reveals as much about the fatigue of the midcentury as it does about me as a reader and Lowell as a poet: To find the magic of hell, albeit a sordid, morbid, even misogynistic magic, is something, anyway, in the tranquillized fifties, and such a discovery helps give "Skunk Hour" its perverse charisma.

Equally, though – and this second point is almost a function of the first – I think I find "Skunk Hour" wonderful, literally full of wonder, because it is one of the few truly "confessional" poems I have encountered. Considering the terms in which I have been describing this work, readers for whom the often abused word "confessional" conjures up either a school of distraught and often alcoholic American poets or a black leather Freudian couch, a gravely psychoanalytic exegete, and a babbling, half-naked artist, may well dispute this point, or at least they will say they are sick of such jargon. But if we use the word "confessional" in its original sense, if we let it evoke that airless, velvet-curtained booth where Roman Catholic Acts of Contrition are still wearily or fervently murmured, then, yes, this is confessional poetry. Implicit in these lines is the attentive priest in his polyester cassock, and here is mother-hating Mephistophilis in drip-dry button-down shirt, khaki pants, and Hush Puppies. Here is the awful Hieronymus Bosch landscape of Sin and Redemption superimposed on (or, rather, merging with) the tidy vacationscape of Maine's Blue Hill. Suddenly understanding the murderous presence of "love-cars," "hermit heiresses," "fairy decorators," and indomitable skunks, I who have summered often in Maine realize that I too have stood on this hill's skull, though my stance as a woman-reader may have been differently anxious. Why this is – and that was – hell, nor are any of us out of it.

At the end of his poem Lowell pauses on his "back steps" and breathes the "rich air." The air of "Skunk Hour" is rich indeed, rich with the seething of ancient powers, rich with moiling Modernist and Postmodernist anxieties. Rich, most of all, with what is finally, odd as it may seem, a kind of nourishment for poets and their readers, a nourishment as necessary to us as "sour cream" is to skunks. For both modern anxieties and ancient powers are transformative: The first tell us who we are, the second teach us who we have been; and the second, in particular, knit us, though we stand on the hill's skull, into the dark fires that burn under the hill, and they are our contemporaries (just as Lowell is) no matter what century we think we are buried in. Finally, then, it seems to me that the ritual Lowell enacts in "Skunk Hour" is not unlike the *rite de passage* enacted by Hawthorne's "Young Goodman Brown." Thinking he lives in an ordinary town, in the fact-littered center of his own age, he goes out into the forests of America and finds not only his contemporary anxieties, not only his community, but himself, more truly and more strange. And I too, as I read and reread this extraordinarily revealing and revisionary poem, find myself more truly and more strange.

NOTES

1 For a different use of the family album metaphor, see Spender 17.

2 Dust jacket of *Life Studies*; quoted in Mazzaro 119.

3 For the *"nil"* of the nineteenth century, see Adams.

4 See, for instance, John Berryman (101–103) and Axelrod (*Robert Lowell* 125–26); and of course Lowell himself commented that "sterility howls through the scenery" in these stanzas ("On Skunk Hour" 107).

5 In the draft reproduced by Axelrod (*Robert Lowell* 250), stanza one of "Inspiration" (later to become "Skunk Hour") is:

> The season's ill;
> Yesterday Deer Isle fishermen
> Threw Captain Greenwright's wreaths into the channel
> And wooed his genius for their race
> In the yachtsmen's yawls. A red fox stain
> Covers Blue Hill.

6 Berryman (103), Mazzaro (117), and Axelrod (*Robert Lowell* 128) all mention Lowell's allusions to Mephistophilis and/or Lucifer/Satan, but none seems to place quite as much weight on this reference as I do here.

7 Although the speaker of *Life Studies* is generally presented as "mentally ill" in a *neurotic* mode, Hamilton has now of course carefully discussed and documented the poet's history of manic-depression; see Hamilton, *passim*.

8 As Axelrod points out, the *"Notebook/History* revision" of "Water," which originally appeared in *For the Union Dead*, reveals that this "rueful" poem about "an unnamed woman [with whom Lowell] proved unable to connect" was a piece about Elizabeth Bishop (*Robert Lowell* 140).

9 For a general discussion of the relationship between feared female power and fearful male impotence as dramatized in a number of crucial (male-authored) Modernist texts, see Gilbert and Gubar.

5

Freud and the Skunks: Genre and Language in *Life Studies*

LAWRENCE KRAMER

Life Studies is famous for two things. First, it marked a decisive break with the formal verse patterns and dense, metaphorical rhetoric of the early poetry that had established Robert Lowell as a leading poet in the high Modernist mode. Second, it repudiated the key Modernist ideal of authorial impersonality on behalf of what seemed at the time (1959) to be barefaced self-revelation, thus ushering in the "confessional" mode that dominated American poetry in the 1960s. It is no wonder that Allen Tate, Lowell's earliest mentor, found the manuscript of *Life Studies* appalling and urged Lowell not to publish it, whereas William Carlos Williams was awestruck by it.[1]

Critical commentary on the volume has naturally tended to take the relationship between its style and subject matter as a starting point, and the results have been remarkably lacking in controversy.[2] *Life Studies* is generally understood as an odyssey of self-understanding in which the poet comes to grips with his oppressive past and madness-ridden present. The process is seen in terms of either heroic (internalized) quest or therapeutic self-analysis; its outcome is a mind gifted with enough inner coherence and tragic awareness to affirm its own troubled continuance. Moreover, that mind does not belong to Lowell alone; Lowell's personal anguish is explicitly bound up with the anguish of his times, so that the capacity of one midcentury poet to endure becomes a model for the capacity of the midcentury reader to do likewise. Lowell's style is commonly regarded as the very thing he needs to carry through his quest for insight. Described as "light," "loose," and colloquial, the language of *Life Studies* supposedly gives the poet the freedom and the flexibility he needs to pass candid judgment on the experiences that have shaped him. Moreover, that language is recognized to be carefully crafted; its conversational aspect is acknowledged to be an effect on the surface of a hidden formalism. The undergirding of form allows the language to articulate the anguish of the volume and at the same time to control it, distance it, tame it for the mind to penetrate. As Lowell himself observed, "All that gives light to these poems on agonizing subjects comes from the craft" (Seidel

20). (Lowell spoke this sentence in reference to the poetry of W. D. Snodgrass, but its applicability to his own work is clear.)

My essay obviously plans to do something uncongenial to this orthodox view; otherwise, there would have been no summary of it. Not that the orthodoxy surrounding *Life Studies* is implausible; on the contrary, it is inevitable, and even indispensable. The pattern of self-overcoming through personal crisis, with a concurrent parallelism of public and private experience, forms the basic plot of autobiographical poetry as it was more or less established by Wordsworth. What the consensus about *Life Studies* really amounts to is a recognition of the book's genre. Not to grasp this pattern, as Marjorie Perloff has pointed out, is to treat the confessional poem "as *confession* rather than as *poetry*" (*Poetic Art* 81). Similar considerations hold true of the volume's language. Wordsworth, with his appeal to conversational norms, once again sets the pattern; the "personal" idiom is meant to mark the authenticity of the "personal" subject matter, and the commonality of the language forms a bridge between the poet and the reader, the private and the public spheres.

My purpose in what follows is not to argue against the orthodox understanding of *Life Studies* but to argue around it, to fray the edges of its necessarily idealizing image of the process of self-understanding in the hope of exposing other processes that are obscured by the generically determined one. My approach will combine rhetorical and psychoanalytic ways of reading, with the intent of reopening the basic questions about the volume and of generating new questions along the way. First, what kind of self-inquisition does *Life Studies* really hold? There is more than one way to explore one's life history before an audience, and each way has its own repertoire of characteristic speech acts. What kinds of speech acts does *Life Studies* imitate, and how does the answer to this question revise the orthodox understanding of the volume? Second, how is Lowell's language here related to the life history that it helps to recount? What motivates his idiom and its characteristic tropes? And how does his rhetoric affect the intention of self-integration determined by the volume's genre? My answers to these questions may make *Life Studies* seem uglier than it already does – which is ugly enough – but they are also meant to recognize real power when they see it. I am orthodox enough myself to believe that *Life Studies* is one of the major accomplishments of its period, and one way to prove this is to take the book unapologetically into the emerging discourses of our own, already different period.

Confessio Amantis

The autobiographical sequence called "Life Studies," taken together with the prose memoir "91 Revere Street," forms the core of *Life Studies* and I will make it my main concern. Most of the poems in the sequence form what might be called confessional monologues; they are seemingly impromptu fragments of autobiography and family history – ironic, heterogeneous, and shameless. It is important to recognize that the confessional force of these poems does not lie in their personal subject matter per se but in how and to whom they present it. To invoke John Stuart Mill's famous distinction, this poetry depends on being heard, not overheard. It is not addressed by the poet to himself or to an intimate, but to a featureless interlocutor who is never represented in the text. This anonymous listener is offered anecdotes, facts, and, where necessary, glosses:

> The farm, entitled *Char-De-Sa*
> in the Social Register,
> was named for my Grandfather's children:
> Charlotte, Devereux, and Sarah.
> No one had died there in my lifetime . . .
> Only Cinder, our Scottie puppy,
> paralyzed from gobbling toads.
>   ("My Last Afternoon with Uncle Devereux Winslow," *LS* 60)

The poetry is descriptive, not introspective; it does not act out a process of recollection but unfolds instead as an inventory of recollections. It is confessional because it models itself on the act of confiding.[3] Just whom it confides in and why are questions whose answers need to be prepared further.

At important moments in the sequence, Lowell fills in the place of the anonymous confessional interlocutor by resorting to the figure of apostrophe. This rhetorical turn regularly represents both a resistance to the mute unresponsiveness that is built into the confessional mode and a concomitant demand for intimacy, dependency, touch. Yet this demand is doomed to frustration by its own rhetorical mode, as the conclusion of "Grandparents" can illustrate:

> Grandpa! Have me, hold me, cherish me!
> Tears smut by fingers. There
> half my life-lease later,
> I hold an *Illustrated London News* – ;
> disloyal still,
> I doodle handlebar
> mustaches on the last Russian Czar.   (*LS* 69)

An apostrophe is always addressed to someone who cannot listen to it. All that Lowell can get of his "manly, comfortable, / overbearing" grandfather ("My Last Afternoon," *LS* 60) is a picture of the assassinated czar, which he defaces partly because it recalls his grandfather too much and partly because it recalls him too little. Elsewhere, Lowell calls out to his dead mother ("Sailing Home from Rapallo," "During Fever") and silently addresses a wife who showers *him* with invective while her back is emblematically turned ("Man and Wife"). When he banters with a daughter too young to understand him, he dismisses the intimacy that he seeks in the very gesture that enacts it:

Dearest, I cannot linger here
in lather like a polar bear.
Recuperating, I neither spin nor toil.
("Home After Three Months Away," LS 83–84)

The apostrophic pattern is most conspicuous in the paired poems "Sailing Home from Rapallo" and "During Fever." "Sailing Home" begins with a three-line apostrophe to Lowell's mother, then turns abruptly to the confessional interlocutor and never turns back:

Your nurse could only speak Italian,
but after twenty minutes I could imagine your final week,
and tears ran down my cheeks. . . .

When I embarked from Italy with my Mother's body,
the whole shoreline of the *Golfo di Genova*
was breaking into fiery flower.   (*LS* 77)

The intimate mother of apostrophe becomes the dead mother's body as the apostrophized grandfather metamorphoses into the Russian czar; mourning is evoked, then averted. "During Fever" tries to make reparation for this half-hostile, half-defensive gesture by reversing the pattern of "Sailing Home." The opening description of Lowell's fevered daughter is shouldered aside by an impassioned apostrophe to his mother, which expands to fill out the entire poem. The vocative "Mother" recurs throughout, yet with each appearance its power to evoke intimacy grows weaker. Lowell finally summons up his mother's smile only to find that it is beset with anxiety and in any case is not for him:

Mother, you smile
as if you saw your Father
inches away yet hidden, as when he groused behind a screen
over a National Geographic Magazine,
whenever young men came to court you
back in those settled years of World War One.   (*LS* 80)

Lowell's apostrophes in *Life Studies* are appealing precisely because they are appeals; their emotional openness seems to transgress refreshingly on the stylized dispassionate candor of the confessional mode. Yet for all that, the apostrophes are chimerical, regressive, distracting.[4] What they do is to set beloved, intimate others in the place of the silent, anonymous Other to whom the poetry of *Life Studies* is really addressed. The significance of this substitution becomes obvious when it is looked at as a psychological process. All of Lowell's substitute interlocutors are explicit representatives of his Oedipal sexuality – the grandfather whom he takes as his true father and in whose bed he "cuddled like a paramour" ("Dunbarton," *LS* 67); the daughter "young enough to be my granddaughter" ("Memories of West

Street and Lepke," *LS* 85) with whom he plays in the bathroom; the mother with whom he shared "unadulterated joy . . . rehashing Father's character" and whose "nuptial bed / was as big as a bathroom" ("During Fever," *LS* 79–80); and the wife with whom he sleeps in "Mother's bed" (*LS* 87). The confessional mode demands that the Oedipal desires embodied in these figures be acknowledged but not indulged, represented but not fantasized. And that, of course, reveals what the confessional mode is and who the Other is – as if we had not known all along.

In his study of Lowell, Alan Williamson points to Lowell's lifelong interest in Freud and suggests that the "method and values" of *Life Studies* are more psychoanalytic than anything else. "[Lowell's] goal," he writes, "is self-understanding, and his principal techniques – the resurrection of early memories, the unsparing objectivity about present behavior, and the increased conscious awareness of interpersonal dynamics – are all common features of the analytic process" (68). Seen in these terms, Lowell's use of psychoanalytic elements in *Life Studies* conforms both to the generically determined goal of self-integration and to the intellectual style of the autobiographical speaker, whom Williamson describes as "a profoundly sophisticated ironist" well-versed in "psychological and sociological ways of thinking" (61). Williamson's description, however, overidealizes the psychoanalytic process in order to preserve the stability of the poem's genre. His account of Lowell's "technique" fails to discriminate between the roles of analyst and analysand, which are separate even in a self-analysis, and his implicit emphasis on control of the insight process assigns it a stability that is never achieved in practice. Furthermore, Williamson leaves out the real core of the analytic encounter: the frustrating, self-renewing struggle over resistance and transference.

More is at stake here, of course, than flaws, however common, in one critic's view of psychoanalysis. Lowell's confessional mode is, as I argued earlier, a mode of confiding. We can now identify it more closely by calling it the singular mode of confiding that is characteristic of the classical analysand. The confessional monologue is addressed to a silent, impersonal other who supersedes the speaker's Oedipal object-choices; it accumulates facts without regard for logical or narrative coherence, except as a passing effect; it regularly includes trivial details next to portentous ones; and it gives the illusion of not censoring material that is embarrassing, humiliating, guilt-ridden, or desire-laden. (The actual censorship, as Ian Hamilton's biography shows in detail, is considerable; we are by no means getting "the *real* Robert Lowell.")[5] In short, Lowell's style in *Life Studies* gives the impression of a discourse that is struggling with some success to obey Freud's "fundamental rule" – the rule that asks the analysand to relax his educated impulses to impose logical, narrative, or moral shape on his experience.

The only trouble is that the cost of this, for the speaker, is a determined disavowal of the emotions attached to the material he brings forth. Two passages that we have already noticed act out this disavowal in the form of curtailed weeping. In each case the curtailment is harsh, abrupt – downright nasty; grief gives way before a regressive, an openly childish hostility that belittles the person who has been loved and lost. In "Sailing Home from Rapallo," the poet's tears change antithetically into "the *spumante*-bubbling" wake of the ship that carries his mother's body (*LS* 77). In "Grandparents," Lowell's tears for his grandfather, Arthur Winslow, "smut" his fingers immediately after his apostrophic outburst, and Lowell, "disloyal still," responds by "smutting" his grandfather's displaced image (*LS* 69). In "Terminal Days at Beverly Farms," the same disavowal is enacted with dry eyes, as the poet describes his father's decline and death in a tone that only departs from affectless neutrality to become a mild derision. The rageful longing for an ideal father, painfully evident in Lowell's worship of his grandfather, is apparent only in the displaced violence of images that purport to describe the landscape:

> They had no sea-view,
> but sky-blue tracks of the commuters' railroad shone
> like a double-barrelled shotgun
> through the scarlet late August sumac,
> multiplying like cancer
> at their garden's border.   (*LS* 73)

   The discourse of Lowell's confessional monologues, then, is not just a replica of the classical analysand's; it is a "realistic" replica that implicates itself in the analysand's unique dilemma – the fact that the discourse that is the instrument of his cure is also the instrument of his resistance to cure, that the language of self-enlightenment constantly manifests itself as the language of self-mystification. In the most general terms, *Life Studies* enacts this dilemma by its rhetorical commitment to the figure of metonymy, a trope that is equivalent to displacement in psychoanalytic discourse. Marjorie Perloff was the first to point out the volume's saturation by metonyms; her analysis shows how, "by presenting his parents in terms of a metonymic series of objects, Lowell creates a devastating image of a tradition gone sour" (*Poetic Art* 98). From the perspective I am developing here, the metonymy acts to deflect attention from one object, one surface, to another, so that Lowell's deadly accurate representation of the props and detritus of three intertwined life histories is also a constant evasion of the emotional meaning and therefore the unconscious influence of those histories.

   Life Studies reflects on the two-edged quality of its own discourse with a series of typically displaced – in this case generalized – images of writing. In "91 Revere Street," the ineptitude of Lowell's father at carving roasts leads to this remark about Commander Billy Harkness, a family friend with exaggeratedly masculine manners: "Nothing could stop Commander Billy, that born carver, from reciting verses" (*LS* 34). The seemingly arbitrary link between carving and poetry has considerable resonance. Various forms of inscription crop up throughout *Life Studies,* and each one of them bespeaks an overdetermination of motives that conforms to the overriding dilemma of the volume's insight process. The inscriptions are all meant to commemorate the significant past, and they all at the same time disfigure what they commemorate. They all mark sites, metonyms of the speaker's whole world, where acts of love or celebration have been fused with suppressed rage, and where the text that acknowledges this is also the text that disavows it. In "Grandparents," as we have seen already, Lowell's doodling on a picture of the Russian czar uses displaced aggression as a defense against grief. In the same poem, the three-ball on the pool table at the Winslow farm both marks and hides the stain formed years before when "Grandpa, dipping sugar for us both, / once spilled his demitasse" (*LS* 68). In "Dunbarton," Grandfather Winslow's cane appears,

> carved with the names and altitudes
> of Norwegian mountains he had scaled –
> more a weapon than a crutch.   (*LS* 66)

For the young Lowell, the cane *is* a weapon, to be "lanced . . . in the fauve ooze for newts." Lowell, who registers his father's inadequacy and mortality with more than a little *Schadenfreude,* finds the same features intolerable in his grandfather. He wields the old man's stick as a hero's sword, scored with runes to defy time, but he only succeeds in lancing the newts, which is as much as symbolically maiming himself:

> I saw myself as a young newt,
> neurasthenic, scarlet
> and wild in the wild coffee-colored water.   (*LS* 66)

The adult Lowell draws on the same arsenal, with more cruelly potent results. At the close of "Father's Bedroom," Lowell reproduces as poetry the writing on the flyleaf of his father's copy of Lafcadio Hearn's *Glimpses of Unfamiliar Japan:*

> Its warped olive cover
> was punished like a rhinoceros hide.
> In the flyleaf:
> "Robbie from Mother."
> Years later in the same hand:
> "This book has had hard usage
> on the Yangtze River, China.
> It was left under an open
> porthole in a storm."   (*LS* 75)

The motherly reproof infantilizes the elder Lowell and deprecates the naval episode that the poet presents as the high point of his father's feckless life. Meanwhile, the "rhinoceros hide" of the Hearn book recalls the "sacred" "rhinoceros hide" chair described in "91 Revere Street," the elder Lowell's favorite object and the symbol of an overbearing masculinity that – to his son's everlasting distress – could never be his. "Cracked, hacked, scratched, splintered, gouged, initialed, gunpowder-charred and tumbler-ringed" (*LS* 17), the chair is a – literally – graphic emblem of the effects of metonymy, of the discourse of displacement. It is also, of course, an enduring surface, like the ego of the analysand, but like that ego again, the chair is too easily alienated. Commander Billy, for one, habitually took possession of the sacred chair at 91 Revere Street, and in one drunken episode, he "sprawled back so recklessly that the armchair began to come apart" (*LS* 38).

I'm Nobody – Who Are You?

One of the most important consequences of Lowell's assumption, in *Life Studies,* of what might be called the speaking part in psychoanalysis, is its impact on the ego of the speaker, and hence on the genre of autobiographical poetry. The confusion of defense for cure can often be read into autobiographical poems, more or less against the will of the author-speaker; much of *In Memoriam,* for example, can be read to suggest that Tennyson had to struggle against a dependence on the figure of Arthur Henry Hallam as a source of charisma or a personified principle of transcendence (see Peckham 35–39 and Kramer, "'Intimations' Ode"). *Life Studies* foregrounds this instability within the genre; it dramatizes its own defense mechanisms as a normal way of proceeding. As a result, the ideal of an integrated, self-affirming ego – the darling of ego-psychology – tends to recede into a mobile, fragmentary, volatile subjectivity. This is true both for general reasons – an ego will seem strong only if its defenses are safely out of sight – and because Lowell's characteristic mode of defense is a flight from the emotional weight of the constellation of family relationships that forms the nucleus of his ego. The autobiographical speaker of *Life Studies* is consequently as empty as his descriptions are full. Robert Lowell is not the speaking subject of his life history; he is only one of its many objects. A passage from "91 Revere Street" is emblematic of this condition:

> The script that I had mastered with much agony at my first school was denounced as illegible [at my second]: I was taught to print according to the Dalton Plan – to this day, as a result, I have to print even my two middle names and can really only *write* two words: "Robert" and "Lowell."
> (*LS* 25)

The accomplishments earned in agony have been deleted, declared meaningless, and linger only in the two words that combine to form the poet's name – words here pointedly separated by "and" and encased in quotation marks. And even the name written in script contains an alien element that epitomizes the intrusion of the external and the other: the two middle names that can only be printed, can only differ from the given and family names. "Robert" and "Lowell" are two words that sometimes enclose, sometimes elide, a void.

This dissolution of the ego takes several forms within the poems themselves. The most obvious is the complete absence of the "I" – the technique of "Father's Bedroom," "Terminal Days at Beverly Farms," and "For Sale," all poems of deferred mourning. More critical is the relentless tendency of the speaker to adopt alter egos, human, animal, and even, tellingly, inanimate replicas of the human and animal: mannequins in the "display windows / of Rogers Peet's boys' store below the State House / in Boston," or "a stuffed toucan / with a bibulous, multicolored beak" ("My Last Afternoon," *LS* 61). The ease and multiplicity of the speaker's identifications reflect the indefiniteness of his own ego and the compulsiveness of his metonymic network. Furthermore, the speaker's identifications are uniformly degrading to him, with the exception of his idealizing identification with Arthur Winslow, which replaces the missing identification with his father. Neurasthenic newts, the famous skunk, a "young Republican" trash collector, the "Mayflower screwballs" of "Waking in the Blue," the "Flabby, bald, lobotomized" gangster Lepke/Buchalter – the litany is depressing. Even the few identifications that offer a compensating dose of normal childish grandiosity turn sour. Napoleon to Lowell at seven is "just my seven years tall!" – but Napoleon "scratched his navel, / and bolted his food" ("Commander Lowell," *LS* 70). Lowell's romantic ancestor Major Mordecai Myers, the heroic "wolf" and "Wandering Jew" of the poet's "adolescent war on [his] parents" is only "a sheepdog in wolf's clothing" ("91 Revere Street," *LS* 12). The speaker is so lacking in basic narcissistic appreciation of himself that he cannot bear the sight of his own reflection. As a boy, he recalls, he watched as "Distorting drops of water / pinpricked my face in the basin's mirror" ("My Last Afternoon," *LS* 61). The painful water drops anticipate the disfiguring tears that the speaker will later repress; meanwhile the boy's own face becomes inaccessible to him as he passively watches. Lowell can only admire his reflection while in a fit of madness; it is in "the house for the 'mentally ill'" that he struts, "Cock of the walk, / . . . in my turtle-necked French sailor's jersey / before the metal shaving mirrors" ("Waking in the Blue," *LS* 82). But even here, the sailor's jersey falsifies the reflection, and hints – it is a *sailor's* jersey – at a botched, hopeless attempt to identify with a figure resembling the despised father.

Continuous identification, it seems, is the only means the speaker possesses to manifest any sort of ego at all. Back from the asylum, he assigns his refurbished self an image of moral and physical deformity: "Is Richard now himself again?" The poem in question, "Home After Three Months Away," ends Part I of *Life Studies* with a rare glimpse of the Lowell ego stripping off its armor of identifications:

> I keep no rank or station.
> Cured, I am frizzled, stale, and small.   (*LS* 84)

The conclusion is humanly intolerable. Without the ability to identify, the speaker is too enervated, too dessicated, to move forward with his life. In compensation, a second conclusion, soon to follow, will slake this interior drought with a hieratic cup of sour cream scavenged by a totemic mother skunk.

"Skunk Hour," in fact, marks the apogee of both displacement and identification in the volume. Generically, the poem should provide at least a qualified moment of self-assertion, and so it does – a truth universally acknowledged. But the poem also fuses this moment with the psychoanalytically determined moment in which the self is most dispersed and its objects most fully denied. This is not to say, however, that the defensive aspect of the volume's move toward closure acts crudely to undercut a "march and affirmation" (the phrase is Lowell's) that is already ambiguous enough ("On Skunk Hour" 107). On the contrary, the power of the "quixotic and barbarously absurd" skunks (Lowell again) is intimately woven into the knot of disavowals that the poem ties.

From this point of view, the most important part of "Skunk Hour" is its first half, described by Lowell as "a dawdling more or less amiable picture of a declining Maine sea town," just as the most important part from the generic point of view is the second half, the record of a voyeuristic prowl that ends with the uncomfortably redemptive sight of the skunks on parade. Lowell's description of his "amiable picture" is suggestively unreliable: "Sterility howls through the scenery, but I try to give a tone of tolerance, humor, and randomness to the sad prospect. The composition drifts, its direction sinks out of sight into the casual, chancy arrangements of nature and decay" ("On Skunk Hour" 107). The telltale word "howls," jarring against the urbanity of these sentences, points to a more turbulent emotional investment than Lowell's reading acknowledges. If we want to know why, we might ask about the tone that Lowell says he tried to achieve. A look at the poetry suggests that tolerance and humor are conveyed less by positive rhetorical means than by the absence of the derisive irony that plays elsewhere around Lowell's references to his father, to himself, and, less consistently, to his mother:

> The season's ill –
> we've lost our summer millionaire,
> who seemed to leap from an L. L. Bean
> catalogue. His nine-knot yawl
> was auctioned off to lobstermen.
> A red fox stain covers Blue Hill.   ("Skunk Hour," *LS* 89)

> Smiling on all,
> Father was once successful enough to be lost
> in the mob of ruling-class Bostonians.
>   ("Commander Lowell," *LS* 72)

This implicit contrast is not an accident but a reparation, because the family constellation of child and parents is the hidden referent of the first part of "Skunk Hour."

Taken as description, the first four stanzas of the poem are, as Lowell suggests, "casual" and "chancy." Taken as displacement, however, they are powerfully overdetermined and constitute nothing less than a symbolic geography of Lowell's distorted Oedipal triangle.[6] The opening description of "Nautilus Island's hermit / heiress" who "lives through winter in her Spartan cottage" and is "in her dotage" (*LS* 89) recalls the description of Charlotte Lowell after her husband's death:

> Ready, afraid
> of living alone till eighty,
> Mother mooned in a window,
> as if she had stayed on a train
> one stop past her destination.   ("For Sale," *LS* 76)

The heiress's son is a bishop; Lowell in his youth was "a fire-breathing Catholic C.O." ("Memories of West Street," *LS* 85) and is now the author of a poem, "Skunk Hour," written to, and after, a Bishop – Elizabeth. Finally, the heiress's thirst for "the hierarchic privacy / of Queen Victoria's century" recalls Lowell's final imaginary placement of his mother "back in the settled years of World War One," with their life of terrible post-Victorian "decency" and repression of "unseemly intimacy / or quarrels" ("During Fever," *LS* 80). The ruined summer millionaire reenacts the financial failure of Lowell's father, and the millionaire's nine-knot yawl, "auctioned off to lobstermen," recapitulates both the elder Lowell's profession of sailor and his selling-out of that profession to the highest bidder "when Lever Brothers offered to pay / him double what the Navy paid" ("Commander Lowell," *LS* 71). Like the millionaire, again, Lowell's father is something of a clotheshorse:

> He smiled his oval Lowell smile,
> he wore his cream gabardine dinner-jacket,
> and indigo cummerbund.   ("Terminal Days," *LS* 73)

That leaves the final figure in the landscape to represent Lowell himself:

> And now our fairy
> decorator brightens his shop for fall;
> his fishnet's filled with orange cork,
> orange, his cobbler's bench and awl;
> there is no money in his work,
> he'd rather marry.   (*LS* 89)

The decorator's fecklessness recalls the Lowell of "Home After Three Months Away," who neither spins nor toils, and the incompatibility between the decorator's homosexuality and his thoughts of marriage recalls the anguish of Lowell's own marriage, which has just been registered in "Man and Wife" and "'To Speak of Woe That Is in Marriage.'" The decorator's brightening of his shop for fall harks back to the dummies – self-images of the young Lowell – in the "imperishable autumn / display windows" of Rogers Peet's boys' store ("My Last Afternoon," *LS* 61). Finally, the homosexuality of the decorator exposes a deep current of early-childhood (Oedipal) homosexuality in the autobiographical speaker, which has manifested itself earlier in the explicitly feminine position taken by the adoring young Lowell toward his grandfather:

> In the mornings I cuddled like a paramour
> in my Grandfather's bed,
> while he scouted about the chattering greenwood stove.
>
>   ("Dunbarton," *LS* 67)[7]

Far from being random, the first half of "Skunk Hour" is luxuriantly related to the most intimate revelations of the speaker's discourse, as intrusively indiscreet as the radio that "bleats, / 'Love, O careless Love'" in the second half (*LS* 90).

By projecting his Oedipal group portrait into the sterile Nautilus Island landscape, Lowell signifies an effort to sterilize that portrait's power to demean and oppress him. The "tolerance, humor, and randomness" of his description are meant to enact a withdrawal, not a repression, of his childhood emotions. The fallen "eyesores" facing the hermit heiress's shore celebrate, in secret, The Fall of the House of Lowell. But the cost of this psychic stratagem – of course there would be one – is a loss of familiar bearings that heightens the already excessive plasticity of the speaker's ego. As a result, identification rules the second half of the poem as displacement does the first.

After describing Nautilus Island, the speaker turns to confront the legacy of the Oedipal drama that is topographically represented there. The Lowell family romance literally constitutes the scene (context, cause, motive) of his climactic struggle to recognize and overcome his "ill-spirit," a self-contempt that seems beyond the pale of love. The struggle is carried on by means of identification. Initially, Lowell's effort is to insert himself in the scene as a deranged pariah, but in a way that simultaneously aggrandizes him to more than heroic proportions, like a latter-day Childe Harold. His self-images – Jesus, Saint John of the Cross, Marlowe's Mephistophilis and Milton's Satan – are outsize figures who are all too clearly linked by antithesis to the earlier newts, dummies, garbagemen, and mobsters. When these phantoms of a trumped-up narcissism pass out of view, only a void is left. Lowell's distraught acknowledgment, "Nobody's here," includes the man who makes it: "nothing himself, [he] beholds / Nothing that is not there and the nothing that is" (Wallace Stevens, "The Snow Man").

The mother skunk who enters this void with her "column of kittens" is a therapeutic inspiration. She provides the perfect compromise between the untenably grandiose identifications of "Skunk Hour" and the intolerably depressive ones that fill the rest of the volume. The skunk is repellent but, for that very reason, formidable. She is "moonstruck" yet full of sane, creaturely purpose; an outcast, yet the nurturing mother of a family; invested with a phallic aspect as she "jabs her wedge-head in a cup," but prolifically female (*LS* 90). Totem, mascot, fugitive from a beast fable – whatever the skunk may be, the speaker gratefully takes her to himself in a moment of antinomian wit, and so both mitigates his predicament and assures its continuation. As to the skunk herself – a "small, attractive black-and-white creature, affectionate and loyal when tame," as John Berryman observed apropos of this poem (99) –

the skunk effects a substantial revision in the autobiographical genre. Thanks to her (with some help from Freud), it is not an epiphany that leads toward affirmation but a creative evasion, not an act of self-possession that proves an anodyne but an act of creative dispossession.

He Do the Police in Many Voices

Given the nature of its confessional mode, what sort of rhetorical process does the celebrated colloquial style of *Life Studies* set in motion? No less striking than the conversational impression the volume makes is the multiplicity of voices its speaker takes up, often shifting from one to another within a single sentence:

> They're altogether otherworldly now,
> those adults champing for their ritual Friday spin
> to pharmacist and five-and-ten in Brockton.
> . . . .
> They're are all gone into a world of light; the farm's my own.
>
> *(LS* 68)

This abridged stanza from "Grandparents" begins and ends with a mingling of Lowell's voice in the traditional "middle style" and Henry Vaughan's voice in a higher lyric one. The first line preserves the elegiac wistfulness of Vaughan's, "They are all gone into the world of light!" but tropes wittily on its phrasing; the last line reverses the process. The second line of the excerpt adopts a cool conversational irony, edged with contempt and flaunting its rhetorical control, only to modulate bathetically into the doggerel of the third line, which states a prosaic fact in conspicuous iambic pentameter. This sort of metrical bathos is frequent in the volume, and so is overt rhetorical bathos. A line describing Lowell's daughter, for instance, begins with an old-fashioned poetic flourish, a simile in inverted word order, and ends with a description that might have been lifted from a mail-order catalogue: "Like the sun she rises in her flame-flamingo infants' wear" ("Memories of West Street," *LS* 85). The colloquial element here is quite different from the upper-crust wit of the line about champing adults; the speaker self-mockingly parrots merchandising jargon, as he elsewhere retails brand names and clichés. For the rest, the volume ranges from Ogden Nash-like doggerel,

> There were no undesirables or girls in my set,
> when I was a boy at Mattapoisett –
>
> ("Commander Lowell," *LS* 70)

to fine-honed lyric compression,

> Azure day
> makes my agonized blue window bleaker.
>
> ("Waking in the Blue," *LS* 81)

to somber figuration,

> Dour and dark against the blinding snowdrifts,
> its black brook and fir trunks were as smooth as masts.
>
> ("Sailing Home," *LS* 77)

As the last pair of excerpts indicates, Lowell echoes at times the gnarled, densely consonantal language of his earlier poems.

How does this polyglot style serve the ends of the volume's discourse, as I have described them? One answer would be that the speaker's volatility of voice is a stylistic acting out of his volatility of ego, which is otherwise represented by his incessant identifications. Repudiating any single voice, the speaker composes himself of many voices; and instead of adding these up into a unified persona or personality, he defines himself as the indeterminate space that envelops them, the unspeaking voice that articulates those that speak. To refurbish an old cliché with a new significance, it is style here that makes the man. Lowell intimates an intention of this sort in a stichomythic bit of dialogue from "91 Revere Street":

> "A penny for your thoughts, Schopenhauer," my mother
> would say.
> "I am thinking about pennies," I'd answer.
> "When *I* was a child I used to love telling Mama
> everything I had done," Mother would say.
> "But you're not a child," I would answer.   (*LS* 20)

What the young Lowell does here is, in effect, to refuse to answer his mother's voice with his own. He self-protectively breaks off bits of her sentences and rebuffs her by handing them back. The "real" child, his mind "blanked and . . . fill[ed] with clammy hollowness," only appears by refusing to speak as, himself. He rejects the identities his mother offers him – Schopenhauer and herself as child – and preserves his opacity to her and to himself. If style makes the man (to whom the child is father), then the man is two-dimensional, as the stylish Uncle Devereux, dying, is "a ginger snap man in a clothes-press" (*LS* 64).

Lowell's congeries of voices also combines with the metonymic movement of the volume to demystify and devalue what is being described. The various levels of bathos serve the same function: Nothing must occupy a center, nothing must mesmerize the speaker enough to be dwelt on, nothing must compel an answer. Unlike his father, Lowell refuses to accept the reification that is implicit in becoming attached to favorite objects in a world that already determines all too much of him. Not for him the talismanic rhinoceros armchair or the "little black Chevie" that is his father's "best friend." He is anxious at the prospect of belonging anywhere; he "hogs" his own house and sees its tiny garden plot as "a coffin's length of soil" ("Memories of West Street," *LS* 85; "Home After Three Months Away," *LS* 84). He longs to be unanchored: As a boy on his grandfather's farm he "picked with a clean finger nail at the blue anchor / on my sailor blouse washed white as a spinnaker," seeking the freedom of the blank sail, the blank page of himself ("My Last Afternoon," *LS* 62). The polyglot style of *Life Studies* is meant to give a kind of phonographic reproduction of the world of Lowell's origins, but like the "rattly little country gramophone" on the old farm, it must distort what it plays back. Lowell loosens his ties to the world that made him by "doing impressions" of it, turning its idioms into "routines" in a virtuosic stand-up repertoire, a vatic vaudeville.

Similar motives attach to what is probably the most privileged rhetorical figure in *Life Studies,* the inventory or catalogue. In his poem, "The Abyss," Theodore Roethke depicts himself as beset by "the terrible hunger for objects," and he launches an apostrophe: "Be with me, Whitman, maker of catalogues." Like the *blazon* which is its ancestor, the catalogue ordinarily appeases the hunger for involvement with the world as a plenitude. The Whitman catalogue is exemplary: Its long-breathed lines sluice the reader from one object to another with quasi-erotic force, satisfying "the curious sense of body and identity, the greed that with perfect complaisance devours all things" ("A Song For Occupations," *Leaves of Grass*). Lowell's inventories do exactly the opposite. Clipped, short-breathed, discontinuous, they isolate the objects they supposedly conjoin, expose the gaps between individual perceptions, feelings, memories. The catalogues of *Life Studies* are haunted by pathos or futility, as delineated by objects that ironically betray those who possess them: Uncle Devereux's spruce clothing, Commander Lowell's *chinoiserie*, Charlotte Lowell's "proper *putti*." Large blocs of material, too, are consistently juxtaposed on this model, jumbled together as isolated segments of an unrealized narrative like bits of bric-a-brac on a flea-market table.

Represented in this way, objects – and object-choices – that were numinous or oppressive in childhood lose their psychic authority. Although they come back in the form of demand, "urgent with life and meaning," they are less than life-sized: "Because finished, they are endurable and perfect" ("91 Revere Street," *LS* 13). They can no longer condemn the present by reviving past feelings of shame or inadequacy, and they can no longer degrade the present by evoking nostalgia for an impossibly idealized past. Of course, both the shame and the nostalgia repeatedly disrupt the exaggeratedly flat surface of *Life Studies*; the volume draws much of its power from the intensity of its struggle to *contain* – meaning both to enclose and to restrict – just those feelings.

The style of *Life Studies,* then, articulates Lowell's often ruthless effort to become more than the sum of his parts, to establish an identity that transcends its origins. Style and psyche prove to have tangled roots, and with a self-consciousness conditioned explicitly by a reading of Freud, the volume reflects on its own style in its portrait of Lowell's relationship to his mother.

Charlotte Lowell is repeatedly presented in terms of her oral dominance over others – the very thing her son is trying to resist in the mother–son dialogue I quoted earlier.

"91 Revere Street" testifies to her brittle, unpleasant manner of speech, its capacity for "gloating panic" and "murderous coolness," its shrilling *"weelawaugh."* Reading to her son in "Commander Lowell," Charlotte grates on him with a voice that is "electric / with a hysterical, unmarried panic," and the son, like his counterpart in Rimbaud's "Les Poètes de Sept Ans," responds with self-wounding defiance: "bristling and manic, / [I] skulked in the attic" (*LS* 70). The son fears his mother's supercharged orality, which seems to awaken primitive fears of being devoured: "[I] cringed because Mother, new / caps on all her teeth, was born anew / at forty" (*LS* 71). (Later, the "old-fashioned tirade" his wife delivers on "Mother's bed" will break over him "like the Atlantic ocean" [*LS* 87].) In retrospect, the mother's oral aggressiveness impresses the son as self-protective. Her shrill grande dame manner is worn like a Yeatsian mask that reverses an inner deficiency – here a lack of "self-assurance for wide human experience" ("91 Revere Street," *LS* 32). But this means that when she speaks, whenever she speaks, she inscribes herself anew within the rigid, archaic social and linguistic order in which she grew up, the ancien régime of the nineteenth-century family.

Lowell is tempted by a nostalgic view of that old order, dominated as it is for him by the figure of Arthur Winslow, and he is tempted, too, by a certain Oedipal seductiveness in his mother, which he recalls longingly in "During Fever." But the very strength of the temptation feeds his determination to be more than a mere echo of his circumstances, to "harden [his] mind against the monotonous *parti pris* of Mother's voice" ("91 Revere Street," *LS* 13). Consistent with this, Lowell's style of speaking in *Life Studies* becomes everything his mother's was not: demotic, polyglot, indecorous, inconsistent. In large measure, these qualities revive the "rowdy" voice of his mother's great antagonist, Commander Billy Harkness, the "rough diamond" who delighted in throwing Charlotte Lowell "off balance" with vulgar patter, virtuoso diatribes, and execrable comic verse. Commander Billy is an unanchored man who had often combed the seas "not knowing what admiral he served under or where his next meal or load of fuel oil was coming from" ("91 Revere Street," *LS* 45). He represents the aggressive side of the ideal father figure Lowell's own father could never embody, just as Arthur Winslow represents the affectionate side: "The man who seems in my memory to sit under old Mordecai's portrait is not my father, but Commander Billy – *the* Commander after Father had thrown in his commission" ("91 Revere Street," *LS* 45). Commander Billy relentlessly exposes the social and sexual failings of the Lowell household, as its young scion would later do in *Life Studies.* He makes the *poète de sept ans* "squirm" with would-be denial – and supplies him with an unrefined form of the language of acknowledgment.

Lowell's shockingly cruel representation of his mother's body in "Sailing Home from Rapallo" becomes intelligible, if not less ugly, in this context. Lowell repays and repudiates his mother's "hysterical," self-maiming voice by recording a condign punishment. The dead mother's identity is effaced by an abuse of language and her person is degraded with an oral image:

> In the grandiloquent lettering on Mother's coffin,
> *Lowell* had been misspelled *LOVEL*.
> The corpse
> was wrapped like *panetone* in Italian tinfoil.   (*LS* 78)

What Lowell attacks here is less his mother than a slip of the pen – or chisel – that epitomizes the power of language over the self. The false, grandiloquent lettering is of a piece with the graveyard inscriptions waiting in the family cemetery behind a "fence of iron spear-hafts," names honed to a "diamond edge" by frost. Fixed, stylized language in any form violates human dignity and need; once inscribed, the letter killeth. As I noted earlier, the next poem in the sequence, "During Fever," makes a certain reparation for this one. That reparation consists less in the poem's staged Oedipal idyll, which is partly a joke on the reader, than in its repeated apostrophes to the now-silent mother and in its affectionate memory of conversation with her. But "During Fever" nevertheless ends by consigning the mother, face fixed in a smile, to the oppressive "old life of decency" that spoke tirelessly through her voice.

Troubling the Waters

In the early phase of its reception, *Life Studies* was widely taken as a book that brought the reader uncomfortably close to the poet's anguish and humiliation, and established aesthetic distance by its control over language and poetic form. Irvin Ehrenpreis's influential essay of 1965 crystallizes the point: "If Lowell had not managed to infuse the despair of his disgust with the humor of his irony, he could not have established the framework that screens the reader from the simple pathos of most confessional verse" (178). Certain ways of reading the volume testify to the felicity of this view, particularly one that emphasizes the way Lowell's uninhibited, not to say Byronic, use of rhyme and half-rhyme sets up the language of the text as a frisky running counterpoint to its own referential melancholy. Nonetheless, though this distinction between style and subject must be drawn, it must also be erased. In this essay, I have tried to show that *Life Studies* invites a reading in which the speaker's troubled experience and his poetic idiom are not antithetical but rather mutually implicated at every point, a reading in which the innocence of form does not mitigate the fallenness of content, but in which each factor is charged with its own independent series of ambivalences. Control or mastery of the personal-historical material is of secondary importance; more urgent is the process of representing the material in a way that is ripe for insight, in both the general and the psychoanalytic sense. The ripeness is all, for the insight is not supplied. It is entrusted to the anonymous Other – not, I think, to any idealized reader – just as the whole discourse trusts to the intelligibility of its variegated *unconscious* motives. Simlarly, the volume constitutes less a cleansing of the speaker's self than an inquiry into the nature and possibility of having a self, and into the question of the self's relationship to language and culture.

As I intimated earlier, Lowell's great contribution in *Life Studies* is to have made these processes, which exist as tensions within all autobiographical poetry, into explicit formal features of the genre. This is felt most strongly at the end, where the incompleteness of closure is turned into a will to continue, a will to live, with only the smallest trace of idealization, thanks to an almost Lawrentian willingness to see a skunk, self-image or not, as a skunk. Of all antecedent poems, perhaps only Coleridge's "Dejection," which *does* idealize as it ends, is so radically noncommittal about its own therapeutic value. So it is fitting that *Life Studies* pays Coleridge a disturbed, self-reflexive tribute:

> The room was filled
> with cigarette smoke circling the paranoid,
> inert gaze of Coleridge, back
> from Malta –   ("To Delmore Schwartz," *LS* 53–54)

The halo is not much; it will not beat Whitman's on Brooklyn ferry. But for all that, it is a halo still. Or, as Captain Billy says:

> *This* reeward, *though small,*
> *Beats none at all.* . . .   (*LS* 35)

NOTES

1   Steven Gould Axelrod notes these opposed responses and gives a detailed account of Lowell's relation to Williams apropos of *Life Studies* (*Robert Lowell* 91–97).

2   The consensus view of the volume cannot, of course, be found anywhere exactly as I put it. Representative discussions would include those in Hugh Staples, *Robert Lowell: The First Twenty Years*; Richard J. Fein, *Robert Lowell*, rev. ed.; Alan Williamson, *Pity the Monsters: The Political Vision of Robert Lowell*; and Stephen Yenser, *Circle to Circle: The Poetry of Robert Lowell*.

3   As Axelrod points out, the term "confession" has a double etymological appropriateness: It "derives from *com* plus *fateri*: to *speak completely*, and also to *speak with*, to *speak together*" (*Robert Lowell* 131).

4   In the essay "Apostrophe," from his *The Pursuit of Signs* (135–54), Jonathan Culler argues that there is an antagonism between apostrophe and narrative, a contention that Lowell's treatment would seem to bear out.

5   In his *Paris Review* interview, Lowell says apropos of *Life Studies*, "The reader was to believe he was getting the *real* Robert Lowell" (Seidel 21).

6   I will have to go into some detail on this point, in part because it requires careful substantiation, and in part because I want to demonstrate the sheer overabundance of metonymy in the volume's final moment.

7   Lowell seemingly takes pains to stress this side of himself. In "91 Revere Street" he describes how he felt at his Brimmer School: "I wished I was an older girl. I wrote Santa Claus for a field hockey stick" (*LS* 27). Also pertinent are these lines from "My Last Afternoon":

> I wasn't a child at all –
> unseen and all-seeing, I was Agrippina
> in the Golden House of Nero.   (*LS* 63)

6

Poètes Maudits of the Genteel Tradition: Lowell and Berryman

MARJORIE PERLOFF

> . . . Really we had the same life,
> the generic one
> our generation offered
> (*Les Maudits* – the compliment
> each American generation
> pays itself in passing):
> first students, then with our own,
> our galaxy of grands maîtres,
> our fifties' fellowships
> to Paris, Rome and Florence,
> veterans of the Cold War not the War –
> all the best of life . . .
> then daydreaming to drink at six,
> waiting for the iced fire,
> even the feel of the frosted glass,
> like waiting for a girl . . .
> if you had waited.
> We asked to be obsessed with writing,
> and we were.   ("For John Berryman," *DBD* 27)

The "generic life," as Lowell candidly defines it in his memorial poem for John Berryman, and as the authoritative biographies of the two poets by Ian Hamilton and John Haffenden and the memoir by Berryman's first wife, Eileen Simpson, relate it, is that of the Baudelairean *poète maudit* turned academic – "first students, then with our own" – the outsider poet, alienated from his society, who is really an insider, the quintessential fellowship holder and prize winner. (Lowell and Berryman each won two Guggenheims, the Pulitzer, the Bollingen, and the National Book

Award, not to mention a score of lesser fellowships and prizes like the Harriet Mon-
roe Poetry Award; unlike Baudelaire, who could not get himself elected to the Acad-
emie Française, they were charter members of the American Academy of Arts and
Letters and of every comparable institution.) Like Eliot's Gerontion, Lowell and
Berryman might have said that they were "neither at the hot gates / Nor fought in
the warm rain. / Nor knee-deep in the salt marsh, heaving a cutlass, / Bitten by
flies, fought." Theirs was not World War II, the terrible war raging outside the
gates of the Ivy League and Southern agrarian universities that nurtured them, but,
by Lowell's own admission, the Cold War, that period of anxious watchfulness in
which the "game of poetical chairs," as Eileen Simpson calls it (203), the cycle of
one-year appointments at Princeton or Harvard, of fellowships and poetry readings,
of writing reviews and, more important, reading the reviews of one's own books
written by one's friends, could continue unabated. This "generic life" was peppered
by enormous doses of alcohol and adultery, and, in Lowell's case (as in that of Theodore Roethke and Delmore Schwartz) by repeated bouts with insanity that resulted
in repeated hospitalization. "We asked to be obsessed with writing," Lowell remarks, and "asked" is the revealing word. Baudelaire, Nerval, Rimbaud – those
archetypal *poètes maudits* did not have to *ask* to be so obsessed; they simply were. But
for Lowell and Berryman and their poet friends, the obsession was less with writing for its own sake (something you do because you have to, never mind the circumstances or rewards, as in the case of Joyce or Pound or Stevens) than for what Berryman called, in the title of his last published book, *Love & Fame*. As Berryman put it
in a Dream Song addressed to Delmore Schwartz:

> You said 'My head's on fire'
> meaning inspired O
>
> meeting on the walk down to Warren House
> so long ago we were almost anonymous
> waiting for fame to descend
> with a scarlet mantle & tell us who we were.
>
> ("Dream Song 152," *The Dream Songs*)

But did fame, which certainly did spread her mantle for these poets, tell them
who they were? The Hamilton and Haffenden biographies, recording as they do
the almost unendurable sufferings of Lowell and Berryman, as well as of their friends,
wives, and mistresses, suggest otherwise. "Who they were" is something we are
only beginning to understand now that forty years have elapsed since the publication
of *Lord Weary's Castle* (1946) and more than twenty since *The Dream Songs* (1964).
Indeed, although neither Ian Hamilton nor John Haffenden draws larger conclusions
from the individual lives examined so relentlessly, both raise important issues about
the relationship of poetry and culture. The myth of the poet as it was disseminated
in the decades following World War II, a myth firmly believed in by what is often

called the "tragic generation" of poets – Lowell, Berryman, Roethke, Schwartz, Jarrell, and, a bit later, Sylvia Plath and Anne Sexton – this is my subject.

I

When John Crowe Ransom died in 1974, Lowell wrote in tribute:

> The kind of poet I am was largely determined by the fact that I grew up in the heyday of the New Criticism. From the beginning I was preoccupied with technique, fascinated by the past and tempted by other languages. It is hard for me (now) to imagine a poet not interested in the classics. (Hamilton, *Robert Lowell* 57)

What this preoccupation with technique and tradition meant in practice can be seen in a 1938 review of Ransom's *The World's Body*, published by the twenty-one-year-old Lowell in the Kenyon literary magazine *Hika*:

> Proudly we declare that common and quotidian experience is beneath the grace of art. . . . Metaphysical poetry makes the miraculous explicit. . . . If the tears [the reference is to Donne's "A Valediction: Of Weeping"] seem to have a cosmic importance, blotting out all else, becoming a flood which destroys the whole world, destroying at last the lovers themselves, such poetry substantiates its hypothesis. It preserves the richness of particulars and can, as in the great religions, make explicit the most supernatural reality, God. (Hamilton, *Robert Lowell* 59)

Lowell's Kenyon training with Ransom and Tate had its Northeast equivalent in Berryman's studies at Columbia. Haffenden reports:

> In April 1936 Berryman enjoyed the splendid honour of seeing four of his poems published in *Columbia Review* alongside 'A Critic's Job of Work' – a review by Mark Van Doren of Blackmur's *The Double Agent* – and 'The Experience of Ideas', a review by Blackmur himself of Allen Tate's collection *Reactionary Essays*. He invited Blackmur to be guest of honour at the annual poetry reading of the Boar's Head Poetry Society, and thrilled to sit with his idol in the Harkness Academic Theatre on 30 April 1936 as Mark Van Doren gave an address on Blackmur's criticism. (74)

And when Allen Tate gave a summer school course at Columbia, Berryman declared, so Eileen Simpson recalls, that he had "the top of my head blown off" by Tate's "brilliance and erudition" (Simpson 127).

The poetry born of these glamorous associations, unlike the early poetry of Eliot and Pound, not to speak of Williams, immediately struck a responsive chord. True, the young Berryman complained a good deal about critical neglect and about his own failure to produce enough first-rate work (Simpson tells us that when he was twenty-six, he said bitterly that "all he had to his name was a *fifth* of a book"), but the fact is that although fame did not come until 1956, with the publication of *Homage to Mistress Bradstreet,* Berryman was always recognized as a serious poet by those whom he respected. "Praise in general meant little to John," says Simpson, "praise from Delmore or Mark, or Allen Tate or R. P. Blackmur was what mattered" (32). As early as 1938, for that matter, Berryman was part-time poetry editor for the *Nation*; as early as 1940, he held an instructorship at Harvard. By 1950, when he was thirty-six, Berryman had received invitations to teach from the universities of Washington, Vermont, Wayne State, Cincinnati, and Princeton.

As for Lowell, the success of *Lord Weary's Castle,* with its brilliant fusions of the dense Symbolist mode of Eliot with the personal, fiery rhetoric of Dylan Thomas, can only be called stunning. Randall Jarrell wrote him that *Lord Weary's Castle* "will be the best first book of poems since Auden's *Poems. . . .* not only that, I think they are some of the best poems anyone has written in our time and are sure to be read for hundreds of years. . . . I think you're potentially a better poet than anybody writing in English" (Hamilton, *Robert Lowell* 103). If we bear in mind that Stevens's *Transport to Summer* was published in the same year as *Lord Weary's Castle,* and that Williams had published *Paterson*, Book I, the previous year, Jarrell's are strong words indeed. But no stronger, of course, than Allen Tate's response to Schwartz's *In Dreams Begin Responsibilities* (1938): "I want to tell you that your poetic style is beyond any doubt the first real innovation that we've had since Eliot and Pound. There's nothing like it, and by comparison Auden and MacNeice are camp followers of easily identified schools" (Atlas 129).

But the "first real innovations" in whatever literary mode usually take some time to be perceived. By 1972, with the hindsight of a poet-critic who had also absorbed the lessons of Black Mountain, of the Objectivists, and of the Beats and New York poets, David Antin remarked:

> . . . the Metaphysical Modernist tradition, which was by no means a "modernist" tradition [was] an anomaly peculiar to American and English poetry. It was the result of a collision of strongly antimodernist and provincial sensibilities with the hybrid modernism of Pound and the purer modernism of Gertrude Stein and William Carlos Williams. Because of the intense hostility to "modernism" of Eliot, Ransom, and Tate, it was not possible for them to come into anything but superficial contact with it except as mediated through Ezra Pound, whom Eliot at least was able to misread as a fellow provincial, chiefly because of Pound's "Great Books" mentality. (120)

The "collision" Antin describes, and which proved to be so celebrated from the late forties to the late sixties, produced, in any case, what we might call the *Wild-Genteel* or *Bad Boy–Professor* tradition in poetry. There is a photograph in Hamilton's biography (facing p. 277) depicting the members of the Kenyon School of

Letters in 1950: Philip Rice, Arthur Mizener, Robert Lowell, Kenneth Burke, Delmore Schwartz, Charles Coffin, William Empson, John Crowe Ransom, and L. C. Knights. Gentlemen all, the writers could hardly look more "clean-cut," as we used to call it in the fifties. With the exception of the bearded Empson, all are clean-shaven; all wear well-cut if slightly rumpled suits or sport coats. The tie, slightly askew in Lowell's case, is *de rigueur.* All but Kenneth Burke wear white shirts. In photograph after photograph, this is the look: the casually worn coat and tie, the stray wisp of hair that is otherwise neatly cut, the glasses, the extended hand holding a cigarette. Frederick Buechner, one of Berryman's students at Princeton in 1943, describes the poet as follows:

> He was slender, pale, dark-haired and rather brittle-looking. He had a chiseled, ascetic face and carried his head slightly to one side. When he walked, he gave the impression of coming at you sideways. He spoke very intently and quite rapidly, picking his way with unusual care between words and pausing from time to time to find the particular one he wanted. . . . In both the manner and the matter of what he said, he struck me always as profoundly considerate and courteous. He was of course very intellectual, very witty, but at the same time a very attentive and responsive listener. In general he seemed above all things donnish. . . . When the weather was cool, he wore an enormously long striped scarf wound around his neck and often read a book as he walked, apparently oblivious of everything else. I remember somebody saying nobody ever *looked* so much a poet. (Haffenden 161; ellipses are Haffenden's)

Both Lowell and Berryman were, in a curious way, perfect preppies. They had been to the right schools (St. Mark's for Lowell, South Kent for Berryman); they assiduously avoided Bohemia (see Peter Taylor's short story "1939" on this subject); and Lowell's brief "rebellion" against Harvard, which brought him first to Vanderbilt and then to Kenyon, should not obscure the simple truth that he was, like Berryman, the ultimate Ivy Leaguer, the educated, genteel intellectual who would spend a good portion of his life on campuses like Harvard or Princeton. Yet the other side of the preppie portrait is that of the Wild Man – the physically violent, deeply neurotic, aggressively promiscuous *macho* poet, whose sensibilities are endlessly at war with the soft-spoken (think of Lowell's slightly Southern accent imposed on Beacon Hill), gentlemanly anti-self.

The "Brooksandwarren" (Lowell's own term – see Hamilton, *Robert Lowell* 76) principle of irony as structure, the New Critical doctrine that every poem is a little drama built around a central paradox, is reflected not only in the early work of Lowell and Berryman, as is generally held, but in the very fabric of their lives. When Robert Penn Warren declared in "Pure and Impure Poetry" that Romeo always needs a Mercutio as a balance, he might have been describing the lives of Lowell or Berryman. Especially Lowell, whose life is the emblem of New Critical tensions:

the New England Puritan aristocrat who is also a relentless womanizer, the conscientious objector who, when near mental breakdown, is fond of extolling the "superman ideology" and lecturing on Hitler's "brilliance" (Hamilton, *Robert Lowell* 209), the "Mayflower screwball" (note the oxymoron) who avoids all contact with the Beat scene. If Lowell had not existed, surely the New Criticism would have had to invent him.

Neither Hamilton nor Haffenden, careful as they are not to make judgments on the lives they narrate so fully and interestingly, makes clear how *different* their subjects were from the preceding generation of Modernist poets. Consider first the question of the place of poetry. For Yeats and Eliot, as for Pound or Williams or Auden, lyric poetry was only one link in the larger literary and artistic chain. The poets either had close contact with the visual artists of their day (Pound, Williams, Stevens), or with composers (Pound, Auden), or with the theater (Yeats, Pound), or with philosophy (Yeats, Eliot, Stevens, Auden), or with the political life of the nation and of the world (Yeats, Pound, Auden). Poetry was still regarded as *one* of the arts rather than as *the* art; it was, in any case, understood to be an impossible source for earning a living. Williams was a physician, Stevens an insurance executive, Eliot an editor and publisher; Yeats, Pound, and Auden wrote for the weekly papers and produced books and articles on such nonpoetic subjects as politics, religion, and cultural history.

What distinguishes Lowell and Berryman and Roethke and Schwartz from their Modernist predecessors is thus their single-minded *literariness.* Neither in his topical sonnets nor in the letters and journals quoted by Hamilton does Lowell give the slightest indication of interest in the dominant art movement of his time, Abstract Expressionism, or in its successors, Pop Art, Minimalism, and Conceptual Art. Lowell lived in New York during the sixties, no more than a fifteen-minute cab ride from, say, Jasper Johns or Willem de Kooning, but there seems to have been virtually no contact with the art world or, for that matter, with the world of avant-garde music or dance. The brief excursus into the theater (with the characteristically "literary" production of *The Old Glory* in 1964) only makes clearer how far removed he was from the experimentation then taking place in the other arts. Berryman's case is very similar: Nowhere does Eileen Simpson record any particular reaction to contemporary art or music, and "good theater" meant fine productions of Shakespeare rather than of, say, Beckett and Pinter.

Within the literary domain itself, both Lowell and Berryman again follow their New Critical teachers in being committed anglophiles. It is not, I think, coincidental that the first biographies of both poets have been written by British authors, for it is toward Britain (as refracted through New England and the South) that Lowell and Berryman face. The Eng. Lit. curriculum of the universities – Shakespeare and Donne and Jonson, Milton and the Romantics – has never so fully dominated poetry as it did in these midcentury years. This anglophilia sheds interesting light on Lowell's *Imitations* (1961), a book about which I have always had reservations. In the preface, Lowell admits to "reckless[ness]" with "literal meaning" in the interests of "get[ting] the tone" of the originals and making "alive English" out of them (I.xi). But unlike Pound reinventing Propertius or Eliot making Baudelaire's unreal city his own, Lowell seems to have little feel for the poets "imitated," the exceptions being Virgil and possibly Montale. Continental Europe seems to have remained, so to speak, "Beyond the Alps." Berryman's case is similar. Haffenden lists Ronsard, Vigny, Lamartine, Mallarmé, Rimbaud, Verlaine, and Laforgue as poets Berryman studied while at Cambridge so as "to keep my sense of values straight" (77), but it is hard to see what real role these poets were to play in Berryman's own poetry. And of course, whereas Laforgue was almost a contemporary of Eliot's – and hence some-one whom Eliot could, so to speak, discover – for Berryman, Laforgue was already a figure from literary history.

Lowell's first trip to Europe was made in 1950 when he was thirty-three. Elizabeth Hardwick remembers it as a period of "gorgeous absorption and infinite passion for Italy and Europe, which both of us were taking in for the first time. . . . We shed tears when we opened the door of the Athens Museum and saw the Charioteer, standing serenely" (Hamilton, *Robert Lowell* 173). And Lowell wrote to Randall Jarrell:

> I feel and talk like a guide book – full of gaps, irrelevencies [sic] and am-nesia. . . . It's like going to school again – I fill up on everything indis-crimently [sic] and hope it will settle – a lot of French and Italian poetry, even some German and Latin, thousands of paintings, a lot of history, plays, opera, ballet – one feels so ignorant, so conscious that one won't have forever, that it's hard to stop. (Hamilton, *Robert Lowell* 173)

Comment after comment reveals what was surely a tourist's Europe – the conscien-tious visits to the great Italian museums, galleries, and churches, the absorption in history. Not surprisingly, Lowell soon tired of France and Italy and wanted to go to Holland, a country more in accord with "my own Protestant New England back-ground" (Hamilton, *Robert Lowell* 175). Culture, in the end, belonged safely at home – in Boston or New York or on the campus where one studied and taught and compared notes with one's friends.

Why does this matter? Why, after all, should Lowell or Berryman have cared about Europe? Again, why should they have concerned themselves with, say, the painting of Pollock or with the new ballets of Balanchine or the New Polish Theater? Perhaps because to be so exclusively literary, so centered on lyric poetry (and Anglo-American lyric poetry at that) created a curious solipsism. To have no outlet but the literary life on the campus or in the quarterlies is not as unconnected as it might seem to the endless cycle of broken marriages and mental breakdowns, of alcoholism and suicide that characterized the lives of what we might call the tragic generation of genteel poets. Let me try to explain this somewhat outrageous assertion.

II

From the Modernists, the poets of Lowell's generation inherited the doctrine, codified by the New Criticism, of the rigid separation of *art* from *life*. As Berryman put it to his psychiatrist in 1947:

> My oblivion [his failure to remember incidents from his childhood] I said I ascribe to two causes: (1) my old belief in the perfect separateness of Life & Art, the poet's life being negligible & to-be-lost (believed dogmatically for years, though no more); (2) a real indifference to my own past life, partly because of my habit of looking back on myself as a hopeless fool prior to the present moment. (Haffenden, 184)

And Ian Hamilton is surely right when he remarks on "how *little* of [Lowell's] life up to 1945 can be construed from the poems of *Lord Weary's Castle*. One can deduce something of his Boston background, his *Mayflower* ancestors – though nothing in the least precise. There are elegies in the book addressed to dead relatives, but these carry little direct feeling, nor do we get from them any clear sense who these people were" (*Robert Lowell* 105). The poem as well-wrought urn, as self-contained artifact, whose structure acts, in the words of Cleanth Brooks and W. K. Wimsatt, as "a combination of concreteness and significance, a reconciliation or simultaneous embodiment of diverse emotive pulls, a way of facing and even asserting something serious while at the same time declining the didactic gambit which nature is always pushing forward" (752–53) – this is the doctrine to which Lowell and Berryman subscribed.

But – and here is, I think, one cause of the peculiar malaise of Lowell's circle – the doctrine of art versus life, which could be accommodated by a Mallarmé or a Joyce, now came to blows with the more deep-seated belief, inherited from the Romantics, who stand, of course, squarely behind the so-called confessional mode of Lowell even as they stand behind Roethke's vegetal animism, a belief in the artist as hero, exempt from ordinary rules and ordinary morality, and its corollary that genius and madness are but near allied. Neither Joyce nor Mallarmé, after all, wrote books like *The Dolphin* or *For Lizzie and Harriet,* that incorporated, without disguise, family letters and other personal documents. But in the case of Lowell and Berryman, the Coleridgean doctrine of organic form ran headlong into the Shelleyan insistence that the poet is the legislator of the world, a prophet who "participates in the eternal, the infinite, and the one." "A man," said Shelley, "to be greatly good must imagine intensely and comprehensively," and, in practice, such "imaginings" easily lead the poet into dangerous waters. For to equate morality with imagination is to abjure responsibility for one's everyday behavior, for one's ordinary relations with men and women and with one's social and political milieu. In these circumstances, suffering becomes a way of identifying oneself as a poet. Thus Lowell writes to Berryman on March 8, 1962:

All winter I've had an uncomfortable feeling of dying into rebirth. Not at all the sick, dizzy allegorized thing such words suggest and which I've felt going off my rocker. But that flat prose of coming to an end of one way of life, whittled down and whittled down and picking up nothing new though always about to. . . .

What queer lives we've had even for poets! There seems to be something generic about it, and determined beyond anything we could do. (*Robert Lowell* 298; ellipses are Hamilton's)

The notion of mental illness as a "dying into rebirth," somehow decreed by fate, somehow "generic," comes up again and again in Lowell's writings. Consider the following letter to Roethke, written on July 10, 1963, less than a month before Roethke was to die from a heart attack:

We couldn't be more different, and yet how weirdly our lives have often gone the same way. Let's say we are brothers, have gone the same journey and know far more about each other than we have ever said or will say. There's a strange fact about the poets of roughly our age, and one that doesn't exactly seem to have always been true. It's this, that to write we seem to have to go at it with such single-minded intensity that we are always on the point of drowning. . . . I feel it's something almost unavoidable, some flaw in the motor. There must be some kind of glory to it all that people coming later will wonder at. I can see us all being written up in some huge book of the age. But under what title? (Hamilton, *Robert Lowell* 337)

This cult of madness as certifying poetic power, as giving *evidence* of greatness, was, in turn, accepted by those close to Lowell or Berryman as a kind of status quo; both poets were regularly excused for their behavior, no matter how cruel, selfish, and outrageous it was. Reading Hamilton's life of Lowell, one is appalled, not so much by what Lowell *did* – poets, after all, have never been known for being Nice Guys – but by how others reacted to it. From the beginning, friends, mistresses, wives, even acquaintances, were quite willing to turn the other cheek. In the summer of 1935, for example, while still a student at St. Mark's, Lowell rented a cottage at Nantucket with his two friends, Frank Parker and Blair Clark. Hamilton records:

[Clark's] chief memories of Nantucket are to do with Lowell's brutal, childish tyranny. . . . On one occasion, Lowell decided that Blair Clark should give up smoking, and when Clark resisted "he chased me around and he knocked me down, to make me give up." On another, it was decided that Experience required the trio to know what it felt like to be drunk. Lowell announced that the brew would be rum mixed with cocoa: I remember I made the cocoa. And we drank it as if we were mainlining heroin. I remember the chair falling over and my head hitting the floor. We got blind drunk in about twenty minutes. Next thing I remember was staggering onto the porch outside – and how I didn't choke on my own vomit, I don't know. Why *did* we go along with it? (*Robert Lowell* 24)

Why indeed did they all go along with it? Why was the same Blair Clark always ready to serve Lowell? In 1962, for example, it was Clark who flew to Argentina, Lowell having cracked up while on a mission for the Congress of Cultural Freedom, and talked the local clinic into discharging the poet "on condition that a doctor and a nurse accompany him to New York, and at a huge cost (Clark recalls) this was arranged" (Hamilton 303). Again, Jean Stafford, whose nose Lowell broke not once but twice, and whom he subjected to endless cruelties in the years leading up to their divorce, later wrote to him:

> My dear, please never castigate yourself for what you call blindness – how blind we both were, how green we were. . . . All we can do is forgive ourselves and now be good friends – how I should cherish that. (Hamilton, *Robert Lowell* 307–8)

And in 1965, when Lowell's affair with the Lithuanian dancer Vija Vetra, with whom he went so far as to set up housekeeping in lower Manhattan under the name Mr. and Mrs. Robert Lowell, all the while telling his friends that his marriage to Elizabeth Hardwick was finished, predictably culminated in the usual breakdown, followed by the usual confinement in the mental hospital, and, in turn, by the usual contriteness and the desire to return home to his family, Hardwick not only forgave her husband but wrote him, "I would kill myself, if it would cure you" (Hamilton, *Robert Lowell* 333).

Hamilton discreetly makes no comment on these incidents, the implication being that poetic genius (so inextricably bound up with madness) cannot be measured by the ordinary rules of behavior, that Lowell's very special charisma atoned for all his sins. It took a simpler, more down-to-earth woman like Vija Vetra to declare when, without any warning from Lowell himself, and just a few weeks after he had declared his undying love for her, she was called to a meeting by Lowell's attorneys and advised to vacate the premises within two days, "Heartless, absolutely heartless. That's the American way. Very ugly" (*Robert Lowell* 319). But then Vija Vetra did not know who the Lowells of Boston were, and she did not fully appreciate that her lover was a Great Poet.

Haffenden's biography of Berryman and Simpson's memoir provide us with similar paradigms, although Berryman evidently did not have Lowell's magnetic appeal or, for that matter, the "potency of the Lowell name" (Hamilton, *Robert Lowell* 6). There *were* women who left him, including "Lise," the Lady of the *Sonnets,* and Eileen Simpson herself, whose story has a happy ending in remarriage and her own career as psychotherapist and writer. Here is Simpson's account of her initial coming together with Berryman:

Crucial to our relationship was his discovery early on that while reading Keats and Byron and Shelley . . . in college, I had, in some woolly way, come to believe that poetry was the most powerful and mysterious form of writing. To be the "helpmate" (wasn't that the word we undergraduates used in the student cafeteria, talking of such things?) to a poet would be the most interesting and useful way for a woman to spend her life.

Perfect! The combination of near ignorance (no wrong-headed notions to be dislodged), eagerness to learn (from what better teacher?), an exalted view of his craft and the promise of devotion, suited John admirably in a companion. (5–6)

Good-humoredly ironic, Simpson does not seem bitter about her marriage. But here is Haffenden's description of that marriage, less than ten years later:

[Berryman] spent a good proportion of his time during the period intriguing for sex. His liaisons were never as untransparent as he wished, and in fact, as Pat Warnock Eden recalls, "his rages and tantrums and affairs were well known and gossiped about [at Princeton]. . . . 'It's all part of my biography, that's all,' he said once, when he was chasing some young woman around, and obviously embarrassing and hurting Eileen." (219)

Again, when in Cincinnati in 1952 Eileen suffered a serious back injury:

Berryman found himself unable to tolerate her incapacitation, not only for selfless reasons of her suffering but also for his own sake. Although he was far from feeling heartless towards her, he was more used to self-engrossment and to receiving attention than to giving it. It distressed him immeasurably to suspend his own needs in favour of the absoluteness of hers. For reasons which were deep and largely unintentional, he considered her disablement a galling burden to himself, and chafed in ways that seemed childish and hysterical at the responsibility. . . . He soon started begrudging her his time and energy in visiting the hospital, a fact which Allen Tate . . . remarked to his family. Eileen persuaded Berryman to use his time as he wished. (Haffenden 231)

The prodigal poet, the unselfish and forgiving wife or mistress – the pattern, similar to Lowell's, is repeated over and over again. Haffenden's biography is full of stories about poetry readings and terms-in-residence at universities all over the country, in the course of which Berryman would cause his hosts acute embarrassment, harass those, like the Anthony Ostroffs of Berkeley, who proffered friendship, and shamelessly pursue the wives of colleagues. When, in 1961, he decided to marry Kate Donahue, he wrote to Saul Bellow, "She is beautiful as well but the best thing about her is Japanese submissiveness, silence & attention. I'm tired of raging egos, especially my own" (Haffenden 300). Which echoes Lowell's famous line, "Everyone's tired of my turmoil" (*FUD* 19).

One can, of course, offer psychoanalytic explanations of Berryman's behavior: Haffenden convincingly relates his treatment of women to the peculiar love–hate relationship he had with his mother, a relationship exacerbated by his father's suicide. Or again, in the case of Lowell, one can argue that his manic-depressive psychosis would now be treated as a physical illness, that had lithium therapy been discovered sooner, Lowell and his loved ones might have been spared much suffering.

But such explanations are never quite satisfactory. For one thing, what was evidently Lowell's worst betrayal of Hardwick – his elopement with Caroline Blackwood – a betrayal that prompted Hardwick to write to Lowell, "My utter contempt for both of you for the misery you have brought to two people who have never hurt you knows no bounds" (Hamilton, *Robert Lowell* 399), came three years after he had been put on lithium. But, more important, the pattern of disturbance, mental breakdown, and suicidal despondency is too pervasive among the poets of Lowell's circle to allow for such individual accounting or justification.

To understand the ethos of this not-quite-tragic generation, we must reconsider the curious split I spoke of earlier between the New Critical doctrine that art and life were wholly separate and the Romantic faith in the artist as inspired lunatic, exempt from ordinary morality. The former stands behind Lowell's obsessive revisions (revisions that, as Jonathan Raban has noted, constituted "a kind of gaming with words, treating them like billiard balls" [Hamilton, *Robert Lowell* 431]), and behind his decision to publish *The Dolphin* regardless of warnings from his closest friends like Elizabeth Bishop that the sonnet cycle about his private drama, incorporating as it does Hardwick's personal letters, was in poor taste and would cause his wife much suffering. When Lowell heard that Auden did not wish to speak to him because of the book, he was "indignant" and, as he cabled Auden, "ASTOUNDED BY YOUR INSULT TO ME" (Hamilton, *Robert Lowell* 425). For was not poetry, as Ransom and Tate had taught him, wholly unrelated to life?

This consciously held conviction, a thin veneer over Lowell's real feelings, clashed with the more deep-seated conviction that of course art *is* life. In 1959, Lowell wrote to Berryman:

> I am just back from Greensboro, where Randall and [I] enjoyed (?) ourselves lamenting the times. It seems there's been something curious twisted and against the grain about the world poets of our generation have had to live in. What troubles you and I, Ted Roethke, Elizabeth Bishop, Delmore, Randall – even Karl Shapiro – have had. I hope your exaustion [sic] is nothing very drastic; these knocks are almost a proof of intelligence and valor in us. (Hamilton, *Robert Lowell* 275–76)

"These knocks are almost a proof of intelligence and valor in us" – here is the Romantic myth of the poet writ large, a myth still widely held today, as the critical response to the new biographies suggests. Reviewer after reviewer has expressed deep sympathy for the terrible sufferings Lowell and Berryman underwent, ignoring, I think, the

possibility that suffering was, in a curious sense, a postwar poetic style – a proper way of being.

The cult of suffering as witness to one's poetic sensitivity is closely related to the political consciousness of Lowell and Berryman. Lowell is generally regarded as an important political poet; his poems, especially the *Notebooks* and *History*, contain much commentary on political figures from Eisenhower to Che Guevara and on events like the Pentagon march. But how deep does Lowell's political analysis go? Commenting on the treatment of Colonel Shaw and his Negro regiment in "For the Union Dead," Robert Pinsky makes an interesting observation:

> For tortuously complex reasons, the poet must evoke an ideal for contrast, and must admire it without professing it. He must imply, with utmost tact bordering on reticence, a comparison between the moral consequences of depending upon slavery and the moral consequences of depending upon gross machines. The point here is, first, that the poet's goals are, indeed, such tact and indirection; second, that he manages the task with brevity and grace by using a device which his readers know so well that they hardly notice it. Attribution, quotation, borrowing of terms, allusion to what someone else hears, sees, said, or might have said – for Lowell these are ways to qualify or refine ironies or allegiances. (17–18)

Qualification and irony – these, rather than passion or commitment – characterize much of the "political" poetry. Still, it comes as something of a shock to read Hamilton on the background of *Land of Unlikeness* (1943):

> . . . three elements in the [poet's] turmoil can be thought of as consistent: Boston, Catholicism, War. The essential drift is that if the worst of Boston could learn from the best of Rome, then wars would at least have dignity and noble purpose. This is crudely put, but the poems don't put it much more subtly: how could they, since Lowell in the spring of 1943 was irritably unsure of his own principles? Most of his childhood heroes had been military heroes, and he had shown himself to have a rare appetite for both tyranny and violence; but he could see little that was splendid in the way modern wars were fought. Could the "good fight" ever be fought with bombs? Lowell had, it is said by Frank Parker, supported the Franco side during the Spanish Civil War, and his conversion to Catholicism had engendered an even fiercer hostility to Communism. Thus, America's alliance with the Soviet Union would have seemed to him a repugnantly high price to pay for the defeat of Hitler. Much of this is conjecture: Lowell's letters of the period are strikingly free of any comment on the war. (*Robert Lowell* 84)

Lowell's decision in 1943 to become a conscientious objector must be understood against this background; it represents a curious amalgam of Puritan high-mindedness, a taste for violence and authority, and a lack of real interest in what was actually happening in Europe. "In 1941," he wrote President Roosevelt, "we understood a patriotic war to preserve *our lives, our fortunes, and our sacred honor* against the lawless aggressions of a totalitarian league: in 1943 we are collaborating with the most unscrupulous and powerful of totalitarian dictators to destroy law, freedom, democracy, and above all, our continued national sovereignty" (Hamilton, *Robert Lowell* 89). But what about the "national sovereignty" of our allies? The tragic events leading up to the war – the fall of Poland, the occupation of France, the Battle of Britain, as well as the battles on the Eastern Front during the war – these seem never to have penetrated Lowell's consciousness, preoccupied as he was in those years with questions of religion (the conversion to Roman Catholicism), poetic craft, and sex.

Berryman's indifference is similar although he had none of Lowell's fascination for military heroes and strong men. Abroad at Cambridge on a Kellet fellowship in 1936, Berryman and his then mistress, "Beatrice," took a vacation trip to Heidelberg:

> . . . they found rooms in Friedrichstrasse. German nationalism was heavy in the air, flags and troops everywhere, and boys who looked hardly older than fourteen bore rifles with bayonets on their bicycles. Berryman began to feel as Rilke had in 1919, when he lamented the loss of that humility he discerned in Dürer's drawings. Taking full advantage of the Reichsfestspiele, the official festival for which Goebbels had assembled all the best actors in Germany, Berryman and Beatrice attended several drama productions including *Romeo and Juliet* at the Castle on 21 July – a massive and magnificent spectacle: "several hundred actors storming in from four angles, brilliant lighting, fireworks at the banquet," Berryman related, "drums & swords & dances & a 20-minute wordless procession to lay Juliet in the tomb – it was very exciting." When they later chanced to meet one of the principal actors and entertained him to tea, Berryman could not contain his hero-worship: "possibly the most satisfying human being I've ever seen, large, powerful, open, brilliantly alive, laughing, magnificent." Another day they went for a ten-hour hike up the Heilingenberg, just across the river from Heidelberg, and observed the massive new Nazi stadium. (Haffenden 94–95)

A year or so later, Berryman wrote to Van Doren:

> More and more, with the decay of the family as a social unit, and the world what it contemptibly is, love and friendship must take on the burdens that the Church and State and general hopefulness once bore and bear no more. Personal relationships and, for some, work – are all. (Haffenden 106)

Love and friendship, personal relationships – these are the big subjects for the *poètes maudits* of the period. Delmore Schwartz, himself Jewish, wrote in his journal of 1939 that the war was a "farcical drama" in which "two raging giants, Germany and

Russia, were certain to destroy each other, and eventually, the world." "The widening of war," moreover, meant "a null period for immortal poetry" (Atlas 148).

In this context, Lowell's later gestures – his refusal to dine at the Johnson White House in 1965 because of the Hanoi raids, his participation in the Pentagon march, his support first of Eugene McCarthy and then Robert Kennedy, must be taken with a grain of salt. In 1958, when he was hospitalized at McLean's outside Boston, Anne Adden, the Bennington girl with whom he had fallen in love, was following a reading program the poet had devised for her. "Hitler," she wrote him, "has the greatest retrospective power" (Hamilton, *Robert Lowell* 249). In 1962, on the Latin American tour that culminated in another manic attack, Lowell was pronouncing himself the "Caesar of Argentina" and telling Keith Botsford, the government representative with whom he was traveling, "I want you to travel with me always. You are my lieutenant" (Hamilton 303).

None of this is to suggest that Lowell had fascist leanings: His remarks about Hitler, like his sudden passion for whatever young girl happened to appear on the scene, were always a signal that he was about to have another manic attack. Nevertheless, the strong-man scenario would not, I think, have shown up as consistently as it did, had Lowell not had, even in his sanest moments, an elitist, isolationist, New England Puritan-turned-Southern agrarian sense of America's destiny. Such isolationism was, of course, not uncharacteristic of the American Modernist poets – one thinks of Wallace Stevens – but the Modernist stance did not manifest the internal contradictions we find in poets like Lowell and Berryman. For a poet like Stevens, the Supreme Fiction was to be sought outside the political or social arena: To sign petitions or to make public pronouncements was to succumb to the "pressure of reality." Lowell, on the other hand, was given to much self-mythologizing as "fire-breathing Catholic C.O." (*LS* 85) and later as scourge of the Johnson regime even as he ruminated on the magical power of a Hannibal or a Napoleon.

The real turn, in Lowell's as in Berryman's poetry, is, in fact, inward. In the classroom civilization in which poets now began to move, there was precious little material to write poems about except the *self*, endlessly dissected by Freudian analysis, the self, falling in and out of love, making friends and enemies, and hopelessly ambivalent about fathers and mothers. True, the self was regularly positioned in a literary or historical field: "Lowell" as Caligula or Ulysses or "Mayflower screwball"; "Berryman" as Anne Bradstreet or as Mr. Bones. But, as in the lives of the poets, so in their art, others were endowed with life primarily so as to function in the poet's own drama.

Such relentless *self-centeredness* accounts, I think, for both the strengths and the weaknesses of "genteel" *poésie maudite*. In the *Life Studies* poems, as later in *Day by Day*, Lowell dispassionately presents his self as a kind of cultural artifact, the product of a particular time and place, the point of confluence of a complex network of psychological, economic, and political circumstances. Take the opening of "Commander Lowell":

> There were no undesirables or girls in my set,
> when I was a boy at Mattapoisett –
> only Mother, still her Father's daughter.
> Her voice was still electric
> with a hysterical, unmarried panic,
> when she read to me from the Napoleon book.   (*LS* 70)

Every word of this seemingly casual account of childhood summers at the beach resonates. The boy, not permitted to associate with "undesirables or girls" in the snobbish summer colony, is ruled by the most undesirable "girl" of all – his Mother, "still her Father's daughter," a woman who has never come to terms with her marriage, going so far as to deny, in her "hysterical, unmarried panic," that the sex act that brought the poet into the world ever took place. Yet this same Mother reads to her son "from the Napoleon book"; in the family, she is the general that Commander Lowell, retired from the service and fired from job after job, could never be.

Lowell might easily have sentimentalized this family portrait, but he is just as hard on himself as he is on his parents: Mother's "hysterical, unmarried panic" is evenly matched by his own "bristling and manic" behavior, "skulk[ing] in the attic" and memorizing the names of two hundred French generals. The self is never allowed to "scape whipping" even as Berryman's Henry Pussycat is presented by his creator as a charming but feckless creature, who regularly confuses sex with religion:

> The glories of the world struck me, made me, aria, once.
> – What happen then, Mr. Bones?
> if be you cares to say.
> – Henry became interested in women's bodies,
> his loins were & were the scene of stupendous achievement.
> Stupor. Knees, dear. Pray.
>
> All the knobs & softnesses of, my God,
> the duckling & trouble it swarm on Henry,
> at one time.   ("Dream Song 26," *The Dream Songs*)

Such poems have lost none of their freshness, their ability to fuse self-scrutiny with ironic distance and subtle humor. But the mode is precarious; it all too easily shades off into the self-pitying postures of Berryman's speaker in *Love & Fame* on the one hand, and a kind of stock response to the public domain on the other. Lowell's "political" poems may now strike us as relying on gesture rather than on substance. Take, for example, the famous last stanza of "For the Union Dead":

> The Aquarium is gone. Everywhere,
> giant finned cars nose forward like fish;
> a savage servility
> slides by on grease.   (*FUD* 70–72)

In the context of the elegiac ode, these lines are nothing if not clever. The "noses" of the compliant fish in the aquarium (stanza 1), and the monument that "sticks like a fishbone / in the city's throat" have been replaced by "giant finned cars [that] nose forward like fish." The innocent "savagery" of the "dark downward and vegetating kingdom / of the fish and reptile" has given way to a "savage servility" – servility rather than the "service" of Colonel Shaw, who is "out of bounds now." And this savage servility "slides by on grease" – a far cry from the "marching through Boston" of Shaw's regiment. "There are no statues for the last war here," the poet tells us high-mindedly; the only "Rock of Ages" our debased civilization has is the "Mosler Safe . . . / that survived the blast." And indeed, "The ditch is nearer." (For a thorough analysis of this poem, see Axelrod, *Robert Lowell* 162–76.)

Imagery, symbolism, ironic contrast, paradox – all these abound in "For the Union Dead" and have made it a near-perfect "classroom poem." But no matter how many ways we can relate "a savage servility / slides by on grease" (with its brilliant alliteration of *s*'s) to earlier passages in the poem, the fact remains that, to be drawn into the world of "For the Union Dead," we must somehow accept its underlying premise, which is that our own world is a debased, commercial, mechanized wasteland, peopled by Mosler safes, "yellow dinosaur steamshovels," and "giant finned cars." Behind the "metaphysical" complications of the poem's surface, there is a logocentric vision of origins, a longing for a landscape uncontaminated by technology.

Such nostalgia for a pastoral world is perhaps the inevitable corollary of the Lowellian faith, expressed in the 1959 letter to Berryman, that "these knocks are almost a proof of intelligence and valor in us." For the genteel *poète maudit* of midcentury, suffering was *de rigueur* and indeed a sign of election. For wasn't it, in the larger sense, not the poet's fault that he suffered but the fault of his age, a late silver age of decaying cities and polluted rivers? The fault of the "tranquillized *Fifties*" (*LS* 85) that succeeded a war neither Lowell nor Berryman had fought in?

Yet – and this is the paradox – it was an age that still made much of its successful poets. When *Lord Weary's Castle* was published in 1946, the *Boston Globe* bore the headline, "MOST PROMISING POET IN 100 YEARS . . . MAY BE GREATER THAN JAMES AND AMY." In the mid-eighties, it is inconceivable that any American poet would receive such an accolade. For who, to the reading public of our own time, are James and Amy that Robert Lowell might be "greater" than they are?

To be crowned a Great Poet in an age of reputed "savage servility / [that] slides by on grease" proved to be, for both Lowell and Berryman (as, in a lesser sense, for poets like Schwartz and Jarrell) a burden rather than a blessing. For the age demanded that the poet *rise above* the tawdry "unforgivable landscape" where "Chemical air / sweeps in from New Jersey" (*FUD* 10). The poet, after all, was supposed to be the youth crowned with the laurel wreath who must triumph over adversity. Not surprisingly, the demand of the Age of New Criticism proved too great.

Accordingly, one reads the new biographies of Lowell and Berryman with a mixture of nostalgia and irritation – nostalgia for the good, gone days when a poet like

Lowell could appear on the cover of *Newsweek* or participate in a presidential campaign, nostalgia for a time of more clearly defined sex roles when poets were sensitive but red-blooded *men*, and women were still willing to play the part of the great man's hostess, wife, or mistress, with no thought of putting their own claims to possible success or greatness first.

But there is also, at least for me, a measure of irritation in the contemplation of these paradigmatic lives of the poets – lives the biographers treat with such reverence. For the term "The Age of Lowell," coined by Irvin Ehrenpreis in 1965, is surely in need of reassessment. From the perspective of the last decades of the century, the accomplishment of Lowell and Berryman now seems a lesser thing than it once was. For one thing, their supposed "breakthrough" to a new "personal" and "prosaic" mode, remarkable as it appeared in 1959 in the wake of a decade of formalist poetry, now seems tame when compared with the great poetic inventions of the early century. For another, such rival groups of the fifties and sixties as the Black Mountain poets, the New York school, and especially the Objectivists are now exerting a much greater influence on contemporary poets than are Lowell or Berryman. And finally, ours is a time of what Elizabeth Bruss has called "beautiful theories," a time when the passionate interest once reserved for a new volume by a leading poet like Lowell has been transferred to other modes of writing, to the new Derrida or De Man or Guy Davenport.

In her excellent survey of Lowell criticism, Norma Procopiow notes that Lowell has always been more popular with academics and professional critics than with the poets of either his own or subsequent generations. She remarks: "The only bloc of poets who consistently supported Lowell were the 'confessionals'" (5–6). Why this is the case and what it means for Lowell's future reputation is a complex question. But I think that, whatever our answer, the "Age of Lowell" can now be understood as marking the end of an era rather than ushering in a new one – "the back-look," as Lowell himself recalls the forties in one of the *Notebook* sonnets (84). Or, as he put it so succinctly in "Grandparents":

> . . . the nineteenth century, tired of children, is gone.   (*LS* 68)

7

Notebook 1967–68: **Writing the Process Poem**

ALEX CALDER

I

Robert Lowell came late to the long poem. By 1967, when he began writing sonnets, adding one to another in a projected "Notebook of A Year," it was not extraordinary to expect such an activity to yield a book-length poem. So many other poets had written or were writing long poems in a broadly compatible way. Lowell could look to Ezra Pound, William Carlos Williams, Louis Zukofsky, Charles Olson, and John Berryman, among others, for principles and strategies that were already well tried and well tested.

Although any poem that fractures distinctions between the process of composition and composition's end product might be called a process poem, in using this term I have only long poems in mind. Understood as a way of writing the long poem, the term "process poem" identifies a compositional feature most high and late modern long poems have in common. The author of a process poem typically begins writing with no clear conception of what the long poem will grow to include. He or she has no specific blueprint, no master plan assigning places to the component parts as they come to be written. So rather than make decisions regarding the disposition of elements that already belong to a series, the poet allows the composition or generation of a series to decide its own constitution and rules of formation. Often allowing for personal change and the intervention of chance events, the poet tends to follow an unordained progression whereby the future integrity of the long poem as a series is discovered largely in the act of writing it. Given time, the process poem attains not a strict order or unity but a jagged shapefulness that marks and records the poem's history in process.

But by 1967, the process poem was necessarily a self-conscious undertaking. Although Pound and Williams did not actually set out to write process poems, their example and method had long since permitted a younger generation of poets to articulate and apply a method they found in the *Cantos* and *Paterson*. Thus, Charles Olson, writing in 1950 observed: ". . . if I think that the *Cantos* make more 'dramatic' sense than do the plays of Mr. Eliot, it is not because I think they have solved the problem but because the methodology of the verse in them points a way by which, one day, the problem of larger content and of larger forms may be solved" (rpt. *Selected Writings* 26). And a year earlier, John Berryman noted: "I have the impression that Pound allowed, in whatever his plan exactly is (if it exactly is, and if it is one plan), for the drift-of-life, the interference of fate, inevitable in a period of violent change; that this may give us something wholly unpredictable in the cantos to come, as it has given us already the marvellous pages of the *Pisan Cantos*" (1949; rpt. *Freedom* 269). Like Pound and Williams, both Berryman and Olson spent more than a decade writing their long poems. Lowell aimed to give just a year to his "notebook." He would eventually spend six years on his sonnets but the future of the poem after *Notebook 1967–68* lay as much in rewriting as in writing. *Notebook, For Lizzie and Harriet,* and *History* continue the project yet they also offer competing versions or stages of the earlier poem. If, in this respect, Lowell's commitment to the process poem appears less thoroughgoing than his predecessors', the date and timing of that first volume suggest his use of the method was also more knowing.

One feature of Lowell's project that may well seem inconsistent with the process poem is his choice of sonnet form. One might argue that in a process poem not only the poem at large but also its component poems should be allowed to find their own form. Since Lowell has discussed the question of sonnet form in an interview, it seems appropriate to have him meet this objection himself.

> I didn't find fourteen lines handcuffs. I gained more than I gave. It would have been a worry never to have known when a section must end; variation might have been monotony. Formlessness might have crowded me toward consecutive narrative. . . .
>
> *Notebook* is in unrhymed, loose blank verse sonnets. . . . It can say almost anything conversation or correspondence can. . . . [The fourteen lines] allowed me rhetoric, formal construction, and quick breaks. . . . One poem must lead towards the next, but is fairly complete; it can stride on stilts, or talk. . . .
>
> Words came rapidly, almost four hundred sonnets in four years – a calendar of workdays. I did nothing but write; I was thinking lines even when teaching or playing tennis. . . . Ideas sprang from the bushes, my head; five or six sonnets started or reworked in a day. As I have said, I wished to describe the immediate instant. If I saw something one day, I wrote it that day, or the next, or the next. Things I felt or saw, or read were drift in the whirlpool, the squeeze of the sonnet and the loose ravel of blank verse. (Hamilton, "Conversation" 13–14)[1]

Although Lowell's choice of the fourteen-line package is at odds with projectivist theory it remains in keeping with a processive method of writing a long poem. One of the more central and ongoing problems of writing a process poem is to accommodate material in such a way that the poem neither merely records a string of compositional occasions nor hardens into a closely regulated system. Poets frequently meet this demand by inventing compositional strategies that oppose cohesive and disjunctive modes of arrangement in order to activate process continually. No matter how the pattern of opposition is framed – it could be in terms of metrics, styles, goals, characterization, and so on – a push–pull effect remains constant. If the writer veers too much toward disjunction the poem may lack impetus, too much toward cohesion and the poet may lack room to move. By utilizing the tension between such poles, a writer can set a long poem in process. For Lowell, to set "the squeeze" of the sonnet against "the loose ravel of blank verse" was a principal method of constantly activating process. Far from proving a constraint, his decision to use sonnet form facilitated a continuous production of individual poems. Moreover, we should be wary of too quickly associating Lowell's use of the sonnet with concepts of fixed form. Can one employ that term and not ground artistic value in an anxiety or will to form the poem as high tensile object? It is a phrase Lowell uses elsewhere in his interview yet his emphasis on immediacy, on avoiding the formal "worry" of variation, suggests it may be more pertinent to view his "sonnet" as an instance of arbitrary form. Insofar as the fourteen-line shape functions as a stencil, formal pressures devolve toward the arrangement rather than the construction of sonnets. If the "Notebook of A Year" was to proceed as a long poem, the sonnets were liable to be organized; if the poem was to retain a processive structure, Lowell's methods of organization would undergo revision and change along with the poem.

In the "Afterthought" to *Notebook 1967–68* Lowell wrote: "As my title intends, the poems in this book are written as one poem, jagged in pattern, but not a conglomeration or sequence of related material" (159). "Are written" is an interesting construction. The past tense, in the form of "were written," would not have been accurate: We will find that Lowell did not begin writing sonnets "as one poem" until certain key areas of the poem-to-be had already been written. Moreover, "are written" usefully collapses a retrospective statement of intention (these sonnets were conceived as one poem) into a situation where the production of the poem has an ontological reference in the present as well as the historical past. We might say that the reader of the process poem is formed as a surrogate writer, as one who retraces the poem's history in process. The poem, in other words, has been written in such a way that it offers itself to a reader as a poem that *is* being written rather than "a conglomeration or sequence of related material." Yet this status has been earned; it is not simply a casual by-product of composition. If we consider *Notebook 1967–68* as an archaeological site, we might say that an account of its writing uncovers twin layers of compositional history. On one level, the poem itself records the development of strategies that instruct a parallel reading of the volume in process terms. Beneath that, the entire body of manuscript material constitutes a second level in which traces of the preparation and decisions underlying the choice of those strategies are preserved. But, as in archaeology, these vertical layers may not be quite flush with each other; some "faulting" may have occurred and a reading of the published volume in process terms may prove to be out of alignment with the actual circumstances of composition. In what follows, I have chosen to concentrate on manuscript material rather than a finished text. This is partly because a "second-level" examination of how *Notebook 1967–68* came to be written is bound to highlight strategies for reading the published poem. More important, though, it is by working with manuscript rather than a finished text that we can best determine the nature and extent of Lowell's commitment to processive methods of writing a long poem.

II

A long poem will have many beginnings. It can begin on the first line, with the first working title, or among the numerous traces preceding overt points of commencement. Lowell's fiftieth birthday marks one beginning. A poem he wrote for that occasion goes through many versions and many draft titles: "Prometheus (For My Fiftieth Birthday)," "March 1 1967," "March 1 1917 and March 1 1967," "Fifty," "Surviving Fifty," and "Half a Century Gone."[2] These are the first drafts in a direct line of continuity with Lowell's later involvement in the long poem. The final typescript – a close precursor of *Notebook 1967–68*'s five-sonnet section "Half a Century Gone" – consists of 101 lines of free verse grouped into stanzas of irregular length. A rough, anacoluthic piece, it might well suit a division into several smaller, independent yet related units. But sonnets? Perhaps even Lowell would have thought the prospect unlikely.

In the summer of 1967, Lowell began another birthday poem. His daughter Harriet was born on January 4, 1957, and on June 4 she would celebrate what Winnie-the-Pooh calls a half-birthday.

> Half a year, the [sic] a year and a half
> then ten and a half – the pathos of fractions!
> I know nothing about the cycles of the Grreeks [sic],
> but time, even on the hottest, stillest –
> so hot, so still, it stops the clock –
> is fire. And we go on looking for the key,
> the one that must be there,
> because it can't be there –
> a face still friendly to chaos.   (ms.)

This is the earliest draft of "Harriet 1," the opening poem of *Notebook 1967–68*. As yet, all Lowell had was a sketch, a sequence of ideas: the daughter growing up, time, the search for a key. For Lowell, however, the process of revision was invariably one of inspiration and discovery. It is so much his way of making poems happen that some account of Lowell as a revising poet is literally inseparable from a study of the genesis and continuation of the Notebook project. The next version of the Harriet poem is in fourteen lines; after the reference to time as fire it continues:

SUMMER (VACATION) 1967

(To Harriet, born January 4, 1957)

I

DO YOU BELIEVE IN GOD?
Half-a-year, then a year-and-a-half,
then ten-and-a-half---the pathos of your fractions---,
all whirled in the chain-saw bite of whatever divided
the earth by name and number---from a sea-slug,
to a man with a hundred servants, to...then
you gave up guessing... Tonight for the hundredth time,
we circle the village easily slicing
through the fog with our headlights on the ground,
as if we were the first philosopher,
as if we were trying to pick up a car key...
It can't be here, and so it must be there
behind the next crook in the road, or fluff of fog,
and dazzled by our feeble beams---
a face still faithful to chaos.

II

HOME

A fly, blue-black, thumb-thick---so large,
its presence here is an impossibility---
loops through the breathless fecklessness
of your nursery bedroom
with the freedom of a plane
scattering insecticide or the Goths---
one of the mighty, one of the helpless,
it bumbles and bumps against this and that,
making its short life shorter:
the life of a summer fly---
yet to be remembered perhaps with joy,
to be pack-ratted away by you---you
on the dizzying brink of discretion,
and fading into fullfillment.

III

STILL AT HOME

A rankness on the air, and waking
you know you are in my barn,
whose loud aluminum-painted walls
have aged, as they should, to weathered wood.
An unacustomed closeness... No, you remember, a fight
about opening the windows has divided
your father and mother in shut rooms---
you are at home. Heart's-ease and nettles,
we rest from discussing, smoking, drinking,
pils for high blood, three pairs of glasses,
the dread of standing our turn as server at tennis...
Offering you our leathery love, or... I don't know, —
but time, even on a summer night,
when the grown-ups stop dead, will take no leave.

Manuscript page of "Harriet" I–III. Courtesy of Houghton Library, Harvard University.

　　　. . . For the hundredth time
we circle the village, easily cutting
through the fog, with our headlights lowered,
solemnly, as if searching for the key,

> the necessary, impossible key,
> the one that must be there, because it can't be –
> except through some hole, some chink,
> some of [sic] a needle derisively narrowing to nothing:
> a face still friendly to the chaos.   (ms.)

The additional details are welcome. The "we" is no longer general but the poet and his daughter driving around the village; a cure for the child's sleeplessness, perhaps, yet also one more circular movement to follow the "Greek cycles" and the mention of a clock. Similarly, the fog is both damp New England fog and a detail furthering the distance between the poet and "the necessary, impossible key."

In a slightly later version, the opening lines about Greek conceptions of time have disappeared and the sonnet has its first title, "Do You Believe in God?"

> Half a year, then a year and a half,
> then ten and a half – the pathos of these fractions,
> the chainsaw bite of whatever reared the earth
> on name and number – from a seaslug,
> to a man // with a hundred servants, to . . . you gave up guessing
> Tonight for (the tenth year and almost) the hundredth time,
> we circle the village easily slicing
> through the fog. . . .   (ms.)[3]

It is a noteworthy feature of Lowell's revision that phrases that seem casually introduced in early drafts often prefigure the poem's subsequent development. The sonnet's second draft, for example, mentioned the action of "easily cutting" through the fog. In the draft just quoted, this becomes "easily slicing," and new lines describe the contrasting "chainsaw bite" of "whatever reared the earth / on name and number." Later, "reared" would become "squares," setting up a further opposition with the movement "around" the village.

The route toward the published ending of the sonnet is also directed by a search for precise detail. Early versions conclude with the paradox of the key: We are circumscribed by time, but is it possible to move out of that circle, to find some redemptive principle or "key" existing outside time? An uncertainty initially expressed in abstract language increasingly gives way to a far richer ambiguity of particulars. In the final version, it is a car key that is sought but the vehicle's headlights pick up "a face, clock white, still friendly to the earth" (*N 1967–68* 3). Although a symbolic reading is warranted, its likelihood is carefully withdrawn: The face belongs to a nocturnal animal as resolutely denotative as Lowell's more famous skunks. Moreover, it is not the key that is found but something quite unlooked for. As the sonnet links an object of discovery with the act of finding, it seems especially apt that it should also become the commencement point for a long poem that stresses these prospective values.[4]

In revising this sonnet, Lowell's tendency has been to move from the abstract to the particular and to cement connections between these particulars. It would be unwise, however, to dismiss his constant revision as perfectionism, as an indication of how little he departed from New Critical strictures about the well-wrought poem. Revision can also be a mark of attention to process: To rewrite is to uncover what remains to be written. In an unpublished note to *Notebook 1967–68* Lowell acknowledged Berryman's influence with the comment: "I can think of us working in much the same way: the intense shaping of a short section, free yet dependent, in that it pointed towards sections already written and suggested others half intuited" (ms.). In practice, even the casualties of Lowell's "intense shaping" pointed toward the early drafts of other sonnets. The third Harriet sonnet, for example, once ended with lines jettisoned from the earliest drafts of "Harriet 1":

> Greek cycles or nothing twice? I don't know –
> time, even on summer nights,
> when the old stop dead, takes no leave.   (ms.)

The conclusion finally chosen for this poem is embedded in drafts of another early sonnet, "Harriet 2."

> Tossing, you wish to be old, to do nothing
> but type and think, and go to movies . . .
> This instant will be remembered perhaps
> with joy then, pack-ratted away by you – you
> on the dizzying brink of discretion,
> and fading into fulfillment.   (ms.)

"Harriet 2" retains fragments of the third, fourth, and last lines; the remainder is transferred to "Harriet 3." During the entire period of composition, from "Harriet 1" through to the last additions to *History,* Lowell's sonnets would maintain this tendency to generate offshoots.

With the earliest drafts of "Harriet 3," the three sonnets began to take shape as a sequence. Two of the earliest arrangements were:

Summer 1967 (To Harriet)	AGES	
1. "Do You Believe in God?"	1. "The Spin (for Harriet)"	
2. "Home"	2. "Home"	
3. "Still at Home"	3. "In My Barn"	(ms.)

These drafts are easily dated: Harriet's half-birthday and a reference to the Arab–Israeli Six-Day War in the second sonnet both point to early June 1967. Lowell's own birthday poem – the "ur-Half a Century Gone" (henceforth "ur-HCG") – probably dates from March 1967, but it seems certain that he was still at work on this poem in June, the month when the Harriet sonnets were written. The evidence requires some explanation. The worksheets for all the *Notebook* sonnets have been arranged into folders at Harvard's Houghton Library. Almost every sonnet is represented by one or more folders containing successive drafts of that sonnet. But since revision is such a paper-intensive operation, one generally finds that the folder for any one sonnet will include drafts and fragments of other sonnets. The "Summer 1967 (To Harriet)" typescript mentioned earlier has, for example, an excerpt from the "ur-HCG" on its reverse side. Lowell seldom dated drafts, but where connections like these are both numerous and reciprocal they enable us to reconstruct the sequence of composition. While there are many such connections between the "Harriet" and "ur-HCG" worksheets, there is also a deeper convergence between these drafts of *Notebook 1967–68*'s earliest poems. On one side of an early "ur-HCG" draft Lowell typed a curious version of "Ages [i.e., Harriet] 1." It begins, "Half a year, then a year and a half, then *fifty* and a half . . .," and continues entirely in the first person (ms.). The "pathos of these fractions" would seem to have weighed heavily with Lowell that summer; indeed, all three Harriet sonnets share themes and ideas with Lowell's fiftieth-birthday poem. The longer draft's more personal concern with time – "with us no man has outlived his wife" – is echoed in "Harriet 3" where, as Frances Ferguson has noted (21), the poet's aging barn and aging marriage are drawn together in a progrression from "wood" to "weathered wood" to "heartsease and wormwood" (*N 1967–68* 4). The "ur-HCG" generates image after image of detritus as the poet considers the ubiquity of death throughout time. It is a viewpoint adopted again in "Harriet 2," a half-comic sonnet about the death of a blowfly:

> I kill it, and another instant's added
> to the horrifying mortmain of
> ephemera: keys, drift, sea-urchin shells,
> packratted off with joy, the dead fly swept
> under the carpet, wrinkling to fulfillment.   (*N 1967–68* 3)

This "mortmain of ephemera" raises the question of whether anything of meaning or value persists through time. Although "Harriet 1" answered negatively, the qualified optimism of that sonnet's response has no counterpart in Lowell's birthday poem. There, only the fact of death is constant in change; to look back through time is to watch death, "the invincible syllogism / expand from proof to proof / on the unprincipled quicksand" (ms.).

It seems that in starting a fiftieth-birthday poem Lowell found himself engrossed in a subject that demanded, and could sustain in verse, further and further exploration. At first, though, he probably had nothing more ambitious than a short sonnet sequence in mind. Every so often, after completing one or two new sonnets, Lowell would include them in a revised typescript of "Ages," the sequence of sonnets begun in June. One early arrangement adds the sonnets "Fogbound" ("Long Summer 4") and "Winter Harbor" ("Long Summer 14") to the three Harriet poems (*N 1967–68* 6, 11). These five sonnets form a coherent, well-unified whole. They appear to be set on one particular summer's day and are linked by imagery derived from that common setting. Thus, the fog in "Harriet 1" is also the fog of "Harriet 3" and "Fogbound," and in the latter poem, the gulls "with groans like straining rope" seem the very ones whose "exaggerated outcry" punctuated "Harriet 3." The sonnets are by no means interchangeable; not only does each one appear to be set a little later than its predecessor, but in "Harriet 1" and "Winter Harbor" the poet has written a definite opening and a strong conclusion for the sequence. The first sonnet begins with summer and the pathos of a child counting her age in fractions of a year. Other sonnets then look further at aspects of the aging process, and their implicit conclusions are drawn together in a final sonnet where the prospect of the poet's own death is viewed in terms of the onset of winter. The movement is entirely toward closure: from summer to winter, from Harriet's fractions to vast expanses of time encapsulated in ice.

Yet Lowell continued to write sonnets. He "completed" the sequence once more with the inclusion of "Long Summer 8" in a new typescript closed with the date, "Summer 1967." The additional sonnet was inserted between the second and third "Harriet" sonnets – a position that preserves the integrity of the earlier arrangement as the newcomer amplifies the list of ephemera in "Harriet 2." The next typescript of "Ages" included "Long Summer 13" as the sixth of seven sonnets: Once more, the sequence withstood an addition. Later versions of the sequence, however, resemble work in progress rather than drafts of an essentially completed project. Drafts and fragments of other "Long Summer" poems litter the worksheets and, in what seems a rapid expansion, the sequence grew from seven, to ten, to fourteen poems. On the way, Lowell decided to drop "Ages" in favor of "The Long Summer" as a working title. The change represents a subtle but decisive shift in Lowell's subject matter. The concern with time, though still pervasive, is less insistent in the new sonnets. In these, we tend to find the poet looking back through time at the motions of history or at his early life. In "Long Summer 5," for example, Lowell seems inclined to dwell on details and images remembered from the past. The pressing concern with time that had prompted him to begin the sequence was now beginning to act as a wedge opening out panoramas of history and autobiography. In consequence, the draft ceases to record the working out of a thematic movement but becomes dynamic, a coil ready to unspring.

The typescript of fourteen "Long Summer" sonnets is notable for its corrections. Lowell split the sequence into two sections, "Harriet, 1–3" and "Long Summer," and penciled in a new title. He called it "A Year's Notebook." With that alteration the concept of the work at hand changed radically. The draft was now prospective; Lowell had discovered that, contrary to all intentions and expectations, he was already writing a long poem. But what might have prompted that recognition? In *The Armies of the Night,* Norman Mailer reports that Lowell began writing a long poem a few days after the Pentagon demonstrations late in October (278). We will see that politics certainly had a part in the development of the Notebook project, but manuscript evidence suggests that the Notebook idea was formulated sometime earlier at a stage when few other sonnets could have been written. The fourth Harriet sonnet is not mentioned on the typescript altering the sequence to "A Year's Notebook," but since this sonnet was in existence toward the end of September when Lowell wrote his next cluster of sonnets (the section, "Through the Night"), I favor that date as the latest formal embarkation point for the project. During the period June to September, Lowell continued work on other poems besides the "Long Summer" sequence. Since 1966 he had been engaged on a poem marking the death of his friend Randall Jarrell. Another poem, "Those Older," had been started by the time Lowell came to write "Fogbound," the fourth sonnet of the "Ages"/"Long Summer" sequences. And there was his own birthday poem, the "ur-HCG." The decision to keep "A Year's Notebook" may well have coincided with a perception that this material could be drawn together, that it provided a ground against which a long poem might be improvised.

Although the manuscript evidence does not point conclusively to a date, it seems fair to assume that all these longer poems were included as sonnets in the "Notebook" before Lowell ventured much further with the project.[5] It is impossible to say how early Lowell knew what the eventual position of these sonnets was to be in the long poem. But, leaving aside the Jarrell sonnets, it should be understood that (whether in sonnet form or not) the very first parts of Lowell's long poem to be written are found at the beginning, almost exactly in the middle, and at the conclusion of *Notebook 1967–68*. Each of these sections – "Harriet, 1–4"/"Long Summer," "Those Older," and "Half a Century Gone, 1–5" – were responses to identical pressures: Each furthers an inquiry into time and death, each is of vital importance to the structure of *Notebook 1967–68* as a long poem. Lowell had a structure available; 1967 and 1968 would see it fleshed out as a process poem.

III

Following the decision to field the earlier sequence as "A Year's Notebook," Lowell's sonnets began to take a different turn. Not time, but the times, became a focus of attention. In October 1967, on the eve of the march on the Pentagon, Lowell happened to meet Norman Mailer at a party. Naturally, their conversation – as reported by Mailer – involved matters of the profoundest literary and political moment.

> "You know, Norman," said Lowell in his fondest voice, "Elizabeth and I really think you're the finest journalist in America. . . ."
>
> "Well, Cal," said Mailer, . . . "there are days when I think of myself as being the best writer in America."
>
> The effect was equal to walloping a roundhouse right into the heart of an English boxer who has been hitherto right up on his toes. Consternation,

not Britannia, now ruled the waves. . . . "Oh, Norman, oh, certainly," he
said, "I didn't mean to imply, heavens no, it's just I have such *respect* for
good journalism."

"Well, I don't know that I do," said Mailer. "It's much harder to write"
– the next said with a great and false graciousness – "a good poem."

"Yes, of course."

Chuckles. Headmastermanship.

Chuckles. Fellow headmastermanship. (31, 32)

Did the two chuckling headmasters have some inkling of how they would write of
that weekend's events? Mailer, the "journalist," was to write under the grand aegis
of "Historian as Novelist/Novelist as Historian" whereas Lowell would adopt a
humbler, though Mailer-like, role for himself. He became the poet as journalist. His
first dispatch, a two-sonnet poem called "The March," appeared in the *New York
Review of Books* on November 23, 1967. It is set in familiar Lowell territory:

> Under the too white marmoreal Lincoln memorial
> the too tall marmoreal Washington Obelisk,
> gazing into the too long reflecting pool,
> the reddish trees, the withering autumn sky. . . .   (*N 1967–68* 27)

This is the architecture of America's "monotonous sublime" (*NO* 16). If this were
a poem from either of Lowell's two previous collections it might well have continued with a moral interrogation of these monuments. Like the Boston Aquarium
and the statue of Colonel Shaw in "For the Union Dead," the Washington monuments might have served as a locus for one of Lowell's characteristically grim ap-
praisals of American life. But the sonnet declines to press home a moral judgment.
As we read on, we realize that the description of these monuments has located point
of view with the demonstrators: The poet is there among them, on alien, possibly
dangerous ground, and his primary concern is to report what it was like to be there,
to be a person participating in these events. Once under way, for example, the progress of the demonstration is recorded by seven bare nouns in succession: "sped by pho-
tographers, / the notables, the girls . . . fear, glory, chaos, rout . . ." It is as if a news-
cameraman has been caught up in the rush – the camera turns but it is impossible
to linger or even focus on a detail. Then, a recovery: Progress is checked so that facing the camera, as unmovable as the institution they defend, stands "the other army,
the Martian, the ape, the hero, / his new-fangled rifle, his green new steel helmet."

Lowell's aim, as in so many Notebook sonnets, was to capture the immediate instant, to get the experience down on paper, quickly and fresh. In time, this process
of note taking might unfold into a long poem. He would have to count on fate or
chance for his next day's copy but, in 1967–68, there was seldom a shortage of news.
Like the "New Journalists" at work at the time, Lowell was less after hard facts than
a personal sense of "the air." As he said of the thirties, it was "air in which events
were hovering over your shoulder at every point," a period when one's writing

necessarily registered the times (Alvarez, "Robert Lowell" [Aug.] 39). The detached tone and chiseled quatrains of Lowell's last collection, *Near the Ocean,* belonged to an earlier stage of concern over the war. But as Marvell, the presiding genius of that volume would appreciate, it was now "time to leave the books in dust / and oil the unused armours rust" ("An Horatian Ode upon Cromwell's Return to Ireland"). That "air" of the late sixties valued the present moment: It demanded – and so often got – experiments with provisional form.

But that did not mean *Notebook 1967–68* would be a diary of sonnets. The project would ultimately rely on a diarylike entering of new material, but the sonnets, as they came to be written, were likely to suggest modes of arrangement that did not necessarily follow the actual sequence of composition. If the "Notebook" was to work as a process poem, these methods of organization would respond to the shifting requirements of a long poem written over a period of time.

In *Notebook 1967–68*, Lowell's pair of sonnets on the Pentagon march are part of the larger "October and November" section. The title seems to promise a holdall, but the six sonnets form a well-unified whole. In the second sonnet Lowell recalls, on a visit to Caracas, driving "through another of our cities without a center . . . / past the 20-foot neon sign / for *Coppertone* on a church, past the population / earning $700 per capita / . . . and on to the White House / of El Presidente Leoni . . ." (26). It would be difficult to miss the irony of his concluding remark: "This house, this pioneer democracy, built / on foundations, not of rock, but blood as hard as rock" (26). Yet the comment assumes more than the preceding twelve lines as its province – its application is sectionwide. The sonnet "Charles Russell Lowell: 1835–1864," for example, concerns an ancestor who was killed in the American Civil War. While that blood-"relationship" affirms an imperative behind Lowell's Vietnam–South American protest, a sonnet on the death of Che Guevara points to another connection between blood spilled and what is called the defense of democracy. Thus, the section's intersecting details and thematic consistency grant "October and November" a particular coherence over and above that of the poem at large. However, this coherence is also dependent on Lowell's having incorporated only six of the thirty or so sonnets actually written during October and November into that section. The arrangement postdates the composition of the sonnets themselves. Although Lowell tended to write the earlier sonnets in groups, he seldom wrote with a clearcut sectional arrangement in mind: In general, only the final one or two drafts of a particular sonnet is associated with a section heading. Neither did he work out this pattern of organization as a final stage in the composition of the poem. He once put forward an eccentric theory about Shakespeare's sonnets: The couplets, he thought, might well have been written "in a single dashing afternoon" (Hamilton, "Conversation" 14). The division of *Notebook 1967–68* into a number of sections happened not on one but on a number of dashing afternoons. In part, it was a way of clearing the deck, of taking stock of what had been produced so far; in part, it was one of the principal ways he structured the poem as he wrote it.

Lowell's aim, as he said, was to capture the immediate instant, to describe private moments and public events as they happened. A series of sonnets recording immediate instants would naturally construct a durational time scheme as a by-product of composition. In *Notebook 1967–68*, the passage of time is so heavily marked by reference to seasonal change and the shifting concerns of national life that the order of sonnets seems to duplicate an original sequence of composition. But the achieved time scheme is not entirely authentic. Of the sonnets in the 1967 area of the poem (i.e., from "Harriet, 1–4" to "Christmas and New Year" inclusive), I estimate that some seventy-one were actually written during that time.[6] *Notebook 1967–68*, however, includes twenty-five additional sonnets at the same point in the poem; thus, more than a fifth of the sonnets apparently written in 1967 were composed later in 1968 and 1969.[7] Even so, a majority of sonnets are actually in accord with the poem's durational time scheme. Of all the sonnets written during 1967, only those belonging to "Those Older" and "Half a Century Gone" have been placed in later sections of the poem. Once a sonnet was assigned a place in the developing poem, it tended to keep that position. But the arrangement produced was not fixed – Lowell could always make adjustments by adding new sonnets. "Autumn in the Abstract," for example, was written during the autumn of 1968 but, given its position in the poem, it appears to belong to autumn 1967. Since the addition of four sonnets under that section title strengthens the poem's formal time scheme, it contributes to the illusion that we are following a natural sequence of composition. One addition has quite the opposite effect. "Munich 1938" follows two sonnets on Randall Jarrell and precedes the "October and November" section. The sonnet is clearly well placed: No doubt it seemed apt to follow the Jarrell sonnets with one recalling John Crowe Ransom at Kenyon College; apt, also, to slot "Munich 1938" in before "October and November" as if marking an anniversary of that conference. However, Lowell has published the date of that sonnet – August 22, 1968 – and destroyed an otherwise seamless addition. It is neither the date of the conference nor the date of Ransom's eightieth birthday; there is no apparent reason for the acknowledgment. But, as we shall see, the contours of this process poem actively demand some subversion of the poem's durational time scheme.

The addition of new sonnets had a striking effect on the sectional arrangement of this area of the poem. Sonnets dating from 1967 are usually found in groups of three or more and tend, like "October and November," to cohere strongly as units. The experience of reading one such group after another is radically unlike reading the first ninety-six sonnets of *Notebook 1967–68*. There the presence of additional sonnets has generally subverted the sectional integrity of those written in 1967. "My Grandfather," for example, is a one-sonnet section inserted between two larger, relatively well unified groups, "The Charles River" and "Names." The new poem is an eye-and-hook sonnet. Because it deals with Lowell's grandfather, it offers a link back to the second and third sonnets in "The Charles River" sequence, while a concern with portraiture and a reference to Cato proffer hooks to the "Names" section. The sonnet "For Mary McCarthy," on the other hand, disrupts an otherwise natural transition.

This poem, together with several of the "Dream" sonnets, adds a jagged edge to what was once a smooth, gradually widening meditation on time extending from "Harriet, 1–4" to "Through the Night, 1–7." Lowell also added sonnets to existing sections. "Christmas and New Year" was originally written as a tightly knit group of four poems: "Snake," "Christmas Tree," "Descendant," and "Bird." The inclusion of four extra sonnets undermines the section as a well-ordered whole; what was once a coherent unit becomes a unit that balances coherence with disjunction. As in my previous examples, the adjustment is functional. Had he wished, Lowell could have added these sonnets to others more recently written. Instead, he disguised the natural sequence of composition and altered the original contours of *Notebook 1967–68* by placing these sonnets among those written earlier in 1967. With each adjustment, he subordinated the individual sonnet or section to a larger principle of organization, that of the one poem.

Over the first five or six months of composition Lowell would have been mindful of two problems. He needed to build a momentum that, unwinding, would see the project through to its conclusion. Yet as he had written relatively few sonnets he would have been uncertain how well or exactly in what way *Notebook 1967–68* was continuing to take shape as a long poem. Later he could afford to relax but, throughout 1967, he would probably have been cautious, inclined to favor tight areas of organization, to connect sonnet to sonnet rather than add them piecemeal to the pile. Less attentive procedures risked stagnation or the discovery that he had spent months pursuing a fruitless line of development.[8] It was necessary, then, in reviewing this area of the poem, to add sonnets and so ease the overly insistent section divisions and punctuate the opening meditation on time. In this way, Lowell gave the poem a looser pattern of unfolding consistent with his later, more informed, overview of the poem.

IV

Sometime in September or October 1968, twelve or more months after beginning "A Year's Notebook," Lowell drafted a table of contents for the work so far produced. Although the list is eighty-three sonnets short of *Notebook 1967–68*'s total, Lowell had, in a sense, finished the poem. He had written an "Afterthought" and had decided how the poem was to end. The section heading, "Circles," defines the ending strategy and the overall curvature of the poem itself. *Notebook 1967–68* would end as it had begun, with summer, with thoughts on time and death.[9] "Obit," the final sonnet, is both outside and congruent with this movement. Undated, it marks the occasion of its author's death with the following testament:

> In the end, every hypochondriac is his own prophet.
> Before the final coming to rest, comes rest
> of all transcendence in a mode of being, stopping
> all becoming. I'm for and with myself in my otherness,

in the eternal return of earth's fairer children,
the lily, the rose, the sun on dusk and brick. . . .

(*N 1967–68* 156)

In another sonnet, "Reading Myself," Lowell referred to his work in progress as "this open book . . . my open coffin" (*N 1967–68* 128). "Obit" gives that book the firmest of conclusions while allowing it to remain open. The lines just quoted constitute a gestural avoidance of closure but they also leave the structure of the work elastic. Until the coffin lid shuts, until the obituary finds a date, the poem has not come to rest; it is open to the inclusion of further sonnets. But, exactly as in Berryman's *Dream Songs,* it is the middle of the poem that is extendable; any additional sonnet must be placed before this final poem. As Lowell wrote in "Afterthought": "The time is a summer, an autumn, a winter, a spring, another summer; here the poem ends, except for turned-back bits of fall and winter 1968" (*N 1967–68* 159). Thus, we might consider the subversive dating of "Munich 1938" and other sonnets as a further announcement drawing attention to these necessary "turned-back bits."

Since the project was due for completion, any differences between the draft table of contents and the published version are likely to reflect the pressure of new material as much as a need to adjust some area of the poem. After a year of writing, Lowell had become so accustomed to writing sonnets he found it hard to stop writing them. His attitude toward the sectional organization of sonnets changed with this developing ease of production. Later sections tend to be larger and more diffuse than those written in 1967. "Circles," for example, seems open to the inclusion of sonnets on almost any subject; its component poems do not form a subentity but are read only as part of the long poem. Twenty-five sonnets were listed under this heading in the first draft table of contents. Although the section occurs at a point in the poem most open to the addition of new sonnets, if Lowell was to include many more he would risk overstating the progression from the early, relatively tight arrangement of sonnets to the relatively loose and extendable sections found later in the poem. This was a natural feature of composition and he wished to preserve it, to balance one area of the poem against the other without abandoning the principle of sectional arrangement altogether. As he rarely discarded sonnets – on the whole, everything written was judged relevant – there was only one solution. As Lowell continued to write sonnets, what was once one section became three: "Circles," "The Races," and "Summer." Over several drafts, four sonnets were shunted from "Circles" to "Summer" before reaching their final destination in "The Races."

These shifts from section to section were not characteristic of earlier stages in the poem's composition. The policy of sectional arrangement answered several problems associated with writing a long poem in sonnet form but, after a year of writing sonnets, the conditions that prompted this method of organization had virtually disappeared. Back in 1967, Lowell sometimes could not place all he wanted to say within fourteen lines and so wrote pairs or triplets of sonnets. Now, rather as a film director might learn to organize his or her field of vision in terms of a rectangular screen,

Lowell had developed an instinct for blocking out his material in terms of a fourteen-line unit. Earlier on, Lowell needed subpatterns of organization. Without them, a process of accretion would have built a thicket of sonnets at precisely that point when he most needed a clear sense of where the poem was coming from and where, with that impetus, it was headed. By October 1968, Lowell had a fairly detailed overview of the poem. He believed the project was nearing completion and rather than lead the poem toward a development out of the "Notebook of A Year," he preferred to stay within the original framework. It made sense to do so because, in October 1968, that framework could still withstand the addition of new sonnets. In the regrouping of "Circles," Lowell was able to keep the principle of sectional arrangement intact simply by forming new sections. This method had limits. In theory, he could continue to follow the pattern of seasonal change by introducing another autumn section, another winter section, and so on. His carefully worked-out ending strategy, however, was aided by the symmetry of beginning and closing with a summer. Moreover, he did not expect to be writing the poem for much longer. But far from proving a hindrance, Lowell's earlier use of a durational time scheme actually helped him place these sonnets that, like it or not, he found himself writing.

April and May, for example, were busy months for Lowell. Six weeks of that time he was on the campaign trail with Eugene McCarthy so it is not surprising that, in the first draft table of contents, the April–May sections are represented by only fifteen sonnets. It was an area ripe for expansion, and, in successive drafts, it doubled and tripled in size, new sections being added as necessary. One annotation seems especially symptomatic: After penciling in two additions to the "April" section, Lowell drew a line underneath the enlarged list of sonnets and wrote, in big capital letters, "STOP!" The note went unheeded. Lowell kept writing sonnets, and a subsequent annotation indicates that four sonnets were to be withdrawn and placed with a new group, "Poetry and Power."

This section – it appears as "Power" in *Notebook 1967–68* – was one of the last to be written. Its thumbnail sketches of "the powerful" also represent the type of sonnet that sits least comfortably in a poem that needs to value immediacy, needs to align thoughts on time with the passage of time in order to work as a process poem. Indeed, Lowell's later decision to select and republish a chronological sequence of these sonnets under the title "Heroes" would initiate the eventual recasting of *Notebook* as *History*. With Lowell's developing interest in writing the sonnet-portrait we can locate a third force that, along with the growing redundancy of sectional arrangement and the durational time scheme, urged a radical remodification of the original format. But *Notebook 1967–68*, published at last in May 1969, was able to make use of these pressures. As a process poem, its logic of development required setting impulses toward order against the circumvention of order.

The compositional history of a process poem will inform a reading of the poem so produced. In some respects, of course, *Notebook 1967–68* is read as if it had been written as a process poem: The poet seems to have recorded the drift of life but he has relied heavily on more artificial forms of arrangement to produce "one poem, jagged in pattern" (*N 1967–68* 159). Even so, these strategies and devices were always sensitive to the present needs of the poem, and an account of how *Notebook 1967–68* came to be written at least casts a silhouette of the achieved jagged pattern. The volume begins with a long meditation on time that diffuses to a point where other subjects – the times, marriage, history, literature, autobiography, writing the poem, etc. – are foregrounded. But that concern over time never quite disappears. In any lengthy section we will read one or two sonnets anchoring these wider concerns to Lowell's ongoing pursuit of what it means to exist in time. Halfway through the poem, in the sections "My Death" and "Those Older," these issues return to the center so that, momentum recovered, the poem may fan out once more until the closing sections. Accompanying this movement, we notice that an early tendency to write well-defined sections dissolves to a point where sectional arrangement itself is arbitrary – a silhouetted feature of the poem representing both its inclination to sprawl and its ability to encompass. The volume formally locates itself within the chronology of its own composition. Lowell's poem does, as he claimed, "roll with the seasons" (*N 1967–68* 159): Dates, section headings, details of seasonal change insistently record the passage of time from summer through to summer. Although the poem concludes with its author's undated obituary sonnet, the inclusion of sonnets delimiting the poem's formal time scheme reaffirms its processive nature. Finished but unfinished, *Notebook 1967–68* invites the presence of further sonnets.

V

Notebook, the poem's third and much expanded edition, took up that invitation. Ninety-nine new sonnets were added: "I couldn't stop writing," explained Lowell, "and have handled my published book as if it were manuscript" (*N* 264). The new poems, he wrote, were "not placed as a single section or epilogue. They were scattered where they caught, intended to fulflesh my poem, not sprawl into chronicle" (*N* 264). But the original framework was incapable of sustaining quite so massive an enlargement. Although the poem's major structures had approached redundancy during the composition of that earlier volume, Lowell had been able to field the resulting contradictions as an intrinsic aspect of the poem's history in process. That option could not be extended. The poem had reached a point where the various structures that had once facilitated composition were now swamped by the sonnets produced. Although Lowell painstakingly preserved a time scheme and the principles of sectional arrangement, he could not effectively maintain *Notebook 1967–68*'s ongoing meditation on time in the new *Notebook*. A core of sonnets had once informed the movement of the poem as a whole; under the weight of addition, these sonnets became local events in the poem and engaged only like sonnets. *Notebook* claims an organic development but the only structures it reveals coincide with accidentals of process – a time scheme, a pattern of sectional arrangement. The poem does not so much "roll with the seasons" as resemble a circular clothesline on which Lowell has continued to pin laundry. But *Notebook* is not an unqualified failure. Although the volume may not work as a process poem, it perhaps had the sort of utility we more commonly associate with draft tables of contents or other provisional forms of arrangement. As a way of trying the poem out, *Notebook* at least demonstrated that Lowell's earlier schemes had outlived their usefulness, that new action had to be taken.

A prefatory "Note" to *History* states: "My old title, *Notebook,* was more accurate than I wished, i.e. the composition was jumbled. I hope this jumble or jungle is cleared – that I have cut the waste marble from the figure" (*H* 9). The contents of *Notebook,* which Lowell had been revising ever since publication, were divided between two volumes, *History* and *For Lizzie and Harriet.*[10] The dispersal occurred largely according to subject matter yet the two "new" long poems are marked by much deeper divisions. In *For Lizzie and Harriet* one finds, almost intact, the discarded exoskeleton of *Notebook.* As a series, *For Lizzie and Harriet* is a *Notebook* pared back to its earliest processive structures. From summer section through to summer section, the sonnets retain an ongoing meditation on time. In *History,* however, Lowell has found another way to formulate series.

History is not a process poem since it eschews the organicist structures on which that method is based. In *History,* the sonnets – or sonnet titles since time is often stacked "ply on ply" in an individual sonnet – are arranged in rough chronological order yet they do not constitute a chronological series. Unlike the *Notebooks* or *For Lizzie and Harriet, History* does not rely on an exterior line of events, such as a real or supposed time of writing, to cohere as a long poem. *History*'s chronological order is indexical – more like the alphabetical order of a telephone directory than the organic shapefulness of a process poem. This leads to a further distinction between *History* and Lowell's other long poems. Our reading of the *Notebooks* and *For Lizzie and Harriet* is bound to be cued by section headings and the season-to-season chronologies of the poems at large. It is always possible, therefore, to say who speaks in any particular sonnet. We come to identify the speaking voice of the process poem with "Robert Lowell," with a sensibility placed on record over a period of time. But *History* does away with that whole elaborate fiction. There are no section headings like "April" or "Midwinter," and very few references to the time of writing survive as such in the new volume. Furthermore, Lowell's massive revision – only one sonnet, "The March 1," makes the journey from *Notebook* to *History* unchanged – is not just a matter of improving the quality of individual sonnets. The target of revision is very often some sort of deictic marker; by altering a pronoun or demonstrative here, a tense or set of quotation marks there, Lowell has undermined the various cues that direct a reader toward a univocal source for the utterance. As *Notebook* became *History,* the pattern of revision radically altered the extent to which that earlier figure of narrative authority could be produced in the text.

As a long poem, *History* is a series that no longer depends on the continuities occa-sioned by a given subject writing over a period of time. Perhaps a more positive parallel for the method and structure of *History* can be found in what Foucault, echo-ing Nietzsche, describes as genealogy (see Foucault, *Language* 139–64). A genealogy, for Foucault, is a critical examination of patterns of descent and emergence, a method of thinking and writing about history which relates a poststructuralist understand-ing of textuality, subjectivity, and the formation of historical series to questions of power. *History* invites exploration in all these areas. First, as a study of descent, *His-tory* is like a family tree in which a genealogy of "the poet," of the person of "power-ful vision," traces tyrants as well as artists as ancestral types. As Foucault suggests, this form of genealogy might well parody the uses to which traditional history is put (*Language* 160–64). Lowell, for example, is writing about "great men of history" but they do not stand as monumental figures representing high points or low points in the onward march of civilization; rather, they tend to illustrate how closely "in-stinct, passion, the inquisitor's devotion, cruel subtlety and malice" are implicated in a "will to knowledge," which is also a will to power (*Language* 162). Where a traditional history would invite us to identify with great figures from the past, Lowell's lineup of the powerful functions as a kind of anti-identity parade.[11] An author ought to be directing the lineup but "he" so often appears inside the proces-sion, there can be no separating out of identities. Even in the final, more autobio-graphical, sections of the poem, the text forms "Robert Lowell" less as a secure speaking subject than as the shiftiest character in that parade.

I have already suggested that the pattern of revision is partly responsible for the displacement of a secure speaking subject. While Lowell's revision exemplifies a sense of textuality that is prepared to forget the motives and intentions of prior composi-tional occasions, a new title poem, added after most of the revision had been com-pleted, acknowledged how thoroughly the formation of a speaking subject had been compromised.[12] It is as if "Robert Lowell," the figure of narrative authority in the *Notebooks,* could be reformed only as a shell, as the emblematic skull of the poem's opening sonnet. When "History" admits a first-person pronoun – "two holes, two holes, / my eyes, my mouth, between them a skull's no-nose" – the emphasis is pre-cisely on what is not there in a skull (*H* 24). These are gaps and holes, an interstitial presence doubling as lack, as absence. We cannot look to the presence of a speaking subject "behind" the words of this sonnet. As a displaced or deconstructed figure of narrative authority, the skull both signifies the lack of presence and compensates for that lack by coupling absence with presence. Neither evidently there nor evidently not there, the "Robert Lowell" of the *Notebooks* has been interred in a text aware of its status as writing.[13]

I have said that Lowell came late to the long poem, that he took on an approach toward writing the long poem that his contemporaries had already developed. Al-though *Notebook 1967–68* is a process poem, my account of its compositional history has stressed the artificiality of its achieved processive structures. Although all process poems make concessions toward artifice, few make so many as *Notebook 1967–68*. The structure of *Dream Songs,* for example, centers on the unfolding of a personality: Briefly, a limited minstrel persona dramatically establishes Henry as a persona who in turn allows a further complex to emerge, Henry-as-Berryman. The shifts, moreover, are stylistically marked: in *77 Dream Songs* Berryman invents idioms for Henry, in *His Toy, His Dream, His Rest* he finds an idiom for Henry as himself. The development comes to rest as the Henry complex assumes another more limited role; Henry is the author of the dream songs so that, in a final song, poet-character and poet-person take leave of each other. In comparison, Lowell's guiding structure linking thoughts on time with the passage of time must seem an easy organicism. It is as if *Notebook 1967–68* represents a formalist's commitment to the process poem rather than a method of composition that has subverted that allegiance. In this respect, *Notebook 1967–68* would seem to have even less in common with book-length poems written by a younger generation of poets. But although volumes like Creeley's *A Day Book* and Dorn's *Slinger* would certainly offer a more thoroughgoing application of a process aesthetic, their position vis-à-vis the late modern long poem may well be in keeping with Lowell's. Dorn's poem, for example, reworks the process poem method not as epic but as mock-epic; Creeley's sense of ambition and scale is domestic rather than epic. In the opening pages of *A Day Book* (1972), Creeley considers: "Some sense obviously of when does the story start, or more, what point the going on and on. I can do that, i.e., know it can be an exercise I simply continue till I'm altogether bored with it, or have to assume it can't come to more than such boredom." *Notebook 1967–68* is like the "exercise" Creeley knew he could write and wanted not to write. Like Dorn's mock-epic and Creeley's "domestication" of the long poem, Lowell's Notebook volumes also signal the calcification of a late modern method of writing the long poem.

Yet although the process poem method was available to Lowell as a convention, the manner in which that convention was appropriated also points a way toward *History.* I have suggested that *History* is a genealogy, a form of epic that owes little to the example of Lowell's late or postmodern contemporaries in America, but which shares some of the concerns of a poststructuralist writer like Michel Foucault. It may well be significant that, unlike Olson or Ginsberg say, Lowell placed little emphasis on the breath, on the dynamics of oral performance. Or that, unlike Berryman, Lowell did not take the unfolding of a personality as the primary goal of a process poem. Instead, the production of a speaking subject in the Notebook volumes depended more on formal devices than organic structures of consciousness mapping; the "kinetics" of Lowell's long poems arose out of writing, out of a process of constant revision rather than a process more committed to speech as a model. Even so, writing in the two Notebooks ought to have been transparent, the sonnets ought to have been a series of frames that would hold and restore a plenitude of vanished moments. But Lowell's excessive reliance on artificial and redundant methods of organizing a serial long poem would not allow *Notebook* to be read in that way. The composition was "jumbled"; a narrative contract could not be drawn correctly. Had Lowell been less of a formalist he might never have written himself into a corner with *Notebook*. But had he subscribed more wholeheartedly to a process aesthetic, he might never have had to question the sovereignty of a speaking subject, never have had the opportunity to revalue his sonnets as *writing*. It was as a revising poet that Lowell began his involvement with the long poem. It was a knowledge gained from that constant rewriting, most of all, that permitted Lowell to discard an entire process poem convention along with the particular structures of the Notebooks.

NOTES

1 I have run together responses to several questions put to Lowell by Hamilton.

2 Mss., the Robert Lowell Papers, Houghton Library, Harvard University, Cambridge, Mass. All manuscripts cited belong to this collection and appear by permission of the Houghton Library and the Lowell estate.

3 The reproduction of this draft incorporates Lowell's penciled corrections and additions to the typescript.

4 See Stephen Yenser, *Circle to Circle: The Poetry of Robert Lowell* 288. I am indebted to Yenser's reading of this poem.

5 The textual evidence hinges on drafts of the Jarrell poem. We know that Lowell wrote drafts of "Harriet 4" soon after the decision to make the sequence "A Year's Notebook." An early draft of the sonnet was written on the second page of the Jarrell poem. But by late September or early October, when Lowell was at work on "Through the Night," the Jarrell poem was almost certainly in sonnet form. Second, two separate drafts of the Jarrell sonnets appear on the same sheets as drafts of one of the "Half A Century Gone" sonnets, suggesting that both longer poems were reduced to sonnet form at much the same time. It should be noted, however, that the worksheets lose sight of "Those Older" and that the links between the other various mss. are by no means so numerous they constitute proof. However, if we suppose that Lowell may have wanted to clear his desk of half-completed work before progressing further into the new project, the inclusion of those longer poems as sonnets would have been an attractive solution to the problem.

6 This total is approximate since it is subject to the previously described limitations of a method that examines the coexistence of drafts through various worksheets. Ian Hamilton provides independent (though undocumented) confirmation: "By Christmas, 1967, he had written over seventy such pieces [i.e., sonnets]" (*Robert Lowell* 368).

7 The sonnets written later are: "Long Summer 12"; "For Mary McCarthy"; "Dream of the Fair Women"; "Five Dreams, (1–5)"; "The Muse, (1–2)"; "Munich 1938"; "Autumn in the Abstract, (1–4)"; "Symbols 4, 5, & 6"; "The Heavenly Rain"; "My Grandfather"; "The Literary Life, A Scrapbook"; and "Christmas and New Year 3, 4, 5 & 6."

8 As, for example, Charles Olson discovered in September 1953 when he wrote to Cid Corman that his process poem "had got off its proper track" (cited in *Olson Journal* no. 6:1).

9 For an account of circular organization and motifs in *Notebook 1967–68* (and Lowell's work generally), see Yenser 273–97.

10 For an account of how *Notebook* was revised and the production of the three following volumes, see Hamilton, *Robert Lowell* 408–9, 419–27. I am also indebted to Frank Bidart, who explained the genesis of *History* to me in an interview, November 1981.

11 Cf. "No longer the identification of our faint individuality with the solid identities of the past, but our 'unrealization' through the excessive choice of identities" (Foucault, *Language* 161).

12 Frank Bidart has informed me that "History" was written while Lowell was examining proofs for the soon-to-be-published volume – that is why it appears with its companion, "Man and Woman," on a verso the publishers planned to leave blank.

13 Cf. Derrida's deconstruction of the "supplement" in texts by Rousseau in ". . . That Dangerous Supplement . . ." (*Of Grammatology* 141–64).

8

Illegible Lowell (The Late Volumes)

CALVIN BEDIENT

Lowell in the Contact Zone

If Robert Lowell is closer to us than T. S. Eliot, Pound, Yeats, Wallace Stevens, or even cautious Robert Frost; if he is the most inexhaustible of our recent poets, it is partly because he deliberately placed himself in the daily sphere that M. M. Bakhtin, in his essay "Discourse in the Novel," called "the contact zone," with whatever consequent "weakening and degradation of the capacity to generate metaphors," so as to create a discourse "more concrete, more filled with everyday elements" (345). Yet what a resistance to the task! What a grumbling technique! The indignity of opening the poetic gates to (the word as heavy as a convoy of trucks) heteroglossia! Beginning with *Notebook 1967–68*, Lowell found himself writing a poetry craw-crammed with quotation, with what Eugene McCarthy and Bobby Kennedy had said, and Irving Howe, and Mary McCarthy, not to mention Randall Jarrell, Pound, Frost, Tate, Ford Madox Ford, Jean Stafford, Caroline Blackwood, Harriet and Lizzie – above all, Lizzie.

That Lowell was both personally and poetically outrageous enough to compose whole poems from Elizabeth Hardwick's private letters to him may suggest a downright eagerness to violate what Bakhtin calls the "unitary and indisputable discourse" of poetry (286); but Hardwick's words enter Lowell's volumes as depicted things, like the words of a character in an epistolary novel (Lowell's shamefaced "plot"), and I think Lowell begrudged every line lost to the language of others, even Hardwick's. How could this competition of discourses within the echoing walls of his work fail to upset his balance, muddy his sense of himself? Should "the language of the poet [not be] *his* language," and should he not be "utterly immersed in it, inseparable from it," making use "of each form, each word . . . as a pure and direct expression of his own intention" (Bakhtin 285)? Forced into the contact zone of the quoted "outside" of language and of unresolved contemporaneity by his contradictory project – that of a poetic notebook – Lowell remained famished for what was "virginal" and still "unuttered" (Bakhtin 278): the province of the poetic image. He wrote like one wakened by human voices[1] and beginning to drown.

The resulting hit-and-miss accuracy, the slickness, and the slapdash, indifferent writing may have been "spontaneous" but lacked his special wild genius (strong medicine though the latter was). Journal keeper he may have appointed himself, but each line seemed to want to start up from the desk and abandon the project, whether for silence or for an absolute poetic authority. If Lowell half wished to find the actual day still amazingly here, it was to be "like lightning on an open field" (*DBD* 53), and lightning is mercifully quick, spitting its relationship. "A nihilist," Lowell famously said, "has to live in the world as is," but he added, with deadpan sabotage, "gazing the impassable summit to rubble" (*H* 193). For Lowell, to enter into mere "reality" was to pulverize it. The caged bear all but wrecked the cage.

In *Robert Lowell: Nihilist as Hero*, Vereen Bell skillfully extracts a Lowell for whom "'grace' and 'accuracy' (an accurate rendering of the world) may turn out to be the same after all" (232). But "accuracy" is not a word I would naturally associate with Lowell – with any part of his poetic operation. When Lowell says "But we must notice – / we are designed for the moment" (*DBD* 118), it is partly protest and only makes one reflect on how ill-designed he himself was for the moment – how distracted, miserable, restive. "These days," he says in the same piece, "of only poems and depression – / what can I do with them? Will they help me to notice / what I cannot bear to look at?" Finding himself "elbow to elbow on the rush-hour train," he nonetheless writes "on the back of a letter, / as if alone":

> "When the trees close branches and redden,
> their winter skeletons are hard to find –"

What he wants is not to notice, not to be kept from the skeleton of the incurable. Accordingly, his reaction to spring is fey: "Is this what you call a blossom?"

For Lowell to seek the "grace of accuracy" was to work against the grain. In any case, he seemed to go about it the wrong way, with whomps from his incorrigibly savage plane, startling the air with flying chips. To apply what he wrote in "Jean Stafford, a Letter" (*DBD* 29), "[He] pretended [his] impatience was concision." While appearing to settle down like a husband of Accuracy, in metonymic fidelity, Lowell nonetheless undermined the arrangement with nights out and with daily complaints of "misalliance" (*DBD* 127). His graceless *in*accuracies speak of the boredom of having to restrict memory, his eye, his genius for glancing organization, his heated brain, to something so everyday as "photographic" fact and to thoughts arranged like knives and forks around servings of description. In his pronouncements about his fourteeners, Lowell played the model husband: "I had a chance such as I had never had before, or probably will again," he said in "After Enjoying Six or Seven Essays on Me," "to snatch up and verse the marvelous varieties of the moment" (114). Ian Hamilton, in *Robert Lowell: A Biography*, quotes Frank Bidart on "the aesthetic of *Notebook*": that art "be . . . more connected to fleeting feelings, insights, perceptions, marginal half-thoughts." But, notes Bidart, "he was not . . . happy with that aesthetic. And also he was . . . not happy with the writing" (420).

That he was not happy with the aesthetic is plain from the poems, which sweat out their confinement to snapshot rapidity and rectilinear form. Indeed, they sweat everything. Much of the writing is feverish. Take the temperature of some of the aphorisms ("A false calm is the best calm"; *DBD* 97) or similes ("You lie in my insomniac arms, / as if you drank sleep like coffee"; *DBD* 96) and you find that they cannot be in their right mind. His description is all daubs, a virtuosic impatience. "A border of thistles hedges the drive," he writes in "Milgate" (*DBD* 63) – then adds, after a semicolon, "children dart like minnows." This jars like a mixed metaphor; the semicolon lacks padding. "Like minnows" leaps ahead to "troutbrook" in the next line: "They dangle / over the warm, reedy troutbrook." But by that point the children are dangling, not darting. The description is all live wire, snapping and dancing to a wild rhythm of its own. Often it is covertly metaphoric, the images like a mind troubled by something unconscious. "Shifting Colors" (*DBD* 119) speaks of "universal consolatory / description without significance, / transcribed verbatim by my eye," but what it describes is Lowell's despair of breaking free from depression ("ducks splash deceptively like fish; / fish break water with the wings of a bird to escape") and his static rage ("A hissing goose sways in stationary anger"; "an ageless big white horse, / slightly discolored by dirt . . . / unmoving"). Lowell summarizes: ". . . nature is sundrunk with sex"; on the contrary, the ducks, fish, horse, goose, and so on seem acutely constricted. The Eros in Lowell looks out on the natural world with blind envy; but, trussed-up, small and "ageless" as an eternal, dirt-discolored boy, it sees its own unexamined torment.

Similarly, Lowell's lines and stanzas have to each other a symptomatic, not a logical, relation. The celebrated "moment" often proves a conceptually centerless whirl in which past and present, Lowell and something other, object and metonymically dead-adjacent object, wonder to find themselves in the same world, the same poem. (If this is no less true of *Day by Day*, at least its short stanzas often have the saving lightness of skipped stones.) Some of the disjointedness aspires to leap from helter-skelter metonymy to montage trope; and at times it does. The rest seems to concede that the "year runs out in the movies" anyway (*H* 207). If time reels off into oblivion, why not throw poetry to the dogs of metonym? The conflict, relentless and even for the reader exhausting, resulted in verse that seems to lack love for what it says – to say it quickly and hurry on.

Lowell virtually created a new species of poetry, poetry-on-the-run. Brilliance is passed on to us like a hot potato. The first line of "Fever" (*H* 166), "Desultory, sour commercial September," hurls three unexpected modifiers at September, and the effect is both energetic and bewildering – bewildering, that is, if you stop to ask whether only a certain September is meant, and whether the month itself is desultory and sour, or only the poet during that month, and whether September is more or less commercial than other months. Again, in the second line, "lies like a mustard plaster on the back," the simile of the mustard plaster passes only if you pass by it, not wondering if it is relevant that a mustard plaster is a cure. "Pavlov's dogs, when tortured, turned neurotics. . . .": This line, the third, jostles you to notice what the first two lines are hinting, yet tries to appear, at the same time, offhand. Nor do matters improve with the next two lines: "If I see something unbelievable in the city, / it is the woman shopper out in war-paint –." The stridency of "something unbelievable in the city" is inversely matched by the anticlimactic triteness of "the woman shopper out in war-paint."

After a brilliant line, "the druggist smiles etherealized in glass" (the *l*'s help make this druggist seem silly in his benign detachment from the tortured in the street), the poem goes on to reveal just how ill the speaker himself is:

> Sometimes, my mind is a rocked and dangerous bell;
> I climb the spiral stairs to my own music,
> each step more poignantly oracular,
> something inhuman always rising in me –
> a friend drops in the street and no one stirs.

The selfishness of that oracular "rising" as "a friend drops" unaided is faced straight on, humanly and helplessly. Lowell's Bartlebean *would prefer not* – his gape holes and throwaway similes – emerges as the reverse side of his manic *would prefer to be God*. Yet this God does not write English: "Even if I should indiscreetly write / the perfect sentence, it isn't English – / I go to bed Lord Byron, and wake up bald." So the verse rocks between *would prefer not* and *but must*, is neither Lord Byron nor bald, neither silent nor a dangerous music. It is speech-harsh, brilliantly blurty.

A marveling immediacy? On the contrary, the ideology that reigns in Lowell's late volumes, dully surviving every erotic shudder, is the one Georg Lukács, misled by taking Kafka as a model, ascribed to literary modernism: despair of history, the reduction of experience to the static and sensational, the solitary and asocial – to "what people were to feel in the air raid shelters," in words Lukács quotes from Hanns Eisler (37). This ideology – which in fact describes what is now called Postmodernism[2] – shades from the stunning reversal of trope in "if we see a light at the end of the tunnel, / it's the light of an oncoming train" (*DBD* 31) to the sad characterization of the present as "the infection / of things gone" (*DBD* 57) and on to the pat negativism of

> . . . No sound; no talk;
> dead matches nicked the water and expired
> in target-circles of inverted sky,
> nature's looking-glass . . . a little cold!
> Our day was cold and short, love, and its sun
> numb as the red carp, twenty inches long,
> panting, a weak old dog, below a smashed
> oar floating from the musty dock. . . .   (*H* 134)

Although Lowell was not an exemplary nihilist (he was too sexual, dependent, infatuate, human: "We shiver once a moon," he wrote, "whenever Eros arcs into the Virgin"; *H* 75), he was yet unhappy enough, perverse enough, to write in "Seventh Year" (*DBD* 100):

> This early January
> the shallow brown lakes on the drive
> already catch
> the first spring negative of the birds.

The negative of January is a positive? With Lowell, one cannot be sure. He had just written, of his "dream of putting [a] place on its feet," "I see it clearly, / but with the blind glass eyes of a doll." This concentration of reversals suggests a zeal to "crash," like the "oxweight cows" in the same poem, "foot over foot through vine and glass" – to make a shambles of the ideal order of things.

"A drastic experimental art is now expected and demanded," Lowell said in his memory-note on William Carlos Williams in the *Hudson Review* (536). The year was 1961 and "drastic" was perhaps an overstatement, for what R. P. Blackmur called the pyrotechnics of modernism had already died down the darkening air (*Primer* 16). But Lowell was responding to his own increasing compulsion to do something desperate to poetry, or with it – something to match the extremity of his personal feeling. To turn "blind glass eyes" (the redundancy may be a deliberate infelicity, but with Lowell how can one tell? Was not this uncertainty his "drastic" experiment?) – to turn such eyes on what is "clearly" seen is confusing enough to serve as an apt characterization of Lowell's experiments.

To put this more strictly, Lowell chose to see feverishly, or not at all. Naturally, this exposed him to distortions, to hastiness, to slash-and-burn tactics. It led (as will be noted) to inspired impetuosity, and it led, even more, to dubious phrasing and structuring – poetry that left the reader wondering who was missing what. Certain it is that, as if expecting the contact zone to trap him anyway in its target-circles of inverted transcendence, Lowell flicked some of his lines off like dead matches (including the pointless, pushing double negative of "dead matches . . . expired" in the poem quoted earlier). The revisions in *History* and *For Lizzie and Harriet* of most of the poems in *Notebook* ("And also he was . . . not happy with the writing") laid bare, for those who cared to pursue the matter, just how sodden and crumbly many of those matches originally were. In part, the problem was vexation (whether political anger or the philosophical nihilist pique Hegel thought endemic to modern persons). The first perhaps led Lowell to write of "women dissolved on the line" (*N* 241), when, as the subsequent revision suggested, he had seen "women hosed down stairs" (*H* 61). And the second may explain the bathos and blur in "Marlowe": "Tragedy means to die . . . / for that vacant parsonage, Posterity, / tabloid stamped in bronze, our deeds in dust" (*N* 167). In *History* (65), the last line is at once truer and memorably "stamped," classical in its antithetical poise: "my plays are stamped in bronze, my life in tabloid."

For whatever reasons, often we find first a kind of woozy inattention that Lowell then sought to rectify.[3] For instance, "racing your cooling grindstone to ambition," in "Randall Jarrell" (*N* 116), is rubbed to clarity in "racing the cooling grindstone of your ambition" (*H* 135). Vereen Bell can hardly be blamed for deducing that "her agile thigh" in "Wind" (*N 1967–68* 195) refers to the female snail mentioned in the preceding line, though one may have suspected that it referred, instead, to the young woman, mentioned four lines back, "rowing her boat since early morning." The revised poem (*H* 58) secures the thigh to the woman, leaving the snail, now male and still mawkishly stumbling "like the blind," with its traditional foot.

The numerous reversals in *History* and *For Lizzie and Harriet* of statements in *Notebook* make one exclaim that Lowell could have held so lightly his own memory and the "poor passing facts" that his new manner affected to find compelling, indeed "marvellous." "Ford Madox Ford" reads first "In time, he thought, I might live to be an artist" (*N* 120), then "Ford doubted I could live and be an artist" (*H* 118). One of these versions denies Ford his own mind. In *Notebook* (80), a local Harvard emulator of Paul Claudel says, " '*L' Académie Groton, eh, c'est une école admirable*" and in *History* (180), " '*L' Académie Groton, eh, c'est un école des cochons.*" The same pretender's vocabulary is first "poorer than Racine's," then "a vocabulary to mortify Racine." "Red and Black Brick Boston" first has "The sun baking the red and black brick red" (*N* 137), then "The arctic brightness bakes the red bricks black" (*H* 205). If the latter is aurally a crisply superb rout of the first version, it leads to another revision that contradicts it: "I glow with the warmth of these soiled red bricks." This chokes the boast, in the same poem, of a "senseless originality for fact."[4] These whirls lead nowhere unless to the conclusion – a real clinker – that Lowell was ready to say almost anything, then take it back and replace it with its opposite. "I want to make / something imagined, not recalled," he said in "Epilogue" (*DBD* 127) but in fact he seemed to remake everything he recalled.[5]

If some of the reversals suggest an intellectual self-deconstruction, a philosophical or mathematical game of heads or tails, the results are mostly idle, or worse. Lowell first slightly misquotes Melville in *Notebook* (153): "There's a wisdom that is woe / but there is a woe that is madness."[6] This is altered in *History* (41) to "There's a madness that is woe / and there is a wisdom that is madness." "True, under certain conditions x equals y, and y equals z," so the poet might be mumbling, "but under other conditions z equals y, and x equals z." Lowell's scrambling of Melville leads to the (re)discovery of a wisdom that is madness but gives rise to the truism "There's a madness that is woe." Elsewhere, Cleopatra's barb against Antony, after he forswears his thirst for her, is first, "If God / did not exist, this prayer [Antony's oath] would prove He did" (*N* 158), and later "If God existed, this prayer would prove he didn't" (*H* 46). The former may pass as a passionate woman's heavy, bitter wit; the latter is just bitter and heavy.

Some of the reversals, it is true, work to bring a statement more in line with the poem – as when the rhubarb "Often the player's outdistanced by the game" (*N* 238) is replaced by "Often the player outdistances the game" (*FLH* 37) as better gracing a poem on a twentieth wedding anniversary ("we smell as green as the weeds that bruise the flower"). Frequently, too, the tinkerings sharpen description and bear out Bell's sense (held in regard even to *Notebook*) of Lowell's "labor of deference to . . . empirical identity" (Bell 181). For instance, the change from "You rival the renewal of all seasons / clearing the puddles with your last-year books" (*N* 92) to "You rival the renewal of the day / clearing the puddles with your green sack of books" (*FLH* 21) rightly drops the technical (and puzzling) "last-year" as a description of books and adds the felicitous "green," which proves at once metonymic, the color of actual book bags, and metaphoric (of "renewal," spring). The abstraction "all seasons" gives way to something it is easier to rival while clearing puddles, the more lightly leaping "day." Affection and intimacy supplant intellectual distance. If the world did not exist, such revisions would prove it did.

But, again, though there are many such nice adjustments, the writing nonetheless retains its dismay at having to cross the Alps, as Lowell said Robert Penn Warren had done in *Brother to Dragons,* and, "like Napoleon's shoeless army, [enter] the fat, populated riverbottom of the novel" (Lowell, "Prose Genius" 621). What was the imaginative tyrant, Lowell, doing in the metonymic contact zone where "crowding kills the soul" (*H* 103), where "in splinter elms" the shrill "annual fledgelings with spikey necks . . . say to man his road is mud, or nothing" (*H* 98), and where "When their barn has been burned, / cows will look into the sunset and tremble" (*H* 61)? Despite the vernacular whip in his hand, which he could wield so flexibly, was he really ready to rival Warren's "prose genius in verse," which he found "so startling"? Or did he not, rather, brood, and balk, and go through mere motions of "deference to . . . empirical identity"? Did he surmise that his genius was only slumming there, a captain disguised as a shoeless enlisted man who, knowing the exigencies of the poetic struggles of his day, was doing his tour in the contact zone, with every tin plate of beans increasing his resentment, indeed nausea, and confirming the thought that he would rather be God?

O to Break Loose

Lowell wanted to write with "the directness that catches / everything on the run and then expires": "I would write only in response to the gods, / like Mallarmé who had the good fortune / to find a style that made writing impossible" (*DBD* 120). If, instead, he had to place rocks around the base of his arrowing signposts till "reality," or the reader, could catch up, it was natural for him to feel impatient, even vindictive. Here and there in the late volumes, one is reminded of Lowell's comment on Allen Tate: "Out of splutter and shambling comes a killing eloquence. . . . How often something smashes through the tortured joy of composition to strike the impossible bull's eye!" ("Visiting" 559). Lowell himself conveys no joy except when he smashes through. The title poem of *History* (24) contains – barely contains – the lines "O there's a terrifying innocence in my face / drenched with the silver salvage of the mornfrost." These imaginatively queer lines strike me as more truly "Lowell" than anything to which the gold star "accuracy" could attach. Hallucinatory, surreal, they catch his hysteria and his power – an odd manic-depressive will to override, with both a creator's joy and a suffering man's restiveness, the well-behaved metonymic limits of "description."

Everyone will recall moments when Lowell "smashes through" even in the fourteeners – moments when the very backbone of language suddenly "swims in the sperm of gladness" (*FLH* 17). "On my great days of sickness," Lowell remarked with lyrical wryness, "I was God . . . short half-holiday" (*H* 139). Such are the occasional half-holidays of his language, language thinking for a moment it is God. In "A Bronze Head," Yeats speaks of bringing "Imagination to that pitch where it casts out / All that is not itself," and so it is with those lines of Lowell's that, in Seamus Heaney's words, strike "the bronze note, and perhaps even the brazen note, of artistic mastery" (Heaney 37).

A modest-enough example closes "The Charles River 1" (*FLH* 18):

> if we leaned forward, and should dip a finger
> into this river's momentary black flow,
> infinite small stars would break like fish.

This perhaps overdeliberate fantasy – restrained but magical – illustrates the grandiosity often latent, when not manifest, in Lowell's break-out lines. Here the simile, "like fish," brings the remote charmingly near and turns the mineral instantly vital, set leaping by the mere dipping of a finger: a diffident boy's tentative phallic stir toward living interaction with the cosmos; and poetic genius as *logos spermatikos*. Most of Lowell's whiplash lines ascribe force to *something*, whether a power-saw moon ("The circular moon saw-wheels through the oak-grove"; *H* 112), winter blowing sparks in the face of God (*H* 88), sex ("the body of man's crash-love, and her affliction"; *H* 46), poetry ("If words were handled like the new grass rippling"; *H* 146), or "the true shark, the shadow of departure" (*D* 77).[7]

Like Yeats and Robert Penn Warren, Lowell conceived of life as in essence violence, a conviction that owes much to suppressed rage at not being seen for what one is, loved unconditionally. Many things mirror this inner vehemence, even time: "Randall, the scene still plunges at the windshield, / apples redden to ripeness on the whiplash bough" (*H* 126). In *History* we find as well "the minotaur steaming in a maze of eloquence" (180), a poignant, minatory expression of the brute anger stamping within Lowell's own art. We find "seeing my thoughts / stream on the water, as if I were cleaning fish" (25), with its somewhat sickening, self-abusing surprise, eased only by the flow of internal rhyme. And we find "white-faced, predatory, / the beautiful, mist-drunken hunter's moon ascends" (24), where (manically) Lowell finds his own shock-white face mirrored in the moon, while his lurching voice goes lustily after the sounds of "mist-drunken hunter's moon ascends." I like "his mason's chisel on the throat of stone" (167): Here the artist-thug opposes both a mother-sculpted identity and the flint-throated muse. And marvel at "to love the flesh of our youth, / V-mouth of the pike" (168), the capitalized, crotch-like V taking on the chomping force of Eros. "Cézanne left his spine sticking in the landscape" (191) lays bare both the bodily projection and the physical cost of art, including the sexual (if the mermaid does not pick the spine, the muse will). Lowell's lines of "killing eloquence" – "Shoot when you get the chance," Tate directed, "only shoot to kill" (*H* 122) – betray aggression either of or against the flesh, even when, as in "we yearn to swoop with the swallow's brute joy" (*H* 99), they imagine the impossible happiness of health.

It was Lowell's conviction of being "not right" in the mind that led him to curb, perhaps even flout and punish, his genius. His was a childhood in which everything pointed "to non-existence except existence" (*H* 74). How, then, should he presume to turn his mind, or the American language, into a blaze of meaning, or at the least make the absence of transcendence, or even of everyday coherence, at the drop of a sizzling match, the occasion for a dazzling figure? He had better take for his special province the meeting of the metaphoric with the metonymic plane as a cross where the desire for metaphoric consummations bleeds metonymy, and where metonymic realism suffers from the sense of a dying divinity of metaphor.[8]

On the other hand, it was precisely the rage to exist that led to Lowell's impetuous outbursts of metaphor. And never was his genius for metaphor more wonderful than when it remembered the first being who presented herself as an image of inaccessible beauty and happiness: his mother, the original mermaid of his memory.

To such as Lowell, childhood is at best a marbling transcendence, unforgettably enchanting, unforgivably false – an "it will never begin" and a "now it's over" (as in Beckett) that led to such gnomic pronouncements as, "if you want to make the frozen serpent dance, / you must sing it the music of its mouth" (*N* 105). Lowell hinted at this fate in one of his most quotable fourteeners, "The Nihilist as Hero":

> "All our French poets can turn an inspired line;
> who has written six passable in sequence?"
> said Valéry. That was a happy day for Satan. . . .
> I want words meat-hooked from the living steer,
> but a cold flame of tinfoil licks the metal log,
> beautiful unchanging fire of childhood
> betraying a monotony of vision. . . .   (*H* 193)

Here fiction is formidably entangled with fact. As Stephen Yenser remarks, "The very image of 'words meat-hooked from the living steer' has at once a repugnant power and a certain imprecision that exemplify his desideratum." Yenser adds, "And the following lines, so difficult to relate directly to those that precede and follow, seem to flaunt their intransigency in the face of the phrase 'six passable in sequence.'" (280). Yet what the following lines say, I think, is precisely that Lowell cannot have what he wants (even as he seems to commandeer it). He is not Attila "mounted on raw meat and greens" and galloping "to massacre in his single fieldmouse suit" (*H* 51). For the flame of *his* being is false – cold tinfoil (and the *l*'s in the line "but a cold flame of tinfoil licks the metal log" answer with an ever-famished licking). Childhood set in him a decorous unliving fire in place of the real thing, nor has the situation changed ("childhood, closer to me than what I love"; *H* 115). His mother, he says (*DBD* 124), goes on "cleaning house / for eternity, and making it unlivable," and even the log and flame in the fireplace are sootless and smokeless metal.

So the truth – or is this now the myth? – is that Lowell's table is bare, that he has hooked no live meat – that, in any case, he has no fire to cook with. He cannot ride upon the "now," for he began life with the sense that the beautiful might-have-been was already engraved on his dead, if unfinished, time. Somewhere the spirit, so he writes of Israel Citkovitz, "led the highest life," and "all places matched / with that place / come to nothing" (*DBD* 40). An uncannily sensitive child, Lowell came hoveringly near to enjoying emotional intimacy with his mother, but the latter, sea-hearted, a remote deficiency, a false plenitude, eluded him. Why should he honor the lovely might-have-been, with its "monotony of vision"? Only weakness requires ideal perfection. But he *is* weak. Not for him the hermaphroditic self-sufficiency of the cornstalk-flame, the other ideal of a living perfection:

> Life by definition breeds on change,
> each season we scrap new cars and wars and women.
> But sometimes when I am ill or delicate,
> the pinched flame of my match turns unchanging green,
> a cornstalk in green tails and seeded tassel . . .   (*H* 193)

This fragile illusion of "unchanging green" steadies only in the stalled air of prostration. There is nothing for it but passivity: "A nihilist has to live in the world as is." But, really, passivity is intolerable. The unwanted child in Lowell has his pride, his spite. On all that presents itself to him as mockingly transcendent, he will practice, then, an emotional demolition: "A nihilist has to live in the world as is, / gazing the impassable summit to rubble."

So a myth is born. Commentators find in the poem either a cowboy poet of "immediacy," hooking words from the living steer, or the nihilist as hero – really a sort of sci-fi anti-hero with a razing gaze. But if Lowell in *History* is a bit of both, he is, even more, the often impotent nexus of their contrary intentions. "The Nihilist as Hero" is full of regret, not vindictiveness; it is a poem all pathos, with nothing of the bloodletter's whoop. Perhaps Lowell really would have liked to live up to Nietzsche's flattering notion that the artist is a powerful animal, full of surplus energy, his life "a kind of youth and spring, a kind of habitual intoxication" (Nietzsche 421). And certainly his poem reveals an artist's sensual joy in making – as betrayed, for instance, when "rubble" ruthlessly compacts the sounds of "impassable summit," or with its ripe long vowel "gazing" stands out raptly among words with rubbly short ones.

By such evidence Lowell is not really willing to live in the world, or the word, as is; he continues making even as he pretends to be unmaking. What drives Lowell to write – in part a will to dazzle, a will to power – wars with his willful ideology of nihilism. (Often, his Humpty Dumpty poems are not really in pieces but, at the end, are still sitting on the wall, rocking with calculated dangerousness.)

Nonetheless, the ideology is still there, hanging around in the poems, unwashed and sulking, an unwanted child. Lowell's depression can be tracked back to attention of the wrong kind, in which his own feelings were left out, as if they were weeds that might bruise the flower. "You . . . resigned perhaps from the Navy," he wrote of his father, "to be an airhole – / that Mother not warn me to put my socks on before my shoes" (*H* 116). "In her presence," Elizabeth Hardwick said of Charlotte Lowell, "all the joy goes out of existence . . . there is not even a little corner left which you can fill up with affection or humor or respect or pleasure" (Hamilton, *Robert Lowell* 198). Alice Miller says in her book *Prisoners of Childhood* that a deficient narcissism – the illness from which Lowell seems to have suffered first and last – is usually caught from off a mother whose remote self-absorption and brusque domination is itself the result of insufficient self-love. Such a mother communicates to her children, *sotto voce,* that she really does not want to have any children, that now she has them they had better give her a minimum of trouble and a maximum of flattering attention and security, or else she cannot answer for the consequences. Miller notes that, in order to get into her good graces, the children of such a mother often transform themselves into tuning forks responding to her every need – that, in fact, the relationship fosters genius. Yet in the child a hidden rage slowly gathers – rage that he is not being perceived, corroborated, loved as the person he really is. To control his depression, he may decide – like the boy Paul in D. H. Lawrence's story "The Rocking-Horse Winner" – that he will astound his mother, indeed the world, with his self-discovered grandiosity (Miller 30–63).

In Lowell's case it was at first a deliberately ugly grandiosity, reserved for the small fry at school, over whom he passionately tyrannized. Later, his adult manic-depressive cycles alternately blew up into nightmarish proportions both the rage of Caliban at not seeing his face in the family mirror and the contriteness of the naughty child, who now gives himself up to female jaws to be "nibbled at recess in the marathon." (Not that the two states were always distinct: Lowell once shouted "Cut off my testicles" while policemen subdued him; Hamilton, *Robert Lowell* 156.) In his poetry Lowell is still a grotesque jack-in-the-box of bullying power or of nihilism, or else hooked on women, the "wetfly breathed into [his] belly – / broken whiplash in the gulp of joy" (*H* 83). He is still a prisoner of childhood, "a terrifying innocence" in his face. "The soul groans and laughs," he said, "at its lack of stature" (*FLH* 33).

For me, a rough rule of thumb is that Lowell's poetry is better when grandiose than when depressed (better when fiery than when soggy) and best when negotiating the treacherous, beautiful waters in between – those of the sexual marathon. A still rougher rule: It is better when predominantly metaphoric, not metonymic (an observation correlative with the first). How eloquent Lowell is when recalling, however indirectly, the tyrannical mermaid who had impersonated his mother, a creature "stonedeaf at will" (*D* 36), and stone-deaf often. "I've searched the rough black ocean for you . . . I thank the ocean that hides the fearful mermaid": These lines were written for Caroline Blackwood, "Rough Slitherer in [her] grotto of haphazard" (*D* 37), but Lowell had searched the black ocean for such a creature at least once before. His most passionately metaphorical lines would, as counter-Sirens, call the fearful mermaid from the remotenesses that hide her. "I almost doubt," Lowell said, "if you exist" (*D* 37).

Such regions of experience are perforce metaphoric, the image a divination, a sounding-line. A poet loves a metaphor because it is "virginal," language at its most seductively pristine. Lowell is hardly an exception, and if in "Epilogue" (*DBD* 127) he implies that, as poet, he is a poor metonymic photographer, he nonetheless does so in the sexy language of metaphor. "Pray for the grace of accuracy," he says, perhaps confusing "what happened" with what art alone can say:

> Pray for the grace of accuracy
> Vermeer gave to the sun's illumination
> stealing like the tide across a map
> to his girl solid with yearning.

But not only has Lowell, with inspired inaccuracy, invented this "Vermeer" (Bell suggests that it is "a composite of several of Vermeer's paintings"; 243, n. 10); he has the painter, via the sunlight, steal like a lover to "his girl." And since water is never far from Lowell's imagination in relation to a "girl" or to "yearning," the sun's illumination steals, what is more, "like the tide," let all the world lie between though it will ("across a map"). To Lowell, what is most "living" ("We are poor passing facts," he concludes the poem, "warned by that to give / each figure in the photograph / his living name") is lit by Eros, the father of metaphor.

For Lowell, because of the deadly example of his mother, the seductive, elusive woman "sings the Kill-river of no cure." But when was Lowell ever more imaginative, ever more excited, than when taking the plunge? Nietzsche in *The Will to Power* attributed the artist's "embellishing power" to his sexuality: "As man sees woman and, as it were, makes her a present of everything excellent [by exaggerating her beauty, grace, and so on], so the sensuality of the artist puts into one object everything else that he honors and esteems – in this way he *perfects* an object ('idealizes' it)" (424–25). For all his grumbling about imperfection, his harping on threadbareness, Lowell was still capable, in his last years, of this embellishing power, and never more so than in the "name" of a woman:

> My Dolphin, you only guide me by surprise,
> forgetful as Racine, the man of craft,
> drawn through his maze of iron composition
> by the incomparable wandering voice of Phèdre.   (*D* 78)

(If this last is not perfect, it may be something just as good. Lowell's characteristically forgetful syntax suits the meaning, putting the reader too in a maze, forcing a backup from the false lead between "forgetful" and "you." More problematical, it must be said, is Lowell's bullish offhand way with paradox, which here causes "forgetful" to forget "iron composition"; this last, in turn, forgets "by the incomparable wandering." But in Lowell's own lines it is precisely the absence of "iron composition" that draws us on, promising and offering magic, a way into its marvelously recessive maze.)

The element that elates and fascinates Lowell is, again, the one that will drown him – fascinating him, in part, because it has that power. Eros, he perceives, is bafflingly but willingly related to Thanatos, just as, in *The Dolphin,* the playful dolphin, she who "When I was troubled in mind, . . . made for my body / caught in its hangman's knot of sinking lines" (78) metamorphoses, in a wink, into the mermaid who "serves her winded lovers' bones in brine" (35). In health, Lowell once wrote beautifully under the aegis of a flamy Eros:

> O when will I sleep out the storm, dear love,
> and see at the end of the walk your dress glow
> burnt-umber, as if you had absorbed the sun?   (*FLH* 27)

But for the most part, Eros surrenders him to "the mermaid / and her singeing conjunction of tail and grace" (*D* 35). Because (with reason) he feared his mother, and so dreaded women, the oceanic unconscious, the unknown, he was chary of enlarged and enlarging images, cresting metaphors, flow . . . yet he never loves his craft so much, never writes more undulantly, than when, catching his breath and leaving pick-work metonymic "reality" behind, he enters the deep uncharted erotic swell. Then, with a half-horrified, half-willing rush to destruction, he goes to greet the mermaid who waits in the refreshing depths to ply her "knife and fork in chainsong at the spine" (*D* 35).

The image is a woman, the woman an image. Both are spontaneous and seductive, strong and elusive. With both, one "loses one's head." To create an image is, like offering oneself up as a prey to Venus, to invite death. Lowell cannot dip up an image of three or four lines without finding in it bits of bone, probably a lover's. For him, in fact, to write is only the most beautiful way to die. He may once have fancied himself a sailor – in "Waking in the Blue" (*LS* 81) he struts in his "turtle-necked French sailor's jersey" among other "victorious figures of bravado ossified young." Nonetheless, by some malignant fatality, he became an "Underseas" fellow (*LS* 53), a poet who has drowned in his own vocation.

To put this another way, Lowell's verse confirms that he is already dead, for what good is all his "genius" but to reveal that he accidentally died in childhood, as if his mother had left him momentarily unattended in the bath? And what are his happiest inspirations if not hopeless regressions to the time when "I nightly enjoyed my mother bathing – / not lust, but the lust of the eye" (*DBD* 36), as he too protestingly puts it, as if he might be, after all, Oedipus in Boston, an old theme.[9] "Genius hums the auditorium dead," he wrote in *The Dolphin* (15):

> Any clear thing that blinds us with surprise,
> your wandering silences and bright trouvailles,
> dolphin let loose to catch the flashing fish. . . .
> Poets die adolescents, their beat embalms them,
> . . . .
> genius hums the auditorium dead.

Women are let loose to catch the flying fish, but poets hum the auditorium dead – this last as against "winning the dolphin from the humming water" (*DBD* 125). Lowell goes on to distance himself from this sudden letdown, this discovery of his catchless genius, with a few drifting, inessential lines ("the archetypal voices sing offkey; / the old actor cannot read his friends, / and nevertheless he reads himself aloud"). But then he returns, by way of a pun on "line," to confront his sense of his fated death by and for love of a seawoman and by and for poetry:

> The line must terminate.
> Yet my heart rises, I know I've gladdened a lifetime
> knotting, undoing a fishnet of tarred rope;
> the net will hang on the wall when the fish are eaten,
> nailed like illegible bronze on the futureless future.

The fish will be "eaten" because the dolphin has been "let loose" both by nature and by the poet's own longing for her, his admiration of the way she nips the phallic small sports from the air. ("For Peter Taylor 1" repeats that classic male nightmare, "vagina like a jaw"; *H* 119.) "Failure keeps snapping up transcendence," Lowell says elsewhere in the book, characterizing "the mermaid"; phallic "Deficiency served her" (*D* 35). Odyssean phallus though the poet may be, fish breaking the water as "with the wings of a bird" (*DBD* 119), he will nonetheless go under to "the insatiable fiction of desire" (*D* 35). If "transcendence" is out of the question, if transcendence is all that remains, he can hardly hope to compete with the mermaid at the muddy bottom, comic figure as he is, a "Bullfrog boating on the surface, / belly lustily lagging three inches lowered" (*D* 35). Or he can go under but "None swims with her and breathes the air" (*D* 35).

Has he even left the shore? Is he not really, in Joyce's phrase, "Penelope stayat-home," knotting, then undoing his own language-shroud? Yes, that is how it is – as the last poem in *Dolphin* obliquely acknowledges. He has sided with the female against his own pent-up phallic rage, his book "an eel-net made by man for the eel fighting." His eye sees what his hand has done: how he has knotted his tar-defiled, tar-toughened noose against his own criminal hope of becoming real, transcendent, through manic outrage. (In his poem "Louisiana State University in 1940" [*DBD* 25]

Lowell asks: "Can poetry get away with murder, / its terror a seizure of the imagination / foreign to our stubborn common health?") He will be destroyed without ever venturing from the shore, save for a few lines at a time, lines of gladdening blind surprise. Once lifted free of his insatiable desire, his lines, dripped dry, weather hardened, will be decorative at best, uncooperatively mum about him, "illegible" (as Whitman once famously complained his own lines were: Whitman who was also in love with the fierce maternal sea).

Lowell's poetry will survive, so he envisions, in a future as futureless as the political present of his own times, and as futureless, too, as the psychological prison he had always lived in: the unmirrored, unechoed child and proved father to the man, a small fry whose fate it was to be eaten without having first been loved, seen, prized as the flashing creature, the transcendent genius, he thought he was, and was. ("O why was I born of woman?" he laments in "Hudson River Dream" [*H* 124]: "Never to reach their eye-level.")

For me, Lowell's most moving cry remains the first stanza of "Waking Early Sunday Morning" (*NO* 13):

> O to break loose, like the chinook
> salmon jumping and falling back,
> nosing up to the impossible
> stone and bone-crushing waterfall –
> raw-jawed, weak-fleshed there, stopped by ten
> steps of the roaring ladder, and then
> to clear the top on the last try,
> alive enough to spawn and die.

Here, again, is the sexual marathon, if synoptically viewed, and here again his incomparable Neptunian metaphoric genius – in this instance without concern to be majestic, simply sinewy and powerfully active, if half-subdued by the burden of metonymic description introduced by the *like*-phrase. Incomplete as a sentence, this elaborate expletive, this naturalist's lyrical prayer, nonetheless inscribes a whole destiny. The end may be mute and inglorious, a mere finish, but the arc is cohesive and satisfyingly complete, and steeled by an austere pathos: The poet counts the costs, and seems glad of them. Gone are the torments of psychology, of genius: What is contemplated with an appropriative longing is the universal fate of all born to spawn and die.[10]

In this joyously composed stanza, every degree of rhyme, every hyphen and caesura, is intensely implicated. From the vibrating sustained roundness of "O," that phonemic figure for a completed cycle, to the plosive "break," "like," and "chinook" and the countering, much-desired absence of restraint in the sound of "loose," to the jumping and falling rhythms of the second line, and the nosing action and despairing line-break of the third, and so on, the writing makes us know every part of, want, and want the end of, the struggle. Lowell never wrote with more passionate knowledge-by-enactment. Perhaps unfairly, for no one could consistently write at so high a pitch, the stanza makes one feel how regrettable and unnecessary the throwaway gestures are in much of Lowell's later poetry – how they but bump against the bottom of the roaring ladder.

The secret of this stanza, as of "Fishnet," "Mermaid 1," and "Dolphin," or of Lowell's whiplash lines, or of his quatrain on an absurd, macabre, yet familiar and almost endearing rage,

> I see even in golden summer
> the wilted blowbell spiders
> ruffling up impossible angers,
> as they shake threads to the light   (*DBD* 62)

or even on a due and welcome celibacy,

> After many lives in marriage,
> bedrooms blood-temperature,
> my joy in making this room arctic –
> a solitary barrenness
> finds the cold spots in the bed,
> and cherishes their expiring chill   (*DBD* 37)

– the secret is that Lowell has put aside his wizened child's play and assumed the courage of his actual power, and stopped the show. These lines take the full brunt of his imagination. If success of this kind often eases the inhibitions on his eroticism only to turn it aggressively against himself or others, the lines do not fend the reader off, but command corroboration.

Art, it seems, has no use for a negativity that seeps into its fibers, and still less for one brutally directed against them. It thrives only on impulses of its own validation, and in that way is like a child. When Lowell substitutes his art for his mother and sees it reflecting back the positivity of his feelings – his real rage or his real love; when he makes these last fit to be seen, beautiful, astonishing, and admirable, then the gods high on beaked prows, "their fixed archaic smiles smarting with salt," reach out to him, as to his terrifyingly innocent Helen, "indulgent arms."

NOTES

1 In "Our Dead Poets" (*H* 137), he writes, touchingly: "Sometimes for days I only hear your voices."
2 My view of postmodernism (if not of modernism) accords with the one David Lodge proposes in his essay "Modernism, Antimodernism, Postmodernism" in *The Modes of Modern Writing: Metaphor, Metonymy, and the Typology of Modern Literature.*

3   Perhaps there is not much more of this inattention, if any more, than would be average in first drafts. But was Lowell publishing first drafts? (And if he was, should he have been?)

4   Randall Jarrell had used the phrase "senseless originality" in his review of *Lord Weary's Castle*: "The things in Mr. Lowell's poems have, necessarily, been wrenched into formal shape, organized under terrific pressure, but they keep to an extraordinary degree their stubborn, unmoved toughness, their senseless originality and contingency" (25).

5   In introducing this poem at a poetry reading on December 8, 1976, at the Poetry Center of the 92nd St. Y, in New York City, Lowell said that he was "not sure" of the distinction between the remembered and the imagined. "Obviously," he said, "a poem has to be more than just memory," even though "memory is genius, really" (*A Reading*).

6   Herman Melville, *Moby-Dick,* ch. 96: "There is a wisdom that is woe; but there is a woe that is madness."

7   Some of the outstanding lines, it is true, are calm, even gentle – for instance, in *History,* "With a bull's moist eye, / dewlap and misty phallus, Cuyp caught the farthest glisten, tonnage and rumination of the sod" (62); "Spring the echo of God's single day" (97); "often the old grow still more beautiful, / watering out the hours, biting back their tears, / as the white moon streams in on them unshaded" (114); "Mother, we are our true selves in the bath" (115); "Red leaves embered in the blue cool of fall" (119); "love, . . . / it's all that kept off death at any time" (122); "the Joyful the creatures find no word to sing" (196); and "The slush-ice on the east bank of the Hudson / is rose-heather in the New Year sunset" (207).

8   For a discussion of the balance Lowell had earlier achieved between metaphor and metonym, see Marjorie Perloff's discussion of "Man and Wife" in *Poetic Art* 84–99.

9   Lowell's various lines on his mother frequently associate her with water, particularly baths.

10   Perhaps the lines half remember a passage in Robert Penn Warren's "The Ballad of Billie Potts": "The salmon heaves at the fall, and, wanderer, you / Heave at the great fall of Time, and gorgeous, gleam / In the powerful arc, and anger and outrage like dew, / In your plunge, fling, and plunge to the thunderous stream: / Back to the silence, back to the pool, back / To the high pool, motionless, and the unmurmuring dream." They also parallel Robert Duncan's description of poetry in "Poetry, a Natural Thing" as "a spiritual urgency at the dark ladders leaping. / This beauty is an inner persistence toward the source . . . salmon . . . at the falls battling, inarticulate, / blindly making it."

9

Going Back, Going Down, Breaking: *Day by Day*

ALAN HOLDER

I

My title is meant not to designate a chronological sequence but to name a series of recurring gestures or states central to the book of poems Robert Lowell brought out shortly before his death. Mapping a life whose end he believed was near, Lowell's *Day by Day* repeatedly goes back to crucial elements of his past, as well as to earlier poems that addressed those elements. Occasionally linked to this retrospective or revisionary urge is his concern with experiences of a going down, that is, of falling from conditions of promise, beauty, or vitality. Such gloomy descents are thematically related to a motif of breaking, employed, paradoxically, to dramatize both Lowell's sense of one-time power and its replacement by a feeling of current powerlessness. Although such a shift is not new in the Lowell canon, it acquires an unprecedented weight in *Day by Day*.

"Ulysses and Circe," the opening poem of the book, allows Ulysses to speak for himself throughout its fifth section. It initiates his doing so in lines that constitute a revision of a passage from a poem Lowell published many years before. The indebtedness of those lines to the earlier work is underscored by their encasement within quotation marks. Lowell thus carries further the blurring of the distinction between his protagonist and himself that "Ulysses and Circe" has already effected. Lowell-Ulysses is quoting Lowell, enacting on a verbal level what Ulysses is enacting in deed – he is going back, to his own words. Strikingly enough for the reader who has flipped through the poet's volumes to locate lines he thinks he has seen before, the poem to which Lowell is returning (in *For the Union Dead*) is itself entitled "Returning."[1]

Fully a third of the poems of *Day by Day* incorporate the element of returning, in one sense or another. This is reflected in part by several of the titles: "Homecoming," "Phillips House Revisited," "Return in March." Other titles – "Ulysses and Circe," "Off Central Park," "Turtle," "For John Berryman," "Marriage" – echo titles of works found in previous collections. Again and again in the volume, Lowell takes up subjects he has dealt with in earlier books, and so not only returns to persons, places, and experiences that have figured as important presences in his life, but also, at least implicitly, to his earlier renderings of them. In one way this going back – to his personal past, his poetic past – is not a series of discrete, reverse traversings through time, but the presentation of an ongoing continuum. For Lowell, "What was is," as he tells us at the start of "Homecoming," driving home the point by employing in that poem a first stanza that, like "Ulysses and Circe," uses materials originally found in "Returning." The notion that the past persists is given the grimmest of formulations in "We Took Our Paradise":

> the present, yes,
> we are in it;
> it's the infection
> of things gone . . .   (*DBD* 57)

To put it another way, Lowell conceives of himself as having been caught in a movement that presumably had sent him forth into a future, into change, but that has brought him back to an ever-confining past. The final passage of "Ulysses and Circe" describes his protagonist in related terms as Ulysses gets ready to slaughter the suitors:

> his gills are pleated and aligned –
> unnatural ventilation-vents
> closed by a single lever
> like cells in a jail –
> ten years fro and ten years to.   (*DBD* 10)

At the very moment of his potent attack, seemingly the expression of will and choice, sharklike Ulysses is seen as the prisoner of his physiological mechanisms. His bodily cells amount to jail cells.[2] This sense of captivity is reinforced by the last line of the passage (and of the poem), which suggests that Ulysses is caught in a circular career that has returned him to his point of departure.[3] Moreover, the line, with its repeated use of "ten," makes for a kind of return to the opening of the poem – "Ten years before Troy, ten years before Circe," – as well as to an inverted form of itself in the middle of the work: "ten years to and ten years fro." For Ulysses, fro and to come down to the same thing. For the reader, the work has moved forward only to end with a reminder of its beginning, which in turn insistently focuses on the element of "before," that is, on the past. The effect is something like that described in the closing sentence of *The Great Gatsby:* "So we beat on, boats against the current, borne back ceaselessly into the past."

Thus, while the title of *Day by Day* suggests a plodding forward, the book, for its maker and readers, is often a series of returns to texts and the experiential contexts that engendered them and those at hand. It is almost as though *Day by Day* has taken as its model the process by which writing, and verse in particular, is produced, the continual going back to and starting again from the fixedness of the left-hand margin, effected, when one is typing, by hitting the key marked "Return."[4]

There is a sense in which the element of return marks the verbal texture of a number of the book's lines. *Day by Day* furnishes several pronounced instances of a means (apart from end-rhyme, which is rarely employed here, and outright repetition, which is) that creates the effect of a poem going back to itself even as it moves forward: the use of one word to echo another that has shortly preceded it. We have already seen one example of this in the "ventilation-vents" of "Ulysses and Circe." Closely matching that phrase is "The torch-pipes wasting waste gas all night" (the opening of "Louisiana State University in 1940," *DBD* 25), the overlapping wording helping to convey the sense of excessive use. Two other examples, providing an etymological as well as a sound yoking, are Lowell's speaking of "the generic [life] / our generation offered" (in his wonderful tribute, "For John Berryman," *DBD* 25), which heightens the effect of one's being conditioned by circumstances as well as one's genes, and his wondering if the English country house will "predecease its predecessor, / the cathedral" (*DBD* 55), which startles us into a reminder of what "predecessor" literally means. "Domesday Book," the source of the last quotation, also has Lowell describing William the Conqueror as having "made anarchy anachronism," and asking if the country houses will "fall / under the ax of penal taxes. . . ." (To match what might be called the prominence of these various sound returns, one might well have to go back to the verse of Edward Taylor or Gerard Manley Hopkins.) A conjunction of two sound returns is reinforced by a linking assonance in "Shadow": "I have found the shadow of the crow, / a Roman omen . . ." (*DBD* 116). Contrasting with all of the foregoing is the subtle effect to be found in "Home":

> Less than ever I expect to be alive
> six months from now –
> *1976*
> a date I dare not affix to my grave.   (*DBD* 114)

Following the comparatively obvious return of "six" in "1976," we have the cross-rhyme of the latter term in "af*fix*." The near burying of this effect corresponds to the poet's reluctance to presume living into 1976.

Such returns as I have just been describing are of course willed, part of Lowell's manipulation of his medium. But the kinds of returns I am chiefly concerned with, and wish to explore further, are the sorts that appear to be compulsions of his sensibility and memory, recalls, perhaps in some cases unconscious, of situations or images appearing in earlier works. For example, when, in "Morning after Dining with a Friend," he speaks of "the eternal autumn of youth" (*DBD* 93), is he aware of echoing "the imperishable autumn / display windows / of Rogers Peet's boys' store," to be found in *Life Studies* (61)?[5] In "Ulysses and Circe," Lowell-Ulysses, waking beside Circe at dawn, describes the rising sun as "a red bonfire." His curious application of the term "uxorious" to his situation somehow falls into place when we think of the opening of "Man and Wife" in *Life Studies,* with its nonmythological couple lying abed, while "the rising sun in war paint dyes us red" (87). "Man and Wife" goes on to incorporate, ironically, the mythical – "in broad daylight [Mother's] gilded bedposts shine, / abandoned, almost Dionysian," whereas "Ulysses and Circe" moves toward the domestic. The two poems may each be said to constitute an anti-aubade, pulling against whatever suggestions of myth and passion each invokes (both so different from that earlier anti-aubade, Donne's "The Sunne Rising," with its lovers' sense of self-sufficiency and perfect union).

In "Suicide," the speaker goes to the window and sees that

> five floors down, the trees are bushes and weeds,
> too contemptible and small
> to delay a sparrow's fall.   (*DBD* 16)

This passage echoes and may be thought of as eerily completing that moment in *Life Studies,* in "Home After Three Months Away," when Lowell, before going on to register a sense of himself as shrunken, notes that

> Three stories down below,
> a choreman tends our coffin's length of soil,
> and seven horizontal tulips blow.
> Just twelve months ago,
> these flowers were pedigreed
> imported Dutchmen; now no one need
> distinguish them from weed.
> Bushed by the late spring snow,
> they cannot meet
> another year's snowballing enervation.   (*LS* 84)

In both passages we have a looking out a window at some sorry vegetation. But the chief thing to be noted is that the subliminal suggestion of the earlier poem's "coffin's length of soil," perhaps passed over in our original experience of it, is crystallized by the later poem's open confrontation of the possibility of suicide. The morbid measuring of that garden miniplot can now be seen as the act of a potential plunger.

The frequent use of numerical specification in *Day by Day,* for example, "Suicide" 's "five floors down," recalls the practice of the poems of *Life Studies.* (Witness the use of "Three," "seven," and "twelve" in the passage just cited.) Indeed, can one find another poet who has so filled his lines with particular numbers? Their use to designate ages, Lowell's own or those of others, abounds in *Day by Day,* and this marks a return to the practice of *Life Studies.* More generally, his predilection for numbers may be part of an attempt to incorporate the irreducible factuality of existence in his verses, but can also be seen as a means of mastering a threatening or disturbing world. An act of counting occurs, as we have just seen, in a poem about suicide, and can also be found in two poems published years before, one about a restless night and the other about pain.

The two poems in question, "Myopia: A Night" and "Going to and fro," appeared in *For the Union Dead,* a volume that, like *Life Studies,* is implicated in the series of returns being investigated here. For one thing, that book had its own versions of going to and going fro, of movement and its reversal generating overtones of futility or entrapment, remarked on earlier in connection with "Ulysses and Circe." The speaker in "The Scream" says "Mother kept coming and going – with me, without me!" (*FUD* 8). Three pages later, "Fall 1961," a poem about the fear of nuclear war, opens with this stanza:

> Back and forth, back and forth
> goes the tock, tock, tock
> of the orange, bland, ambassadorial
> face of the moon
> on the grandfather clock.   (11)

(As with "Ulysses and Circe," the ending of this poem circles back to its beginning.)[6] The conclusion of the very next poem in *For the Union Dead,* "Florence," pictures sympathetically the severed head of the Gorgon – it "swung / like a lantern in the victor's hand" (14). "Going to and fro," coming later in the volume, assigns that motion to Lucifer and associates it with an act of counting that might release him from a sense of being trapped on earth.

For the Union Dead is again recalled by *Day by Day* when we come across "Turtle" (98–99). Here Lowell pictures himself as an old turtle, vulnerable, looking foolish in the persistence of its amorous impulses. Lowell's present turtlelike status, he seems to be saying, is an appropriate punishment for his having "hunted them in school vacations." Turtle and poet, originally joined in the poem by metaphor and memory, split apart, their one-time roles reversed. In a nightmare vision, Lowell is caught in a turtle's beak, being pulled underwater and clawed to pieces "small enough to swallow." Beginning the poem by praying for memory, Lowell has gotten more than he bargained for. The movement from memory as a deliberately invoked good to its eruption as a pain-giving power parallels the course of Shakespeare's "When to the sessions of sweet silent thought." Lowell is, in some sense, drowned by his summoning up remembrance of things past. For the student of Lowell, the poem cannot help summoning up remembrance of "The Neo-Classical Urn" in *For the Union Dead,* which recorded the original victimization of the turtle.[7] There, too, we find Lowell's identification with his victims through metaphor, along with the ambiguous syntax of the closing lines:

> . . . I rub my skull,
> that turtle shell,
> and breathe their dying smell,
> still watch their crippled last survivors pass,
> and hobble humpbacked through the grizzled grass.   (48)

In "Turtle," as elsewhere in Lowell's poetry, memory bringing guilt and/or fear is compounded by the recall of its earlier manifestations.

Where "Turtle" opens with Lowell praying for memory, "Grass Fires" begins with what appears to be a self-admonition about recalling the past:

> In the realistic memory
> the memorable must be forgone;
> it never matters,
> except in front of our eyes.   (85)

These lines can be taken as a warning that what has been thought important, "memorable," must be seen as less than that, either because our subjective view has magnified it unduly, or because it was of consequence only at the time of its original occurrence. Going on to say "We cannot recast the faulty drama," Lowell proceeds to do just that, using a stanza that, first seeming to be the report of a present action, modulates into a memory of his having set grass afire as a child. He glories in having put out the conflagration: "I snuffed out the inextinguishable root." This claim to mastery (decidedly uncharacteristic of *Day by Day,* as we shall see), already made precarious by its oxymoronic formulation, is swept away by the ensuing lines, where Lowell says he can do "as little now as then, / about the infernal fires − / I cannot blow out a match" (86). The recording here of the unconquerable infernal fires (which should be regarded as internal) can be seen as a reworking of "Eye and Tooth" in *For the Union Dead* (18–19). There, Lowell describes himself as chain-smoking through the night, "learning to flinch / at the flash of the matchlight," as though trying to overcome his natural fascination with fire. The poem, which suggests that his typical mode of seeing is linked with the fiery and infernal ("My whole eye was sunset red / . . . I saw things darkly"), concludes by declaring that there is no hope of dampening this combustion, exhausting though it may be to the poet and those around him:

> Nothing! No oil
> for the eye, nothing to pour
> on those waters or flames.
> I am tired. Everyone's tired of my turmoil.

The intense, pain-causing component of his nature is a given, insuperable. It constitutes an "inextinguishable root," to return to "Grass Fires," but the root so designated can also be taken as remembrance of past experiences that no effort by "the realistic memory" will eradicate.

"Grass Fires" is not the only work in *Day by Day* that recalls "Eye and Tooth." In the earlier poem the pain associated with seeing was connected to boyhood voyeurism:

> No ease for the boy at the keyhole,
> his telescope,
> when the women's white bodies flashed
> in the bathroom. Young, my eyes began to fail.

We are reminded of this when "Art of the Possible," which seems to trace stages of Lowell's sexual life, devotes a much longer stanza to the same sort of activity:

> In my parents' townhouse,
> a small skylight-covered courtyard,
> six feet by nine,
> lit two floors of bathrooms –
> their wanton windows clear glass above,
> and modestly glazed below.
> There for a winter or so,
> when eleven or twelve,
> one year short
> of the catastrophic brink of adolescence,
> I nightly enjoyed my mother bathing –
> not lust, but the lust of the eye.   (*DBD* 36)

Here, as with "Suicide" and "Turtle," we find an echoing poem carrying a greater charge than the original, in this case through a heightening of the "confessional" element. The object of illicit looking is not now anonymous women, but Lowell's own mother, gazed at *every night* for a winter or so. (Note the proliferation of numerical notation in this rendering of a loaded experience.) It is as if, in *For the Union Dead,* Lowell had not been prepared to tell all.

The sense of *Day by Day* filling us in on disturbing materials suppressed or partly so earlier in his career is conveyed as well by "St. Mark's, 1933." While he had noted in the prose portion of *Life Studies,* "91 Revere Street," his marginal position in the Brimmer School – "To be a boy at Brimmer was to be small, denied, and weak" (27) – this is as nothing compared to the barrage of insults he records having endured at his prestigious prep school (e.g., " 'Cal is a slurp,' / 'A slurp farts in the bathtub' "; *DBD* 89). We learn from this piece that two terms that appear in *Life Studies* and give the impression of being part of an invented self-deprecating diction had their source at St. Mark's. "Dunbarton" opens with the lines "My Grandfather found / his grandchild's fogbound solitudes / sweeter than human society" (65). The first stanza of "During Fever" quotes Lowell's daughter: " 'Sorry,' she mumbles like her dim-bulb father, 'sorry' " (79). "St. Mark's, 1933" shows that both "fogbound" and "dim-bulb" were among the epithets Lowell had to endure at the hands of his schoolmates. It seems he was called a good deal more than "Cal" (for "Caligula" as well as "Caliban") in Southboro, Massachusetts (see Hamilton, *Robert Lowell* 20).

Life Studies is again echoed and in some sense completed by three more works in *Day by Day:* "To Mother," "Unwanted," "Robert T. S. Lowell" (Lowell's father). Both parents figure prominently in the earlier book, handled for the most part from a chilly distance that can still make readers uncomfortable. The last direct views of each in *Life Studies* are unforgettably reductive. Here is Charlotte Lowell as rendered in "Sailing Home from Rapallo":

> In the grandiloquent lettering on Mother's coffin
> *Lowell* had been misspelled *LOVEL.*
> The corpse
> was wrapped like *panetone* in Italian tinfoil.   (78)

Even in death, Charlotte has been brought down through her married name (compare the way, earlier in the poem, the family motto on the gravestone of Lowell's father had "seemed too businesslike and pushing" among the maternal Winslows and Starks). Her misnaming was presumably produced by a careless workman, but the humiliating simile of the last line is the deliberate construct of her own son. As for Lowell's father, witness his description in "Terminal Days at Beverly Farms":

> Father's death was abrupt and unprotesting.
> His vision was still twenty-twenty.
> After a morning of anxious, repetitive smiling,
> his last words to Mother were:
> "I feel awful."   (*LS* 74)

Here is no memorable deathbed pronouncement, but the commonest of expressions, in keeping with the mediocrity *Life Studies* has assigned to him. His claim to fame is his perfect vision. Placing the passage in context further reduces him, for it echoes an earlier line in the poem:

> He smiled his oval Lowell smile. . . .

This mouth-coercing line, with its combination of assonance, consonance, and ghost of an internal rhyme, mimics and mocks the father's characteristic act, and his final word, "awful," can be seen as a parody of "oval."

Day by Day appears to be doing penance for these earlier parental portraits. "To Mother" (which may be said to complete the association of Charlotte and Napoleon found in *Life Studies*) testifies to the close connection Lowell still feels with his mother and to his recognition of her characteristics in himself. He longs to be with her. Still, a certain irony tinges the mood of acceptance. Although he does not wish to count the minutes he imagines spending in her parlor, neither does he wish his visit to last "forever," and he concludes the poem by saying:

> It has taken me the time since you died
> to discover you are as human as I am . . .
> if I am.   (*DBD* 79)

Phrased this way, the self-deprecation casts some doubts on his mother's humanness.

"Unwanted" reveals a source of anguish for Lowell, his being told while he was in college that he was an unwanted child. At the same time, it attempts a reconciliation with his mother. Lowell wonders whether it is the "fear of not being wanted" rather than his mother's not desiring a child that constitutes "the one unpardonable sin"

(*DBD* 124). Reminding one of Hardy's "Channel Firing," which pictures the scouring of Hell's floor as a punishment, he comically asks: "For this, will mother go on cleaning house / for eternity, and making it unlivable?" The humor suggests he has been able to forgive his wounding parent.

"Robert T. S. Lowell" goes further than the mother poems of *Day by Day* to dissolve the distance and mockery that characterized Lowell's portrayals of his parents in *Life Studies*. There is a long way to go. Who can forget the picture of ex-Commander Lowell booming "Anchors Aweigh" in the bathtub (*LS* 71)? The mode of "Robert T. S. Lowell" (*DBD* 80–81) is itself a sharp departure from the earlier volume. In *Life Studies*, Lowell's father, like almost all other persons in the sequence, had been permitted only bits and pieces of utterance. Here, after an initial stanza spoken by "Son," the poem is given over entirely to a monologue by "Father."[8] In delivering it, he acquires not only the pathos that was almost the only thing Lowell could afford him in *Life Studies*, but an eloquence, dignity, and scope he had never approached in the earlier book.[9] The poem's conclusion, even while separating the son's experience from the father's naval career, establishes common ground: "it's your life, and dated like mine."[10]

"Robert T. S. Lowell," the capstone to the series of poems Lowell wrote about his father in the course of his career, provides one illustration of what the poet may mean when he declares (in "To Frank Parker"): "The past changes more than the present" (*DBD* 92).[11] That is, with the passage of time, we revise our former judgments of what we experienced. The revision of the image of Lowell's father, the replacement of *Life Studies'* inclination to hold him up detachedly as an ineffectual buffoon by the empathetic and respectful treatment of "Robert T. S. Lowell," is one of the chief moral achievements of *Day by Day*. The poem marks perhaps the single clearest indication in the volume that returning to the past can result in something other than a renewal or intensification of the disturbance, guilt, or pain previously associated with it.

II

Day by Day is a good deal more than the book of returns to a relatively distant personal and poetic past that I have been describing. Not only does it reflect large events of Lowell's life comparatively close in time to his writing about them – his marriage to Caroline Blackwood, his fathering a son, the disintegration of the marriage, his stays in a mental home in England – but also, sometimes drawing on these, it attempts to focus on narrowly defined experiences, isolated fragments of the immediate, conceived of as *days* or *minutes* or *moments*. (This sort of focus is one of the meanings of the book's title.) "Last Walk?" for example, recounts the events of an "unhoped-for Irish sunspoiled April day" (*DBD* 13). The opening poem of Part Three of *Day by Day* (that section bears the same title as the book) is called simply "The Day." "Sheridan" begins with "Another day of standstill heat" (68), "The

Withdrawal" with "Only today and just for this minute" (72), "The Downlook" with "For the last two minutes" (125). A walk through Lowell's native city is called "Bright Day in Boston." These concentrations on the immediate, the moment at hand, may be *attempted* escapes on Lowell's part from the burden of memory, from the sense of carrying always within himself a determining past ("What was is").[12]

Consider the opening lines of "The Day":

> It's amazing
> the day is still here
> like lightning on an open field,
> terra firma and transient
> swimming in variation,
> fresh as when man first broke
> like the crocus all over the earth.   (53)

In spite of everything, of all that one has been through, there are still available spaces, beginnings, bloomings. Here we are, in the present moment. In "Sheridan" 's single summer day Lowell observes flowering chestnut trees, and in the particular minute of "The Withdrawal" he notes a different, but apparently more treasured foliage, suggestive of autumn, "my favorite season." In this poem, too, we find a "moment" associated with the freedom available, if only temporarily, to children. "Seventh Year" pictures the poet swayed by "the hard infatuate wind of love" in the course of a divided "minute" (101).

These poems of days and moments that please or enthrall tend to be marked by brightness or illumination, taking the form of lightning and sunlight in "The Day," of sunlight alone in "Last Walk?", "The Withdrawal," "Logan Airport, Boston," "Bright Day in Boston," and "Sheridan," of the light of the full moon in "The Downlook." The association of light with the present moment assumes its most intense embodiment near the end of "Marriage" (which, on the whole, is not in the same category with these other poems). There, Lowell speaks of the "miracle of lighting / for the photographer's sacramental instant" (*DBD* 71). What makes for the sacramental, it might be ventured, in addition to the heavenly air that seems to inform the married couple in question, is the instantness caught by the photographer, the moment unencumbered by past or future, pure nowness.

Composing poems, in whole or part, of days, moments, light, may be said to constitute Lowell's version of *carpe diem*. But although notable, this element of *Day by Day* is virtually swamped by more familiar components of his sensibility. The day of "Last Walk?", whatever its pleasures, seems to mark the end of his marriage, registering the consciousness that seven years have come to almost nothing. "The Day" starts out focused on the "amazing" day, available and immediate. But shifting its lines back and forth between present and past, the poem comes to rest with the elegiac, another acknowledgment of failure. Euphoria does not necessarily accompany even moments or minutes in *Day by Day*. "Ten Minutes" recounts a night of apparent, if not actual, insomnia, and includes a memory of "five-minute spells" (108) of total recall by Lowell's mother, during which she would exhaustively itemize examples of his alleged selfishness. The "instant" may be "sacramental" in "Marriage"; however, in "Bright Day in Boston," it is not synonymous with a seized or seizing magical present, but located deep in the past: "An epoch ago the instant / when one could live anywhere / unendangered . . ." (83). This undoes the "joy" that has marked the first two stanzas of the poem, and Boston comes to be described as "a city of murder, an American city." The contexts of "instant" are also gloomy in "Turtle" and "Seventh Year." The first of these has Lowell, in "the awful instantness of retrospect" (99), imagining himself being victimized by a turtle, while the second opens with "Seven years ago, my instantly dispelled / dream of putting the place on its feet" (100). These examples show how much pressure the past exerts on the present moment, how what has happened can take over Lowell's *carpe diem* vocabulary. Even when the past does not exert its darkening presence, a focus on the moment is no guarantee of pleasurable experience. In "Shadow," Lowell speaks of "this pending hour, this tapeworm minute . . ." (116).

Lowell's moments, even when made up of peak experiences, like those "moments / of the Great Day, / the *dies illa*, / when we lived momently / together forever / in love with our nature," are, like anybody's, only momentary, their brilliance all too temporary, "flash-in-the-pan" ("The Day" 53). Moreover, that brilliance is considerably different from the characteristic light of the world in *Day by Day*. The "light of day" in "Art of the Possible" (36) serves only to "melt" the union of lovers, and "noonday light" in "Suburban Surf" (97) shows cars, earlier associated with sexual intercourse, as "a farce / of their former selves at night." The perception of the favored autumn season afforded by the sunlight in "The Withdrawal" is fleeting, the "true angle" of "sunslant" replaced by an illumination of the heavens described as "melodramatic" (72). The career of light is complicated in "Logan Airport, Boston" (74–75), a poem that seems to mark an exception to the characteristic failure of illumination in *Day by Day*. While its opening effect of brilliance is replaced by a search for the sun through the windows "in the brown air of our rental," brightness returns at the end of the poem, at least through metaphor ("Bright sun of my bright day, / I thank God for being alive"). However, even this apostrophe has to contend with the preceding stanza, which focuses on the absence of the beloved woman in question, on what is only remembered brilliance, "the undrinkable blaze / of the sun. . . ." "Ulysses and Circe," which, standing at the beginning of the book, anticipates a number of its thematic and verbal elements, has Ulysses saying "'I found my exhaustion / the light of the world'" (7), and tells us "He has seen the known world, the meanness and beacons of men . . ." (9).

And what does Lowell himself see? "I see even in golden summer / the wilted blowbell spiders / ruffling up impossible angers, / as they shake threads to the light." "Nothing" in the season "is gold" ("This Golden Summer" 62). In "Homecoming," gold is associated with blight. Gold is thus subverted by Lowell, absorbed into the prevailing absence of brilliance.[13] So, too, is whiteness. "Last Walk?" ends with a scene of "all whiteness splotched" (14), and the animal the poet regards as his double in "Shifting Colors," "an ageless big white horse," is described as "slightly discolored by dirt" (119). But if any color is shifted away from its traditional potency or honorific associations, undermined by the failing light of Lowell's present world, it is red.

Returning after forty years to Phillips House at Massachusetts General Hospital, in a winter season showing "its usual luminous lack of warmth," Lowell relegates brightness to an earlier time, something possessed by his grandfather when *he* was sick and associated with the color red. His grandfather had a "reddish tan" and "was slipped / champagne and oysters / by a wild henna-dyed niece . . ." ("Phillips House Revisited" 87–88). But red, that hue traditionally emblematic of brilliance, beauty, passion, figures quite differently when associated with Lowell himself and those with whom he identifies. A reminiscence about a youthful sense of kinship with the Indian – "we once claimed alliance with the Redskin" – is sandwiched between a description of garden grass "thin[ning] to red clay," and a pondering of what has been "won by surviving / if two glasses of red wine are poison" ("To Frank Parker" 92). Red is the color of complexions blotched by the artistic efforts of a lifetime ("our book-bled faces / streak like red birds") or the ravages of aging and alcohol ("our unchangeably sunset / and liver-invigorated faces"). The first of these quotations is from "Our Afterlife I" (21), the second from "Sheridan" (68), in which the poet sees his young son separated from his own condition by a brilliance that would seem to be formidable but is rendered reductively as "only the eternal midday. . . ." The implication here seems to be that the boy will grow beyond the stage of apparent invulnerability, and acquire his own indelibly red-streaked face.

A red face suggestive of embarrassment is also to be found in *Day by Day* and is most significant. In "Our Afterlife I" Lowell notes:

> This year killed
> Pound, Wilson, Auden . . .
> promise has lost its bloom,
> the inheritor reddens
> like a false rose –

We may take the inheritor as Lowell himself, hailed, at least in the earlier part of his career, as successor to the great line of Modernist writers, but here exhibiting discomfort over his supposed position in literary history. Not only has brightness fallen from his world, but from the poet as well.

This reading is consistent with the strain of self-deprecation that pervades *Day by Day*, manifesting itself partly in Lowell's sense of failure as a human being, but even more so as a poet. He sees his medium as having let down its materials or as having violated them. "[N]o truth" is to be found "in this processing of words" ("Ten Minutes" 108). He does, somewhat hesitantly, point to a power once held:

> I was surer, wasn't I, once . . .
> and had flashes when I first found
> a humor for myself in images,
> farfetched misalliance
> that made evasion a revelation?   ("Unwanted" 121)

But the penultimate line here and "evasion" dilute, at least partially, the claim to "flashes" and "revelation." Now Lowell seems to be haunted by the fear of exhibiting only a "helpless paperishness" ("In the Ward" 40). Although Mary, Queen of Heaven, may never have doubted that "the divided, stricken soul / could . . . / . . . rob the devil with a word," Lowell's words, for him, have no such potency; in fact, he imagines himself having a dialogue with the devil, "not knowing which is which . . ." ("Home" 114–15). In "Epilogue" he is impatient with his poetry even as it conveys a view he apparently respects:

> I hear the noise of my own voice:
> *The painter's vision is not a lens,*
> *it trembles to caress the light.*   (127)

The slight dissonance of the *noise–voice* internal rhyme heightens the effect of self-oppression. In "Thanks-Offering for Recovery," placed just before "Epilogue," he seems to identify with a primitive head, "solemn as a child," whose "shallow, chiseled ears" are "crudely healed scars lumped out / to listen to itself . . ." (126). The image is a knotted one, perhaps a parody of the notion put forth by Edmund Wilson in *The Wound and the Bow* that a deeply painful childhood experience contributes to the making of an artist. Here the healing (evidenced by the scars)[14] has taken the form of a dubious self-preoccupation. Lowell may also be identifying with another instance of aural self-preoccupation, the most notorious of our times: Nixon listening to "his drab tapes play back his own voice to him, / morning, noon, and night" ("George III" 135).[15] As well as being oppressive to his ears, his poems are, for Lowell, minimal, mere observations, "description without significance, / transcribed verbatim by my eye" ("Shifting Colors" 119). "Epilogue," a meditation on his poetry, speaks of "the threadbare art of my eye" (127).[16]

Given this dismissing view of his poetry, why does he continue with his writing? Because, like his sympathies and cruelties, it comes of itself, beyond his will, though to no good purpose, well removed from the Blakean concept of creative fire, more akin to those "infernal fires" he can do so little about:

> the dull, instinctive glow inside me
> refuels itself, and only blackens
> such bits of paper brought to feed it . . .[17]   ("Ten Minutes" 108)

It would appear that Lowell could not get much gloomier about his art than characterizing it as nothing more than a spoiler of paper, but the view of his poetry is even bleaker in the following lines, though this may not be immediately evident. Having been released from a mental hospital, with even the name of his doctor forgotten, he says:

> I am free
> to ride elbow to elbow on the rush-hour train
> and copy on the back of a letter,
> as if alone:
> "When the trees close branches and redden,
> their winter skeletons are hard to find –"   ("Notice" 118)

The passage delivers its point when we realize that it has made a return within *Day by Day*: The lines in quotation marks are Lowell's own, and come, with one tiny alteration, from "Suicide," a poem found earlier in the book. No longer in the institution where, "Notice" has already informed us, he experienced "'days of only poems and depression'" – here he is quoting what he said to the doctor – he is free, while commuting uncomfortably, to concern himself with poems *of* depression. One form of self-quotation has been replaced by another, even darker.

The dejection to be found in Lowell's view of his art is of a piece with the general temper of *Day by Day*, and the process we undergo in moving from the initially unconditioned assertion of "I am free," in the lines just quoted, to the discovery of the contents of that freedom is characteristic of more than a dozen passages in the book. Repeatedly we find that to read down the page in *Day by Day* is to experience a psychological going down, a fall from the effects of power, vitality, beauty, promise, that the poetry may first offer us.

Lowell initiates this series of falls as early as the second and third lines of the book's opening poem, "Ulysses and Circe":

> things changed to the names he gave them,
> then lost their names: (3)

This effect of first establishing a verbal potency, and then dissolving it, though applied to Ulysses, might well be Lowell's view of himself. Not very much further along in the poem we find:

> . . . The sun rises,
> a red bonfire,
> weakly rattling in the lower branches –
> that eats like a locust and leaves the tree entire.   (3)

As though the sun as bonfire has not already been subdued enough, the passage proceeds to give it to us as "dull changer of night to day, / itself unchanged, in war or peace." The sun is thus reduced, in Lowell's undoing hands, to a trivial version of the Unmoved Mover.[18] Something too weary to be called bitterness is at work here, as is the case in other instances of the "falling" effect. Here are some more specimens:

> Her then unspectacled eyes were stars –
> a cornered rabbit . . .   ("Ulysses and Circe" 8)

> We sat and watched a mother swan
> enthroned like a colossal head of Pharaoh
> on her messy double goose-egg nest of sticks.   ("Last Walk?" 14)

> O Baton Rouge, your measureless student prospects,
> rats as long as my forearm regrouping toward
> the sewage cleansing on the open canals –
>   ("Louisiana State University in 1940" 25)

And in a passage already discussed:

> . . . it was I put out the fire,
> who slapped it to death with my scarred leather jacket.
> I snuffed out the inextinguishable root,
> I –
> really I can do little,
> as little now as then,
> about the infernal fires –
> I cannot blow out a match.   ("Grass Fires" 85–86)

What might be called the implication of such descents is that life promises what it does not keep, that to live is to suffer a fall or series of falls. As in "Ulysses and Circe," dawn goes down to Domesday. It is eminently right for *Day by Day* that Lowell should have followed "The Day" with "Domesday Book" and that he should have entitled one of the other poems in the volume "The Downlook," a name that reminds us of what he had called years before, in *For the Union Dead*, "the downward glide / and bias of existing . . ." (68). As far removed as his characterization of childhood is from that in Wordsworth, as much as he can see the damage done in his early years, he can still attribute enough gladness to his younger self to allow space for a plunge into despondency and madness. The hope held by that self can recur in later years, but only sets Lowell up for more such falls. Thus, going down, or falling, joins going back and going to and fro as an essential motion of the world of *Day by Day*.

III

Lowell has trouble, as already suggested, in finding a cushion against that falling in his art, for it too is conceived of as having experienced a descent. We can fill in his conception of his poetry by investigating the ways in which "breaking" operates in the book. In "Robert T. S. Lowell," it figures as an annoying but relatively inconsequential activity, a manifestation of childhood energies; there, Lowell's father describes the poet's children as "climbing and breaking." It can also be found associated with early energy (though here combined with an ominous overtone) when Lowell says of the young in "Homecoming": "they break themselves against the surf" (12). Breaking acquires a content of would-be destructiveness in "St. Mark's, 1933," where Lowell describes his backbiting of classmates:

> I broke one [friend] on the other –
> but who could break them,
> they were so many,
> rich, smooth and loved?   (90)

But it is in "Ulysses and Circe" where breaking is endowed with its strongest negative meaning. Ulysses, poised to slaughter the suitors, is unsparingly rendered as

> a vocational killer
> in the machismo of senility,
> foretasting the apogee of mayhem –
> breaking water to destroy his wake.   (9)

(The sound interplay of *breaking–wake*, combined with "destroy," might well remind us of that earlier statement about violence in the poem, "I destroyed Troy.")[19]

What has any of this to do with Lowell's conception of himself as a fallen poet? Consider "Off Central Park." Lowell, back at the New York apartment he once shared with his second wife, Elizabeth Hardwick, surveys its furnishings, including the contents of a bookcase:

> the same radical reviews
> where we first broke into print
> are still new to us.   (44)

The phrase "first broke" acquires an added honorific charge when we find it again, intensified by a kind of cross-rhyme, in "The Day," where Lowell notes that the day in question is

> fresh as when man first broke
> like the crocus all over the earth.   (53)

An initial breaking, then, is associated with creative energy, including that of his younger years.[20] The creative aspect of breaking is intertwined with destructiveness as Lowell ponders the nature of poetry in "Louisiana State University in 1940." In a passage reminiscent of Wallace Stevens's association of poetry with "a violence from within," Lowell asks:

> Can poetry get away with murder,
> its terror a seizure of the imagination
> foreign to our stubborn common health?
> It's the authentic will to spoil,
> the voice

> haunted not lost,
> that lives by breaking in
> berserk with inspiration,
> not to be shaken without great injury,
> not to be quieted by ingenious plotting –   (25–26)

The poem-making impulse, seizing the poet, injurious to others, cannot be resisted without injury to oneself. Its violence, its breaking, here appear to be accepted, perhaps even embraced. But in other poems of *Day by Day*, the acceptance of the poetry–violence complex, with its attendant notion of self-protection, is severely questioned. Lowell certainly seems to regret, in the following passage, the harm his words have done:

> How often have my antics
> and insupportable, trespassing tongue
> gone astray and led me to prison . . .   ("The Downlook" 125)

The verbal trespasses may of course be those of life situations, but can also be seen as those of his poetry in, say, *Life Studies* or *The Dolphin*.[21] Lowell's rejection of Ulysses' physical violence, clear enough from the description of him already cited, is underlined when, in "Homecoming" – the poem immediately following the homecoming scene of "Ulysses and Circe" – we find that "sore-eyed" Ulysses, who "circles" like a shark preparatory to slaughter, is at once evoked and displaced by the poet:

> Sometimes
> I catch my mind
> circling for you with glazed eye –
> my lost love hunting
> your lost face.   (11)

Murderous doing has given way to tender remembering. The juxtaposition of "Ulysses and Circe" and "Homecoming" suggests an attempt on Lowell's part to purge his one-time attraction to violence, to assign it to Ulysses, who is then cast off. The treatment of Ulysses is relevant to the matter at hand not only because of Lowell's at least partial identification with him, first noted early in this essay, but because Homer's hero appears to be associated in Lowell's mind with poetry: "things changed to the names he gave them. . . ."

Ulysses may be linked to other instances of masculine aggression or assertiveness in *Day by Day*, all of them disowned by Lowell.[22] In "Domesday Book," William the Conqueror is described as having had French clerks who tore hundreds to shreds, feeding them "to berserk hawk and baron" (54). Going "berserk," which is tied to the breaking in of "inspiration" in Lowell's characterization of the poetic impulse in "Louisiana State University in 1940," has nothing to recommend it here (and remember Lowell's conception of himself as a victim being torn apart prior to being eaten in "Turtle"). Moreover, where, in the "Louisiana State" poem, the resistance to the poetic impulse was seen as capable of causing injury to the poet, it is the yielding to this impulse that is seen as having drained Lowell in "Our Afterlife I." At the very least, his poetry is regarded as not having saved him from hurt, from *being* broken. Although he raises the possibility that art "is a way to get well" (124), the book repeatedly reminds us of his falling away from mental health. Employing the breaking motif once again, Lowell responds to what is presumably a doctor's comment in "Home":

> "Remarkable breakdown, remarkable recovery" –
> but the breakage can go on repeating
> once too often. (113)

Breakage occurs *within* the hospital: "Cups and saucers stamped with the hospital's name / go daily to the tap and are broken." However much Lowell has opened himself to the breaking in of his creative energy, he still finds himself in a mental home, thinking about being "lucky" enough to end up among the shards of common people and common objects in the National Museum.

IV

The image of *Day by Day* offered thus far is a good deal gloomier than that to be found either in Steven Gould Axelrod's *Robert Lowell: Life and Art* or Vereen Bell's *Robert Lowell: Nihilist as Hero.* Axelrod, in the comparatively brief treatment of *Day by Day* at the end of his book, states that the title sequence has as its "overriding theme . . . the power of the individual, despite age and illness, to bear his life, to learn to understand and even prize it" (235). In his reading, "Epilogue," the final poem of the sequence, "affirms the artistic ideal of *Day by Day,* and implicitly of all [Lowell's] poetry, even while denigrating his actual achievement" (239). Able to agree only in part with these formulations, I find that Axelrod has yielded to the common wish to find *something* affirmative even in our gloomiest works of literature and to the common temptation to give our perorations an upbeat flavor. The same elements, which will not be entirely escaped by the present essay, are at work in Bell (though he allows himself a last-minute drop). Impressively formulating much of what makes for the book's bleakness, he still finds that *Day by Day* is at least qualifiedly affirmative, that it locates "margins" that are "open," if not human (of what use are these?), that it sends "the living dream, still alive, free into the world" (225, 232). In his view, the book does this, to a large extent, by its structure, which he sees as manipulating the chronology of Lowell's life so as "to get the worst of the *life* story over at once and to allow the volume to end on a note that, though not exactly buoyant, is at least open to possibility" (209). But *is* this the effect of the book's structure? In the closing pages of the "Day by Day" sequence, the section of the book Bell has in mind, we have Lowell describing himself as "a thorazined fixture"

(113), expressing a desire to die, seeing the shadow of a crow crossing his "shaking hand" (116), experiencing "'days of only poems and depression'" (118), revealing that he was an unwanted child, telling us that he is "in days of the downlook" (125), and claiming that his "trespassing tongue" (125) has put him into a prison. He does wake at night to find himself "mysteriously in full health," but the poem in which this occurs goes on to speak of "unhealth" and to indicate that he is apparently in an asylum; the final image is of hospital attendants reassuring the sick (116–17). Virtually the only things left to counteract the downward glide of these closing pages are "Thanks-Offering for Recovery," whose "affirmation" is almost entirely confined to its title, and the highly ambivalent "Epilogue."

In "Epilogue" Lowell seems disheartened that his art is now less akin to painting than to photography. A kind of ambiguous context for this characterization has been established by five or six references to photography scattered through the book. We might first look briefly at these before considering "Epilogue" in and of itself. In "Our Afterlife I," Lowell speaks of "the account," presumably of his own life, which he connects to "50 years of snapshots" (22). The last term, which might mean either actual photographs or the mental pictures of a lifetime, seems modest enough, but is numbered by Lowell among the "riches" of middle age. "Realities" alludes to "the golden age of photographs" (65), and "Marriage," fusing a painting of a married couple by Van Eyck with a family photograph of Lowell, his third wife, and three young stepdaughters, speaks of "a miracle of lighting / for the photographer's sacramental instant" (71). All these serve to give photography favorable associations. But "Square of Black" begins with "a sad, black, actual photograph / of Abraham Lincoln" and his son Tad, going on to talk of the president's premonition of his own death (32). "Suicide" provides an enigmatic linkage of a successful suicide attempt and the improving of one's skills in taking pictures (16). (Perhaps this is an obscure version of the notion that perfection of one's art is only achieved at great cost to one's life.)[23] "Riches," "golden," "sacramental" on the one hand, death by assassination or suicide on the other – a curiously sharp split, to say the least, in Lowell's associations with photography. "Epilogue" itself oscillates between negative and positive poles in its handling of photography in relation to Lowell's art.

Early in the poem Lowell speaks of his desire "to make / something imagined, not recalled. . . ."

> But sometimes everything I write
> with the threadbare art of my eye
> seems a snapshot,
> lurid, rapid, garish, grouped. . . .   (127)

The strong falling rhythm and staccato effect of this last line convey a tone of impatient self-dismissal. His photographic art seems, as does photography itself when compared with painting, at the mercy of the given, "paralyzed by fact." He goes on to say "All's misalliance." Here he is echoing a piece of self-criticism found three poems back in "Unwanted," where he had characterized even the "flashes" of his earlier poetry (note the possible allusion to photography in this) as guilty of "far-fetched misalliance." But having used the first fourteen lines of "Epilogue" to denigrate himself, Lowell effects a turn, defending the art of recall, the art tied to the facts of his experience: "Yet why not say what happened?" No sooner is this in place than he prays that his poetry achieve a quality found in painting, in Vermeer;[24] so, in effect, the photographic is again subordinated to the painterly. The poem performs a final flip, with the now famous lines:

> We are poor passing facts,
> warned by that to give
> each figure in the photograph
> his living name.

Here the photographic is accorded status, a vital function, in a variant on the eternalizing conceit of Elizabethan poetry.

This final reversal in the poem's characterization of Lowell's art gives a hundred and eighty degree turn to the characterization of the "facts." In its first occurrence in the poem, "fact" possesses a constricting power, the ability to "paralyze" the poet, preventing him from achieving his desired imagining. In its second occurrence, the factual is weak, the stuff of transience, in danger of simply disappearing. In this transformation from power to pathos, focused on a word, we find a possible analogue for the place *Day by Day* occupies in relation to Lowell's career as a whole.

His poetry long showed a fascination with power, even while eager to point to its abuses or limitations. He himself attempted to *be* powerful in the charged, portentous lines of his early verse, which he might well have been referring to when he spoke of "my intemperate, apocalyptic terms . . ." (*H* 70). That Lowell wrote on stilts and packed his poetry with willed energy in *Lord Weary's Castle* and *The Mills of the Kavanaughs* need scarcely be argued. Even when and after "his own vulnerable humanity [was] forced in on him" in *Life Studies*,[25] he maintained ties with his earlier, high oracular voice and grand allusions. Witness, in *Life Studies*, the classical references in "Beyond the Alps," and the identification with no less a figure than Milton's Satan in "Skunk Hour." *For the Union Dead* retained "Beyond the Alps," a sense of connection with Satan (in "Going to and fro"), and displayed Lowell's prophetic mode (though altered from its earlier manifestations) in its title piece. That mode dominated much of *Near the Ocean*, which begins with Lowell longing to possess the power of the salmon flinging itself up the "stone and bone-crushing waterfall" (*NO* 15). *Notebook 1967–68* included a section entitled "Power," which appeared in expanded form as "The Powerful" in *Notebook*. In the "Afterthought" of the first of these books, reproduced in the second, Lowell said he feared he had not been able to avoid "the gigantism of the sonnet" (*N 1967–68* 160, *N* 263). But gigantism in some sense was what he had frequently pursued, and he continued to do so. Taking over, with much revision, most of the contents of *Notebook* and greatly adding to them,

History generated a sense of inclusiveness, of sweeping through much of Western civilization, focusing on notable figures, historical and literary. The respective sequences "Power" and "The Powerful" in the *Notebook* volumes had ended with almost identical versions of a poem about Lowell, thus placing the poet himself under those categories. He chose to conclude *History* with this same work (in yet a third version), which, whatever its self-directed irony, presents its maker in a grand manner:

> One more annus mirabilis, its hero *hero demens,*
> ill-starred of men and crossed by his fixed stars,
> running his ship past sound-spar on the rocks. . . .   (*H* 207)

The Dolphin begins and ends with images of the poet as net maker; in the first instance the net is hardened into a kind of enduring memorial plaque, in the second it figures as an heroic tool, "an eelnet made by man for the eel fighting –" (*D* 78). At this late date, Lowell was still keeping his poetry tied to power.[26]

With *Day by Day,* he foregoes entirely this connection. Marital dissolution, deaths of friends and relatives, physical deterioration, mental illness have brought him down. He thinks of his "flashes" as relegated to the past, and, long simmered in suffering, he exhibits, in Helen Vendler's apt phrase, "the humility of the generic" (*Part of Nature* 167). His Ulysses may in fact refute the mediocrity he has been assigned by the suitors (to whom, comically, "he is Tom, Dick, or Harry" (10)), "breaking water to destroy his wake" (10), meaning, perhaps, attempting to obliterate his past sufferings and humiliation by an outburst of power. But in doing so he is repudiated by Lowell (whose last persona in the book is a woman questioning whether glory is to be identified with the exercise of military might). Instances of powerlessness repeatedly engage the poet of *Day by Day:* Horace unable to hold the river into which a girl he is pursuing has flung herself, Lowell's cousin Harriet Winslow permanently paralyzed, his wife required to lie in only one way because of her spine, her ex-husband having his feet wired above his head in a hospital, Lowell himself incapable of doing one thing or another – the book features the word "cannot." The poet is no longer an imperious, wide-ranging creator, but a limited creation, made "to be given away" (126). He has joined the rest of us in our state as poor passing facts, "designed for the moment" (118). "Breaking" has moved from a transitive action to something that must be endured; Lowell himself is one of the broken, a victim of what he had already called, in *The Dolphin,* "this breaking life" (*D* 55).

The sense of powerlessness or at least the sense of relinquishing claim to power may be seen in the format of *Day by Day's* poems. If we count *Notebook 1967–68* and *Notebook* as separate works, Lowell gave us no fewer than five consecutive volumes of sonnets, or at least fourteen-line poems. However diverse the materials, however large the subjects, he compelled his verses to parade before us in those strictly defined units, probably the longest forced march in contemporary poetry. With *Day by Day* he has let go of this willed packaging. The poems come to us in all sizes, in lines that may use one word or ten. The insistence on formal shaping, on the explicit presence of the poet's controlling hand, has been yielded up.

I am arguing not that the emergence of a sense of powerlessness is new in Lowell but only that it has never been so pervasive. Its triumph, understandably, makes for dispiritedness. This is clearly evident in *Day by Day*'s epigrammatic passages. A gift for epigram might be regarded by a poet as a manifestation of his powers, a means for getting back at what has first gotten at him, and doing so in a self-delighting way. Lowell's epigrams are surely memorable, but unmistakably glum, as when he calls a "responsible" daily newspaper "an anthology of the unredeemable world" (125), or when he says "if we see a light at the end of the tunnel, / it's the light of an oncoming train" (31).

A poet who has identified his art with power, sometimes with the energy of the "manic," now to a greater degree than ever has to make poems out of his depression. It is his achievement in *Day by Day* that he is able to do more than succumb to the falling nature of things and take us down with him. He shows himself capable of humor, tenderness, empathy, appreciation, coming to terms with old grievances, and surviving. His poetry could not necessarily save him from his depression, and frequently produces just that feeling in the reader. But *Day by Day* gives us, if not flashes, then nuggets that gleam amid the prevailing gloom, albeit darkly.

NOTES

1 In quoting himself, Lowell can be seen as slyly displacing the matter of Troy with the matter of Lowell. Just as much as Homer, he himself is now the basis for allusion. Helen Vandler (*Part of Nature, Part of Us: Modern American Poets* 169) has remarked on the relative absence of allusion to other poets in *Day by Day*. "Returning," incidentally, is echoed not only in "Ulysses and Circe" but also in the very next poem of *Day by Day*, "Homecoming" (11).

2 Vendler suggests that the bedroom in which Ulysses is lying with Circe is a prison (*Part of Nature* 137).

3 Stephen Yenser's *Circle to Circle: The Poetry of Robert Lowell* makes much of circular movements in the Lowell canon. Yenser's book, of course, was published before the appearance of *Day by Day*.

4 An earlier stage of Lowell's career was marked by what might be called massive returns to earlier work, but not in the sense I am interested in here. *Notebook 1967–68* was hardly out before Lowell went back to it to produce *Notebook*. He went back to *that* to produce *History* and *For Lizzie and Harriet*. The returns I am concentrating on arc back over much greater periods of time and are something other than a matter of verbal revision.

5 The wistfulness of both passages, particularly the latter, is underlined when we read *Day by Day*'s declaration that "Autumn is my favorite season – / why does it change clothes and withdraw?" ("The Withdrawal" 72).

6 Here I find myself in disagreement with both Steven Gould Axelrod and Helen Vendler, who contend that the ending of the poem offers relief (Axelrod, *Robert Lowell* 150; Vendler,

"Lowell's Last Poems" 81). In my reading, "Fall 1961" consciously offers too puny an ending to counteract the poem's oppressiveness.

7   For a similar linkage of the two poems, see Bell, *Robert Lowell: Nihilist as Hero* 210–12.

8   The difference in treatment is exemplified by the way "tiptoe," employed in *Life Studies'* "During Fever" to suggest Lowell Senior's marginal position in his house, is here appropriated by him for his own use.

9   With one exception: Lowell's father is given a touch of the heroic at the end of "Commander Lowell."

10   It might be noted that another father and son in *Day by Day*, Abraham and Tad Lincoln, are said to have, in a photograph of them made in 1861, "amost matching silver watch-chains" (32). In "For Sheridan," where the use of a photograph is not entirely clear, Lowell again points up a connection between parent and child, perhaps referring to his father, himself, and his son: "Three ages in a flash: the same child in the same picture, / he, I, you, / chockablock, one stamp . . ." (82). "Middle Age," in *For the Union Dead*, can be seen as occupying a kind of middle ground between *Life Studies* and *Day by Day* with respect to Lowell's portrayals of his father. There the poet records his "meetings" with his parent, already dead. He addresses him in a parody of the Lord's Prayer, but the closing stanza is entirely serious and gives the father a sudden magnitude: "You never climbed / Mount Sion, yet left / dinosaur / death-steps on the crust, / where I must walk" (7). "Robert T. S. Lowell" furnishes a curious verbal overlap with this: "It would take two lifetimes / to pick the crust / and uncover the face / under our two menacing, / iconoclastic masks" (7). We might see this nearly impenetrable crust as echoing a section of "Charles River" (later "Mother and Father 1"), in which Lowell says that an apology he made for having struck his father "hardly scratched the surface of his invisible / coronary . . . never to be effaced" (*N 1967–68* 37; *N 68*; *H* 114). "Robert T. S. Lowell," in its reconciliation with the father, also recalls "Father in a Dream" and "To Daddy," printed consecutively in *History* (116).

11   Compare Lowell's statement in his essay "After Enjoying Six or Seven Essays On Me": "From year to year, things remembered from the past change almost more than the present" (113).

12   As Bell has said, "noticing, living in the moment, and innocence of perspective . . . come to symbolize for Lowell a desired status in the world" (228).

13   "Gold" can retain its favorable associations in *Day by Day*, but as such it tends to be placed in the past. "Our Afterlife II" says "America once lay uncropped and golden" (23), and "Realities," referring to a generation or generations before the poet's own, speaks of "the golden age of photographs" (65).

14   Lowell associated scars with his vocation in the final poem of *History*, where the carbon copies of his poems are described as "scarred with ciphers" (207).

15   Another sort of depressing presidential self-listening with which Lowell may identify figures in the volume when Lincoln is described as hearing his voice in a dream "saying over his own dead body: / 'Lincoln is dead'" ("Square of Black," *DBD* 32).

16   Compared with its earlier version, the phrasing of this line stresses Lowell's sense that he offers us merely the results of what he sees. The poem, as it appeared in *Salmagundi*, reads "I write / with dim eyes and threadbare art" ("After Enjoying" 115).

17   In "Harriet's Donkey," section 6 of "Winter and London" in *The Dolphin*, Lowell pre-

sents a similarly contemptuous image of his writing: "On this blank page no worse, not yet defiled / by my inspiration running black in type . . ." (46).

18   I wrote this before reading Robert Fitzgerald's "Aiaia and Ithaca." Fitzgerald also links the sun to the notion of an unmoved mover, but does not talk of the falling pattern I am placing it in.

19   Both these phrases, particularly "I destroyed Troy," can be thought of as examples of sound returns, discussed earlier.

20   Compare the use of the word to designate presumably admired energy in "Shifting Colors": "fish break water with the wings of a bird to escape" (*DBD* 119).

21   In the title poem of the latter book he says: "I have sat and listened to too many / words of the collaborating muse, / and plotted perhaps too freely with my life, / not avoiding injury to others, / not avoiding injury to myself – / to ask compassion . . ." (*D* 78).

22   Specifically: the ruthless William the Conqueror of "Domesday Book," the intoxicated baron of "Ear of Corn," deluded about his irresistibility, the "barracuda" critic of "Death of a Critic," and the male swan of "Last Walk?", who has escaped the "matriarchal pond" to go down the river, "smirking drunkenly."

23   In the second section of "Hospital" in *The Dolphin,* Lowell writes: "I mark my proofs, a sheaf of tapeworms . . ." (20). The final stage in the production of his poems is seen as consuming him.

24   Derek Walcott tells us that he asked Lowell "what painter he imagined to be his complement, and he said Vermeer" (30).

25   The comment was made by Randall Jarrell, quoted on the book jacket of *Notebook 1967–68.*

26   He may, however, be questioning that tie in *The Dolphin,* at least in the sense of questioning his commitment to a high-flown intensity. He says in that book, in "Summer Between Terms," "I have stood too long on a chair or ladder, / branch-lightning forking through my thought and veins . . ." (28).

10

Lowell and the Visual Arts

HELEN DEESE

Introduction

Derek Walcott once asked Robert Lowell "what painter he imagined to be his complement," and Lowell answered, "Vermeer" (30). In "Epilogue," the poem that closes his last collection, *Day by Day*, Lowell affirms that sense of similarity in their artistic intention:

Pray for the grace of accuracy
Vermeer gave to the sun's illumination
stealing like the tide across a map
to his girl solid with yearning.   (127)

We can see that Lowell perceived a common method in the design of paintings and the design of poems. His informal but systematic study of painting began during his school years at St. Mark's, just when he was also becoming interested in writing poetry. He described those beginnings to Frederick Seidel:

My school had been given a Carnegie set of art books, and I had a friend, Frank Parker, who had great talent as a painter but who'd never done it systematically. We began reading the books and histories of art, looking at reproductions, tracing the Last Supper on tracing paper, and studying dynamic symmetry, learning about Cézanne, and so on. I had no practical interest in painting, but that study seemed rather close to poetry. And from there I began. (16)

That passage suggests that Lowell first became interested in painting and the other visual arts less because of their symbolic meaning or story-telling capacity than because of their composition, the way their interacting colors and shapes could achieve visual effects. What he found close to poetry was the "dynamic symmetry" of art, the effects of composition that are more than sums of the parts.

Meaning may seem inescapable when words are put together or when colors are juxtaposed on flat space. A viewer or reader will inevitably detect meaning in his or her experience of a poem or painting because meaning looked-for always appears. But the artist concentrates first on the means to his or her achievement, "the dynamic symmetry." In Leonardo da Vinci's *Last Supper*, for example, "the compositional structure does much more than hold together a picture of great size. It is itself an expressive factor and . . . the strongest one" (Canaday 167). Although an artwork's final, elusive totality of meaning can be completed only by the viewer or reader, a study of the artist's means can make that completion a richer, more complex, and even, paradoxically, a more mysterious psychological experience.

This essay is a study of Lowell's integration of visual art, especially paintings and photographs, into his poetry, both within individual poems and within sequences. After looking at "For the Union Dead," "91 Revere Street," and "Cranach's Man-Hunt," we will study some of Lowell's most significant late texts. We will relate the juxtaposition of visual and verbal elements in *Day by Day*'s "Epilogue" to that in *History*'s "Rembrandt," *Day by Day*'s "Marriage," and finally to the composition of *Day by Day* as a whole. Lowell's integrated images of pictorial representation in the poems of *Day by Day* become even richer expressive factors when their complexity is understood within the volume's unifying pastoral pattern.

Although some critical attention has been given to Lowell's use of sculpture – it is difficult to ignore Augustus Saint-Gaudens's bas-relief in "For the Union Dead," for example – very little has yet been written about Lowell's verbal representations of paintings. Lowell, particularly in the collections beginning with *Notebook 1967–68*, absorbed and transformed images from the visual arts into his poetic texts, not as homages of description, nor as exemplary allusions whose specificity can be ignored by the otherwise attentive reader, but as visually enriched units of grammar. Synecdochically, he embedded whole pictures, often with the artist's technique and concept included, into a sentence. Sometimes the picture became a whole piece of poetic structure. In "Marriage," for example, Lowell's rendering of Jan Van Eyck's *The Arnolfini Marriage* makes up more than half the poem. It is an intertextual poem: The texts he joins, however, are not words with words but visual images with verbal images, pictures with words.

Michael North has interestingly studied Lowell's use in "For the Union Dead" (*FUD* 70–72) of Saint-Gaudens's monument to Robert Gould Shaw and the Massachusetts Fifty-Fourth Infantry Regiment. North, however, misses a significant dimension of Lowell's practice: He interprets Lowell the poet as responding not to the physical art of Saint-Gaudens but exclusively to symbols, ideas, and history. The visible art becomes invisible. North apotheosizes both words and bronze into a timid abstraction of pure spirit: "Shaw is Lowell's aspiration to a life free of the flesh and an art above the violence of society" (283). But Lowell the poet always keeps a physical representation in sight. When he writes "Their monument sticks like a fishbone / in the city's throat," his "their" refers to Shaw and the black soldiers, and his metaphor derives from Saint-Gaudens's specific imagery: The slanted bayonets on the soldiers' rifles make a pattern much like that of a fishbone. Saint-Gaudens's colonel is, as Lowell suggests, "as lean / as a compass needle"; his upper torso rises vertically, with "gentle tautness," from the saddle, pointing, within the frame of the bronze relief, due north like a compass needle. Formally Shaw's back is the major vertical in a sculpture that is remarkable for its achieved sense of movement, so it appears that "when he leads his black soldiers to death, / he cannot bend his back." The point is that the poem records both Saint-Gaudens's bronze imagery and Lowell's perception of the young colonel's bronzed, "angry wrenlike vigilance" and the "bell-cheeked" soldiers whose bronzed blackness sticks in the craw of a newly race-conscious city. To experience the poem fully one should be aware, moreover, of the history of the monument (related in Axelrod, "Colonel Shaw," and Hansen). Indeed, the poem calls our attention to that history: "William James could almost hear the bronze Negroes breathe." But the specificity of Lowell's written words should not be ignored in the wish to achieve a grandly abstract interpretation. The words, however suggestive, represent very physical bronze images.

Stephen Tapscott dismisses Lowell's inclusion of visual artifacts in his poems as mere objective correlatives, and he mistakenly reports that Lowell made poetic use of sculpture more than of paintings: "Lowell, who writes of public statuary more than of pictures, renders his Puritan tombstones and Civil War monuments directly, as civic relics that objectify an estranged past" (38). The newer poets who are writing poems of memory, says Tapscott, depict "a single scene, as if in memory or in a clear dream" (38), and often the scenes are responses to, not descriptions of, photographs or paintings. These poets are "less overtly derivative" than are William Carlos Williams ("Pictures from Brueghel," "The Blue Nude"), W. H. Auden ("Musée des Beaux Arts"), John Berryman ("Winter Landscape"), and Robert Lowell. "Overtly derivative" seems an unnecessarily reductive phrase for these poems by Lowell and the others who make visual art the material of their verbal art. These poets do render particular paintings carefully to create certain verbal effects, but the poems are not homages. They are equal to the paintings, just as Charles Demuth's *I Saw the Figure 5 in Gold* is equal to Williams's poem "The Great Figure," not derivative of it as an illustration would be. Wallace Stevens uses Picasso's *The Great Guitarist* to begin a set of variations on a theme, transforming reality with the imagination; David Hockney, in turn, responds to Stevens's "The Man with the Blue Guitar" with a set of etchings that he conceived "not as literal illustrations of the poem but as an interpretation of its theme in visual terms. Like the poem, they are about transformations within art."

Lowell's imagination, similarly, transforms visual compositions to verbal composition, making motif and metaphor out of his experience of art. Tapscott is factually wrong in saying that Lowell made limited use of paintings. For example, Lowell opens the first section of "91 Revere Street" (*LS* 11–46) with a vivid picture: the portrait of Major Mordecai Myers in his "sanguine War of 1812 uniform with epaulets, white breeches, and a scarlet frogged waistcoat." Apotheosized in the boy's eyes "by the sunlight lighting the blood smear on his scarlet waistcoat," visually exciting the young Lowell's admiration for military costuming and Jewish difference, the portrait recurs in the last scene of the prose memoir. There it hangs over the seated Commander Billy Harkness rather than over Commander R. T. S. Lowell. The portrait not only structurally opens and closes "91 Revere Street" but also specifies the contempt that qualifies the boy's unhappy love for his father.

The same "For the Union Dead" that contemplates Saint-Gaudens's bas-relief foreshadows *Day by Day*'s concern with photographic images in two haunting verbal representations of pictures from the camera: a commercial photograph of "Hiroshima boiling / over a Mosler Safe" and a television shot in which the "drained faces of Negro school-children rise like balloons" (*FUD* 72). The memory poems of *Life Studies*, meant to seem "as open and as single-surfaced as a photograph" (Hamilton, "Conversation" 32), also attest to his interest in photography as a stylistic metaphor. In addition, beginning with *Notebook 1967–68*, Lowell writes into his text more and more painterly images from the walls of the great galleries of Europe and America. To name only the most obvious, he uses Titian, Holbein, Dürer, Cranach, Potter, Cuyp, Constable, Velasquez, Ryder, Turner, Renoir, Degas, Cézanne, and Manet.

Those names suggest much rich material for study, for Lowell uses no painting casually. Consider, for example, his association of Anne Boleyn with the cows of Peter Potter and Aelbert Cuyp ("Anne Boleyn," *H* 62) – odd until one associates Potter's famous and massive *Young Bull* with Henry VIII. Or consider Lowell's association of Lucas Cranach's *Stag Hunt* with a commemorative photograph of a group "composed, you will say, for our forever friendship, / almost one arm around our many shoulders" ("Cranach's Man-Hunt," *H* 63). These are "friends" bound to each other "by birth and faith . . . one German outing." They are also "game for the deerhunt, aged five to ninety." I believe that Lowell is looking at a real photograph of real people, people who are about to die "on this clearing of blown, coarse grass." And because they are photographed (as game), we know they are from our time, not that of Lucas Cranach the Elder (1472–1553), who rendered *The Stag-Hunt of the Elector Frederick the Wise* in 1529. The details of the photograph merge into the details of Cranach's etching, suggesting that the first derives from the second, that the manhunt descends from the staghunt. The "stream of the photograph" becomes the "choppy, lavender stream" of the etching, where the stags are hunted from ambush by "the Kaiser Maxmillian" (of Austria), by his host, Frederick, the "wise Saxon Elector" (whose palace was in Wittenberg), and by assorted horsemen, picadors, and their "beautiful, verminous dogs." Frederick was called "Wise" because he provided the political support for Luther's Reformation. Cranach was court painter for Frederick and the unofficial court painter for Luther and the Reformation. Surely, the merging of photograph and etching, manhunt and staghunt, becomes a visualization of a truth: The Holocaust had a significant source in Luther's exhortations that Jews be hunted out from the German communities. The last line of the sonnet, however, extends the hunting victory to the rest of militant Christianity: "this battle the Prince has never renounced or lost," the prince being the "Prince of Hades" or perhaps the "Prince of Peace."

In "Cranach's Man-Hunt," Lowell has used visual artifacts that are information-ally complex in themselves and rich with associations in order to open out his strict sonnet form – or, to put it a contrary way, in order to bring in density, to invest his language with great chunks of the outer world. There is much to be learned, as I have said, by closer study of Lowell's poems that slip one art into another. But be-cause of the limitations of space, this study will focus on the visual representations suggested directly and indirectly by "Epilogue." These will be paintings by Vermeer, Rembrandt, and Jan Van Eyck, as well as several photographs. Each painting has a woman in it; each photograph, like that in "Cranach's Man-Hunt," has an aura of death about it. Lowell uses that contrast, as I shall show, to enhance the elegiac tone of *Day by Day*'s second section and the consolatory tone of its third (and last) section.

Describing Women

Although, as he told Derek Walcott and implied in "Epilogue," Lowell felt Vermeer to be his closest complement in the visual arts, the two artists were, in one respect, radically different: Lowell created poetic vitality from misalliance, whereas Vermeer drew his visual energy from the seeming stillness of light. On the other hand, both Vermeer and Lowell composed their art from what they ob-served. Vermeer painted the appearance of what he saw; Lowell told "what hap-pened" ("Epilogue," *DBD* 127). In addition, the art of both very often focused on women. (In this connection, it may be significant that Lowell apparently derived his phrase "Why not say what happened?" from the conversation of his second wife, Elizabeth Hardwick [see Alvarez, *Observer* 19].) But to understand "Epilogue," and Lowell's descriptive poetry in general, we need to examine in more detail the charac-teristics of the Dutch painting that attracted him.

Elizabeth Hardwick, in *Sleepless Nights*, her barely fictionalized reflection on her life with Lowell, describes a book in their library as being "Fromentin on the Dutch painters in a neat Phaidon edition" (103). Fromentin, a nineteenth-century artist and historian of excellent insight, writes about the seventeenth-century Dutch painters thus:

> If you take away Rembrandt – an exception in his own country and every-where else – you will see but one style and one method in all the studies of Holland. The object is to imitate that which *is*. (100)

Dutch painting is an art, he continues, "which adapts itself to the nature of things . . . nothing preconceived, nothing which precedes the simple, strong, and sensitive ob-servation of what is" (128).

Svetlana Alpers, in her admirable study, *The Art of Describing: Dutch Art in the Seventeenth Century*, agrees that the Dutch artists showed immense respect for the thing itself, and a delight in the appearance of things. One of her major themes is that Dutch art

> can best be understood as being an art of describing as distinguished from the narrative art of Italy. "Descriptive" is indeed one way of characterizing many of the works that we are accustomed to refer to casually as *realistic* – among which is included the pictorial mode of photographs. (xx)

Among the Dutch painters, Jan Vermeer was the most accurate in rendering the natural appearances of things and persons, in representing the effects of light passing from objects to retina, in recording compositionally what the eye has seen. "The description," according to Lawrence Gowing, "is always exactly adequate, always completely and effortlessly in terms of light" (19).

Gowing was, during Lowell's lifetime, the most accessible, significant, and widely known scholar on Vermeer. It seems probable that Lowell was familiar with his commentary. Gowing's thesis in *Vermeer* is that Vermeer paints light, light revealing form and being, especially feminine being. In the characteristic Vermeer painting,

> the nature of things is perfectly visible; objects receive the light as if by habit, without welcoming or shrinking. . . . Often it is not matter that occupies the eye, so much as the reciprocal play of nearness and distance. . . . Along with window frames, across the floor, the perspective pattern extends until, against the wall, framed in its rectangular divisions, the human inhabitant is discovered. She has no thought in particular, no re- markable occupation. Her mooning is caught in a mathematic net made definite at last, part of a time-less order. (18)

The energy levels of the two artists – Lowell and Vermeer – differ radically: Lowell's poems do seem at times, as he says, "lurid, rapid, garish, grouped, / heightened from life" (*DBD* 127). But some things echo from one artist to the other: the dy- namic symmetry and perhaps the woman as an instance of some kind of an order that transcends generational time.

Most of Vermeer's thirty-four or thirty-five paintings represent women. As Gow- ing says, "So long as Vermeer has a positive subject, his subject remains the attention that man pays to woman" (52). His paintings, Gowing explains later, "expound a dual view of female nature, challenging and receptive" (55). Alpers agrees that "Ver- meer effectively determines the woman observed, woman as the object of male atten- tion, to be the painter's subject" (223). When Lowell in "Epilogue" affirms a sense of similarity to Vermeer, surely he has in mind the painter's reciprocal interplay in design, his visual acuity, and his attention to women:

> Pray for the grace of accuracy
> Vermeer gave to the sun's illumination
> stealing like the tide across a map
> to his girl solid with yearning.

The details in those lines prescribe a Vermeer picture with three particular details: the sun's illumination, a map, a young woman. A closer reading suggests that the sunlight enters the picture's room from one side, partially illuminating first a map and then a woman. It is to this light that Vermeer gives the "grace of accuracy," the light in which all things are seen, the illumination that in turn gives visible existence to the map and the woman. Gowing writes that "the grace of Vermeer's world is to wear to the last the garment of a retinal impression, to claim no greater depth than the play of light" (61). Yet the woman, to Lowell, seems "solid" in her being, substantial "with yearning."

Not one, but five of Vermeer's paintings contain the three required details of Lowell's poem – the sun's light, a map, a young woman. Lowell was undoubtedly familiar with all five. Probably this is why Vereen Bell concludes that the details seem to represent "a composite of several of Vermeer's paintings, not a particular, identifiable one" (243). I believe, however, that, although all five are probably in the subtext of "Epilogue," only one of the five paintings precisely meets the specificity of the poem's detail.

The five paintings are, as titled by Gowing, *Soldier and Laughing Girl, A Lady with a Lute, Young Woman with a Water Jug, An Artist in His Studio*, and *Woman in Blue Reading a Letter* (see Figs. 1–5). Lowell had ample opportunity to know each of these paintings directly, not merely in reproduction. *Soldier and Laughing Girl, Lady with a Lute*, and *Young Woman with a Water Jug* all hang in New York City. *An Artist in His Studio* is in the Kunsthistorisches Museum of Vienna, not far from Salzburg where Lowell taught in the summer and fall of 1952. The last painting, *Woman in Blue Reading a Letter*, hangs in the Rijksmuseum in Amsterdam where Lowell and Hardwick lived in 1951.

The commonality of detail among these pictures might indeed suggest that the poem refers to a composite, as Bell supposes, if composites were Lowell's usual subject. Lowell's habitual, metonymic specificity, however, and his fidelity to visual fact argue that he is describing a specific painting. As we have already seen in "For the Union Dead" and "Cranach's Man-Hunt," Lowell expects the details of a visual artifact, even the unstated details, to function dynamically within his poetic composition. The question then is, Which picture of the five functions most effectively within Lowell's poem?

In *Soldier and Laughing Girl*, the entire map is brightly lit by the sun's light at full tide, and the woman's broad smile seems pleased with something other than yearning. In *Lady with a Lute*, the woman seems sufficiently yearning, but the sun's illumination steals across her to the map, not the other way around. In *Young Woman with a Water Jug*, the sun's light again brightens the woman before it reaches the map.

An Artist in His Studio seems at first to fit Lowell's lines fairly well, if not precisely. Norma Procopiow has stated without qualification or discussion that "the painting referred to in 'Epilogue' is Vermeer's *The Artist in His Studio*" ("Day" 9). But in this painting the sun's illumination does not steal "like the tide across a map / to his

Fig. 1. Vermeer, *Soldier and Laughing Girl.* Copyright The Frick Collection, New York.

girl. . . ." The sun's light touches the woman's hand before it reaches the map's border. Indeed, in the moment of the painting's time, the sun is simultaneously lighting up her hand, face, and the entire map. Furthermore, the spatial focus is not on the woman but the distance between the painter and his model. The two, painter and model, are – like the lovers on Keats's Grecian urn – bound eternally in the rendered moment of the painting and are forever at a distance.

The Vermeer painting embedded in "Epilogue" is *Woman in Blue Reading a Letter.* Only this painting matches Lowell's details exactly. The visual focus of *Woman in Blue* is immediately and clearly on the woman who so solidly occupies the center

Fig. 2. Vermeer, *A Lady with a Lute*. The Metropolitan Museum of Art, bequest of Collis P. Huntington, 1900 (25.110.24).

area and the middle distance of the painting. The light, flowing in from the left of the picture through an unseen window, is indeed a "tide" of illumination stealing across the map to that woman solid with pregnancy, a feminine condition in which the present visibly contains the future for which it yearns. Vermeer has eternalized a quiet, enclosed, passing moment of a woman's life, but one that silently suggests the existence of a world external to the picture. The light steals in from an outer, unseen source; the map charts the geography of a recently independent nation. The letter carries words from an unseen writer, and the pregnancy involves an unseen husband, perhaps the letter writer.

Fig. 3. Vermeer, *Young Woman with a Water Jug*. The Metropolitan Museum of Art, gift of Henry G. Marquand, 1889 (89.15.21).

That letter, whose contents are unknown to us, can tell us no story. But it does connect the painting – if only by implication – to composed texts. We cannot see the words on the letter, but the activity we do see – physically a very still activity – is reading. Lowell's poem contains a picture, and that picture contains a text. Visual image and verbal image slip in and out of each other. The map, too, is a type of text as well as a type of picture. Of necessity, if it is to be useful, a map is an accurate text-picture of a particular part of the external world.

Howard Nemerov reminds us that poetry and painting may have a common derivation in the human activities preserved in cave drawings, which are both representations

Fig. 4. Vermeer, *An Artist in His Studio*. Kunsthistorisches Museum, Vienna.

and signifiers. And he suggests that some day poetry and painting might come back together, fusing "their very different but immense powers . . . into something not really much like either." Nemerov says that we "already have an instance in which this happens: the making of maps, charts, diagrams, blueprints . . . where the representing of the visible, at which painting is supremely capable, is accomplished in parallel with the strict and abstract syntax of writing" (107). Vermeer, like most

Fig. 5. Vermeer, *Woman in Blue Reading a Letter.* Rijksmuseum-Stichting, Amsterdam.

Dutch painters, commonly represented texts as letters, words, titles, and maps in his paintings (Alpers 169–221), integrating abstract signifiers into his representations of the visible.

Lowell himself was integrating the representation of the visible into his written texts as early as "Charles the Fifth and the Peasant" in *Lord Weary's Castle.* As that sonnet progresses through various revisions in *Notebook 1967–68, Notebook,* and *History,* its picture – Titian's mounted *Charles the Fifth,* studio painted and not from life – and its text integrate with each other ever more accurately. But Titian's portrait itself is not a realistic rendition; it is more a glorification:

> The sunset he tilts at is big Venetian stuff,
> the true Charles, done by Titian, never lived.
> The battle he rides offstage to is offstage.   (*H* 63)

Although Lowell obviously admired Titian, his own poetic aesthetic of "accuracy" in image and word brought him closer to the realism of Vermeer and the Dutch painters, and to their easy, unselfconscious integration of the verbal and the visible.

Vermeer's *Woman in Blue* is reading a letter we cannot see, so the verbal possibilities must be inferred. In another painting that attracted Lowell, a woman has also received a letter, but in this case we know the contents. The painting is *Bathsheba,* and it is one of four Rembrandt paintings of women that Lowell uses in his sonnet "Rembrandt" (*N 1967–68* 85; *N* 143; *H* 69). In the painting, the naked Bathsheba, her bath completed, is resting on a draped seat. Her hand holds her letter against her knee; she seems to be gently pondering it. A servant is drying Bathsheba's feet (see Fig. 6). Here is Lowell's description of Rembrandt and his Bathsheba, a biblical figure painted as an ordinary woman:

> The Dutchman was a sack, his woman a sack,
> the obstinate, undefeated hull of an old scow;
> but Bathsheba's ample stomach, her heavy, practical feet,
> are reverently dried by the faithful servant,
> his eyes dwell lovingly on each fulfilled sag;
> her unfortunate body is the privilege of service,
> is radiant with an homage void of possession. . . .   (*H* 69)

In his chosen details, Lowell leaves out the letter, just as he leaves out the letter in the Vermeer painting, but anyone familiar with either work knows just how significant the letters are. Viewing the Vermeer, we can only guess at the text, but we know the contents of Bathsheba's letter. The letter is from King David who, from his roof, saw her bathing:

> And David sent messengers, and took her;
> and she came in unto him, and he lay with her.   (2 Samuel 11.4)

Eventually, after her husband is conveniently killed in battle, she will marry King David and mother the son who will succeed him – Solomon. It is a momentous letter. The painting, however, focuses our eye more on the woman than on the story.

The woman in the painting is called Bathsheba, but the woman is also Hendrickje Stoffels. Hendrickje first came into Rembrandt's home as a servant but she became, after his wife's death, his mistress, his model, and eventually his common-law wife.

Fig. 6. Rembrandt, *Bathsheba*. Cliché des Musées Nationaux, Paris.

Those male eyes that the sonnet tells us "dwell lovingly on each fulfilled sag" belong neither to King David nor the painted servant but to Rembrandt himself. In Lowell's interpretation, it is Rembrandt's painterly "homage void of possession" that makes her "unfortunate body" "radiant."

The sonnet creates other pictures of women. Read as a whole, it becomes a verbal gallery of Rembrandt paintings of women. I want to identify the paintings and then show how, using the images from the paintings and some language borrowed from Kenneth Clark, the sonnet connects to Lowell's last sequenced poem, "Epilogue." First, let me repeat the sonnet in its entirety:

Rembrandt

His faces crack . . . if mine could crack and breathe!
His Jewish Bridegroom, hand spread on the Jewish Bride's

Fig. 7. Rembrandt, *The Jewish Bridegroom.* Rijksmuseum-Stichting, Amsterdam.

bashful, tapestried, level bosom, is faithful;
a girl, half-shadow, gives soul to his flayed steer.
Her breasts, the snowdrops, have lasted out the storm.
The Dutchman was a sack, his woman a sack,
the obstinate, undefeated hull of an old scow;
but Bathsheba's ample stomach, her heavy, practical feet,
are reverently dried by the faithful servant,
his eyes dwell lovingly on each fulfilled sag;
her unfortunate body is the privilege of service,
is radiant with an homage void of possession. . . .
We see, if we see at all, through a brown mist
the strange new idol from the marketplace.   (*H* 69)

The first line reminds us of how old paint looks on a canvas, finely crackled. Lowell's verbal faces, however, having no concrete existence, cannot change with time, as paint does – or as breathing people do.

   Lines two and three, concerning the "Jewish Bridegroom" and "Bride," evoke a painting that is sometimes titled *The Jewish Bridegroom,* sometimes *The Jewish Bride* (Fig. 7). Whether this is a portrait of real people or of Isaac and Rebecca in seventeenth-century dress, no one knows, but either is possible. Although, as in *Bathsheba,* the woman's figure is central, the emotion studied in the painting is that between a man and a woman. The bridegroom is gently embracing the bride: His left arm is draped protectively about the shy woman's shoulders; his right hand rests, palm down, on the woman's flat-bodiced breast. The position of that hand, erotic and protective, immediately catches the viewer's eye. Rembrandt's bridegroom, however realistically painted, seems a portrait of ideal masculine fidelity and protecting love, while the bride seems just as ideally compliant and shy. Both faithful groom and shy bride are at an ironic distance from Lowell and his own experience with women.

Line four refers to a powerful but strange picture, Rembrandt's *The Slaughtered Ox,* which hangs in the Louvre in Paris (another version hangs in Glasgow). The picture is of a slaughtered steer, flayed and eviscerated and hanging in a slaughter-house. A young woman, half in shadow, is looking up at the bloody carcass. Lowell has changed the reference from "ox" to "steer," probably because the steer is a cas-trated ox or bull. Lowell's line alludes to the male as victim – but not as victim of the woman. She gives it (or him) soul, something beyond the physical.

Line five describes yet another Rembrandt image of a woman, an image somewhat more difficult to identify. She is obviously nude. Rembrandt's most sensual nude, more erotic if less haunting than Bathsheba, is *Danae* (Fig. 8). Here is yet another possibility in the relationship between man and woman – possession by a god. Danae was visited by Jupiter in a shower of gold and from that visitation conceived Per-seus. In the painting, she is lying on her bed, smiling. The simile of snowdrops, especially as the flower, could well describe her breasts, and she has survived the golden storm of Jupiter's love.

The fourth feminine image in the sonnet is, of course, Bathsheba-Hendrickje, beloved by King David and beloved by Rembrandt. Compositionally Lowell's sonnet balances two clothed women against two nude ones. There seems a progression of feminine sexuality, caught as images in male eyes, from the flat-breasted Bride to Bathsheba's belly-sagging maturity.

The sonnet's final two lines comment chorically on this visual male attention to women:

> We see, if we see at all, through a brown mist
> the strange new idol from the marketplace.

The remark is mysterious and allusional. Lowell, in these lines, is borrowing imagery and metaphor from texts more than from paintings. Line thirteen, of course, evokes Paul's first epistle to the Corinthians (13.12): "For now we see through a glass, darkly." Lowell's "brown mist" suggests, in an extension of Paul's "darkly," the brownness of Rembrandt's shadows and his golden light. Line fourteen derives from Francis Bacon's third class of idols. Bacon's "Idols of the Marketplace" are not, as we moderns might assume, the ambitions of merchants. Rather they are words, abstract signifiers that create unsubstantial images or "false notions" (335), words that "wonderfully obstruct the understanding. . . . throw all into confusion, and lead

Fig. 8. Rembrandt, *Danae*. The Hermitage, Leningrad.

men away into numberless empty controversies and idle fancies" (337). Bacon himself derives the term "Idols of the Marketplace" from Paul's experience in the marketplace of Athens, a city "wholly given to idolatry" (Acts 17.16). In the marketplace,
Paul disputed "daily with them that met with him" – the Epicureans, the Stoics, the
Athenians who "spent their time in nothing else, but either to tell, or to hear some
new thing" (Acts 17.17–21). So the old Idols of the Marketplace are the words "that
so beset men's minds that truth can hardly find entrance" (Bacon 335).

But Lowell's "strange new idol *from* the marketplace" (my italics) cannot be words,
for the idol is something seen. It is woman, sometimes bought and sold, who besets
men's minds, woman whom they see through "a brown mist" if they see her at all.
To understand this sonnet, which is both an examination of the ways of men with
women and an affirmation, as in "Epilogue," that word and image should be accurate, we must look at its other textual borrowings.

Some of Lowell's words depicting Bathsheba derive from Sir Kenneth Clark's discussion in *The Nude* of Rembrandt's unidealized style of painting. (In the "Afterthought" to both *Notebook 1967–68* [16] and *Notebook* [263], Lowell admits generally to borrowing from Clark without telling us just what he borrowed; Jack Branscomb has identified the source [120].) I have italicized the pertinent phrasings:

> Rembrandt's greatest painting of the nude is of a young woman, clearly intended to be physically attractive. This is the Bathsheba in the Louvre, one of those supreme works of art which cannot be forced into any classification. The composition is derived from the combined memories of two antique reliefs, which Rembrandt had seen in engravings but his conception of the nude is entirely unclassical and, in fact, must represent his beloved Hendrickje. Now, when the dogmatic insistence of early etching has been abandoned, we feel the value of Rembrandt's humble and scrupulous honesty. For this *ample stomach,* these *heavy, practical* hands and *feet,* achieve a nobility far greater than the ideal form of, shall we say, Titian's *Venus of Urbino.* Moreover, this Christian acceptance of the *unfortunate body* has permitted the Christian *privilege* of a soul. The conventional nudes based on classical originals could bear no burden of thought or inner life without losing their formal completeness. Rembrandt can give his *Bathsheba* an expression of reverie so complex that we follow her thoughts far beyond the moment depicted; and yet these thoughts are indissolubly part of her body, which speaks to us in its own language as truthfully as Chaucer or Burns. (439–41)

Clark is pointing out that the facts of Rembrandt's woman speak a human thought more moving than the beauty of idealized femininity. Her body itself is visual language.

Clark goes on to compare Rembrandt's "miracle" of *Bathsheba* – "the naked body permeated with thought" (*Nude* 41) – to one of the most "horrifying images . . . ever put before us" (443): a painting by Georges Rouault of a naked prostitute, blank-eyed, square-jawed, drooping at the shoulders, with heavy breasts and belly. The prostitute, says Clark, is imaged like a cult object, like the primitive carvings of the ancient Aphrodite or the old Mexican mother goddesses with grossly exaggerated feminine body parts. And Clark uses the word "idol" that Lowell has picked up and enriched by embedding it in the Baconian context:

> She is a monstrous idol inspiring us with fear rather than pity. In this respect Rouault is also entirely unlike Rembrandt, whom he so greatly admires. . . . Rembrandt's approach was moral, Rouault's is religious. This is what gives his menacing prostitute her importance for us. Her hideous body is ideal because conceived in a spirit of awe. (446)

Lowell's "Rembrandt" is a marvelously rich sonnet, its connotative and layered meanings on the attention men pay to women not fully sayable in critical prose. Its women and its idol and the visions of its poet and painter seem a long distance from Vermeer's young woman in "Epilogue." Yet there is a connection, again through Kenneth Clark and Lowell's imaginative transformations of borrowed phraseology.

In *Rembrandt and the Italian Renaissance,* Clark compares Rembrandt's warmly human *Danae* (the woman with breasts like snowdrops in line five of "Rembrandt") to Titian's more coolly idealized *Venus of Urbino*:

> The head of Titian's Venus is without expression; and her body is inert and self-contained, a kind of monstrous fruit, incapable of movement or sensation. The Danae is warm, responsive, open, outward turning. Her gaze and the gesture of her hand, at once welcoming, defensive and surprised, have the complexity of a real human response, and her body is equally far from the vegetable inertia of Titian's Venus. (108)

Continuing his evocation of the Danae's nude body, Clark uses other words that Lowell takes up and, characteristically, transposes. The Danae's nude body

> is more sensuously compelling, partly because it is more natural, and partly because the *light*, which she greets as her lover, passes over her body like a *caressing* hand. (108)

The two words I have italicized reappear, transformed, in the italicized lines of "Epilogue":

> *The painter's vision is not a lens,*
> *it trembles to caress the light.*

I do not know if the first line has a separate derivation; I have not been able to find one. I believe that, in truth, Lowell may have associated *both* lines with the entire passage from Clark on the Danae and Titian's Venus. In Clark's words, the light caresses the woman's body; in Lowell's line, the painter's vision trembles to caress the passing light, as if in erotic response to it. Surely Lowell's poetic imagination seems to associate the painter's vision with the natural, human Danae – "warm, responsive, open, outward turning." And it associates the mechanical lens, no matter how amazing in reduction or magnification, with Titian's Venus – "inert and self-contained . . . incapable of movement or sensation."

Marriage

The explicit sexuality of *Bathsheba* and *Danae* is matched by the implicit sexuality of Vermeer's pregnant *Woman in Blue*. In her comfortable, civilized setting, she is a solid, yearning instance of natural sexual power. Lowell, in "Epilogue," seems no longer to be pitying the monster as he did in "Florence," nor fearing her as he did in "Near the Ocean." He makes the pregnant woman the central human image in his last poem with the same attentive tone Vermeer achieved in his painted images of women.

In another important poem in *Day by Day*, "Marriage" (69–71), Lowell writes about two other pregnant women – his wife, Caroline, and Giovanna Arnolfini from Jan Van Eyck's 1434 painting of *The Arnolfini Marriage*. The women, however, are no longer alone; in this poem the central image is of family, the man and pregnant woman posed together in a formal pictorial statement.

Lowell's "Marriage" divides into two parts, like a visual diptych. In the first half, a visibly pregnant Caroline Blackwood, her three small girls, and Robert Lowell are posing "in Sunday-best" for a "formal family photograph in color." Although Lowell refers to himself and Caroline as "patriarch and young wife," they are legally married only by the implication of the photograph. In the second half of the poem, Giovanni Arnolfini and his pregnant Giovanna are posing, hand in hand, for the painter Jan Van Eyck (Fig. 9). Lowell describes this remarkable painting, which hangs in London's National Gallery, in greater detail than he gives to any other painting in his canon.

The painting is remarkable not only because, as Lowell said (*A Reading*), it is the first great realistic painting, but also because it is a document. It is all picture except for one line of text – "Johannes de Eyck fuit hic" (John of Eyck was here) – that affirms the painter's presence. This text transforms the painting into a document, a recording of a marriage taking place. All the details in this painting that seem so casually natural, so accurately rendered – especially the actions of the unidealized, particularized man and woman – constitute the language of a document. The painting, as Panofsky suggests, was apparently made to function as a marriage certificate. By putting both family portraits, the Lowells' and the Arnolfinis', into the same poem, Lowell makes a public affirmation of his private marriage, an affirmation that is not literally legal but legal enough to legitimize Sheridan.

From his own experience with Catholicism, Lowell knew that the words and actions of witnesses or even of a priest are not essential to the sacramental validity of a marriage. They only attest to its legal validity.

> Marriage is a sacrament which is immediately accomplished by the mutual consent of the persons to be married when this consent is expressed by words and actions: "Actus exteriores et verba exprimentia consensum *directe faciunt* nexum quendam qui est sacramentum matrimonii," as Thomas Aquinas puts it. (Panofsky 122–23)

In the "Age of Faith," before the Reformation and before the Council of Trent "prescribed the presence of two or three witnesses and the cooperation of a priest" (Panofsky 123), marriages performed through the private words and actions of the bride and groom were quite common. According to Panofsky, these words and actions were traditional and richly symbolic:

Fig. 9. Jan Van Eyck, *The Arnolfini Marriage.* Reproduced by courtesy of the Trustees, The National Gallery, London.

Firstly: an appropriate formula solemnly pronounced by the bride as well
as by the bridegroom, which the latter confirmed by raising his hand. Sec-
ondly: the tradition of a pledge ("arrha"), generally a ring placed on the
finger of the bride. Thirdly, which was most important: the *"joining of
hands."* (123)

Here is Lowell's description of Van Eyck's Giovanni:

His wife's with child:
he lifts a hand,
thin and white as his face
held up like a candle to bless her . . .
smiling, swelling, blossoming. . . .

And of Giovanna:

They are rivals in homeliness and love;
her hand lies like china in his,
her other hand
is in touch with the head of her unborn child.

These seemingly natural actions that Lowell describes – the lifting of a hand, the
joining of hands – are part of a ritual solemnizing marriage.

From Van Eyck's rendering of the bridal bedroom, Lowell picks out several images
to which he refers deceptively as "petty facts," deceptively because these ordinary
items are actually important medieval symbols:

The picture is too much like their life –
a crisscross, too many petty facts,
this bedroom
with one candle still burning in the candelabrum,
and peaches blushing on the windowsill,
Giovanni's high-heeled raw wooden slippers
thrown on the floor by her smaller ones . . .
dyed *sang de boeuf*
to match the restless marital canopy.

Lowell's earlier simile of Giovanni's hand "Held up like a candle to bless her" connects blessing to the "one candle still burning in the candelabrum." The illumination
of the burning candle represents "the all-seeing wisdom of God," and "not only was
. . . required for the ceremony of taking an oath in general, but also had a special
reference to weddings" (Panofsky 126). The "peaches blushing on the windowsill"
suggest the innocence of love in the Garden of Eden (Musper 66). The fact that the
couple are unshod, though otherwise fully dressed, derives from God's command-
ment from the burning bush to Moses: "Put off your shoes from your feet, for the

place on which you are standing is holy ground" (Exodus 3.5). Giovanni and Giovanna have discarded their slippers because they, too, are standing on holy or sacramental ground – a nuptial chamber (Canaday 28). What Lowell ironically refers to as "petty facts" he knows to be small and ordinary items, but ones that are not petty in meaning. They are sacramental. Lowell's gently ironic tone in his description of the Arnolfini's scattered artifacts and "restless marital canopy" secures the poem from sentimentality, yet allows the solemnity of one nuptial chamber to reflect on the other.

Readers who know Van Eyck's portrait well can include the whole painting in the comprehension of the poem. Such readers can supply two visual facts that Lowell leaves out: the mirror on the wall and the line of text above that mirror. In the mirror are reflected the backs of the couple, their joined hands, and the witnesses of their vows – the painter recording the scene and another man. Jan Van Eyck's inscription above the mirror – "Johannes de Eyck fuit hic (1434)" – transforms this marvelous painting into a pictorial testament establishing the legal validity of the marriage.

In point of fact, the couple had undoubtedly solemnized their marriage some time before, then commissioned the painting. They must have posed for it over a period of time, for a painting is not a snapshot; painting takes weeks of work to record what will seem an eternalized moment of time. Lowell's next-to-last stanza understands this and uses a contrasting photographic image to loop the poem's ending, and all our knowledge of Van Eyck's *Arnolfini* portrait, to the poem's beginning:

> They wait and pray,
> as if the airs of heaven
> that blew on them when they married
> were not a common visitation,
> not a miracle of lighting
> for the photographer's sacramental instant.

The first, photographic, half of Lowell's poetic diptych begins with words that directly relate Lowell and his new family, and their gritty middle-class realism, to Van Eyck's couple, and their common fact of bridal pregnancy:

> We were middle-class and verismo
> enough to suit Van Eyck,
> when we crowded together in Maidstone,
> patriarch and young wife
> with our three small girls
> to pose in Sunday-best.
> The shapeless comfort of your flowered frock
> was transparent against the light,
> but the formal family photograph in color
> shows only a rousing brawn of shoulder
> to tell us you were pregnant.

Lowell's "formal family photograph" is the modern equivalent to the Arnolfini formal family portrait. Caroline Blackwood and Robert Lowell were not legally married until after the birth of Sheridan (Hamilton, *Robert Lowell* 429–30). Lowell's poetic formalization of their marriage, his verbal interplay of painting and photograph, had to take the place of a more ordinary legalization that circumstances made difficult. The photographer's flash becomes a "miracle of lighting," creating the "sacramental instant" of marriage. Subtextually, Lowell seems aware of the fragility of his common-law marriage. In the Arnolfini portrait, the "airs of heaven" have become "a common visitation," unlike the photographer's sacramental flash, holy but common, tenuous.

The last two lines of "Marriage" return the Arnolfini couple from their eternalization in the verbal–visual portrait to the particular facts of their human mortality:

> Giovanni and Giovanna,
> who will outlive him by twenty years.

Clearly, Lowell senses that the facts of his own union will prove similar.

Photography's Truth

The poet's vision, like the painter's, may tremble to caress the light, but the unremitting fact is that the words are not paint – they cannot reflect light. They can only talk about it. A poem is a series of marks representing a string of sounds, melodic or harsh. Always, writes Lowell, "I hear the noise of my own voice" (*DBD* 127). The genius of poetry is its ease with metaphor, with the alliance and misalliance of visible facts and emotional statement. But pure picturing is difficult for words. Accuracy in imaging is hard. "Epilogue" is Lowell's final assessment of his art and of his own poetry. He talks about it in metaphor from the other two picturing arts – painting and photography.

Characteristically, paintings and photographs are silent. Howard Nemerov, in his 1971 essay in *Prose,* a journal in which Elizabeth Hardwick also published and with which Lowell was undoubtedly familiar, expresses the somewhat anxious envy of a poet in the presence of visual images:

> The poet walks through the museum, and among so many and so diverse conceptions and manners of treatment he sees, he hears, especially two things: silence and light. (102)

The poet, continues Nemerov, "sees also that the light in these rectangles seems to come from within" (102), and then, "His own art, in the comparison, begins to seem the merest, most pitiful chatter, compounded of impatience and opinion" (103). Poems about paintings, notes Nemerov, who himself has composed a poem after René Magritte's *The Human Condition* (I), "speak about the silence of the paintings" and if lucky say no more than "It is so, it is as it is." Nemerov finally restores poems to a separate, independent status:

> The poem, too, when it works, is a concentrated shape illumined by an
> energy from within; its opinions do not matter, but it matters. (104)

As we have seen, Lowell's poems do more than "speak about the silence"; Lowell
transforms both image and silence to text, energizing his poems through the dynamic
symmetry, the tensions of composition.

Yet "Epilogue" does express his poet's anxiety about the thin, harsh quality of
his compositions, his anxiety that the art of his eye is "threadbare." Now Lowell
switches from the visual images and silence of painting to the visual images of photography, silent but quick, stopped.

> But sometimes everything I write
> with the threadbare art of my eye
> seems a snapshot,
> lurid, rapid, garish, grouped,
> heightened from life,
> yet paralyzed by fact.

The illuminating energy may issue from compositional dissymmetry, disturbance:
"All's misalliance."

In "Suicide," Lowell makes a disturbing juxtaposition between suicide and amateur photography:

> Do I deserve credit
> for not having tried suicide –
> or am I afraid
> the exotic act
> will make me blunder,
>
> not knowing error
> is remedied by practice,
> as our first home-photographs,
> headless, half-headed, tilting
> extinguished by a flashbulb?   (*DBD* 16)

The snapshot metaphor of the poem makes two immediate associations: The first
likens picture taking to killing – "headless," "half-headed," and "extinguished"; the
second foreshadows the likening in "Epilogue" of picture taking to poem making.
Perhaps the poem, like the headless snapshot, is a killing agent when it is inaccurate,
when it leaves out the essential identifying emblem of whatever it is representing.

The fear that snapping a person's picture takes something from that person is a
primitive one (Frazer 223–25) and comes from believing that one's image in the photograph is an essential part of oneself. In *On Photography*, Susan Sontag goes on to dif-
ferentiate this familiar primitivism from "the true modern primitivism" that makes
our reality a reflection of remembered photographic images.

Reality has come to seem more and more like what we are shown by cameras. . . . While many people in non-industrialized countries still feel apprehensive when being photographed, divining it to be some kind of trespass, disrespect, a subliminated looting of the personality of the culture, people in industrialized countries seek to have their photographs taken – feel that they are images, and are made real by photographs. (161)

People seek to freeze their reality in their photographed image.

Roland Barthes, like Lowell in "Suicide," sees the snapping of the photograph, the moment of catching and stopping the image on film, as a kind of killing, the transforming of living subject into object:

The Photograph . . . represents that very subtle moment when, to tell the truth, I am neither subject nor object but a subject who feels he is becoming an object: I then experience a micro-version of death (of parenthesis): I am truly becoming a specter. . . . when I discover myself in the product of this operation, what I see is that I have become Total-Image, which is to say Death in person. (14)

Paradoxically, the essential feature of photography, Barthes explains, is that it attests indisputably to someone having lived or to something having existed. "Someone has posed in front of the tiny hole" (78), and light has passed the image into the tiny box and onto photographic film.

Painting can feign reality without having seen it. Discourse combines signs which have referents, of course, but these referents can be and are most often "chimeras." Contrary to these imitations, in Photography I can never deny that *the thing has been there*. (76)

This is the point of photography's truth: "that someone has seen the referent (even if it is a matter of objects) *in flesh and blood,* or again *in person*" (79). So "Every photograph is a certificate of presence" (87).

In actuality, the photograph rarely kills or preserves life. What it promotes, provided it does not cut off heads, is remembrance. Photographic film is ultimately subject to decay, as are verbal images in poems, but both can endure much longer than a human being. One's image in a picture or a poem is the key to remembrance. The inaccurate or dishonest poem or picture can, in that sense, kill: The person's image is lost in falsity, whether it be the falsity of idealization or trivialization or little lies. When Lowell speaks of his poems as snapshots, he is speaking of his poetry as a poetry of remembrance, of recollected images. And in "Epilogue," he suggests that if he has, in his earlier work, distorted the images, heightened them from life, made them "lurid, rapid, garish," still the images are from "facts" that did exist, and now exist, although "paralyzed," in poetry.

A photograph is an emanation of a past reality, a disturbing reminder – actually it is direct evidence – of the transiency of existence. What has been caught on film, paralyzed in image, is already gone, is nonexistent a split second later. The filmed image, however, continues and we can look at it when we will; so it is the photograph we remember effortlessly, not the now absent reality. The same is true of poems, when poems are "snapshots."

On the Deaths of Poets and Others

Most of Lowell's significant photographic images – with the exception of the "formal family photograph" in "Marriage" and references to negatives in "Sheridan" (82) and "Seventh Year" (100), and, of course, "Epilogue"'s snapshot – are gathered into Part II of *Day by Day,* and the images have much to do with the passing of life, with dying and death. Indeed, the poems of Part II express the very darkest mood of the whole collection. Whereas the poems of Part I introduce Ulysses as wanderer and the poet as wanderer, Part II mourns, with wry deprecation, the death of poets, now and in the near future, and even the death of a critic.

In Part II, Lowell uses the photographic image to picture the commonness of passage, the paper record of what has been. The section's first two poems, "Our Afterlife" I and II, are addressed to Peter Taylor. The first "Afterlife" – noting the eminent literary dead of its year (1972–73) – Ezra Pound, Edmund Wilson, W. H. Auden – likens Lowell's own diminishing life to "fifty years of snapshots" ripening one by one into his present image (21–22). The second "Afterlife" begins with faces reflected in a street puddle; one is Lowell's, the other a photograph – "Taylor's face / on the cover of your *Collected Stories*" (23). Lowell goes on to describe an episode of illness possibly like Taylor's own recent heart attack (Hamilton, *Robert Lowell* 440) and ends anticipating both his own and Taylor's death in an ironic visual image taken from a stained glass panel of an "afterlife" that is at once the Psalmist's, Virgil's, and Aubrey Beardsley's:

> In a church
> the Psalmist's glass mosaic Shepherd
> and bright green pastures
> seem to wait
> with the modish faithlessness
> and erotic daydream
> of art nouveau for our funeral.   (24)

Lowell continues in his dark, elegiac mood through all of Part II, the photographic images stimulating his meditations on the passage of human life. In "Square of Black" (32–33), he meditates upon "a sad, black, actual photograph / of Abraham Lincoln and Tad in 1861." The photograph is "actual" because it is present testimony that Lincoln and Tad *actually were:* Light radiated an actual image from their real bodies onto a photosensitive plate. "In Photography," says Roland Barthes, "I can never deny that *the thing has been there*" (76).

But the poignant response, inevitable to both snapshot and formal portrait, is that its instant has passed: The event that has been is gone. Lincoln and Tad's picture is "sad, black" because they both died soon after its taking. As Barthes puts it, "The photograph tells me of death in the future. In front of the photograph of my mother as a child, I tell myself: she is going to die: I shudder . . . *over a catastrophe which has already occurred.* Whether or not the subject is already dead, every photograph is this catastrophe" (96). The response, continues Barthes, is "vividly legible in historical photographs: There is always a defeat of Time in them: *that* is dead and *that* is going to die" (96).

Photographs and poems that are snapshots play with time and life: Past and future, being and nonbeing move in and out and there is no still point, for both viewer and reader are also moving along a living time line. Lincoln's dream of death, capsulized in the poem's first stanza, becomes Lowell's own "dream inconsequent" of death: "Last night I saw a little / flapping square of pure black cloth" (32). In the dream's explanation of itself, the black square becomes a bat, then a mouse to be fed and tamed "with nagging love." This black bat-mouse becomes not poetry but poetry making, which exists only "in my short dream's immeasurable leisure."

The poem that immediately follows "Square of Black" is "Fetus" (34–35). Lowell builds this poem from meditations on three types of photographic images – the news photo, the X ray, and the billboard. The poem begins with details from the *Boston Globe*'s front-page picture on February 19, 1975. The photo shows Dr. Kenneth C. Edelin and his lawyer, William P. Homans, joyously greeting reporters in front of the Suffolk Superior Courthouse. Dr. Edelin had been convicted on February 15 of manslaughter for neglecting to sustain life in a fetus he had aborted by caesarian section on a thirteen-year-old girl. The fetus was variously estimated to be between twenty and twenty-eight weeks old. The newspaper quoted one juror as saying, "We thought that the fetus was alive when he (Edelin) went in (the mother's uterus) and he neglected to save life. . . . We all thought that was negligence" (*Boston Globe,* Feb. 16, 1975; I: 1, 1b). In the front-page picture of the paper for February 19, Edelin and Homans are smiling broadly, even laughing, "lost in the clouds," because the "friendly" court has just imposed a mere token sentence – one year of probation. In contrast to Lowell's gentle imagery in "Epilogue" of the sun's illumination moving like a tide across the map to the pregnant woman in blue, the hard language of Lowell's verbal snapshot of doctor, lawyer, smeared sunlight, and building hurts:

> The convicted abortion-surgeon
> and his Harvard lawyers are Big League,
> altruistic, unpopular men lost in the clouds
> above the *friendly* municipal court.
> The long severe tiers of windows
> are one smear of sunlight multiplied;
> the new yellow brick has a cutting edge.

The news photo is black and white, of course, so the color, the yellow of the brick, must be supplied from Lowell's mind. The lines sharply and quickly summarize the picture yet suggest in their tone ambivalent feelings about the altruism of aborting a nearly seven-month fetus.

Lowell probably never saw the photograph, shown at the trial, of the dead fetus, but the jury did, and I presume that Lowell read their comments in the story accompanying the front-page photograph.

> The jury's decision, said Holland [a juror], hinged on whether they believed the fetus was a person.
>
> "It couldn't be manslaughter unless he (the fetus) was a person," Holland said. "Everybody in the room made up their minds that the fetus was a person."
>
> Holland said the picture, which the jurors viewed without visible emotion at the trial, made an impression. "I personally don't believe it's a person from conception, but maybe the picture helped people draw their own conclusions."
>
> Mrs. Conlin said the picture disturbed her: "It looked like a baby." (*Boston Globe,* Feb. 16, 1975, I.16)

Instead of this photograph of the dead fetus, Lowell is looking, in this poem, which shows some understanding of Mrs. Conlin's emotion, at a fetal X-ray image, deriving from his imagination or, more likely, from a reference book of some kind:

> yet we are shocked a fetus can be murdered –
> its translucence looms to attention
> in bilious X-ray.

Lowell is meditating, seriously if sardonically, on a moral question that always attends abortion: Is the fetus a human being? The militant antiabortionists, looking at the X ray's image of fingers and toes and tiny sex organs, speak of the fetus as an *innocent* human life. But Lowell, with characteristic ironic acuity, thinks of guilt as the criterion of humanness. The fetus is only "our germ" because it has "no number in the debtbook / to say it lived." On the other hand, the fetus's X-ray image already forecasts its acquisition of full human status in sneakiness and sin:

> Like the fetus, the homunculus,
> already at four months, one pound,
> with shifty thumb in mouth –
>
> Our little model . . .

The line "Our little model" shifts the focus of the poem from the no longer germinating miniature to another kind of model, a pictured woman on a billboard who is also dead:

> The girl high on the billboard
> was ten years my senior in life;
> she would have teased my father –.

But as a picture, she is "unkillable, unlaid," a model who "cannot lose her looks." Dead, she's ironically in some kind of an advertisement for Easter buying. But except in image, she is gone, "born a decade too soon for any buyer."

Almost every poem in Part II ends with a "dying beat" (Lowell, *A Reading*) that toughens out the sentimental. The elegiac mood darkens from poem to poem. The mourning – or rather the recognition, controlled, sardonic, by name – is for writers recently gone (John Berryman, Ezra Pound, Edmund Wilson, W. H. Auden), for others newly dead (Israel Citkovitz [Caroline Blackwood's first husband], an unnamed critic [Lionel Trilling?]), and even for a crow named Charlie (41). And for those who will go (Jean Stafford, Robert Penn Warren, Peter Taylor, and himself). The endings of Part II's last two poems – "Death of a Critic" and "Endings," rather appropriate titles – honestly state Lowell's apprehensions about his own dying, not apprehensions of not-being, or of that undiscovered country, but about dying itself:

> I ask for a natural death,
> no teeth on the ground, no blood about the place . . .
> It's not death I fear,
> but unspecified, unlimited pain.   (48)

And:

> My eyes flicker, the immortal
> is scraped unconsenting from the mortal.   (50)

Then immediately, with the turn of the page, comes a wonderful turn in the mood, a new section, a surprise:

> It's amazing
> the day is still here
> like lightning on the open field.   ("The Day" 53)

Lowell was always a skillful composer, a careful arranger aware of the reader's experience in going from poem to poem. "I believe in chronology," he said (*A Reading*). He believed in patterns, in "dynamic symmetry." One leaves Part II with flickering eyelids, the immortal being scraped away; and one begins the very next poem (the beginning of the "Day by Day" sequence per se) with open eyes, seeing that "It's amazing / the day is still here. . . ." And it is a country day, tenuous "like lightning on the open field" but fresh with nature's energetic possibilities:

> terra firma and transient
> swimming in variation
> fresh as when man first broke
> like the crocus all over the earth.

The poem puts the individual into the daily and evolutionary cycle: We and the cows seen from the train window are "flash-in-the-pan moments / of the Great Day," the diurnal cycle, the evolutionary whatever,

> the *dies illa*
> when we lived momentarily
> together forever
> in love with our nature.

But then the last stanza reminds us that individually we can never escape "being absolutely safe," being absolutely dead. We are moments in a continuum.

"Universal consolatory"

Lowell's understanding of our humanly awkward place in nature's day is traditional even if his tone and language are contemporary. Lowell, as a poet, has always written modern tensions and anxieties into traditional forms; his experiments with sonnet form, especially successful in *History,* have not yet been sufficiently studied and understood. Nor has the form of *Day by Day.*

Lowell's *Day by Day* remembers pastoral elegy, not mockingly but with poignant, if ironic, seriousness. Ever since the "Lament for Bion," commonly attributed to the second-century Mochus of Syracuse, poets have used pastoral metaphor to express regret for the death of poets: Virgil for Gallus, Spenser for Sidney, Milton for Edward King, Shelley for Keats, Matthew Arnold for Arthur Hugh Clough.

Milton, a scholar-poet like Virgil, and Spenser and Lowell, made his poem into a rich, seventeenth-century Christianization of the Greeks – Theocritus, Bion, and Mochus – and of Virgil's Eclogues V and X. "Lycidas" is divided into three parts: the introduction of the poet-shepherd; the lamenting for the dead poet-shepherd; and the consolatory vision of the dead poet's entrance into heaven and his apotheosis on earth as "the Genius of the Shore," a guide to sailors on the Irish Sea, welcome in heaven and useful on earth. Similarly, but for a very different audience and with very different expectations about an afterlife, Lowell divides his collection into three parts: the introduction of the poet-wanderer, going from woman to woman; the meditations on the deaths of individuals, especially poets and friends; and the consolation, minimal but reasonable, in the daily continuance of life as "flash-in-the-pan moments," and the poet's useful recording of those moments, gracefully transforming them from mere "passing facts" to verbal life ("Epilogue"). Lowell's wry tone in the "Day by Day" section is a long distance from Milton's certainty of the soul's salvation. In his consolation, Milton's Lycidas is married to the Bridegroom and "hears the unexpressive nuptial Song"; Lowell's first poem in *his* consolatory Part III is hardly comforting in that way, for it concludes with the acknowledgment that "in the end" we marry "with nothingness." The other poems of "Day by Day" repeatedly contrast, as does the "Lament for Bion," the brevity of poets' lives, of all our lives, with the cyclical burgeoning of nature:

> Only when we start to go,
> do we notice the outrageous phallic flare
> of the splash flowers that fascinated children.

> ("Domesday Book" 56)

Not unexpectedly, the consolatory theme in "Day by Day" turns out to be art itself, not only as a means to fame but as a means to life and understanding. In Part II, Lowell used photographs for meditations on the dead and dying. In Part III, he uses photographic images in a different way. He employs the negative as a generative image because the negative is the continuing source of prints. In "For Sheridan" (82), Lowell refers to his father as "the lost negative." The poet is looking at a photograph of his father, as a child, in which the father-child as image continues to exist although the negative is lost. The father as source (and nothing) and the negative as source (and nothing) are both "lost":

> In the lost negative
> you exist,
> a smile, a cypher,
> an old-fashioned face
> in an old-fashioned hat.

In a sense, death is also "lost." The "you" that exists in the print is not only Commander Lowell, the "lost negative," but also Sheridan, a print from the grandfather, a genetic descendant. And the poet too, as son and father, was also fixed, in the camera's instant on the silverized paper:

> Three ages in a flash:
> the same child in the same picture,
> he, I, you,
> chockablock, one stamp
> like mother's wedding silver –.

But then the poet moves to pure metaphor to express his understanding of the intrinsic character of the three succeeding Lowell males: "gnome, fish, brute, cherubic force." And we realize that the poem, much more than the camera, records the significance of Lowell's remembered "passing facts."

Lowell again uses the double meaning of negative as a generative metaphor in "Seventh Year" (100–1). A bird's shadow on a winter lake forecasts the renewing power of nature's coming spring:

> This early January
> the shallow brown lakes on the drive
> already catch
> the first spring negative of the birds.

The poem goes on to consider famous American poets, contrasting the longevity of Longfellow and the other "New England Augustans" with the short life of Hart Crane. The poem links the New England poets, whose pictures hung on school-room walls and decorated the backs of the cards in the *Authors* game, with hackneyed images of immortality – Zeus, laurel boughs, the Senate-elected god, Augustus. These are images that have little to do with poetry. Lowell associates Hart Crane, however, with the drunken Dionysus, the renewing god whose death and rebirth inspired the celebratory rites of tragedy and comedy. Poetry itself is the consolation, the human renewing force – not the fame in honored pictures on schoolroom walls.

Lowell himself is the final image, a half-drunk poet, swaying at the end of his party, dividing the moment like Zeno in order to create a paradox of microinfinity from the finite moment. He is unsteadied by alcohol and "swayed [too] / by the hard infatuate wind of love" that the dead poets can no longer hear.

What is that love? Surely, Lowell had in mind Hart Crane's "The Broken Tower" about the poet's words that, like the tolling bells, are instants in the wind:

> Have you not heard, have you not seen the corps
> Of shadows in the tower, whose shoulders sway
> Antiphonal carillons launched before
> The stars are caught and hived in the sun's ray?
> . . . .
> And so it was I entered the broken world
> To trace the visionary company of love its voice
> An instant in the wind (I know not whither hurled)
> But not for long to hold each desperate choice.

Crane's bells toll for us and toll us toward both death and the ultimate source where "the stars are caught and hived." The poet's voice, like the bells, may be "an instant in the wind" but it can build "within, a tower that is not stone." The poem suggests that the tower can reach to immortality: "The commodious, tall decorum of that sky / Unseals her earth, and lifts love in its shower."

In Lowell's "Seventh Year," his poetic power makes him drunk like Dionysus and Hart Crane; even though it may be only half-filling his "glass in each hand," that is enough to keep him swaying like the bells. Most of the poems in the last grouping within "Day by Day" darkly and painfully express Lowell's awareness of his mental and physical decline. But that expression is the consolatory sense of "Day by Day" – the writing itself, the touching of his, and our, perceived mortality with poetry. Even in the hospital he writes.

Lowell makes a complex duet out of two hospital poems: "Notice" in Section III (118), and "Suicide" in Part I (15). He associates the two poems, through his metaphor, with the renewing power of nature itself. "Suicide" is one of his bleakest poems, recalling poets who died from choice and his own thoughts of suicide. And yet it contains an image of spring that lightens the poem's mood. From his window in the hospital, the poet looks out at trees that "close branches and redden": "their winter skeletons are hard to find." This metaphor of regeneration derives from the precise observation that the branches of fruit trees turn red before they sprout leaves and blossoms in the spring. Then in "Notice," after telling us that he wrote those lines while riding home on the train from the hospital, he asks, "Is this what you would call a blossom?" The question is rhetorical. Both poems are blossoms, sprouting after the winter in the hospital. Poetry is as regenerative in human thought as flowers are in nature. The last lines of the poem, however, return us to the brevity of our lives: "we must notice – / we are designed for the moment."

What is interesting in the final thought is not the commonplace that our existence is momentary, but that we are *designed;* like the blossoms, we are momentary facts in a *pattern.* "Day by Day"'s very next poem, "Shifting Colors" (119–20), perceives life's design as a shifting, moving pattern of active life, nature significant in itself, "sundrunk with sex," busily turning the sun's energy to life forms, facts for the moment. And that, perhaps, is the extent of Lowell's faith. He is, he says in *A Reading,* a man of faith although he is thought not to be. Robert Frost's "Design" suggests that any pattern we perceive may be a "design of darkness to appall," but Lowell seems to find solace in the ever-shifting design of nature.

The surest solace, however, is art, in the transcription (to use Sir Philip Sidney's words) of nature's "brazen world" to poetry's "golden" one (100). In "Shifting Colors," Lowell likens himself, as the observer and poet, to a landscape painter, noticing and responding with an artist's training:

> I fish until the clouds turn blue,
> weary of self-torture, ready to paint
> lilacs or confuse a thousand leaves,
> as landscapists must.

He sees and transcribes natural facts into words, confusing the facts with metaphor just as the landscape painter must confuse (or muddle) the leaves:

> Ducks splash deceptively like fish;
> fish break water with the wings of a bird to escape.
>
> A hissing goose sways in stationary anger;
> purple bluebells rise in ledges on the lake.
>
> a single cuckoo gifted with a pregnant word
> shifts like the sun from wood to wood.

Ducks, fish, birds, geese, and bluebells – each a genus of nature, each trying to be other than it is. The poet himself is like the cuckoo, "gifted with a pregnant word," and, like the cuckoo, a little crazy.

> Horse and meadow, duck and pond,
> universal consolatory

description without significance,
transcribed verbatim by my eye.

Is this transcription a failure of imagination? Of course not. What Lowell must mean by "verbatim" is that he imposes no arbitrary meaning. The fish is not a symbol for Christ. Lowell's verbal snapshots of his landscapes are as gently interpretative (through organization and visual acuity) as a Constable sketch. Constable, writes Lowell, "can make us *see* a breeze" (*H* 181). And a breeze can only be seen by its effects; it is a relationship, a dynamic symmetry.

In *Landscape Painting*, Kenneth Clark distinguishes between the *landscape of symbol* – medieval and most Italian Renaissance painting except for Bellini – in which the facts of nature are noticed only for meaning something beyond themselves, and the *landscape of fact*, which includes a love for the natural facts in and of themselves. Landscape of fact depends on an accuracy of the transcribing eye and of the responding heart (35).

Clark refers us back to John Ruskin, who divides men and poets into three ranks:

> the man who perceives rightly, because he does not feel, and to whom the primrose is very accurately the primrose, because he does not love it. Then secondly, the man who perceives wrongly, because he feels, and to whom the primrose is anything else than a primrose: a star, or a sun, or a fairy's shield, or a forsaken maiden. And then, there is the man who perceives rightly in spite of his feelings, and to whom the primrose is forever nothing else than itself – a little flower, apprehended in the very play and leafy fact of it, whatever and how many soever the associations and passions may be, that crowd around it. And, in general, these three classes may be rated in comparative order, as the men who are not poets at all. . . . who feel nothing, and therefore see truly; the men who feel strongly, think weakly, and see untruly (second order of poets); and the men who feel strongly, think strongly, and see truly (first order of poets). (162–63)

The point is to see the primrose as a significant other in itself – not as a psychic projection, and not *merely* as an objective correlative. The primrose and the ageless "white horse" of "Shifting Colors" may seem to the reader and poet to objectify feeling, even unspecified emotion, but they are not merely emblems. The painter or poet of the first order respects the material existence of other forms of being, aware that existence in form itself is significant.

But Ruskin also recognizes the rare "poet of genius" who goes beyond even that first order through a leap in the intuitive imagination. Similarly, in *Landscape Painting*, Clark defines the grace in painting that transcends the merely accurate description:

> Facts become art through love, which unifies them and lifts them to a higher plane of reality; and, in landscape, this all embracing love is expressed by light. (16)

I cannot say for sure that Lowell knew this work, but his demonstrated familiarity with Clark's *Rembrandt* and *The Nude* suggests that he did. And there is some commonality of word and idea, as if Lowell recognized in Clark's vocabulary some of his own thinking. About Vermeer's most famous landscape, Clark writes, "In one instance the rendering of atmosphere reached a perfection that for sheer accuracy, has never been surpassed: Vermeer's *View of Delft*." And he adds, knowing of course of Vermeer's use of a lens within a camera obscura, that "this unique work is certainly the nearest which painting has ever come to a coloured photograph." But then Clark distinguishes the achieved painting from any mere accuracy:

> But the more we study the *View of Delft* the more artful it becomes, the more carefully calculated its design, the more consistent all its components. No doubt truth of tone adds to our delight, but this could not sustain us long without other qualities, and perhaps could not, by itself have reached such a point of perfection, for the mood of heightened receptivity necessary to achieve it cannot be isolated from that tension of spirit which goes to the creation of any great work of art. (32–33)

Or, as Lowell put it:

The painter's vision is not a lens.

Nor is the poet's:

It trembles to caress the light.

"Epilogue"

Lowell's faith in an ongoing design perceived in nature's continuity may seem minimally comforting, but nevertheless it is a faith. He is neither despairing nor nihilistic, as long as he is writing. In "Thanks-Offering for Recovery" (126), the poem that directly precedes "Epilogue," Lowell contemplates a small wooden sculpture, a head, a pagan carving, created as a votive offering for recovery from a head injury. Elizabeth Bishop had sent it to him from Brazil. It seems to the poet to be both Catholic and pagan, "a head holy and unholy, / tonsured or damaged." Its "stern eyes" frown "as if they have seen the splendor / times past counting." In a way the wooden head, "solemn as a child is serious," becomes, in the poet's consideration, much like the poet himself:

> its shallow, chiseled ears,
> crudely healed scars lumped out
> to listen to itself. . . .

The poet's scars are only "crudely healed," but *Day by Day* does not end in a plunge into the void. In "Thanks-Offering," he says "goodbye" twice to the "wooden winter shadow" of "nothing."

The final image of *Life Studies* is of a mother skunk who "will not scare," a stubborn instance of the natural order of things, comic and female. The central visual image of "Epilogue" is Vermeer's *Woman in Blue,* "solid with yearning," and pregnant like Caroline Blackwood and Giovanna Arnolfini. Much of Lowell's poetry has responded to the guises of women: as Queen of Heaven, mother, lover, monster. "Epilogue" resolves those antithetical figures into this calm bearer of life. The *Woman in Blue* is Aphrodite – domesticated but beyond possession.

The poem ends, however, by emphasizing the traditional poetic consolation for our brief lives – the endurance of art. Lowell modernizes poetry's "universal consolatory," reducing the Renaissance's proud conferring of fame to a self-justifying process of recognition and naming:

> We are poor passing facts,
> warned by that to give
> each figure in the photograph
> his living name.

Poetry thus serves simultaneously as a photograph of life and an interpretation of that photograph – a record and a figurative design laden with meaning.

Lowell wrote at the outer moving point of literary tradition, always aware of and using what went before and yet pushing out beyond. His poetic sequences of the 1970s revise traditional forms, especially the sonnet and pastoral elegy, and reinscribe traditional poetic ideas: the past contained in the present; apotheosis through love; the passing of beauty, youth, and life; the difficulty of poetry; the attention men pay to women; the endurance of art. And more than any other twentieth-century poet, including Williams, Stevens, and Auden, Lowell transcribes another tradition – that of the visual arts – into his own. Williams and Auden describe particular paintings with chosen details, forever bonding poem to painting in the reader's remembrance. Stevens works into his poems the ordering, creative principles of two other arts, painting and music. Lowell embeds paintings and photographs in his poetic grammar. Like nouns and verbs, their images engender a structure of significance. The reader must supply, from his or her own experience, the remembered image or else understand the poem only partially. Not to see in the mind's eye Vermeer's *Woman in Blue* is not fully to see "Epilogue"; and not to understand Vermeer's art of describing in painting is not fully to understand Lowell's art of describing in words. For Lowell, the "grace of accuracy" is the artist's gift of love – both to the art and to the fact.

11

Day by Day: **His End Game**

A. KINGSLEY WEATHERHEAD

I

The claims made for Lowell's last volume of poems, that it is a "late flowering of [his] genius" (Symons), that "we are back with the fascinating, superbly gifted poet of *Life Studies* and *For the Union Dead*," and that "the book rings absolutely true" (Simpson), are misleading, because in many of the poems the manifestations of genius are not remarkably abundant and the qualities they possess are of a different order from those of the two earlier volumes named. And most often the details of "the life of the poet" to which the book is purported to ring "absolutely true" would strongly resist identification. I am contending in this essay that in the poems of *Day by Day*, as in some of the poems of the *Notebook* volumes and *History*, affliction has forced on the poet a style different from the styles in which he made his earlier achievements, and that, within the texture of these latest poems, he obliquely weighs the merits of the later style against those of the earlier and in the end finds it wanting. The powers of imagination manifested earlier in his career, first in the fusion of the parts of a poem and later in the superb outreach of figurative language, are missing. There are occasional flashes of the old panache: A swan is like a colossal head of pharaoh; watching ants is like "a Goth watching a game of chess"; and so on. But among other losses that form a repeated motif throughout this volume, the failure of imaginative power is recorded.

One figure under which that failure is noted is loss of color, which had been used in an earlier volume for the same thing. "Water," the opening poem of *For the Union Dead* (3–4), concerns the memory of an occasion with a woman friend (identified as Elizabeth Bishop when the poem reappeared in *Notebook* and *History*) that had earlier been colored by the imagination. But now, at the time of the poem, the poet is no longer crowned, in Gabriel Pearson's phrase, with the "glamor of madness" (11); his imagination cannot maintain the fictional coloring of which it had previously been capable. And so "Water" displays a series of images that suggest the withdrawal of poetic power: the boatloads of hands pushing off for the granite islands, leaving bleak frame houses; the trapped fish; and the dream that disintegrates. And among these images is the rock that had seemed the color of iris but was only gray. The poem ends on the flat bathetic note: "the water was too cold for us." Now again in *Day by Day,* poems occasionally introduce the loss of color quite casually but surely with a similar resonance: In "Louisiana State University in 1940," "your reminiscences have more color than life" (25); in "To Frank Parker," the English garden has "no color" (92). In "Last Walk?" the poet refers to a "faded colorist" (13), himself perhaps. And in "Death of a Critic," there is this:

> In the old New York, we said,
> "If life could write,
> it would have written like us."
> Now the lifefluid goes
> from the throwaway lighter,
> its crimson, cylindrical, translucent
> glow grows pale –   (46)

On a number of occasions, especially toward the end of the volume, the failure of his poetic power is recorded overtly: "I was surer, wasn't I, once . . ." the poet tenuously asserts in "Unwanted," "and had flashes when I first found / a humor for myself in images" (121); or, in "Shifting Colors," "I am too weak to strain to remember, or give / recollection the eye of a microscope" (119). The eye of the microscope, which like the creative imagination brings detail into staggering proximity in amazing light, he listlessly resigns. He is capable only of literal description, and the poem proceeds to record what he sees as merely "description without significance, / transcribed verbatim by my eye." Lowell has surrendered, a critic charges, to the "siren song of mere description" unenlivened by ideas (Di Piero 361). But, as will appear, it is a recourse, rather than a surrender, and he himself is dissatisfied with it.

"The Downlook" opens with an image of the full moon, a ubiquitous symbol for the imagination, which is retiring before the matutinal chirping of sparrows. Toward the end of the poem the poet refers to his "insupportable, trespassing tongue" (125); and, recognizing his repeated practice, discussed later, of linking the ends of poems to their beginnings, we may consider whether with imagination gone he is associating himself in his diminished role with the chirping birds.

It is not certainly so. In a volume where an unambiguous interpretation is a luxury rarely available, the clearest statement of loss comes in "Epilogue," which has been frequently quoted. It is set at the end of the volume (except for an appendix of three "translations") and opens with lines that distinguish between descriptive poetry that merely recalls experience and that which is imagined:

> Those blessèd structures, plot and rhyme –
> why are they no help to me now
> I want to make
> something imagined, not recalled?   (127)

Description is still available, imagination not. And for this loss the poet does not pretend there is any compensation.

II

The process that has brought the poet to the style of *Day by Day* may have begun as early as the 1950s with the afflictions he endured. He has described his deliberate rejection of the style of *Lord Weary's Castle* ("On Skunk Hour" 108; Seidel 17–19). But at the same time, he may have felt, momentarily or at one time or another, that the style he generally adopted in *Life Studies* was a substitute for the other, not so much a chosen alternative but a replacement for what he had lost. Like the painter Edvard Munch who, cured of his mental ailment, was relieved also of his genius, Lowell records, in one poem of that volume, "Home After Three Months Away," that "Cured, [he is] frizzled, stale and small" (*LS* 84).

The lost power was that supplied by the faculty Coleridge called the esemplastic imagination, from εἰς ἕν πλάττειν, to shape into one. Coleridge quotes two lines from "Venus and Adonis" – "Look! how a bright star shooteth from the sky, / So glides he in the night from Venus' eye" – and asks, "How many images and feelings are here brought together . . . in the beauty of Adonis, the rapidity of his flight, the yearning, yet hopelessness, of the enamored gazer, while a shadowy ideal character is thrown over the whole!" (*Complete Works* 4:48). An imagination with that same power of fusion is at work in *Lord Weary's Castle*, bringing the elements of each poem into unity. In "The Death of the Sheriff" (65–67), for example, there is a "blending of classical and Christian myths and personages of the modern state and the Roman state, of the problems of poet as Christian and poet as man" (Vogler 84); and these elements are accompanied by repeated references to the stars, the constellation of the Plough, in particular, of which the various alternative names occur as functional images – Great Bear, Wain, Dipper, Plough. The poet is not concerned that we see even the outlines of these items that are molded to accommodate the theme of the poem. In the following lines from the same poem, for example, ". . . the *Parmachenie Belle* / That I am scraping with my uncle's file," the poet does not pause to describe the trout fly, in itself an exquisite little fabrication. Its function is to embody the idea of murderous beauty and to accompany references to Helen of Troy, another beautiful lethal snare. Similarly, in "The Quaker Graveyard in Nantucket," though it sprawls, the symbolism of the whale and the Atlantic and the literary allusions are fused by the heat of the esemplastic imagination into a unified work, although critics who have found that Lowell's fusions lead to confusion (see Perloff, *Poetic Art* 140–45) will no doubt recall that Coleridge found that excess of imagination led to mania.

When he turned from *Lord Weary's Castle* to *Life Studies*, Lowell had for the most part resigned or lost the ability for strategies that produced overall meanings in his poems. The latter volume is a series of individual anecdotal studies that individually lack narrative coherence and together do not make up a life. Shrewd criticism has discovered unifying elements in the volume, and some years after its publication the poet himself told me that it was of the same species as "Hugh Selwyn Mauberley." But its production must have been a risk taken in the hope that the disparate details themselves would, in their brilliance, please, or that the fragments of life would satisfy curiosity inasmuch as they were fragments of the life of Robert, the apostate New England Lowell: As he says of Ulysses in *Day by Day*, "Risk was his métier" (8). And the risk paid off because few readers and fewer critics are proof against the attraction of anecdotes from the life of any poet, from the tragic experiences of this poet especially. And it paid off also no doubt because the book so brilliantly indulges the taste for clear-edged autonomous images, unregimented by their role in structure, a taste created in this century, though not shared by Allen Tate, who regretted the "unassimilated details" and found the poems inferior to Lowell's earlier work (quoted in Hamilton, *Robert Lowell* 237).

In *Life Studies* the intense pressure of the fusion felt repeatedly in the earlier volume is generally lacking. But neither volume, of course, is homogeneous. A poem such as "The Ghost," in *Lord Weary's Castle* (50–52), is anomalous: "Would it have strained your purse / To scatter ten cheap roses on my hearse?" does not belong with the Miltonic claws that

rush

At the sea's throat and wring it in the slush
Of this old Quaker graveyard. . . .   (*LWC* 9)

Nor, on the other hand, is the texture of *Life Studies* by any means consistent. Generally, as suggested, the imagination seems in abeyance. Certainly the power of imaginative fusion is inoperative in "My Last Afternoon with Uncle Devereux Winslow" (*LS* 59–64), a series of recollections, gathered originally into unimpassioned prose, among which the symbolic images of earth and lime seem to have been tacked on as afterthoughts and in which the symbolic values of these and other minerals are hardly an insistent structural force. Again, in "Terminal Days at Beverly Farms" (*LS* 73–74), autonomy of detail prevails: The poet's eye is "kept staringly on the object" (Bayley 80). In "Father's Bedroom" (*LS* 75) only one word, "punished," holds out a slight possibility that the catalogue of furnishings might be imaginatively welded into meaning; but it is of the very nature of the catalogue in poetry that the concreteness of things named dampens the instinct for interpretation (see Middlebrook 16). On the other hand, there is surely more than a flicker of the old maniacal imaginative power at work in "Sailing Home from Rapallo" (*LS* 77–78), in which, in the images and especially in the present participles associated with them, the sense of relief breaks through the conventional grief at his mother's death, and color and euphoria prevail. Given, however, all the inconsistencies and incongruities of this human document, the broad range is clear: The force of the esemplastic imagination, lethal to the autonomy and anatomical precision of detail, is replaced by respect for details, *relatively* unselected and unmolded. The details are not necessarily factually true, but they are clear, novelistic, and vivid.

Sometimes, however, drawn with a flick of the wrist as if out of thin air, images are apparently lucky creations that casually, surprisingly, or shockingly jog into presence the latent argument of a poem. So the lobotomized Czar Lepke appears in "Memories of West Street and Lepke" (*LS* 86); so, some have argued, the stuffed duck in "To Delmore Schwartz" (*LS* 53–54); certainly the skunks in "Skunk Hour" (*LS* 90), which appear there suddenly *ex nihilo* following a context that does not anticipate them, provide a resolution for both the poem and the volume: "Somewhere in my mind was a passage from Sartre or Camus about reaching some point of final darkness where the one free act is suicide. Out of this comes the march and affirmation, an ambiguous one, of my skunks in the last two stanzas" (Lowell, "On Skunk Hour" 107–8). Such images may provide a kind of crowning unity. But they are a world away from the earlier kind rendered in imaginative fury that lends unity to themes, such as "The mast-lashed master of Leviathans" in "The Quaker Graveyard" (*LWC* 11), which, at even a modest accounting, is a combined embodiment of two marine heroes and the first and second persons of the Trinity. On the other hand, what has been pointed out of a passage in "The Scream" in *For the Union Dead* is true of images of a wide range of poems written in the late fifties and sixties: of

> the dressmaker crawled on the floor,
> eating pins, like Nebuchadnezzar
> on his knees eating grass,   (*FUD* 9)

Hayden Carruth notes that the Nebuchadnezzar simile is a "brilliant extraneity" that has "only the remotest connection with the scene" (441). Like this one, many other sensational images in the poems of Lowell's middle phase have been snatched from beyond the reach of logic and are brilliant, attractive details.

Metaphor and simile must, by nature, both depart into what is extraneous and involve some degree of violence in the yoking, such as Dr. Johnson deprecated in the Metaphysicals. In "Unwanted" in *Day by Day*, Lowell designates his own images as "farfetched misalliance" (121). Metaphor, according to Walker Percy, is "wrongest when it is most beautiful" (166); misalliance supplies part of the attractiveness of *Life Studies* and *For the Union Dead*, where excitement is generated by the sudden swerving away into sensational similes or metaphors: The "*Chevie*" is "garaged like a sacrificial steer / with gilded hooves" (*LS* 74); the poet's heart is "tense / as though a harpoon were sparring for the kill" (*LS* 81); he hears his "ill-spirit sob in each blood cell, / as if [his] hand were at its throat" (*LS* 90); a tower "pierces the sky / like a hypodermic needle" (*FUD* 14); "Mary risen [is] gorgeous as a jungle bird!" (*FUD* 56). The excitement is produced also where the extraneous element is not a figure but a vivid image that illuminates a tangential or even irrelevant part rather than a central part of a theme or description: "Murder cut him short – / a kitchenknife honed on a carriage-wheel" (*LS* 5); "Father's death was abrupt and unprotesting. / His vision was still twenty-twenty" (*LS* 74).

In "The Scream," there is, of course, a link, tenuous enough, between dressmaker and King Nebuchadnezzar: a fanciful visual similarity. In *Day by Day*, on the other hand, an image may lack any manifest link at all to any other element in the poem. The volume is no more homogeneous than Lowell's earlier ones, but in general the sweep of the imagination that unifies poems in *Lord Weary's Castle* is lacking; and lacking too are the vivid autonomous images that occur in *Life Studies* to absorb attention individually or to resolve the poems they inhabit. The beginning of the opening poem of *Day by Day*, "Ulysses and Circe," refers to the power of giving names to things:

> Ten years before Troy, ten years before Circe –
> things changed to the names he gave them,
> then lost their names. . . .   (3)

Giving names, referred to again at the end of the volume, is an act of possession and an act of making metaphors of the obscurest and the most creative kind (see Percy 78). But the imaginative power the act demands is one that Ulysses had apparently employed in the past – ten years ago.

It is possible to attribute the features of the style in this final volume to the terrible bequest of drugs, alcohol, and depression and to the associated fatigue. Lowell's earliest volumes without doubt contained flawed lines. But the awkwardness was the inexperience, perhaps even a superfluity of energy – the rambunctiousness, for example, of a line like "the starling and the sea / Gull splinter the groined eyeballs of my sin" (*LWC* 39) or "Buckets of blessings on my burning head" (*LWC* 22), called for by that young man who missed the driveway and hit the gatepost at the Allen Tates'. But in *Day by Day*, an overwhelming weariness seems to pervade the poems. In *For the Union Dead*, the poet frequently reveals himself as tired: He is, in fact, quite often depicted as supine. But now the exhaustion is not only explicitly recorded, it is in the texture of the poetry itself. Repeatedly a sentence dissipates into an ellipsis, an image remains half-formed, a line is a half-articulate mumble. The kind of exertion needed for the transmutation of the poet's experience into poetry – into the kind of literary creation that that word usually designates and that Lowell in his early and middle volumes had habitually supplied with such verve – seems beyond his strength. Thus although such visual accuracy as, say, Marianne Moore's was never a feature of Lowell's poems, we have here a host of would-be images that come only half-realized to the mind: "Double goose-egg nest" (*DBD* 14), "the Atlantic rattling paper" (57), "glow-shadow" (125), "splash flowers" (56), "lemon-squeezer night" (77). The point of an image may be quite impenetrable: "The wandering virus never surmounts the cluster / it never joined" (50). Often it is as if it did not really matter whether an image materialized or not, the snapdragons, for example, in "Lives":

> My unhealthy generation
> their lives never stopped stopping,
> with ursine step,
> one foot bleeding,

without a crutch –
snapdragons,
half-amiable and gallant.   (58)

And then there are lines that on account of their sounds simply cannot be read as poetry: "I cannot believe myself them"; "but vampires are too irreplaceable to die" –
lines against which one recalls the excitement of Lowell's old rhythms, the late cae-
suras and the enjambments that used to bring a catch in the breath. In some poems
the increasing tiredness of the poetry, apparent also in the *Notebook* volumes and *His-*
tory, has become crippling. The poet was never unduly sedulous to avoid repetition;
but in such wasteful and flat passages as this in "For John Berryman,"

Yet really we had the same life,
the generic one
our generation offered
(*Les Maudits* – the compliment
each American generation
pays itself in passing)   (27)

or in this from "Shadow,"

this pending hour, this tapeworm minute,
this pending minute, I wait for you to ring,   (116)

it seems that he simply lacked the energy to seek out the rewards of the *mot juste.*
Common sense must tell us that these lines are not beautiful just because they are
by Robert Lowell. If the style of these poems is not merely the product of an overwhelming weariness, it is perhaps the product of a choice narrowed by fatigue and
failing powers.

It has been suggested that footnotes, to be supplied by someone who had walked
and talked with the poet during these final years and days, might supplement the
spare details of these poems and clarify them as records of parts of his life. Similarly,
D. H. Lawrence thought the facts of his life during the time covered by the volume
Look! We Have Come Through! would enrich a reader's experience of the poems. But
notes to Lowell's poems would inevitably betray them, interpreting them as accounts
of experience, when on evidence, as will appear, the poet was not regularly seeking
to supply a message or a public version of the story of himself.

It has been said of Ezra Pound that if he had not actually undergone the experience
in the Pisan stockade, he would have had to invent it for the sake of the major formal
demands of the *Cantos* (Pearlman 251). Like the *Pisan Cantos, Day by Day* contains a
purgatory of recollected failings and failures: Lowell recalls, among others, unpopu-
larity at school, "relentless selfishness," friendlessness, infatuation, and voyeurism.
And inasmuch as many of these last poems reflect circumstances from the seven-year
period he spent in England at the end of his life, there is something gloomily fulfilling
in the bouleversements of those days, as if he had really "plotted," as he says, with

his life. As Axelrod has pointed out (*Robert Lowell* 239), the poet opened his public career in *Lord Weary's Castle* with "The Exile's Return" (*LWC* 3), in which the exile is poised between two worlds (Staples 33); the volume with which he closed that career begins with "Ulysses and Circe" (*DBD* 3–10) in which Ulysses, circling between Circe and Penelope, returns toward the ancestral hearth (but not quite into the house) and obliquely expresses the predicament of the poet in real life, agonizing between two countries and two wives. Caroline Blackwood described him in September 1977 in a sad charade: ". . . he never stopped moving from room to room. He couldn't make up his mind" (Hamilton, *Robert Lowell* 472), poised once more, one might say, between two worlds. And yet, while it contains a scumbled reflection of a real situation, "Ulysses and Circe" differs in this quality from the *Pisan Cantos* inasmuch as Lowell, rather than directly engaging with personal experience, is deliberately holding it at arm's length. "It's wonderful to write about a myth," he is reported as saying at his public reading of this poem in 1977, "especially if what you write isn't wholly about yourself" (Hamilton, *Robert Lowell* 459).

There are, to be sure, confessions murky enough – those of his school days, for example, in "St. Mark's, 1933" (*DBD* 89). But there hangs over many poems in the volume, obliquely expressed, a sense of the poet's detachment from his own life, as if he would wipe the slate clean and identify no longer with the guilt in that fallen nature that had earlier wielded such superb poetic powers. Hart Crane, Lowell once affirmed, did not want to die when he went overboard; he only wanted "to cool and wet his exhausted body" (McCormick 274). So in *Day by Day,* lines occur that give rise to the suspicion of a similar obsession: "O that morning might come without the day" (4); "He dislikes everything / in his impoverished life of myth" (5); "no dog knows my smell" (12); "We feel the machine slipping from our hands, / as if someone else were steering" (31); "How uneasily I am myself" (67); "My detachment must be paid for" (111); "Do I deserve credit / for not having tried suicide" (16). And then also there are lines that celebrate an innocent childhood, prelapsarian, separate from the present self with its knowledge and the guilt of maturity.

The lines that present the children occur in poems about houses. Part of the personality of this poet has consistently been invested in the house. In "Thanks-Offering for Recovery" (*DBD* 126), the poet, identifying himself with the childlike Brazilian *ex voto,* is cozily at work in a house reduced to the size of a handkerchief. The smallness of the house, though possibly figuring the smallness of the poet as a child, creates also the sense of security. Most often, however, he does not quite belong in one house or another, and he seems thus to be separated from a part of himself. In earlier pieces, "91 Revere Street" (*LS* 14), and "The Old Flame" (*FUD* 5–6), he is pictured as looking into the house from the outside, a voyeur perhaps, like the protagonist in "Ulysses and Circe," who, prevented from entering when "just a step" away, views his wife and evaluates her figure through the window. Much of the time in *Day by Day,* houses are in one or another stage of decay and their gardens are ruined. "Architecture declines" (95); the great houses "are converted to surgeries, polytechnics, / cells of the understaffed asylum" (55). In particular there is Milgate, the house of

Caroline Blackwood, only "kept alive" by her, its garden trampled by cattle. But Lowell was distressed when the house was sold (as he was distressed at the prospect of the sale of the Castine house) (Hamilton, *Robert Lowell* 460, 431). The place they went to in Ireland was uncomfortably large.

Always, in the poems that contain those houses in the states of decay that reflect the poet's own, there are references to children, still innocent and not yet victims of time, to whom the poet, recognizing himself among them, looks wistfully back acknowledging his loss: "We cannot recast the faulty drama / play the child . . ." (85). If he could go through it all again, he says, he would be "a child lost / in unreality and loud music" (65); in one ruined garden the drive is "cratered to save the children from delivery vans" (54). And in a mirage at Milgate he sees the half-naked children in pastoral innocence (63). In "The Withdrawal," the change of house marks the passage of time toward death, the last withdrawal. One section of the poem, in italics, recalls the children in a momentary state of grace, playing *"truant from their tuition."* Later, the poet himself, as a boy ("a boy of twenty-five or thirty," however) is

> moving from house to house,
> still seeking a boy's license
> to see the countryside without arrival.   (73)

III

The work of this aging poet, then, wearied by the ghastly round of sickness, detached not only from his childhood self, as all must be, but also from his own mature self, is characterized by images that cannot be visualized, details without contexts, repetitions, and spiritless lines that limp unrhythmically along. Then also, as if the poet were content to be disengaged from a self concealed behind the poetry, there is the penumbra or the complete obscurity of allusion. In "Jean Stafford, A Letter," a line referring to the poet's poem runs "my ambiguities lost seven cities down" (*DBD* 29) and starts up associations of William Empson and Troy; in "Ulysses and Circe" appears the phrase "the light of the world," which perhaps has associations with the Pre-Raphaelite painter Holman Hunt. But from the significance of these associations the reader is shut out. A kind of semiprivate association that makes a mild subdued joke may be seen in lines like those in "The Downlook," where a highway image is uncertainly associated with sexual activity: "It's impotence and impertinence to ask directions, / while staring right and left in two-way traffic" (125). There is again a semiprivate play in "Last Walk?", a poem related to Lowell's visit to Ireland in April 1977, where under the figure of the male swan the poet has escaped the

> . . . safe, stagnant, matriarchal pond
> and gallanted down the stout-enriched rapids
>   to Dublin,
> smirking drunkenly. . . .   (14)

The half-concealed joke is that the swan, free from its mate, is smirking at the paradox of having escaped the female swan, Caroline, by the agency of the muddy river the color of stout, which is the product of Caroline's family, the Guinnesses, on which he is happily intoxicated.

These examples of the blurred or half-outlined reflections of reality suggest that one must look in the poems of *Day by Day* for a fidelity not so much to facts of "real" life, from which the poet maintains his shy separation, but rather to internal necessities. The poems are literal, in the sense that in each the elements tend not to point to things outside the poem so much as to refer to other elements within it. Thus for a number of them unity is supplied, not as earliest in *Lord Weary's Castle,* by the intensity of a fusing imagination, nor as sometimes in *Life Studies,* by the record of an experience that resolves, but rather, as its most extreme, by a word relating back to an earlier word and creating only a literary consistency within the poem itself. It is possible to imagine that the vision of the skunks and the sight of Czar Lepke were experiences actually resolving the actual complexity, conflict, or distress recorded in the respective poems, even though Lowell warns that the "autobiographical" poems, were "not always factually true" (Seidel 21). The repetition of words or a tenuous relation between words at the beginnings and ends of poems producing only a fragile literary unity is altogether another kind of thing. The kind of reciprocation employed in a number of poems may be illustrated by the beginning and ending of "Logan Airport, Boston." The poem opens with a blinding bright image:

> Your blouse,
> Concord grapes on white,
> a souvenir you snatched at the airport,
> shone blindingly up the gangway. . . .   (74)

Later there is the "brown air" of the apartment and the poet decamping "from window to window / to catch the sun." Finally the blinding light again:

> your absence is presence,
> the undrinkable blaze
> of the sun on both shores of the airport.
>
> Bright sun of my bright day,
> I thank God for being alive –
> a way of writing I once thought heartless.   (75)

Indeed, it is a way of writing that lacks the core that had once characterized his poems. "Last Walk?" presents snow in its opening and concludes with a simile comparing nostalgia to "yesterday's whirling snow / all whiteness splotched" (14). "Fetus" (34–35) dwells at first on a short-lived, aborted homunculus; it concludes with a poster of a model, in life now old but still young looking: a model with a fate different from that of the poor embryo, the human model. The point is clever. But it is a literary effect, superficial to that of earlier poems in which images seemed to be satisfying needs. The end of "Thanks-Offering for Recovery," "This winter, I thought / I was created to be given away" (126), confirms the relationship between the poet and the Brazilian votive offering, because it had been a gift to him; thus the final lines make a conclusion. But they are only words reflecting words, not, as in some earlier poems, experience resolving previously presented complexities. The earlier effects are profounder than these later literary ones. And the difference is comparable with that between the firm rhymes and tumultuous rhythms of *Lord Weary's Castle* and the pleasing assonances and consonances the poet sometimes creates in *Day by Day:* in "Domesday Book," for example,

> Will they fall
> under the ax of penal taxes
> they first existed to enact . . .
> too grand for any gallery?   (55)

or in the single line in "The Withdrawal," "running together in the rain to mail a single letter" (72) – effects that are pretty enough but lack the full-bloodedness of the earlier ones.

IV

What remains when imagination fails is a series of snapshots. In a number of poems it looks as if Lowell has bid the muse go pack and taken painting or photography for a friend, media more likely than words to provide neutral description, "description without significance" (*DBD* 120), of moments that are vivid in the memory. There is mention of pictures, cameras, photographs, and negatives. Poems may convey tableaux or glimpses of frozen action: Lincoln "clad for the moment in robes of splendor" (32); a goose swaying in "stationary anger" (119); details in a Dutch interior. In other places the poet is concerned with the passing moment: "you are hardly there," he records in "Logan Airport, Boston,"

> it's as though I watched a painter
> do sketches of your head
> that by some consuming fire
> erased themselves. . . .   (74)

In "Notice," the poet asks of his poems, "Will they help me to notice / what I cannot bear to look at?" The poem concludes, "But we must notice – / we are designed for the moment" (118). In "The Withdrawal," there is a "minute, / when the sunslant finds its true angle" and "suddenly the green summer is momentary," and there is a momentary escape from the hegemony of time and age when "any illness is chronic" (73).

Sometimes the fleeting moment is a glimpse of an Edenic innocence about which the poet does not want to say too much. There is the evanescence of innocent children, seen earlier here. In "Marriage," the poet speaks of a "miracle of lighting / for the photographer's sacramental instant" (71); in "The Day" there is this:

> It's amazing
> the day is still here
> like lightning on an open field,
> terra firma and transient
> swimming in variation,
> fresh as when man first broke
> like the crocus all over the earth.   (53)

But in "Marriage," mere description is recognized as defeat. Considering the Van Eyck painting of the married pair, a Dutch interior with its resistant outlines, he finds "The picture is too much like their life – / a crisscross, too many petty facts" (70). It would have been the function of the imagination to relieve facts of their pettiness and miscellaneousness by fusing them into an ordered context where, as part of a purpose and a meaning, they cease to be miscellaneous. "Description without significance" is banal.

Finally, in considering the poet's ambivalent valuation of description and the imaginative fusion with which he had once been wont to modify it, it is instructive to compare the two poems that respectively open and close the section "Day by Day," the last part of the volume. The former, "The Day" (53), opens with the suggestion that the day, seen in a fleeting glimpse as if by a flash of lightning (or snapped by a camera), has the quality of paradise: "fresh as when man first broke / like the crocus all over the earth." The poet annihilates time. He is not killing time, as the figure in "The Drinker" (*FUD* 36–37) is attempting to do; he is identifying the day in the present in his advanced age with a day he knew as a child, which in turn is the day of the making of the world, a day that existed before the fatal schism that divided human consciousness from the world and labeled things with arbitrary names.

> From a train, we saw cows
> strung out on a hill
> . . . .
> They were child's daubs in a book
> I read before I could read.
>
> They fly by like a train window:
> flash-in-the-pan moments
> of the Great Day,
> the *dies illa*
> when we lived momently
> together forever
> in love with our nature –

Christopher Morris suggests that in *For the Union Dead* the word "flash" signifies an escape from linear time into *illud tempus* (200).

But then if we turn from "The Day," which opens the last section, to "Epilogue" (127), which closes it, we find the poet weighing in his hands the style of the faithful literalist painter against that which he himself had deployed in the past, the act of naming. He acknowledges that the painter's vision is not a passive reproduction in the manner of "naive empirical realism" (Axelrod, *Robert Lowell* 239). But his own writing, he says, is sometimes paralyzed by fact. Fact, the clear accurate detail of a Dutch interior, ought perhaps to be enough. He might settle for it. But the last lines of the poem revert to an art of greater demand:

> We are poor passing facts,
> warned by that to give
> each figure in the photograph
> his living name.

He is not merely saying, "So may some gentle Muse / with lucky words favor my destin'd urn." "He seeks," says Axelrod, "to restore the lost connections between human beings and the world they inhabit so fleetingly." And it is the imaginative act of naming that will effect that restoration, while "description without significance," the prelapsarian acceptance of things without their names, the act described in "The Day," is not enough. The poet is recognizing at last that there is no substitute for the glorious fallen powers he has lost through infirmity.

Lowell reads his work at Sanders Theater, Boston, May 4, 1977. Photograph by
Stan Grossfeld, courtesy of *The Boston Globe*.

12

"Prose or This": What Lowell Made of a Diminished Thing

GEORGE MCFADDEN

I

It seems to be a fact, unpleasant but almost to be expected, that Robert Lowell's reputation is under a cloud. Thinking about this essay, I had a conversation with a young poet who had actually written a dissertation on Lowell's poetry. He told me he hardly read Lowell any more; he still admired his "strong" style but had lost interest otherwise. The blighting effect of the dissertation, you might say, or the acute need of the artist to get out from under the weight of the previous generation. The latter reason, for a young poet, is cloud enough. But what about the dissertation directors and the critics? If they seem to have been slow in responding to the life-work of a once highly acclaimed American poet who died in 1977, there ought to be some justification.

Perhaps there is. After achieving a lot of favorable public attention in the sixties for some of his strongest writing, and hobnobbing with sympathetic public figures like Eugene McCarthy and Robert Kennedy, Lowell went into a kind of English exile. He fathered a son and married his third wife, and retreated from the American political scene into an odd collection of fourteen-liners he called *Notebook* and then *History*. It was all too obvious that the poet was struggling and that his material was either too intimate or too banal to repay careful criticism, and also that it was being published without much time for licking into shape. *For Lizzie and Harriet* and *The Dolphin* were scandalously intimate; moreover, by this time Lowell's manic-depressive problem was widely known. When his last book, *Day by Day*, appeared at just about the same time as the poet's sudden death, it somehow got lost. Any responsible critic might have hesitated to deal with its final intimacies, until some reliable account of the tangled private life and movements came out. The most studiously anti-biographical believers in the intentional fallacy can still make asses of themselves if they stumble over some unexpected fact about the poet or the poem.

Now, of course, Ian Hamilton's biography has come out. It may be the frankest exposé of a poet's private life ever offered to the public. Hamilton seems to have met with an unprecedented willingness to cooperate on the part of almost all concerned. Quite without prurient emphasis he presents some extraordinarily intimate details – the hour-by-hour notations of Lowell's private nurse, for instance, during one of his last attacks. And, of course, it tells critics much, much more than they need or want to know. For the really unexpected fact is that *Day by Day,* written while the worst of the attacks had hardly passed, is one of Lowell's best books.

Responsible critics will want to treat *Day by Day* very carefully, therefore. They cannot allow it to get lost in the mass of biographical details or in the psychological diagnosis. It would be too bad, also, to fall into the literary-historical trap and greet *Day by Day* as the "third phase" of the poet's career (after the "New Critical" and the "open-verse" phases). The error would be worse yet if abundant leads in *Day by Day* were to beguile critics into a "*Life Studies* Revisited" approach. All this is work that needs to be done, in a strictly scholarly way. A more urgent need now is to recognize that *Day by Day* requires a new kind of critical reading, or at least new for the handling of Lowell.

What one's reading method ought to be becomes clearer if one takes Lowell's working method into account. His own view of his work habits, supported by those who knew him well, was that he persistently, unceasingly wrote, rewrote, and revised. Nevertheless, he was always waiting for something special to happen to him – what Elizabeth Bishop called "a stretch":

> I think all the family group . . . are really superb, Cal. I don't know what order they'll come in, but they make a wonderful and impressive drama, and I think in them you've found the new rhythm you wanted. . . . They all also have that sure feeling, as if you'd been in a stretch (I've felt that way for very short stretches once in a long while) when everything, and anything suddenly seemed material for poetry – or not material, seemed to *be* poetry, and all the past was illuminated in long shafts here and there, like a long-waited-for sunrise. (Hamilton, *Robert Lowell* 236)

Bishop was referring to the family poems in *Life Studies,* in a manuscript version. Much the same ought to be said of *Day by Day.* A lot of meaning is packed into Bishop's phrases, especially the remark about Lowell's vast extension of the poetic material, including the past when subjected to a sudden, present but "long-waited-for" insight.

That anything might be poetry, even something apparently past and done with, is one of the authentic ideas of modernist writing. In Lowell's admired poets, Eliot, Pound, Williams, it was the case. As for insights that lit up the past "like a long-waited-for sunrise," the model for all writers is one of the pillars of modernism, Henry James. The hours of "backward awareness" his people experience came as a new, dramatic resource peculiarly effective in the full-length novel but not at all limited to prose fiction. Isabel's midnight meditation, Strether's awakenings to "life," are lyric as well as dramatic, intensely momentous as well as narrative. In a short space of conscious human time, under enormous pressure, what has taken many pages to represent and suggest is suddenly brought to an emotional point by some image.

Henry James could plan for such moments. Robert Lowell did not, evidently, and probably could not. What he could do was to write what came to him, day in and day out, and when a rare "stretch" came, rewrite, revise, and reorder the short, essentially lyrical poems into a sequence implied by their points of greatest force. The result might be called a plot without a narrative. As things do not need to be "poetic" to be poetry, so one does not need a story to create a fiction. The old prestige attached to epic, because it was closest to history and actually improved on history, broke down centuries ago. Mikhail Bakhtin attached this breakdown in a most enlightening way to the development of the novel, citing the "novelization" of long poems by Pushkin and Byron (4–40, especially 33, 39).[1] I would say that Lowell extended this process to the short poem, first in *Life Studies* and then in *Day by Day*.

As I said earlier, this kind of writing requires and deserves a very full kind of reading. The writer has taken advantage of his opportunity to add, delete, and change his texts according to his art, or perhaps his craft, with all of them laid out before him. This privilege is perhaps not nearly so important, particularly in a "stretch," as the creative artist's preoccupied inner fund of awareness of what has been, what is, and what is to be in the work under his hand. Lowell did not revise significantly poems already published in magazines, it would seem. Rather he seemed to be able to organize with the artist's uncanny power what was coming his way. In this respect, *Day by Day* is (at least so far as I have been able to see) a more striking organization than *Life Studies,* where Lowell relied on the Freudian maturation myth, in the "title sequence," for an almost explicitly serial narrative (see my 1975 essay "'Life Studies'"). This use of an underlying myth, as Eliot pointed out in connection with *Ulysses,* makes the writer's task more feasible. It also makes the reader's job easier. Homer, or Jessie Weston at least, gives the reader a clue. But when no such external program is very much in evidence, as in *Day by Day,* readers must build one. They will need to work back and forth, as the writer did, looking for "relations," to use James's word, and putting them together to form a complex literary structure.

I do not know how to set a limit to the number of readings a text like *Day by Day* requires. It is a matter of what one brings to each reading. Obviously any one reader has a threshold of satiety. Even more there is the extent and depth of shared experience with the writer, lack of which can prevent a person from becoming a reader at all. With literary or scholarly critics, however, we can assume many readings, of poems at least, if not of novels. Qualitatively, I can see four distinct stages, or levels of the readings that critics perform (no doubt there are others I do not see). The first is (or ought to be) a reading for delight, with the reader ready for something new and surprising, as well as for things to be expected on the basis of previous readings and enjoyed, if possible, more fully for that reason. Each successive part of the text will fall on this reader's mind with a pristine effect. The critic reads the text a second time, able now to look for relations visible (or more visible) because he has the shape of the whole in mind. It furnishes him with structures and schemes of organization that he can strengthen, augment, and correct as he reads along. With this kind of grasp, a third reading puts the critical reader in a position to second guess the author and his artistry and to judge the effectiveness of the various literary features and structures and the value of their relations, by whatever means these relations seem to him capable of being formed. It seems to me that there is a fourth stage, too, for the scholar who only presents a text to a class, as well as for the critic who writes an essay. One is bound to make statements that do not apply, do not fit, get things wrong or leave something out. One goes back, over and over, to the text and tries to get closer. Or – and this is what makes multiple readings worthwhile – one suddenly has the critic's moment of "backward awareness" when a lot of things seem to jell in a suddenly new light. This experience well may come from a reading aloud – a fifth stage of reading no poet would want to be omitted. Henry James thought it was owed to prose fiction as well. Another whole, fresh reading after such an experience can be a sad disillusionment or it can be the most delightful enjoyment of all, a rereading that freshly opens up the text – or major parts of it – and provides a whole set of new relations.

The role of shared experience continues to be important at every one of these reading stages and accounts for what has been called the life of the work as distinguished from the biography of the author. Besides all that comes under the heading of reading competence, rereadings enable the critic to share the writing experience as well as the lived experience of the poet, and to build connections back and forth between various poems in a volume where the interlinkage is the result of the handling of certain literary features, first, and much later, perhaps, a recognition as to the "life" we are able to share. Whatever this "life" was in the author's primary experience, it has come to a quite different kind of artistic life in the course of reading and rereading – the reader has shared in its creation. Perhaps even more important is that this cocreative process continues to be fed as new writing appears, by the same poet or even after his death, when we are able to hear echoes or see contrasts that add a further perspective to the original. Thus it seemed, during the seventies, that Lowell's work continued to be a productive influence among British poets, while perhaps in decline at home. Reading the poems does more than merely reinforce Lowell's place in literary history. It enables us to see at many new angles the value of his struggle to find a subject, and his insistent demands on language, however "unpoetic" that subject might happen to be.

Some may think that the multilayered reading experience I have outlined is more appropriate for certain kinds of writing than for others. That is perhaps true. Modernist writing demands it so much that one might be excused for thinking that the minimalist revolt of recent years, or the open-verse movement itself, is meant to rule it out. Close readings of open poetry seem a bit ridiculous. What we are now talking about, though, is not at all the nuclear, implosive "strong force" that New Criticism insisted on confining to the single poem. We are talking about "stretches" of writing over a number of poems, usually appearing within the same published book and written within the same time span, that require the cooperation of the reader in order to be taken as artistic wholes, with all the augmentation of artistic value that results.

A pervasive characteristic of "postmodern" (I should prefer the term antimodernist) writing is the rejection of closure. Yet a large number of important modernist works avoided closure, perhaps retaining thereby what Barthes would have called their modernity, their right to be included in "our modernity." What I have written about the reader's discovery of "stretches" (as Elizabeth Bishop wrote, without particular regard to their actual order in the publication) is a way of defeating closure in the objectionable sense. What the reader does is discover certain accumulative forces at work in the collection, forces not of the coercive and enclosing kind but rather inclusive and with powers of extension.

A theoretically minded critic today might consider that any exploitation of the writer's subjectivity is an unacceptable kind of closure in itself, compromising the intertextuality his work shares with the production of society at large. Aside from the fact that this particular taboo is often violated by its own proponents, a lyric poem without subjectivity is a perfect example of *Hamlet* without the prince of Denmark. Nor does it seem possible for anyone to deny that there is such a thing as lyric poetry, or that Robert Lowell was a lyric poet. It is much more "productive" for the critic to recall Frost's "what to make of a diminished thing," and to inquire what Lowell actually made of his savagely undermined talent when given his last chance. We can start by questioning his modernity.

One central point in a poet's achievement of "modern" status is his ability to relate his subjectivity to his language without relying on already-encoded language or imagery. In Lowell's stretches, his images are what I should call "self-promoting." That is, they are drawn directly enough from widely shared experience, but they are recurrent and interrelated in such ways as to give them a special sense or combination of senses. They acquire additional values, especially the value of creating links of feeling and insight with the poems that come before and after in the volume where they originate. This interlinkage, in lyric poetry, makes for a better "plot" than any story would do. It can accommodate to myth, but a recognizable myth is not necessary. It comes out as a record of one person's consciousness. Such an accretion of meaning and feeling is a legitimate form of growth in poetic time, and it is so experienced by the reader in reading time. It may have been the only form of artistic growth and change available to Lowell; the important thing is that he succeeded with it. He must have disciplined himself, as he worked on a book, to think and even more to imagine his existence in certain terms, not willfully chosen by him or imposed on him either by tradition or by neurotic compulsion. Rather, they would be giftwords, spontaneously carried to him by images with a life in reality, his and ours, "things" as William Carlos Williams would say. Apparently it was because he had been out of touch with images of this quality for a long time that he felt impotent in his poetry.[2]

This factor – Lowell's obsessive, narcissist intensity of self-concern, his investigative reporting on his own psyche with its long-drawn-out revelations of incidents in the family romance – is of no poetic value in itself. This "weak force" of radiation from the concentrated "strong force" of the narcissist nucleus is in need of an entirely transformed poetic concentration. It need not be accomplished in a single poem, nor conveyed in a single myth, as Eliot recommended in connection with Joyce's *Ulysses*. A combination of literary features, especially images, woven together with such genius that the reader will want to traverse them many times and from many directions, is what we are looking for – not a nut to crack or an onion to peel.

II

Lowell had made good use of the Freudian family romance in the best part of his *Life Studies* volume, the "Life Studies" or title sequence of fifteen poems that he preserved in its entirety for his *Selected Poems* of 1976 and 1977. As Freud himself used the term, the family romance is incompatible with narcissism because it is a drama of the dawn of object choice in the maturing child, whereas narcissism is a primary process which antedates object choice. Using the Freudian picture of the psyche (as I do) simply as the most widely available microcosmology of the twentieth-century Western self in literature, it becomes apparent that the subject fixated at the narcissist stage is depressingly lacking in the possibility of development, or of what we might call a life story. His lovers are always made part of himself, the incidents of his biography are but repeated recognitions of his primary self at various ages and in various superficially different situations. The world of reality itself is only the surface in which his own image appears to himself. The latter extreme – perhaps because he continued to work at writing – was never Lowell's case. Like his other books, *Day by Day* records his glimpses of a reality not himself seen in nature, or (very rarely) in other persons.

This is the clue to "Grass Fires," which I am going to take as a program-poem in *Day by Day* (85). It serves the purpose far better than the plodding, incongruously derivative "Ulysses and Circe" that opens the volume. "Grass Fires" is clearly a watershed poem, belonging to a different poet from the Lowell of the sixties. It gathers in and revises while at the same time it deepens previous writing. It recalls "Grandfather," the redemptive figure of the "Life Studies" sequence. This already "promoted" figure is put back into service, with a difference. Grandfather Winslow, no longer in relation to a naive six-year-old Bobby and unconsciously chosen instead of father or mother, is pointedly rejected in favor of something outside the Oedipal system altogether – fire. In this previously unrecalled event Lowell uses the old grandfather image as poetic capital to fund the new mythical force of Promethean fire. The boy Lowell tries to flush rabbits out of their holes by starting a fire. His innocent, conscienceless misdeed for once brings out something spontaneous in Grandpa – a speech quite out of character for him in his previous role: "You damned little fool" – as "the tree grandfather planted for his shade, / combusting, towering / over the house he anachronized with stone" goes up in flames.

This packed little episode of memory is a throwaway reminder of the old Lowell of *Lord Weary's Castle*. Lord Weary, in the old ballad the poet took as his epigraph, had a mason who built his castle but who was never paid. In his last book, too, Lowell seems to identify the writing of poetry with settling into a deeply satisfying house, whether it be Milbank in England, West 67th Street in Manhattan, Marlborough Street in Boston, or Cousin Harriet's house in Castine. For him, to "build" his house would be to live and work productively in it, with a wife and good company for his social evenings. Grandfather's is clearly not such a house. Like much in New England, it is humbug colonial. It is towered over, Babel fashion, by a tree that marks for the poet an end to his innocence, and for Grandpa an end to his comfort in the shade.

An injection of reality gives life to this large dose of prophetic symbolism concerning the poet's future career. Lowell rather plaintively states that he himself put out the fire, before the fire department arrived, by beating at it with his scarred leather jacket. Fully "promoted" after several readings of the whole volume, the boy's scarred jacket becomes the mature poet's thick survivor's hide that made Lowell such a callous lover, husband, and friend. But it is a protection that keeps him from suicide, for it "snuffs," i.e., in the old significance, trims, reshapes, makes more clear-burning the wick or lamp of the poet's Promethean fire, his rebellious, aggressive protest that keeps his gift alive in the service of truth and freedom against humbug. An abusive smoker, he admits he cannot blow out his own matches now. But neither could he ever blow out this Promethean fire he is both blessed and cursed with. Thus the reader's late realization about "Grass Fires" is that it presents the poet's own view of his mission, the nature and importance of his gift, and his determination to live up to it, fool and damned though he may be, destructive and given over to the death wish as he seems.

My somewhat rhapsodic interpretation becomes less fanciful and more unforced after additional readings, not of "Grass Fires" especially, but of *Day by Day* as a whole, including the other poems that precede "Grass Fires." But for this reason it is not a poem to be tucked into an anthology. That Lowell wrote so few first-class specimens of the poem-sufficient-unto-itself is an important trait that perhaps is now working against the accessibility of his poetry. His earlier things did try to be self-contained in the correct New Critical manner, but Lowell came to depend more and more on context within a volume, continually revising material to achieve a better fit (like many other poets, of course). This rather studied, even compulsive contextualism had a good effect insofar as its well-submerged allusiveness allowed individual poems to appear relatively simple, direct, and open-faced, lacking in the closed complexities so prized by Brooks and Warren for their textbook examples. "The poetry of statement" seemed to be reborn as traditional and conventional displays of technique became more and more absent from Lowell's writing.

These words, of course, also describe the life-conflict of most good verse of the modernist kind. The great nineteenth-century poets' mastery of sound, so close to being complete that it seemed to exhaust the register of verse and leave new poets nothing to do, made the free-verse movement not only opportune but, practically speaking, necessary. But it created its own problem. Mastery of regular metrical forms, as Coleridge pointed out, makes even a not very inspired patch of verse catch fire by its impetus of movement. The poets of the twentieth century, once they gave up meter, needed something else; so they relied on the wheels of imagery to ignite their writing. To be successful, an image had to be afire with the sudden, surprising inspiration of momentary insight. Only an almost miraculous, multifarious richness of vibration from the image, operating on the reader's whole faculty of response, memory, and imaginative cocreativity could prolong the line-by-line impact of a modernist poem and integrate it as a whole. This is what took the place of narrative and almost any other form of overt continuity in the longer poems of many fine poets. And these poems tended to be not very long.

When we read that Lowell, even in the middle of a bad manic attack, was "working, as usual," what he was doing was weaving together the momentary image of the "now" into the texture of many "thens," including already-published poems in some cases. The process of composition became his truest life process, the one that allowed him to compensate for his personal destructiveness. I find nothing in this picture to recommend it as an *art poétique*. Still, one has to admire Robert Lowell for hanging on to his life and squeezing out of its sad contents as much poetry as he did. We must also admire his lovers and friends, men as well as women, who sustained him, even while we are reminded of Freud's shrewd comments on the fascination that a narcissist's self-love exercises on those within his circle of power.

It was one of those friends, Elizabeth Bishop, who (as I began by saying) was able to divine when she first read the manuscript that became *Life Studies* that some of its poems must have been written together in a "stretch" of spontaneous inspiration. The importance of such a jet of composition is that it is given to the poet as a free gift, a pledge of his vocation or calling. The proof of inspiration makes his dry periods bearable, as a form of agonizing vigil that enables the poet to hear, or overhear, the lines when they come or the images when they do appear. For they come freely, not as the result of technique or chosen themes or past success – unfortunately, not even as the outcome of personal happiness. There is no "cause." These expected but unforced images, moments of spontaneous release and freedom in a lifelong obsession, are creative in the special sense of offering a fictive support, for poet and reader both, that organizes a certain portion of the "day labor, light denied" of the working poet and gives value to his usual drudgery.

Having failed to find many such organizations in the prolonged dry spell recorded in *History* (Aristotle: "Poetry differs from history"), Robert Lowell appears by 1976 to have been pursuing the new theme of "snapshots." Studying all the photographic images he could collect out of a past that he was struggling to keep his own, he perhaps aimed to celebrate their random momentariness – in the mood of the years 1965–74 this randomness passed for freedom. But his own settled mood by that time was a fated sense that he was only going through the motions of a life that had been written out for him already, in advance. To rebel against the decree of fate would not mean to find accidents, but a different continuity: to rewrite this life for himself as self-made rather than ready-made. For the lifelong narcissist this task is feasible enough. For Lowell, though, it meant giving up a number of poses that he had managed to strike with a becoming vanity. If Lambkin in the old ballad "was a good mason / As ever built wi' stane," Lowell's poetic success had not been built without some veneer of humbug – religious, political, pacifist, ethnic, racial. He was a crowd-pleaser in spite of himself. I cannot see that Lowell was much of a critic-in-general, yet for *Day by Day* he must have performed a remarkable self-critique. Less "confessional" (in the slack sense of that term) than *Life Studies,* the better poems of *Day by Day* are even more of an apologia. That is, they constitute a sturdy defense of a career full of shipwrecks but faithful to its poetic course and finally bringing into home port its cargo of valuable goods. The load that overburdened it had always been Lowell himself, his psyche, the insistent demands and obsessive concern of his narcissistic subjectivity. It was almost an unbearable cargo he took aboard at birth, he thought; but he would work it over during his life, reduce it and shape it into an oeuvre. The life-work of a minor poet, perhaps, but one who stood out among his contemporaries, in America first and then in Britain too, by their own consent.

III

I shall try to show now that Elizabeth Bishop's idea of a "stretch" of composition may be applied to a considerable cluster of the poems in *Day by Day.* Its Part III is dedicated to Caroline Blackwood and identified as the title sequence by the heading "Day by Day" (the other two parts have no such identifying titles). The poems included do not make up so readily detachable a mythic plot as the "Life Studies" sequence. As I have brought out, they form other interrelations than the obvious ones of the Freudian family romance. In fact, it would be quite wrong to suggest a "Life Studies Revisited" approach, as if to appraise the last collection as a return to an already-worked mine and a proof that it had not been worked out. More than this can be claimed for *Day by Day.* It develops a more important theme (to Lowell, as well as to readers in general) than the passage of the boy Bobby to fatherhood and revived poetic potency. The new theme is the nature of modern poetry as Lowell saw it, and the nature of his own gift whereby he was made to be a modern poet. This theme, of course, is a dominant one in the good and great verse of our century, but Lowell prevents his handling of it from becoming banal or redundant by proceeding much further than he did in the "Life Studies" sequence with the realization of a version of himself – Robert Lowell the poet, a figure that is in itself a structuring, organizing fiction.

Its core, perhaps, is Lowell's long effort at self-interpretation. This enterprise would have remained only a Freudian therapeutic project that turned into an obsession had it not been for the death of the poet's commitment to memory, and the anguished passion of his struggle to preserve it. Poets have always been the guardians of memory, for themselves but even more for their fellow humans. *Day by Day* is on almost every page a conquest of memory over the ravages endured by the human psyche. Our mind, its imagination and memory, is the only register of real human time or valid recollection. Lowell, so irresponsible in other ways, is never unfaithful to this poetic work of remembering. Some of his efforts in *Day by Day* are confused and disorganized, but his memory is never extinguished. It is an astonishing victory.

Having made a start with "Grass Fires," we can take up the account with "Turtle." Part III, called "Day by Day," is the largest section (forty-three poems) of the volume *Day by Day*. It is itself divided into three sections of twelve, thirteen, and eighteen poems each. "Turtle" is the opening poem of the final section. At first Robert Lowell sees himself as old, an old amorous turtle, "knight-errant / in a foolsdream of armor," whose only safety would be in submerging. Those snapping turtles the poet hunted when he was a boy, in contrast, were well armed. Once he grabbed one of them by its leg instead of by its tail – he could have lost a finger! Now he is waking from a horrible nightmare:

> the snapper holds on till sunset –
> in the awful instantness of retrospect,
> its beak
> works me underwater drowning by my neck,
> as it claws away pieces of my flesh
> to make me small enough to swallow.   (99)

The dream-recognition here in "the awful instantness of retrospect," expresses the poet's rejection of an opposite view of time, the succession of snapshots, upon which he had appeared to rely for organizing the first two parts of his book. Preceding the passage just quoted are the words "Too many pictures / have screamed from the reel . . . in the rerun," etc. At this point, where the title sequence begins a recapitulation of themes, the poet gives up the running metaphor of the photographic image, random and partial and ill-made, and opposes to it the organic and living art of the poetic master. This new metaphor develops as Lowell's struggle to *remember* – his primal poetic task and gift. He perhaps recognized that his efforts to remember the figures of his own past were dangerous for him both as a psychiatric patient and as a living person with friends and loved ones to hold on to if he could, but also as a poet ambitious for originality and continued growth. Yet these images out of his past were all that he had left to body forth the daily experience of his fifty-ninth year. They were his poetic stock. So, in "Turtle" the "film of dreaming" is a motion picture, a succession of raw, disconnected frames evoking a boyhood scene of danger mixed with scenes of later pain. He sees, as he seems to wake from his nightmare, not one but three snapping turtles in the bedroom. Then "What is dead in me wakes their appetite," and

> with crooked smiles
> and high-school nicknames on their tongues,
> as if they wished to relive
> the rawness that let us meet as animals (99)

they "crack apart."

The picture is of a bygone experience of natural animality that the dreamer would relive if he only could hold its images together, if he could again address his experience directly, as when a child, instead of in the fragmented "awful instantness of retrospect" that followed his latest crack-up. The imagined scene where the dream takes place is a studio projection room, and the day's rushes mean success or failure to the film and its players. So too with the poet – his imaginative life, now that he is an "old turtle" and must "pray for memory," is mostly a matter of reruns. And all the while emotional well-being and even sanity call for submerging into forgetfulness.

A touching aspect of Lowell's real-life struggle is that this poem is a smashing success in the New Critical terms of his youthful prime. He had written to Peter Taylor on the death of John Crowe Ransom in 1974, "He was my teacher and kept me from breaking myself. I'm struggling to write on him" (Hamilton, *Robert Lowell* 441). "Turtle" does unify fragmented, even contradictory, personal experience in giving being and significance to a poetic image of one's life, and the poem fills its meaning with an appalling intensity of feeling. Like a few other poems in *Day by Day,* it would have done honor to *Understanding Poetry.* It has one heretical lapse, though. It refers outside itself to other poems.

The final horrifying image, "it claws away pieces of my flesh," most of all, perhaps, takes us back to "Death From Cancer," one of the few early poems Lowell preserved in *Selected Poems* (11). Thereby its "promoted" horror undercuts the rawly unbearable instantness of the nightmare image, for it links the poet once again with Grandfather. We rereaders are alerted to this particular "rerun" not only because we have already read "Grass Fires" (with its "fool" and "scarred leather jacket" echoed by illusions in "Turtle"), but also "Phillips House Revisited" (87). One only has to know, or guess, that Phillips House is a building at Massachusetts General Hospital. Grandfather lay dying there, and Robert Lowell had his congestive heart condition diagnosed there less than a year before it killed him.

About halfway through the third section of Part III there is a low point of personal devaluation that takes shape in another nightmare. Lowell, now "aimless," "companionless," finds his mother upbraiding him for his "relentless, unpredictable selfishness," and all his friends, "mislaid faces," are accusing him: "you wished us dead":

> Oh hidden in your bubble and protected by your wife,
> And luxuriously nourished without hands,
>
> ("Ten Minutes" 108)

they cry. Then the deeper despair of the poet emerges, caused by the apparent burn-out of his gift, voiding the only amends he could make to friends he had abused:

> there's no truth in this processing of words –
> the dull, instinctive glow inside me
> refuels itself, and only blackens
> such bits of paper brought to feed it . . .

As in several of Lowell's other "waking" poems, there is a final change of mood to joy. But this time "I grow too merry, / when I stand in my nakedness to dress" (109). Are we being reminded of William Carlos Williams and his carefree nudity ("Danse Russe")? Perhaps, but Lowell's "too merry" signals a manic attack, and leads to as funny–sad a poem as he ever wrote, "Visitors," in which the poet is overpowered by male and female police and ambulance attendants and his and Caroline's bedroom is ransacked. Lowell opines to the "visitors" that he is being locked up as "a threat to the establishment" – they laugh heartily at this quaint pose:

> My visitors are good beef, they too make
> one falsely feel the earth is solid,   (110)

as, eyes on their watches, they hustle him out:

> "Where you are going, Professor,
> you won't need your Dante."   (111)

How wrong they are! Professor Lowell of Harvard is making time in Dante's measure:

> I follow my own removal,
> Stiffly, gratefully even, but without feeling.
> Why has my talkative
> teasing tongue stopped talking?
> My detachment must be paid for,
> tomorrow will be worse than today,
> heaven and hell will be the same –
> to wait in foreboding
> without the nourishment of drama . . .
> assuming, then as now,
> this didn't happen to me –
> *my little strip of eternity.*

Seen as a rewrite of Dante's "without hope, we live in desire," these lines become twice as moving, and what precedes is pretty convincing evidence that Lowell's narcissism never made him a happy man. The depressive "detachment" he speaks of here seems to take the form of a new persona, in the nine poems that close out this final section of *Day by Day,* detached from the "I" of the poet and uttering comments in italics. Were it not for the Dante link, this detached italic voice might be mistaken for a schizoid crisis.

The crisis, however, is not psychiatric but deeply personal and poetic. The question is whether the poet will linger in his mirror world of self-reference waiting for his grave, his *"little strip of eternity,"* above which he does not dare to write "1976" (i.e., kill myself), or whether he will admit – or, rather, *dramatize* – the real events of his life. As "Visitors" makes perfectly clear, he chooses the Dantean way of dramatizing the image – the image of himself as he really is to his intruders from outer reality, a cuckoo professor that they cannot waste too much time on but humor anyway. It is the way of attachment to the world through his own poetic vision of it and of his real place in it. For Lowell it is a strangely humble way, and these last poems are unique in his work.

The poem that follows is called "Three Freuds." It was the outcome of Lowell's voluntary stay at The Priory, a private asylum near London founded by a Dr. Wood, whose marble bust looks like a more cheerful Freud, "cured by his purgatory of mankind." The "second bearded Freud" is a patient, not "disinterested" but hungry enough "to pluck up coleslaw in his hands." In one of Freud's "stupid jokes" in the book on wit and humor, a man does the same with his mayonnaise in a restaurant and puts it all over his hair. Lowell does not rewrite the man's explanation as Freud recounts it: "I thought it was spinach." Instead Lowell concludes, again using italic lines of foreboding:

> *When you emerge*
> *it may seem too late.*
> *You chose to go*
> *where you knew I could not follow.*   (112)

This little poem suddenly becomes very mysterious. Who is speaking? Is it the third Freud? No, the third Freud is the real, actual Sigmund Freud, author of *Jokes and Their Relation to the Unconscious* (138),[3] whom the bust of Dr. Wood and the bearded patient both resemble. Is it Caroline, accusing Lowell? No, it is not, as the rest of the last part lets us discover.

"Home," which follows, is one of the longest poems in *Day by Day* and possibly the most moving. "The patients are tediously themselves," as if they were confined in a place reserved for narcissists. This time the poet is in a different, more severe, barred-window hospital, along with "The painter who burned both hands / after trying to kill her baby." He thinks Caroline might be right to fear he will harm her or the children; "it is my failure with our fragility." And then, more italics, words "ears put us in touch with":

> *If he has gone mad with her,*
> *the poor man can't have been very happy,*
> *seeing too much and feeling it*
> *with one skin-layer missing.*   (114)

Is this one of Caroline's backbiting friends, a Job's comforter, pitying in a superior way the poor "knight-errant – in a foolsdream of armor," the shell-less old turtle? No, it is a voice within the poet himself, his own devil:

> I cannot sit or stand two minutes,
> yet walk imagining a dialogue
> between the devil and myself,
> not know which is which or worse,
> saying,
> as one would instinctively say Hail Mary,
> *I wish I could die.*

The most unreligious reader of Lowell's verse would probably admit that there are some religious people in the world and that Lowell was one of them, like Dante's Buonconte:

> There I lost sight and speech, and died saying Maria . . .
> I'll tell you the truth, tell it to the living,
> An angel and devil fought with claws for my soul:
> *You angel, why do you rob me for his last word?*

(I have copied these lines, originally published in *History,* from Lowell's *Selected Poems* [165], italics and all, and I suggest that the psychomachia that gives structure to the best part of *Day by Day* is the poet's dramatization of his fight to survive, as he imaged it: a struggle to snatch one last word from the claws of his personal devil.)

In "Home" the final lines are shattering, but by this point – a new frontier for the poet Lowell – they are strangely unviolent, undeclamatory:

> The Queen of Heaven, I miss her,
> we were divorced. She never doubted
> the divided, stricken soul
> could call her Maria
> and rob the devil with a word.

It seems clear to me that *Day by Day,* a book that begins with a long poem invoking the homecoming of Ulysses and is full of images of exile and return, is itself a *nostos,* a story of the homecoming of its hero; therefore the title of "Home" cannot be merely ironic. In what sense is this Northampton mental hospital, far enough away from Milbank and London to protect Caroline and the children from a violent Lowell, "Home"? One answer seems best: It is the place where the poet realized he could rob his devil with a word.

"Shadow," the poem that follows this piercing cry from the heart, is perhaps even better – more real; it seems to show that the poet has gone across the frontier of exile into new speech that gives voice to simple gratitude for life in the world – even the minimal life of the asylum – and the satisfied longing for another's voice, an awareness of human support:

> Praise be to sleep and sleep's one god,
> the Voyeur, the Mother,
> Job's tempestuous, inconstant I AM . . .
> who soothes the doubtful murmurs of the heart.
> . . . .
> A man without a wife
> is like a turtle without a shell –
>
> this pending hour, this tapeworm minute,
> this pending minute, I wait for you to ring –
> two in unhealth.
>
> Yet the day is too golden for sleep, the traffic too sustained . . .
> twang-twang of the asylum's leaden bass –
> those bleached hierarchies,
> moving and shifting like white hospital attendants,
> their single errand to reassure the sick.   (116–17)

There is an absence of nostalgia here, a willingness on the poet's part to cut loose from Dante's maximal heaven and gratefully accept this minimalist one, in words that take on Walt Whitman's task of praising realities of modern life in modern speech.

Critics have yet to give Lowell credit for denying to himself, in an awakening of the artistic conscience, the maximal rhetoric that served him so very well in his earlier career. In the prolonged dry period after *Near the Ocean* he continued to renounce the somewhat fustian notes that were admired earlier. Everyone seemed always ready to grant he had the best ear of his time in poetry; his "strength" of verse is what those who respond to "Waking Early Sunday Morning," and little else in the later Lowell, still admire. Rhythms like

> to clear the top on the last try,
> alive enough to spawn and die

had become so rare in recent verse that people forgot how much they have been a staple rhythm in Jonson, Marvell, Yeats, Auden. The meter is great for audiences – Norman Mailer captured its appeal in his *Armies of the Night* account of a Lowell reading during the march on Washington against the Vietnam War. But the poet had the grace to be dissatisfied with such easy success. See "Reading Myself":

> I memorized the tricks to set the river on fire –
> somehow never wrote something to go back to.   (*H* 194)

If Lowell had been born a Victorian, like Tennyson, or a Romantic, like Keats, he might have struck his strongly individual verse note without any need to alter the dominant style of the period. As a Modernist progressing toward minimalism he must have been painfully aware, on rereading himself, of his echoes from Yeats and Auden (especially Auden). We should recognize how fully he denied himself the easy exploitation of any traditional vein. A line of straight blank verse

> who soothes the doubtful murmurs of the heart

is *rarissime* in Lowell's mature work.

Looking back over the verse as an oeuvre, one might say that in too many poems cacophony and rather empty verbal violence are allowed, as if to accentuate the writer's freedom from Victorian or Romantic mellifluousness. But even so, Lowell's verse as such practically never sounds less than very good, very distinguished, like nobody else's. What does jar one is the imagery, sometimes piled up like Arctic pack ice, with no particular inside form, only a morbid, querulous, but very generalized feeling that needs to be galvanized by a forced intensity of rhythm. This violence, especially, is what the poet was fighting through during his decade of fourteen-liners. In "Reading Myself" he pictured his renunciation, selflessly if rather morbidly:

> a bee
> adding circle to circle, cell to cell,
> the wax and honey of a mausoleum –
> this round dome proves its maker is alive;
> . . . .
> prays that its perishable work live long
> enough for the sweet-tooth bear to desecrate –
> this open book . . . my open coffin.   (*H* 194)

Lowell ceased to be one of those poets whose metrical momentum, as Coleridge said, sets their chariot wheels on fire. He became a genuine modernist poet of the image. In his work the image is best when drawn from real, often everyday experience as a nodal link in a cluster of perceptions that are organized by the special gift of the poet into a structure of words. The result is that he enriches a phase of shared life by extending to his cocreative readers the new interrelation of sound, image, and feeling, often making possible their own individual and personal interrelatings as they draw on their own experience. The reader learns from the poet how to "promote" his own images into the outlines the poem opens to his imagination.

Two or three of Lowell's final poems movingly show his loyalty to immediate perception, painful as it was to him to hold on to it. In "Notice" the poet prays for help "to notice what I cannot bear to look at," for (last lines) "we must notice / we are designed for the moment" (*DBD* 118). So, after signing himself out from a voluntary hospitalization, he seizes one moment on the rush-hour train to write down "as if alone" an image:

"When the trees close branches and redden,
their winter skeletons are hard to find –"

This act of noticing is "what you would call a blossom," proof that his cure is effected and "the much heralded spring is here." Now those two jotted lines appear a hundred pages earlier in *Day by Day*, in the poem called "Suicide." In direct relation to the most important issue in the book, the poet's resistance to suicide, his noticing, his writing down of images show that he is free – free of the suicidal compulsion because he has his poetry to live for. "After long rest," he has forgotten his medical problems and can freely accept the task of the poet, who cannot choose the moments of solace only but has to keep his awareness at the ready long after it produces only pain.

Robert Lowell felt himself to be one of those *maudits* who had prayed to be obsessed with their art. As in the myths, the god's gift came to them as both a blessing and a curse. Twice in this book, with Mallarmé in mind, he refers to poetic writing as a language of the impossible. I detect a veiled thrust against the poet (hardly a *"maudit"*) who "purified the words of the tribe" in order to make a special kind of writing *possible,* while shielding his poetry from the things of the common world. In sharp contrast, Lowell comes through these final poems as a poet of real life, writing in a language formed out of a human time and place.

IV

The last five poems of *Day by Day,* I suggest, ought to be read as a finale to Lowell's life and his career. "Shifting Colors" comes as a kind of plateau, a static balancing point when drugs, therapy, exhaustion, and rest have done their part and the weakened poet is thrown, hardly conscious of his usual self, on the mercy of nature. A victim disguised as a predator, he feels the healing power of mindless life in the sunlight and air, and utters a sort of palinode of his long-held poetic theory. He is no longer "designed for the moment," but now "ready to paint / lilacs or confuse a thousand leaves, as landscapists must." ("Lilacs," "leaves" – Whitman country!) His poem records a whole day of more or less unconscious awareness of the things of the world, instead of (as before) a few nodal moments. Fishing in a stream, "weary of self-torture," Lowell accepts animals as "more instinctive virtuosi" and no doubt finds a model for himself in "a single cuckoo gifted with a pregnant word" who "shifts / like the sun from wood to wood." For once he is unresponsive while "nature is sundrunk with sex." "I seek leave unimpassioned by my body," he says, "I am too weak to strain to remember, / or give recollection the eye of a microscope." He is passive in the wise, health-giving, recreative, humble Wordsworthian way. But, as if he has lost the special vision that made him a poet, he is only aware now of

universal consolatory
description without significance,
transcribed verbatim by my eye.   (*DBD* 120)

Like the ignorantly accurate monastic scribe, he copies a dead language that has no meaning for him.

Finally, in total abasement, Lowell "shifts" his colors, deserts his old standards of realism, the image, actual human speech, and surrenders to the abstract enemy in these sententious lines:

> This is not the directness that catches
> everything on the run and then expires –
> I would write only in response to the gods,
> like Mallarmé who had the good fortune
> to find a style that made writing impossible.

I would insist here that Lowell is not embracing Mallarmé but exorcising him and his "*sens plus pur.*" There are references in Hamilton's biography to one phase of Lowell's revisionary habit when he would add or remove a negative as a refreshing and piquant emendation (431). Two examples are given, and it seems to me that the word "impossible" that ends "Shifting Colors" is another. It is a clever way of taking up Roland Barthes's point that genuinely poetic writing is unreadable according to the accustomed routine of socially conditioned readership. As for Mallarmé, we know that he was T. S. Eliot's most-read poet, but I doubt very much that he was Lowell's.

"Shifting Colors" is an uncharacteristic poem (compare it with "Skunk Hour," which has much the same place in "Life Studies"). It is a poem of exorcism, much needed when the demon of narcissist possession has been driven out and its former abode is left empty but swept and garnished for some new devil. It is a bad sign that the poet catches no fish: "All day my miscast trout fly buzzes about my ears / and empty mind." He is a "poor measured, neurotic man," and his "double" is "an ageless big white horse, slightly discolored by dirt" – but at the end of this aimless day the horse has cropped a whole field and the poet has somehow secreted (without noticing it) a rather fine poem, with quite mindful lines like

> Ducks splash deceptively like fish,
> fish break water with the wings of a bird to escape.   (119–20)

In a later poem Lowell speaks of telling two kinds of lies, standing and kneeling. In his confession here, as in many other places, the poet is lying. He is as narcissist as ever, and his images are as sharp and momentary. The passive acceptance of unsignifying nature, as if it were unharnessed to the poet's immediate uses, is artfully deceptive – he wants to relax, and so nature must follow. He is lying standing up.

Thus, again, the final homage to Mallarmé appears dubious. Lowell's own means of making poetry "possible" had been what he called a word processing by continual revision, instead of the continued life of direct insight that "catches everything on the run." "Shifting Colors" suggests deserting one's standards for more impressionistic ones, but really it enforces Lowell's inescapable commitment to the shape of things as they are and his faith that allegiance to them would give shape to his poems.

Into the habitation of a mind left empty, the next piece, "Unwanted," intrudes what seems to be a legion of devils. It is a rather long poem, very prosy and novelistic, and has the retrospective effect of tearing the veil of Boston humbug off some of the lies, rather self-serving ones, in the "91 Revere Street" section of *Life Studies*. Dr. Merrill Moore, whom Lowell views with seeming contempt and loathing, is a sort of Old Shepherd figure who reveals the secret of the hero's birth: "you were an unwanted child" (*DBD* 122). Was Dr. Moore "mother's lover," and by seducing her, or being seduced by her, did he not succeed in freeing her from Bobby's incestuous love? Their grotesque affair, however, soon loses all poetic importance. The genesis of Lowell's lifelong narcissism, which has become his final subject, is revealed at last, in the strange tale of Nellie's rosary. Robert, still an infant, had stolen its crucifix and (the poet says) stuffed it down a heat register in their Boston dwelling (124). Again, as we know from Hamilton (*Robert Lowell* 228–30), the poet is lying. Actually he swallowed the stolen object. The episode is a perfect example of what Freud called introjection, that is, the means used by narcissists to short-circuit object choice and retain their fixation on self.

"Unwanted" continues its prosy, circumstantial account of "causes for my misadventure, considered / for forty years too obvious to name" (121), incidents to "give my simple autobiography a plot," for, as he admits, "Alas, I can only tell my own story –" At last, it would seem, the poet is very, very humble. No more the attempt to win friends, to find interesting ancestors, to appeal for sympathy. He turns, in his last hope, to his poetic style:

> I first found
> a humor for myself in images,
> farfetched misalliance
> that made evasion a revelation.

This sounds like a mingling of New Critical wit-imagery with Freud's account of humor. In the late twenties, Freud finally came to recognize humor as the best, perhaps the only, recourse against narcissism, which he saw as the first, last, and worst enemy of the healthy human personality. Freud said humor was one of the very rare indulgences permitted by the superego, in its role as the severe parent, to the ego, which is always a child in its narcissist urges ("Humor" 265–66). These urges take the shape of fantasy, they flout reality, but if they are humorous the superego even welcomes them, for somehow they give more recognition to reality than the narcissist usually does. At the end of his writing career, as at its peak of success in "Life Studies," Lowell used this Freudian standard of behavior, or let us say interpretative model of healthy behavior, to make us understand what kept him going in his vocation.

This time he tells us his "case" from its genesis. His first object-choice was not his mother; in fact, he here consigns her to her own special place in hell: "go on cleaning house / for eternity, and making it unlivable." Nor was Grandfather the boy's object-choice. At first, "the thing I loved most / was the anorexia Christ swinging on Nellie's gaudy rosary." The rest is not true history but what we might call a "standing" lie or fiction:

> It disappeared, I said nothing,
> but mother saw me poking strips of paper
> down a floor-grate to the central heating.
> "Oh Bobby, do you want to set us on fire?"
> "Yes . . . that's where Jesus is." I smiled.   (*DBD* 124)

(Actually, as is usual in such cases of introjection in infants, the object-choice came out in his potty. See the invaluable Hamilton, *Robert Lowell* 229.)

This little story is a pretty good example of Lowell's humor of misalliance and revelation. It allies a central-heating system in Boston with Dante's Inferno, and it allies the old poet's compulsive revisions on strips of paper to the infant's narcissist love-offerings. Since the poet tells us "Unwanted" is a poem that names the obvious, in courtesy to his story we should accept the obvious interpretation: Never convinced he was wanted by his mother, never sure his own wives or children wanted him, the poet clung to a god of suffering and made his poems acts of devotion to a fire smoldering within him. One could cite the "economy" of Freud's humor. It is a "saving," turning the destructive and neurotic components into mockery. The mockery itself may seem very destructive (as in the satires of Donne, Marvell, or Swift), but on the whole the poet presents his victims as "introjected" into his fictions, made interpretable and thus memorable – saved, in other words. So "Mother," who appears in Hamilton's pages as a combination of Mrs. Bennett and Lady Macbeth, or rather Clytemnestra, is genuinely "saved" as a major participant in her son's poetic story.

As support for this line of argument, perhaps not so obvious as it might be, we have the fact that in these last poems humor is mainly to be found in the poet's relation to God. In these poems of recapitulation and summing up, Lowell has moved a long way on his soul's path. If we look back to the Latin epigraph before *Lord Weary's Castle,* he offers the poems of that volume to God like the bread and wine for the Eucharist, in the hope that devotion will free him from blame, as suffering (Christ's and their own) freed the saints and made them glorious. This rather overconfident approach to the Lord makes an amusing contrast to "Thanks-Offering for Recovery," in which there is a pardonably childlike humor. At the same time this poem is one of the most humanly appealing things ever written by a poet about himself and his art. In its summary way it stands as Lowell's last, comic, image of himself as poet.

Elizabeth Bishop (I assume) had sent him an *ex voto* wooden head carved by or for a Brazilian native who survived a bad head injury:

> It is all childcraft, especially
> its shallow, chiseled ears,
> crudely healed scars lumped out
> to listen to itself, perhaps, not knowing
> it was made to be given up.   (*DBD* 126)

Here is Lowell with his poet's ear. Perhaps he accepts as his also the "stern eyes, frowning as if they had seen the splendor / times past counting . . . unspoiled, / solemn as a child is serious –" But his deepest identification is with the poet as *ex voto*, made – and making – something to be "given up": to the fellow humans, for the fellow humans, to God if God would accept:

> Goodbye nothing. Blockhead,
> I would take you to church,
> if any church would take you . . .
> This winter, I thought
> I was created to be given away.

My reading of this *jeu d'esprit* is that Lowell in his last year had gained the power to put his poetic gift into a humorous perspective. His gift was something he could not introject; it was bound to come out of him and be given away, no matter how or where. He could not keep it to himself. It was his personal curse that the material needed by his gift was his own life, so much of it lived in the prison of neurosis, "the unshakable terror that made me write . . ." Mysteriously, however, the gift finally offered must be "free" of the terror and the compulsion. And it is, at the last.

Hamilton records (454) that "Thanks-Offering for Recovery," one of the two poems that end *Day by Day,* was written earlier but placed at the end for the sake of a closure the poet wanted. "The Downlook," which precedes it, may actually be the last-written poem included in the book. It contains some exquisite verse, though not of the old, "strong" stamp:

> nothing lovelier than waking to find
> another breathing body in my bed . . .
> glowshadow halfcovered with dayclothes like my own,
> caught in my arms.
>
> Last summer nothing dared impede
> the flow of the body's thousand rivulets of welcome,
> winding effortlessly, yet with ambiguous invention –
> safety in nearness.   (125)

But the rest of the poem turns to despair, all the deeper for the reversal of Dante's famous line:

> There's no greater happiness in days of the downlook
> than to turn back to recapture former joy.

What is said in *The Inferno* is, "There is no greater grief than to recall happy times in the midst of misery" (V, 121). (Here is another case, perhaps, of the addition or subtraction of a negative.) Both Dante's and Lowell's versions point to the power of contrast – the more intense the happiness, the deeper the misery. "Now the downlook," says the fallen poet. As Dante's *Commedia* was an encyclopedic poem of the

Age of Faith, the downlook of husband and wife "staring right and left in two-way traffic" is

> an anthology of the unredeemable world,
> beyond the accumulative genius of prose or this –

"This" is Lowell's verse, his book, his latter-day encyclopedic *commedia,* with its story of (redeemable?) misbehavior. For once the expression is genuinely contrite:

> How often have my antics
> and insupportable, trespassing tongue
> gone astray and led me to prison . . .
> to lying . . . kneeling . . . standing.

Earlier in this essay I have interpreted this "lying" ambiguously, giving to "standing" lies the favorable sense reserved for poet's fictions. As noted earlier, Dr. Freud himself approved of humor as a kind of wholesome, kindly parental lie practiced by the stern superego on behalf of the childlike ego.

Lowell's final poem in *Day by Day,* "Epilogue" (127), is less of an indulgence and more of a self-analysis, a personal and critical *art poétique,* brief as it is. It acknowledges the mediocrity of much of his verse:

> But sometimes everything I write
> with the threadbare art of my eye
> seems a snapshot,
> lurid, rapid, garish, grouped,
> heightened from life,
> yet paralyzed by fact.
> All's misalliance.

This sounds like a write-off of the "snapshot" approach, and a recognition that the poet's eye without the poet's ear is a weak resource, and that without memory – the dimension of time and life, of identification and meaning – the image is static, fixated, factitious, and unliving. Besides accuracy (sharp immediateness) grace is needed, loving recognition like a caress from the poet's art, akin to the recognition

> Vermeer gave to the sun's illumination
> stealing like the tide across a map
> to his girl solid with yearning.
> We are poor passing facts,
> warned by that to give
> each figure in the photograph
> his living name.

So Lowell's last prayer is neither for forgiveness nor understanding nor love, nor "Those blessed structures, plot and rhyme –," but for grace, the grace the modern artist longs for. It is astonishing how Lowell beats Auden at his own art-historical game, transforming Vermeer's unassumingly secular young woman into the Virgin Mary of a quite modern annunciation. Grace is "what happened" to Vermeer and "his girl," and to Robert Lowell and *Day by Day*. "Why not say what happened?" Not a career of word juggling, troping, and epistemological gymnastics, but of experience shared as the poet found it, "in things" (*Paterson* I, 1), to quote Dr. Williams this time. Lowell gave his name and his life as things to make poetry with. Lies as well as facts turn into images, yearning toward what passes and has passed; but they do achieve the solidity of illumination for the patient rereader.

V

The claims of this essay have been inspired mainly by Lowell's last book of verse. I have assembled some critical evidence to show that his modernity was not a sometime thing resulting from a shift of stylistic allegiance and a lapse into confessional artlessness. Lowell's modernity can be identified with perhaps the most pervasive current of change at work in literary art, one that moves poetry in the direction not of music but of "novelness," that is, of fictions imaginatively related to real life, real persons, and real events. This movement makes poetry more difficult by giving up its once distinguishing subject matter and its identifying conventions, so that it becomes an impossible art, an art without a technique – which is to say not an art at all. Even today's young poets who flirt with meter and rhyme are responding to this current, courting and trying to make poetry of the trivial, everyday, and conventional events of life.

Another of my themes has been the transference in recent decades between short, lyric poems and the long narrative. On one side we often see the clustering of lyrics into sequences that develop organizations, not narrative or mythic in the story sense, but open to various structurings that the reader or – as I contend – the rereader is called on to supply. On the other side we have the rare long poems that almost never rely on narrative for unity or even continuity, nor on epic conventions for magnitude. What holds them together is usually a modest attempt to identify, discover, or rebuild a world, or perhaps merely to celebrate it. Their cosmologies are normally either very personal or very localized; think of *Paterson* or *These States,* even *Leaves of Grass.* Both this long type and the lyric sequence display the tendency to "novelness," and oddly the sequence of short poems appears to have an advantage when it comes to the essential quality of the novel, which Bakhtin called its "double-voicedness" or "dialogic" quality (328–31).

On this line from lyric to novel, even Lowell's earliest poems are already moving beyond Eliot. His imagery belongs to a later mode of contextual promotion (as I have explained), different from the more naive and literal-natural symbols found in the Romantics and normally, I think, in Eliot. Lowell no longer confides in correspondences existent in nature, but takes pains to establish and reinforce each important image verbally. He "promotes" it into significance by repetition in meaningful contexts, sometimes within the poem but more often within sequences of poems whose frontiers are established by the process of recollection, recognition, and relating that the reader also performs, usually in several readings. This method allows for the buildup of a network of images that operate as a system to generate meanings and feelings; it is a fund, so to speak, on which poet and reader may draw. Some of its potential relations are going to be either subliminal or quite dormant. Eluding all present readers, these latent relations will await discovery, perhaps as the by-product of what a future poet will write or a future society will make actual.

Whether one dedicates one's art to complexity or to the principle that less is more, one necessarily begs the questions, Complexity of what? More of what? The "what" is what readers are familiar with or are made capable of reaching out for and discovering. Less is more when one's attention to a simple image like Williams's wheelbarrow or Yeats's old beggarwoman is augmented by one's being already overexposed to many more complicated images. The reader's past experience of poetry receives a kind of cleansing, refreshing bath. It is a fact of human perception in real time: At a certain point complexity ceases to remain in focus; it falls apart, and then the very simple possesses an actually greater intensity of interest.

Such a lack of focus, I think, rather spoils the images in Lowell's earliest volumes. "In Memory of Arthur Winslow" is a sort of protosequence of four interlocked poems, arrived at by the contextual weaving together of many different devices, verbal, imagistic, and mythic, over a period of six years (from 1938, when the poet's grandfather died, to 1944, when Lowell published the four poems in *Land of Unlikeness*). In some ways, the treatment of imagery is like Eliot's. But there is an important difference. In Lowell's use of images the need he felt to make his poetry "dramatic," which corresponds to the dialogic or double-voiced tendency I speak of, led him to attach his symbols to more actualized personae than Eliot ever did in his poems. Baudelaire's original symbols, his albatross or his gibbet, or Eliot's dicing hands and woman on a mountain path, are natural, unplotted images whose impact is immediate, surprising, mysterious, and compelling. But in early Lowell, the verbal or imagistic "symbol" was likely to be little more than a literary device of characterization or organization. Living memory that releases a deep current of feelings might never enter those poems by the route of images. His images tended to be emblems (like the "chalice" of "A Prayer for My Grandfather to Our Lady") or mythic composites drawn from his reading (like the same poem's "black swan"). They are *tours de force* of appropriation and introjection. The *ex voto* wooden head in "Thanks-Offering for Recovery" is a much better symbol than the black swan, because the poet has put together its elements before the reader's eyes, so to speak, rather than borrowing it ready-made from the tradition. By the same token, the reader is allowed to earn his response and not to depend for it on the capital he has inherited from an expensive education. Even the all-important links with Dante we must earn via Lowell's new version of the Divine Comedy.

My third theme has been the issue of Lowell's recurring mania and depression, interpreted as an outcome of narcissist fixation, and the argument that he made this serious reduction of his powers into an asset by clinging to the poetic vocation that was coeval with his unhappy subjectivity. With just a little help from Dante, he created in *Day by Day* an original and very appealing personal myth, with just enough humor to save it from being either ignoble or merely painful to a reader. Lowell's inability to love another wholeheartedly and continuously, without making over the loved one to his own image and uses, are explicable in Freudian terms as the failure to make object choices and introjection. In the terms of his own personal myth, Robert Lowell made his battered self both the victim and the funny–sad hero of a lifelong struggle between his devil and his poetic calling.

NOTES

1   I wish to thank Gaylord LeRoy, Susan Stewart, and Alan Singer, of Temple University, for valuable communications concerning Bakhtin.

2   As he did before *Life Studies* (see my 1975 essay) and before *Day by Day,* when he resorted to publishing made-over personal letters and pseudosonnets. His justification was his poet's need to relieve a "clogged" feeling. See Hamilton, *Robert Lowell* 424. Hamilton in ch. 23 includes a letter from Elizabeth Bishop more remarkable for its heartfelt dissuasive rhetoric than for its critical candor. Lowell, however, thought of it as "a kind of masterpiece of criticism." His new lease on poetic life, I should say, is told by Hamilton in these words: "For nearly seven years Lowell had written only 'sonnets'; between September and December 1973 he wrote nine poems in a relaxed, almost meandering free verse: 'single poems in short free verse lines about being 56–57.' They were also about returning from exile (indeed one of them was a rewriting of a poem from *Lord Weary's Castle* called 'Exile's Return')." (436)

3   In a long note, Freud remarks: "We naturally do not perceive that our pleasure in nonsense jokes arises from our having succeeded in liberating a piece of nonsense in spite of its suppression." He later added the "spinach" story.

Works Cited

PRIMARY

Lowell, Robert. "After Enjoying Six or Seven Essays on Me." *Salmagundi* no. 37 (Spring 1977): 112–15.

Day by Day. New York: Farrar, Straus & Giroux, 1977. (Abbreviated *DBD*.)

"Digressions from Larkin's 20th-Century Verse." *Encounter* 40 (May 1973): 66–68.

The Dolphin. New York: Farrar, Straus & Giroux, 1973. (Abbreviated *D*.)

For Lizzie and Harriet. New York: Farrar, Straus & Giroux, 1973. (Abbreviated *FLH*.)

For the Union Dead. New York: Farrar, Straus & Giroux, 1964. (Abbreviated *FUD*.)

Foreword. *Ariel,* by Sylvia Plath. New York: Harper & Row, 1966. ix–xi.

History. New York: Farrar, Straus & Giroux, 1973. (Abbreviated *H*.)

Imitations. New York: Farrar, Straus & Cudahy, 1961. (Abbreviated *I*.)

Land of Unlikeness. Cummington, Mass.: Cummington Press, 1944.

"Liberalism and Activism." *Commentary* 47 (April 1969): 19.

Life Studies. New York: Farrar, Straus & Cudahy, 1959. (Abbreviated *LS*.)

Lord Weary's Castle. New York: Harcourt Brace, 1946. (Abbreviated *LWC*.)

The Mills of the Kavanaughs. New York: Harcourt Brace, 1951. (Abbreviated *MK*.)

Notebook. New York: Farrar, Straus & Giroux, 1970. (Abbreviated *N*.)

Notebook 1967–68. New York: Farrar, Straus & Giroux, 1969. (Abbreviated *N 1967–68*.)

Near the Ocean. New York: Farrar, Straus & Giroux, 1967. (Abbreviated *NO*.)

The Old Glory. New York: Farrar, Straus & Giroux, 1965.

"On 'Skunk Hour.'" *The Contemporary Poet as Artist and Critic.* Ed. Anthony Ostroff. Boston: Little, Brown, 1964. 107–10.

"Prose Genius in Verse." *Kenyon Review* 15 (1953): 619–25.

A Reading. Recording. Dec. 8, 1976. Caldman TC1569, 1978.

Review of T. S. Eliot's *Four Quartets. Sewanee Review* 51 (Summer 1943): 432–35.

Robert Lowell's Poems: A Selection. Ed. Jonathan Raban. London: Faber & Faber, 1974.

Selected Poems. New York: Farrar, Straus & Giroux, 1976.

Selected Poems. Rev. ed. New York: Farrar, Straus & Giroux, 1977.

"Visiting the Tates." *Sewanee Review* 67 (Oct./Dec. 1959): 557–59.

"William Carlos Williams." *Hudson Review* 25 (Winter-Spring 1961): 530–36.

SECONDARY

Aaron, Daniel. "The Etiquette of Grief: A Literary Generation's Response to Death." *Prospects* 4 (1979): 197–213.

Letter to Jay Martin. June 20, 1984.

Adams, Robert M. *Nil: Episodes in the Literary Conquest of Void during the Nineteenth Century.* New York: Oxford Univ. Press, 1966.

Alpers, Svetlana. *The Art of Describing: Dutch Art in the Seventeenth Century.* Chicago: Univ. of Chicago Press, 1983.

Alvarez, A. "Robert Lowell in Conversation." *London Observer* July 21, 1963: 19.

"Robert Lowell in Conversation." *Review* no. 8 (Aug. 1963): 36–40.

"A Talk with Robert Lowell." *Encounter* 24 (Feb. 1965): 39–43.

Anthony, E. James. Letter to Jay Martin. May 7, 1984.

Antin, David. "Modernism and Postmodernism: Approaching the Present in American Poetry." *Boundary 2,* 1 (Fall 1972): 98–133.

Anzilotti, Rolando, ed. *Robert Lowell: A Tribute.* Pisa: Nistri-Lischi, 1979.

Atlas, James. *Delmore Schwartz: The Life of an American Poet.* New York: Farrar, Straus & Giroux, 1977.

Auden, W. H. Introduction. *Faber Book of Modern American Verse.* London: Faber, 1956.

Axelrod, Steven Gould. "Colonel Shaw in American Poetry: 'For the Union Dead' and Its Precursors." *American Quarterly* 24 (Oct. 1972): 523–37.

Robert Lowell: Life and Art. Princeton: Princeton Univ. Press, 1978.

Bacon, Francis. *The New Organon,* I:XLII. In *Francis Bacon: A Selection of His Works.* Ed. Sidney Warhaft. Toronto: Macmillan, 1965.

Bakhtin, M. M. *The Dialogic Imagination.* Ed. Michael Holquist. Trans. Caryl Emerson and Michael Holquist. Austin: Univ. of Texas Press, 1981.

Barthes, Roland. *Camera Lucida: Reflections on Photography.* Trans. Richard Howard. New York: Hill & Wang, 1981.

Bayley, John. "Robert Lowell: The Poetry of Cancellation." *London Magazine* ns 6 (June 1966): 76–85.

Bell, Vereen. *Robert Lowell: Nihilist as Hero.* Cambridge, Mass.: Harvard Univ. Press, 1983.

Berryman, John. *The Freedom of the Poet.* New York: Farrar, Straus & Giroux, 1976.

"On Robert Lowell's 'Skunk Hour': Despondency and Madness." *The Contemporary Poet as Artist and Critic.* Ed. Anthony Ostroff. Boston: Little, Brown, 1964. 99–106.

Blackmur, R. P. "Notes on Eleven Poets." *Kenyon Review* 7 (Spring 1945). Rpt. as "Review of *Land of Unlikeness*" in *Robert Lowell: A Collection of Critical Essays.* Ed. Thomas Parkinson. Englewood Cliffs, N.J.: Prentice-Hall, 1968. 38–39.

A Primer of Ignorance. Ed. Joseph Frank. New York: Harcourt, Brace & World, 1967.

Bloom, Harold. *Agon: Towards a Theory of Revisionism.* New York: Oxford Univ. Press, 1982.

A Map of Misunderstanding. Oxford: Oxford Univ. Press, 1975.

The Breaking of the Vessels. Chicago: Univ. of Chicago Press, 1982.

Boston Globe. "Jurors say 'Negligence' was Basis," Feb. 16, 1975: I.1 +. "Edelin Sentenced to Year's Probation," Feb. 19, 1975: I.1 +.

Bowlby, John. *Attachment and Loss,* III: *Loss: Sadness and Depression.* New York: Basic Books, 1980.

"The Making and Breaking of Affectional Bonds.' *British Journal of Psychiatry* (1977), I: 130, 201–210; II: 130, 421–31.

"Pathological Mourning and Childhood Mourning." *Journal of the American Psychoanalytical Association* 11 (1963): 500–41.

"Processes of Mourning." *International Journal of Psycho-Analysis* 42 (1961): 317–40.

Branscomb, Jack. "Robert Lowell's Painters: Two Sources." *English Language Notes* 15 (Dec. 1977): 119–22.

Brooks, Cleanth, and W. H. Wimsatt. *Literary Criticism: A Short History.* New York: Knopf, 1959.

Bruss, Elizabeth W. *Beautiful Theories: The Spectacle of Discourse in Contemporary Criticism.* Baltimore: Johns Hopkins Univ. Press, 1982.

Canaday, John. *What is Art?* New York: Knopf, 1980.

Carne-Ross, Donald. "The Two Voices of Translation." *Robert Lowell: A Collection of Critical Essays.* Ed. Thomas Parkinson. Englewood Cliffs, N.J.: Prentice-Hall, 1968. 152–70.

Carruth, Hayden. "A Meaning of Robert Lowell." *Hudson Review* 20 (Autumn 1967): 429–47.

Chapman, A. H. "The Concept of Nemesis in Psychoneurosis." *Journal of Nervous and Mental Disorders* 129 (1959): 29–34.

Clark, Kenneth. *Landscape Painting.* New York: Scribner, 1950.

The Nude. Garden City, N.Y.: Doubleday Anchor, 1956.

Rembrandt and the Italian Renaissance. London: John Murray, 1966.

Coleridge, Samuel Taylor. "Shakespeare: A Poet Generally." *Complete Works.* Ed. W. G. T. Shedd. New York: Harper, 1853–54, 4: 46–56.

Collingwood, R. G. *The Idea of History.* 1946. Rpt. London: Oxford Univ. Press, 1956.

Culler, Jonathan. *The Pursuit of Signs: Semiotics, Literature, Deconstruction.* Ithaca, N.Y.: Cornell Univ. Press, 1981.

Derrida, Jacques. *Of Grammatology.* Trans. Gayatri Chakravorty Spivak. Baltimore: Johns Hopkins Univ. Press, 1976.

Dickinson, Emily. *Selected Letters.* Cambridge, Mass.: Harvard Univ. Press, 1971.

Di Piero, W. S. "Lowell and Ashbery." *Southern Review* 14 (Spring 1978): 359–67.

Duffey, Bernard. *Poetry in America: Expression and Its Values in the Times of Bryant, Whitman, and Pound.* Durham, N.C.: Duke Univ. Press, 1978.

Ehrenpreis, Irvin. "The Age of Lowell." *Stratford upon Avon Studies* 7 (1965). Rpt. in *Robert Lowell: A Portrait of the Artist in His Time.* Ed. Michael London and Robert Boyers. New York: David Lewis, 1970. 155–86.

Eliot, T. S. Introduction. In *Selected Poems.* By Ezra Pound. London: Faber & Gwyer, 1928.

Erikson, Erik H. *Childhood and Society.* 2nd ed. New York: Norton, 1963.

Everson, William. *Earth Poetry: Selected Essays and Interviews.* Ed. Lee Bartlett. Berkeley: Oyez, 1980.

Fein, Richard J. *Robert Lowell.* Rev. ed. Boston: Twayne, 1979.

Ferguson, Frances. "Appointments with Time." *American Poetry Since 1960: Some Critical Perspectives.* Ed. Robert B. Shaw. Cheadle, England: Carcanet Press, 1973. 15–27.

Fitzgerald, Robert. "Aiaia and Ithaca: Notes on a New Lowell Poem." *Salmagundi* no. 37 (Spring 1977): 25–31.

Foucault, Michel. *Language, Counter-Memory, Practice.* Ed. Donald F. Bouchard. Trans. Donald F. Bouchard and Sherry Simon. Ithaca, N.Y.: Cornell Univ. Press, 1977.

The Order of Things. 1966. Trans. and rpt. New York: Vintage, 1973.

Freud, Sigmund. "Humour." Trans. Joan Rivière. In *Character and Culture.* New York: Macmillan, 1963.

   Introductory Lectures on Psycho-Analysis (1917). Standard ed. 16. Rpt. New York: Norton, 1966.

   Jokes and Their Relation to the Unconscious. Trans. James Strachey. New York: Norton, 1963.

Frazer, James G. *The Golden Bough.* Abridged ed. 1922. Rpt. New York: Macmillan, 1963.

Fromentin, Eugene. *The Masters of Past Time.* Trans. Andrew Boyle. Ed. Horst Gerson. New York: Phaidon, 1948.

Gelpi, Albert. *The Tenth Muse: The Psyche of the American Poet.* Cambridge, Mass.: Harvard Univ. Press, 1975.

Gilbert, Sandra M., and Susan Gubar. "Tradition and the Female Talent." *Literary History: Theory and Practice.* Ed. Herbert Sussman. Proceedings of the Northeastern University Center for Literary Studies, 2. Boston: Northeastern Univ. Press. 1–28.

Gowing, Lawrence. *Vermeer.* 1952. Rpt. New York: Harper & Row, 1970.

Haffenden, John. *The Life of John Berryman.* Boston: Routledge & Kegan Paul, 1982.

Hamilton, Ian. "A Conversation with Robert Lowell." *Review* no. 26 (1971). Rpt. *Modern Occasions* 2 (Winter 1972): 28–48.

   Robert Lowell: A Biography. New York: Random House, 1982.

Hansen, Chadwick. "The 54th Massachusetts Volunteer Black Infantry as a Subject for American Artists." *Massachusetts Review* 16 (Fall 1975): 746–55.

Hardwick, Elizabeth. Letter to Jay Martin. April 29, 1984.

   Sleepless Nights. New York: Random House, 1979.

Harvard Advocate [Lowell issue] 113 (Nov. 1979).

Heaney, Seamus. "On Robert Lowell." *New York Review of Books* 25 (Feb. 9, 1978): 37–38.

Heymann, C. David. *American Aristocracy: The Lives and Times of James Russell, Amy, and Robert Lowell.* New York: Dodd Mead, 1980.

Hockney, David. Dust jacket of *The Blue Guitar.* London: Petersburg Press, 1977.

Holbrook, David. *Sylvia Plath.* London: Athlone, 1976.

Jacques, Elliott. "Death and the Mid-life Crisis." *International Journal of Psycho-Analysis* 46 (1965): 502–14.

Jarrell, Randall. "From the Kingdom of Necessity." *Nation* 164 (Jan. 11, 1947). Rpt. in *Robert Lowell: A Portrait of the Artist in His Time.* Ed. Michael London and Robert Boyers. New York: David Lewis, 1970. 19–27.

Kees, Weldon. Letter to Norris Getty. April 11, 1949.

Klein, Melanie. *Contributions to Psycho-Analysis 1921–1945.* London: Hogarth Press, 1948.

Kramer, Lawrence. "The 'Intimations' Ode and Victorian Romanticism." *Victorian Poetry* 18 (1980): 315–36.

Kunitz, Stanley. "Talk with Robert Lowell." *New York Times Book Review,* Oct. 4, 1964: 34–39.

Lewis, R. W. B. *The American Adam.* Chicago: Univ. of Chicago Press, 1955.

Lodge, David. *The Modes of Modern Writing: Metaphor, Metonymy, and the Typology of Modern Literature.* Ithaca, N.Y.: Cornell Univ. Press, 1977.

Lukács, Georg. *Realism in Our Time: Literature and the Class Struggle.* Trans. John and Necke Mander. New York: Harper & Row, 1964.

Mailer, Norman. *The Armies of the Night.* Harmondsworth: Penguin, 1970.

Mazzaro, Jerome. *The Poetic Themes of Robert Lowell.* Ann Arbor: Univ. of Michigan Press, 1965.

McCormick, J. "Falling Asleep over Grillparzer: An Interview with Robert Lowell." *Poetry* 81 (Jan. 1953): 269–79.

McFadden, George. "'Life Studies' – Robert Lowell's Comic Breakthrough." *PMLA* 90 (Jan. 1975): 96–106.

Middlebrook, Diane Wood. *Walt Whitman and Wallace Stevens.* Ithaca, N.Y.: Cornell Univ. Press, 1974.

Miller, Alice. *Prisoners of Childhood: Drama of the Gifted Cild and the Search for the True Self.* Trans. Ruth Ward. New York: Basic Books, 1981.

Morris, Christopher. "The Ambivalence of Robert Lowell's *For the Union Dead*." *Modern Poetry Studies* 1 (1970): 199–224.

Musper, H. T. *Netherlandish Painting from Van Eyck to Bosch.* Trans. Robert Allen. New York: Abrams, 1981.

Natanson, Maurice. *Literature, Philosophy and the Social Sciences.* The Hague: Nijhoff, 1962.

Neff, Emery. *The Poetry of History.* New York: Columbia Univ. Press, 1947.

Nemerov, Howard. "On Poetry and Painting, With a Thought of Music." *Prose* Fall 1971: 101–8.

Nietzsche, Friedrich. *The Will to Power.* Trans. Walter Kaufman and R. J. Hollingdale. New York: Random House, 1967.

North, Michael. "The Public Monument and Public Poetry: Stevens, Berryman, and Lowell." *Contemporary Literature* 21 (Spring 1980): 267–85.

O'Connor, Flannery. *The Habit of Being: The Letters of Flannery O'Connor.* Ed. Sally Fitzgerald. New York: Farrar, Straus & Giroux, 1979.

   Mystery and Manners. Ed. Robert and Sally Fitzgerald. New York: Farrar, Straus & Giroux, 1969.

Olson, Charles. Letter to Cid Cormen. Rpt. *Olson: The Journal of the Charles Olson Archives* no. 6 (Fall 1976): 1.

   Selected Writings. Ed. Robert Creeley. New York: New Directions, 1967.

Panofsky, Erwin. "Jan van Eyck's *Arnolfini* Portrait." *Burlington Magazine* 64 (March 1934): 117–27.

Pearce, Roy Harvey. *The Continuity of American Poetry.* Princeton: Princeton Univ. Press, 1961.

Pearlman, Daniel. *The Barb of Time.* New York: Oxford Univ. Press, 1969.

Pearson, Gabriel. "Robert Lowell." *The Review* no. 20 (March 1969): 3–36.

Peckham, Morse. *Victorian Revolutionaries.* New York: Brazillier, 1970.

Percy, Walker. *The Message in the Bottle.* New York: Farrar, Straus & Giroux, 1975.

Peretz, David. "Development, Object Relations, and Loss." In *Loss and Grief: Psychological Management in Medical Practice.* Ed. Bernard Schoenberg, et al. New York: Columbia Univ. Press, 1973. 3–19.

Perloff, Marjorie. *The Poetic Art of Robert Lowell.* Ithaca, N.Y.: Cornell Univ. Press, 1973.

Pinsky, Robert. *The Situation of Poetry: Contemporary Poetry and its Traditions.* Princeton: Princeton Univ. Press, 1976.

Poirier, Richard. "Our Truest Historian." *Book Week* Oct. 11, 1964: 1, 16.

Pollock, George H. "Anniversary Reactions, Trauma, and Mourning." *Psychoanalytic Quarterly* 39 (1970): 347–69.

   "Mourning and Adaptation." *International Journal of Psycho-Analysis* 42 (1961): 341–61.

Procopiow, Norma. "*Day by Day*: Lowell's Poetics of Imitation." *Ariel* 14 (Jan. 1983): 5–15.

   Robert Lowell: The Poet and the Critics. Chicago: American Library Assoc., 1984.

Rahv, Philip. *Image and Idea.* New York: New Directions, 1957.

Reed, Allan W. "Anticipatory Griefwork." In *Anticipatory Grief.* Ed. Bernard Schoenberg, et al. New York: Columbia Univ. Press, 1974. 346–57.

Riddel, Joseph. "Decentering the Image: The 'Project' of 'American' Poetics?" In *Textual Strategies: Perspectives in Post-Structuralist Criticism.* Ed. Josué V. Harari. Ithaca, N.Y.: Cornell Univ. Press, 1979. 322–58.

Ruskin, John. *Modern Painters.* 4 vols. New York: John Wiley, 1892. Vol. 3.

Samuels, Ernest. *Henry Adams: The Middle Years.* Cambridge, Mass.: Harvard Univ. Press, 1958.

Seidel, Frederick. "The Art of Poetry III: Robert Lowell." *Paris Review* 25 (Winter-Spring, 1961). Rpt. as "Robert Lowell" in *Robert Lowell: A Collection of Critical Essays.* Ed. Thomas Parkinson. Englewood Cliffs, N.J.: Prentice-Hall, 1968. 12–35.

Sherwin, Oscar. *Uncorking Old Sherry: The Life and Times of Richard Brinsley Sheridan.* New York: Twayne, 1960.

Sidney, Sir Philip. *An Apology for Poetry.* Ed. Geoffrey Shephard. Edinburgh: Nelson, 1965.

Simpson, Eileen. *Poets in Their Youth: A Memoir.* New York: Random House, 1982.

Simpson, Louis. Quotation on the back of the paperback ed. of *Day by Day.* New York: Farrar, Straus & Giroux, 1978.

Sontag, Susan. *On Photography.* New York: Farrar, Straus & Giroux, 1977.

Spender, Stephen. "Robert Lowell's Family Album." *New Republic* 140 (June 8, 1959): 17.

Stafford, Jean. "An Influx of Poets." *New Yorker* (Nov. 6, 1978): 43–58.

Staples, Hugh. *Robert Lowell: The First Twenty Years.* London: Faber & Faber, 1962.

Symons, Julian. Quotation on back of the paperback ed. of *Day by Day.* New York: Farrar, Straus & Giroux, 1978.

Tapscott, Stephen. "The Poem of Trauma." *American Poetry Review* (Nov.–Dec. 1984): 38–47.

Tate, Allen. Introduction to *Land of Unlikeness.* 1944. Rpt. in *Robert Lowell: A Portrait of the Artist in His Time.* Ed. Michael London and Robert Boyers. New York: David Lewis, 1970. 1–2.

Toynbee, Arnold J. *A Study of History.* Abridged ed. London: Oxford Univ. Press, 1946.

Vendler, Helen. "Lowell's Last Poems." *Parnassus* 6 (Spring–Summer 1978): 81.

Part of Nature, Part of Us: Modern American Poets. Cambridge, Mass.: Harvard Univ. Press, 1980.

Vogler, Thomas. "Robert Lowell: 'Payment Gat He Nane.'" *Iowa Review* 2 (Summer 1971): 64–93.

Walcott, Derek. "On Robert Lowell." *New York Review of Books* 31 (March 1, 1984): 25–31.

Williamson, Alan. *Pity the Monsters: The Political Vision of Robert Lowell.* New Haven, Conn.: Yale Univ. Press, 1974.

Wilson, Edmund. *The Wound and the Bow.* New York: Oxford Univ. Press, 1941.

Woodward, Bob, and Carl Bernstein. *The Final Days.* New York: Simon & Schuster, 1976.

Yeats, W. B. *Mythologies.* London: Macmillan, 1959.

Yenser, Stephen. *Circle to Circle: The Poetry of Robert Lowell.* Berkeley: Univ. of California Press, 1975.

Index

266   *Index*

Lowell, Robert *(cont.)*
works of *(cont.)*
"Drinker, The," 228–29
"Drunken Fisherman, The," 57, 60
"Dunbarton," 33–34, 86, 91, 162
"During Fever," 73–74, 77, 82–83, 96, 162, 178
"Ear of Corn," 179
"Endings," 36, 209
"Epilogue," 23–24, 69, 144, 150, 168, 173–75, 180–81, 184–91, 196, 198–99, 203–7, 215–16, 218–19, 229, 252–53
"Exile's Return, The," 64, 224
"Eye and Tooth," 76, 161
"Falling Asleep Over the Aeneid," 10
"Fall 1961," 160, 177–78
"Father in a Dream," 178
"Father's Bedroom," 41, 86, 87, 220
"Fetus," 207–9, 226
"Fever," 141–42
"Fishnet," 152–54
"Five Dreams," 130
"Florence," 160
"For Anne Adden," 46
"For Aunt Sarah," 34
"Ford Madox Ford," 144
"Ford Madox Ford: 1873–1939," 37
"For John Berryman" *(DBD),* 39, 158, 223
"For John Berryman" *(H),* 15
For Lizzie and Harriet, 106, 118, 134, 143–46, 177, 231
"For Mary McCarthy," 129–30
"For Peter Taylor," 152
"For Sale," 87, 90
"For Sheridan," 178, 211
For the Union Dead, 12, 19, 67, 68, 115, 160–62, 175, 217, 221–22, 229
"For the Union Dead," 19, 20, 24, 66–67, 68, 111, 114–15, 127, 181–83
"Fourth of July in Maine," 35–36
"George III," 18–25, 168
"Ghost, The," 220
"Going to and fro," 160, 175
"Grandparents," 34, 82, 85, 86, 116
"Grass Fires," 161, 236–37, 241
"Half a Century Gone," 123–24, 126, 137
"Harriet," 120–26, 130, 137
"Harriet's Donkey," 178–79
History, 19, 46, 111, 118, 132, 134–38, 141–49, 155, 176, 177, 210, 217, 223, 231, 239, 244

"History," 135, 138
"Home," 69, 158, 168, 173, 243–44
"Home After Three Months Away," 5, 83, 88, 90, 159, 219
"Homecoming," 157, 166, 172
"Hospital," 179
"Hudson River Dream," 153
Imitations, 12, 24, 52, 104
"In Memory of Arthur Winslow," 32–33, 52, 54–56, 58, 60, 254
"In the Cage," 52
"In the Ward," 168
"Jean Stafford, a Letter," 46, 225
"Jonathan Edwards in Western Massachusetts," 22
Land of Unlikeness, 10, 18, 31, 51, 53–54, 67, 111, 254
"Last Walk?" 164–65, 167, 179, 218, 225, 226
Life Studies, 11–12, 16–17, 19, 33, 36, 38, 41, 43, 52, 57, 64, 67, 71–72, 80–98, 113, 158–59, 162–64, 172, 175, 183, 216, 217, 219–21, 232–33, 236, 238–39, 255
"Life Studies" sequence, 11–12, 65, 68, 81–97, 233, 236, 239–40, 248–49
"Lives," 222–23
"Logan Airport, Boston," 165–66, 226, 227
"Long Summer," 124–26
Lord Weary's Castle, 10, 16, 18, 31, 51–64, 65, 66, 67, 68, 100, 102, 106, 115, 175, 219–20, 226–27, 237, 250
"Louisiana State University in 1940," 152, 158, 171, 218
"Man and Wife," 77, 82, 90, 159
"Man and Woman," 138
"March, The," 127–28
"Marlowe," 143
"Marriage," 165, 174, 181, 199–203, 206, 228
"Mary Winslow," 33, 52
"Memories of West Street and Lepke," 221
"Mermaid," 154
"Middle Age," 41–42, 46, 178
"Milgate," 141
Mills of the Kavanaughs, The, 10–11, 15, 18, 52, 64, 175
"Mr. Edwards and the Spider," 52
"Morning after Dining with a Friend," 158
"Mother and Father," 178
"Mother Marie Therese," 11
"Munich 1938," 129, 131

DATE DUE

PRINTED IN U.S.A.